Financial Markets, Banking, and Monetary Policy

Founded in 1807, John Wiley & Sons is the oldest independent publishing company in the United States. With offices in North America, Europe, Australia and Asia, Wiley is globally committed to developing and marketing print and electronic products and services for our customers' professional and personal knowledge and understanding.

The Wiley Finance series contains books written specifically for finance and investment professionals as well as sophisticated individual investors and their financial advisors. Book topics range from portfolio management to e-commerce, risk management, financial engineering, valuation and financial instrument analysis, as well as much more.

For a list of available titles, visit our website at www.WileyFinance.com.

Financial Markets, Banking, and Monetary Policy

THOMAS D. SIMPSON

WILEY

Cover image: © iStockphoto.com/LeeYiuTung
Cover design: Wiley

Copyright © 2014 by Thomas D. Simpson. All rights reserved.

Published by John Wiley & Sons, Inc., Hoboken, New Jersey.
Published simultaneously in Canada.

No part of this publication may be reproduced, stored in a retrieval system, or transmitted in any form or by any means, electronic, mechanical, photocopying, recording, scanning, or otherwise, except as permitted under Section 107 or 108 of the 1976 United States Copyright Act, without either the prior written permission of the Publisher, or authorization through payment of the appropriate per-copy fee to the Copyright Clearance Center, Inc., 222 Rosewood Drive, Danvers, MA 01923, (978) 750-8400, fax (978) 646-8600, or on the Web at www.copyright.com. Requests to the Publisher for permission should be addressed to the Permissions Department, John Wiley & Sons, Inc., 111 River Street, Hoboken, NJ 07030, (201) 748-6011, fax (201) 748-6008, or online at www.wiley.com/go/permissions.

Limit of Liability/Disclaimer of Warranty: While the publisher and author have used their best efforts in preparing this book, they make no representations or warranties with respect to the accuracy or completeness of the contents of this book and specifically disclaim any implied warranties of merchantability or fitness for a particular purpose. No warranty may be created or extended by sales representatives or written sales materials. The advice and strategies contained herein may not be suitable for your situation. You should consult with a professional where appropriate. Neither the publisher nor author shall be liable for any loss of profit or any other commercial damages, including but not limited to special, incidental, consequential, or other damages.

For general information on our other products and services or for technical support, please contact our Customer Care Department within the United States at (800) 762-2974, outside the United States at (317) 572-3993, or fax (317) 572-4002.

Wiley publishes in a variety of print and electronic formats and by print-on-demand. Some material included with standard print versions of this book may not be included in e-books or in print-on-demand. If this book refers to media such as a CD or DVD that is not included in the version you purchased, you may download this material at http://booksupport.wiley.com. For more information about Wiley products, visit www.wiley.com.

Library of Congress Cataloging-in-Publication Data:

Simpson, Thomas D., 1942-
  Financial markets, banking, and monetary policy / Thomas D. Simpson.
    pages cm. — (Wiley finance series)
  Includes index.
  ISBN 978-1-118-87223-9 (hardback); ISBN 978-1-118-872468 (ePDF); ISBN 978-1-118-87205-5 (ePub)
1. Capital market. 2. Banks and banking. 3. Monetary policy. 4. Finance. I. Title.
  HG4523.S568 2014
  332—dc23
                                                                    2014012264

Printed in the United States of America.
10 9 8 7 6 5 4 3 2 1

To my partner in life, best friend, and wife—Cindy.

Contents

Preface	**xvii**

CHAPTER 1
Introduction	**1**
What You Will Learn in This Chapter	1
Overview	1
Where We Are Going in This Book	2
Contributions Made by the Financial System	4
Transfers of Resources from Surplus to Deficit Units	4
Other Contributions	8
Recurring Themes in the Chapters Ahead	11
Resources	12

CHAPTER 2
Overview of the Financial System	**17**
What You Will Learn in This Chapter	17
Introduction	17
Features of an Effective Financial System	17
Direct Methods of Finance	18
Investment Banks	19
Debt versus Equity	20
Money versus Capital Markets	21
Asymmetric Information	21
Adverse Selection	21
Moral Hazard	22
Indirect Methods of Finance	22
Primary versus Secondary Markets	27
Primary-Market Transactions	27
Secondary-Market Transactions	28
Trading Platforms	29
Brokers	29

CHAPTER 3
The Special Role of Commercial Banks	**33**
What You Will Learn in This Chapter	33
Background	33
Commercial Bank Balance Sheet	34
Assets	35
Liabilities	35
Net Worth (Capital)	36

Payment System and Money	36
Commercial Banks and the Payment System	36
Payment System Infrastructure	40
Credit and Stored Value Cards	40
Payments Media in the Money Stock	41
Velocity (Turnover of Money)	42
Liquidity Provision	44
Dealing with Asymmetric Information	46
Maturity Transformation	46
The Safety Net and Regulatory Policy	47

CHAPTER 4
The Pricing of Financial Assets — 55

What You Will Learn in This Chapter	55
Background	55
Present Value	56
Value of a Single Future Payment	57
Value of a Coupon Security	58
Other Applications	59
Solving for Yield to Maturity	59
Solving for Fixed Payments	60
The Special Case of a Consol	61
Maturity and Price Sensitivity	61
Holding Periods versus Maturities	63
Return versus Yield	63
Duration	64
Nominal versus Real Yields	66
Appendix A: Variations of the Valuation Relationship	69
Appendix B: Solutions Using a Financial Calculator	70
Future Value	70
Future Value—A Higher Interest Rate	70
Present Value of Single Cash Flow	71
Lottery Choice	71
Current Price of a Coupon Security	71
Price of an Aasset Providing Uneven Cash Flows	71
Yield to Maturity	72

CHAPTER 5
Factors Affecting Yields — 75

What You Will Learn in This Chapter	75
Background	75
The Term Structure of Interest Rates	76
The Expectations Hypothesis	77
The Term Premium Hypothesis	81
Market Segmentation Hypothesis	83
Implicit Forward Rates	84
The Role of the Term Structure	85

Credit Risk	85
Credit Rating Agencies	86
Investment-Grade versus Below-Investment-Grade Debt	87
Cyclical Behavior of Credit Risk and Spreads	88
Credit Default Swaps (CDSs)	89
Changing Investor Tolerance for Risk	90
Liquidity	90
Taxation	91
Embedded Options	91
Flights to Safety	92

CHAPTER 6
Principles of Portfolio Selection and Efficient Markets — 97

What You Will Learn in This Chapter	97
Overview	97
Uncertainty, Expected Return, and Risk	98
Selecting a Portfolio	99
Expected Return	99
Risk	99
Interpreting the Expression for Risk	100
An Illustration	101
These Principles in Practice	102
Efficient Portfolios and Risk-Return Trade-Offs	103
Efficient Markets Hypothesis	104
Implications for a Random Walk	106
Other Implications	106
Asset Bubbles	106
Evidence	107

CHAPTER 7
The Money Market — 111

What You Will Learn in This Chapter	111
Background and Basic Features of the Money Market	111
Pricing	112
Treasury Bills	114
Auction Procedures	114
The Role of Primary Dealers	114
Purpose for Issuing Bills	115
Commercial Paper	115
Credit Quality	115
Maturities	116
Asset-Backed Commercial Paper (ABCP)	116
Retreat of the ABCP Market	116
Commercial Paper Placement	117
The Role of Commercial Banks in the Money Market	117
Letters of Credit and Bankers' Acceptances	119
Monetary Policy Effects on the Money Market	120

CHAPTER 8
The Bond Market — 125
- What You Will Learn in This Chapter — 125
- Background — 125
- Treasury Notes and Bonds — 126
  - Maturities — 126
  - Features of TIPS — 127
  - Placement — 127
  - When-Issued Trading — 127
  - STRIPS — 128
  - Secondary-Market Trading — 128
  - Reopening — 128
  - Purposes for Issuing Coupon Securities — 129
  - Credit Quality — 129
- Corporate Bonds — 129
  - Placements — 130
  - Tension between Bond and Shareholders — 130
  - Indentures and the Role of Covenants — 131
  - Credit Default Swaps (CDSs) — 132
  - Below-Investment-Grade Market — 132
  - Private Placements — 133
  - Secondary-Market Trading — 133
- Munis — 133
  - Tax Considerations — 134
  - Credit Risk and Liquidity Differences — 134
  - General Obligation versus Revenue Bonds — 134
  - Placement — 135
  - Indentures — 135
  - Ratings — 135
- Government-Sponsored Enterprises (GSEs) — 135
  - Fannie Mae and Freddie Mac — 136
  - Federal Home Loan Banks — 136
  - Features of GSE Bonds — 136
- The Impact of Monetary Policy on the Bond Market — 136

CHAPTER 9
Securitization — 143
- What You Will Learn in This Chapter — 143
- Background — 143
- Obstacles to Overcome — 144
  - Asymmetric Information and Adverse Selection — 144
  - Corrective Measures — 145
  - Regulatory Capital on Ordinary Loans — 145
- Beginnings of Securitization—MBSs — 146
  - Ginnie Mae — 146
  - Illustration of the Process — 146
  - Fannie Mae and Freddie Mac — 147
  - Secondary-Market Trading — 148
  - Other Mortgage Pools — 148

Contents   xi

    Other Securitized Loans—Consumer ABSs   148
        Auto ABSs   148
        Credit Card ABSs   149
        Other Consumer ABSs   149
        Common Features   149
        The Effects of the Financial Crisis   150
    ABSs Involving Business Credit—CDOs and
        Structured Securities   150
        Standard Types of Pools—CLOs, CBOs,
            and CMBSs   150
        Structured Securities   150
        CMOs   151
        Senior-Subordinated Securities   152
        Effects of the Financial Crisis   152
    Securitization and the Integration of Credit Markets   152
    Monetary Policy and Securitization   152

CHAPTER 10
The Mortgage Market   155
    What You Will Learn in This Chapter   155
    Background   155
    Home Mortgages   156
        Homeowner Choices   156
        Standard Features of Home Mortgages   159
    Commercial Mortgages   163
    The Mortgage Market and Monetary Policy   163

CHAPTER 11
The Equity Market   167
    What You Will Learn in This Chapter   167
    Background   167
    Equities as a Source of Corporate Finance   168
    Preferred versus Common Shares   168
        Types of Preferred   169
    Primary and Secondary Markets   169
    Valuation of Individual Shares   170
        Basic Model   170
        Dividend Growth   170
    Price-Earnings   171
        Some Implications   172
    Extending These Principles to the Stock Market   173
    Monetary Policy and the Stock Market   178
    Indexes of Stock Prices   178

CHAPTER 12
Central Banking and the Federal Reserve   183
    What You Will Learn in This Chapter   183
    Background   183
    Origins of Central Banks   184

Constitutional Foundations	184
The Century and a Quarter without a Central Bank	185
Creation of the Federal Reserve	186
Early Years of the Federal Reserve	188
Reforms of the 1930s	189
Fed Independence	190
Central Bank Accountability and Transparency	191
Central Bank Responsibilities	193
Monetary Operations	196
The Demand for Reserves	196
The Supply of Reserves	196
Market Equilibrium	198
Setting the Federal Funds Rate through Open Market Operations	198
Permanent versus Temporary Transactions	200
Payment of Interest on Excess Reserves	201
The Effect of the Financial Crisis on the Reserves Market	201
Interaction of Policy Instruments in the Reserves Market	202

CHAPTER 13
Monetary Policy: The Basics — 211

What You Will Learn in This Chapter	211
Background	211
Effects of Monetary Policy on Output and Prices	212
The Goal of Price Stability	212
The Dual Mandate in the United States	212
The Operational Counterparts to Maximum Employment and Price Stability	213
Maximum Employment	213
Price Stability	214
Aggregate Demand and Aggregate Supply	215
Aggregate Supply	215
Aggregate Demand	216
Monetary Policy and Aggregate Demand	218
The Model	219
Steady Inflation	219
Rising Inflation	220
Falling Inflation	220
The Important Role of Inflation Expectations	220
Actual and Potential Output in Practice	221
Addressing Inflation	221
Addressing a Shortfall in Output	223
Okun's Law	224

CHAPTER 14
Monetary Policy: Challenges Faced by Policymakers — 231
What You Will Learn in This Chapter — 231
Background — 231
Other Forces Affecting Output and Inflation — 232
Lags and Other Complications — 234
    Need to Be Forward Looking — 234
    Importance of the Expected Path of Short-Term Rates — 235
    Forward Guidance — 236
Policy Rules — 237
    Money Stock Rule — 237
    Taylor Rule — 237
Expectations and Central Bank Credibility — 239
Inflation Targeting — 240
The Zero-Bound Constraint and the Slow Recovery
from the Great Recession — 241

CHAPTER 15
Financial Crises — 247
What You Will Learn in This Chapter — 247
Background — 247
Classic Banking Panics — 248
The Nightmare of the Great Depression — 250
    Gold Standard Restraints — 250
    The Stock Market Crash — 251
    Bank Runs — 251
    Massive Damage — 252
Broader Financial Crises — 252
    Big Drop in Asset Values — 253
    Runs on Suspected Institutions — 253
    Fire Sales — 253
The Financial Crisis — 254
    Background Factors — 255
    Proliferation of Nonstandard Mortgages — 255
    Growing Exposures of Key Financial Institutions — 256
    The Unraveling — 257
    Shadow Banking Stress — 257
    Major Credit Crunch — 258
    Policy Responses — 258
    Dodd-Frank — 259
Common Threads — 259

CHAPTER 16
The Foreign Exchange Market and Exchange Rate Regimes — 263
What You Will Learn in This Chapter — 263
Background — 263
Features of the Market — 264
The Relation between Spot and Forward Exchange Rates — 266

Long-Run Exchange Rate Relationships	267
The Real Exchange Rate	269
Exchange Rate Determination in the Shorter Run	269
Demand Schedule	270
Supply Schedule	271
Equilibrium	272
Floating Exchange Rate Regime	273
Fixed Exchange Rate Regime	275
An Undervalued Exchange Rate	275
The Dynamics of an Undervalued Currency	276
An Overvalued Currency	278
Variations on Fixed Exchange Rate Regimes	280

CHAPTER 17
Depository Institutions — 285

What You Will Learn in This Chapter	285
Background	285
Organization of Commercial Banks and Other	
Depository Institutions	286
Commercial Banks	287
Savings Institutions	291
Credit Unions	292
Economic Functions of Depository Institutions	293
Payment Services	293
Liquidity Provision	293
Providing Credit When There Is Asymmetric Information	293
Maturity Transformation	293
The Balance Sheet of the Commercial Banking System	294
The Balance Sheet of Savings Institutions	295
The Balance Sheet of Credit Unions	296
Deposit Insurance	296
Regulation and Supervision of Depository Institutions	297
The Regulators	297
The Focus of Regulation and Supervision	298
Capital Standards	298
Liquidity Standards	299
Depository Institutions and Monetary Policy	300

CHAPTER 18
Mutual Funds — 305

What You Will Learn in This Chapter	305
Background	305
History	306
SEC Regulation	307
Role of Mutual Fund Complexes	307
Types of Funds	309
Open-End Funds	309
Exchange-Traded Funds	314
Closed-End Funds	314
Mutual Funds and Monetary Policy	315

CHAPTER 19
Hedge, Venture Capital, and Private Equity Funds — 319
What You Will Learn in This Chapter — 319
Background — 319
Commonalities in Structure — 320
Hedge Funds — 321
    Role of the Prime Broker — 322
    Leverage — 322
    Entry and Redemption — 322
    Types of Hedge Funds — 322
    Economic Value and Hedge Fund Risk — 323
Venture Capital Funds — 324
    Types of Firms Selected for Financing — 324
    Risks Involved — 324
    Size and Stages of Financing — 325
    Exit — 326
    Economic Value Provided by VC Funds — 326
Private Equity Funds — 326
    Leverage — 327
    Exit — 328
    Economic Value Provided by Private Equity Firms — 328
Alternative Investment Funds and Monetary Policy — 328

CHAPTER 20
Large Institutional Investors — 333
What You Will Learn in This Chapter — 333
Background — 333
Pension Funds — 334
    Defined Benefit (DB) Plans — 335
    Defined Contribution (DC) Plans — 336
    Social Security — 338
    State and Local Government Pension Funds — 338
    Federal Government Retirement Funds — 339
Life Insurance Companies — 339
    Life Insurance — 339
    Annuities — 340
    LICO Assets — 340
    Reinsurance — 341
Property and Casualty Insurance Companies — 341
Large Institutional Investors and Monetary Policy — 342

About the Author — 347

Index — 349

Preface

The financial system—financial markets along with commercial banks and other institutions—can be likened to a mosaic. The individual pieces appear to be dissimilar and unrelated when they are set apart. However, when they are put together, they represent a coherent and magnificent system. This system is affected in a major way by monetary policy, and monetary policy is transmitted through the financial system to the economy and inflation. The recent financial crisis and the ensuing Great Recession amply demonstrated the dependence of the economy on a well-functioning financial system. Disruptions in certain parts of the financial market spread throughout the financial system and led to the most severe economic downturn and loss of jobs since the Great Depression of the 1930s.

In this book, I introduce and develop the role of each major financial market and institution, and describe how each becomes part of the greater mosaic of the financial system. I also describe important features of central banks—which have been given primary responsibility today for achieving macroeconomic goals—and how they go about pursuing goals for inflation and the economy. A special focus is placed on the nexus of monetary policy and the financial system, most notably the commercial banking sector. While much attention is placed on the United States, the book develops principles in a generic manner that applies to other financial systems and economies.

My approach is to base the material of each chapter on sound economic principles—those developed at the principles of economics level—and to center some of the core material on the key term structure of interest rates relationship. Notably, attention is given to how the term structure relationship plays a vital role in the conduct of monetary policy. I also develop a framework for understanding financial crises and the systemic risk entailed, and how financial disturbances affect achievement of monetary policy goals. This includes an examination of the evolving integration of central banks' methods for conducting monetary and financial stability (macroprudential) policies.

This basic approach underlying the book helps to deepen reader understanding. To further help the reader, I begin each chapter with a list of points that inform the reader of what he or she will learn from the chapter, with a series of statements about the importance and everyday relevance of chapter material to motivate the reader to want to go on. Throughout the book, I have worked in the critical interconnection between financial markets and institutions, monetary policy, and performance of the economy. In addition, each chapter has a well-distilled summary. The concluding section of each chapter contains challenging questions that help the reader better learn the material and develop the ability to apply that material to new situations as they are encountered.

The book has quite a number of illustrations that are worked into the text. Some are analytical charts that I have developed to make the concepts easier for readers to understand, while others present actual data showing how concepts developed in the text work in practice.

Throughout the book, material is presented in a way that only someone with my considerable experience working in the field of financial markets, banking, and monetary policy could accomplish.

Overall, this book will take the reader to a new higher level of understanding of how the financial sector of the economy works and how monetary policy is conducted. This level of understanding will enable the reader to follow ongoing discussions of monetary policy and important financial developments that are experienced each day. For instructor materials, please go to wiley.com

Thomas D. Simpson
Wilmington, North Carolina
January 2014

CHAPTER 1

Introduction

WHAT YOU WILL LEARN IN THIS CHAPTER

- What is meant by the financial system.
- What is meant by monetary policy.
- The ways in which the financial system contributes to economic well-being—by transferring resources from surplus to deficit spending units; by providing a variety of financial instruments to participants; by providing a reliable and efficient payment system; by providing for a better allocation of risk in the economy; and by imposing discipline on business management.
- Some basic features of the financial system that will keep coming up in our study.

OVERVIEW

Financial markets, banks, and monetary policy all touch our lives in numerous ways. Perhaps you have been able to be in school because of a student loan or money that your parents saved while you were growing up. When you last bought a jacket from a clothing store, you paid for it with cash in your wallet or with a check, debit card, or credit card. Chances are that the car you are driving was bought with an auto loan. Before long, you are likely to be in the market to purchase a home and will need a mortgage to make it happen. Prior to that, you could well be looking for an apartment, and the owner of that property took out a mortgage to buy the building.

Once you launch your career, you will be considering a savings program to meet future goals, such as accumulating a nest egg for retirement. Speaking of your career, the prospects for easily finding the job you are seeking will depend importantly on the state of the economy when you begin your job search, as will the opportunity for a summer job or an internship this summer. This, in turn, is affected by the central bank's monetary policy, which has an important influence on interest rates and the stock market. Central banks also attempt to ensure that the financial system is sound and stable, which fosters the availability of financing for homes, cars, and businesses whose products and services you like to buy. We could go on with examples of the many ways the financial system and monetary policy affect your life.

By *financial system* we mean financial markets, such as the markets for bonds, stocks, mortgages, and foreign exchange, and financial institutions, such as commercial banks, pension funds, and mutual funds. Connecting these and the broader economy is the payment system, which contains the infrastructure for making payments for purchases of goods, services, and financial assets.

For most people, the financial system and central banking[1] are highly arcane—they seem very complicated, confusing, and opaque. Moreover, financial and monetary matters conjure up many images and a range of emotions—Wall Street, pinstripes, closing the big deal, complex and inscrutable instruments, extravagance, greed, avarice, bailouts, and so forth. For some, the financial system also seems parasitic—living off the rest of the economy and not itself contributing to the public's well-being.

The financial crisis of 2008 and accompanying Great Recession have changed perceptions of the linkage between the financial system and the economy. That recession was brought on by the financial crisis—which was of an order of magnitude that rivaled that causing the Great Depression of the 1930s. It drove home the point that a malfunctioning financial system—whatever the cause—can bring down an economy, driving millions of people from the workforce to the unemployment lines. The major reason why the near collapse of the financial system in 2008 did not cause another Great Depression was enlightened public policy—primarily, actions taken by the U.S. central bank, the Federal Reserve—informed by the mistakes of the 1930s and driven by a dogged determination to avoid reliving that horrible chapter in U.S. and world history. The financial crisis has led to a variety of changes in the financial system, many stemming from modifications in the behavior of financial market participants prompted by that shock and others from changes in public policy and the way the financial system is regulated.

Monetary policy—in the United States, the province of the Federal Reserve System (the Fed)—has come to be the primary policy for macroeconomic stabilization around the globe. In the United States, the Fed is entrusted with achieving price stability and high and sustainable levels of aggregate output and employment. This prominent place for monetary policy is based on decades of research and experience that shows that monetary policy can be highly effective in achieving these results and that price stability fosters the highest level of economic performance. Monetary policy works through financial markets, the banking system and other parts of the financial system, to influence spending decisions by businesses and households—that is, aggregate demand.

Research also shows that economies having sound and well-developed financial systems perform better and are able to achieve higher standards of living. As a consequence, considerable attention is given these days to improving the functioning of the financial system. At the same time, much attention is being given to identifying the causes of financial crises—and the contagion that adds to their severity—and ways to prevent the next one and avoid the damage to economic well-being that would result. For central banks, achieving financial stability has taken on a priority comparable that of monetary policy.

WHERE WE ARE GOING IN THIS BOOK

In this book, we begin our journey with a look at the various ways in which the financial system contributes to our well-being—that is, how it creates economic value. In Chapter 2, we develop a helpful framework for identifying the different types of financial markets, such as bond and stock markets, and financial institutions, such as commercial banks, life insurance companies, and hedge funds, and the respective roles that they play. Because commercial banks traditionally have been the most important part of the financial system—and still dominate the financial systems of many economies today—they are singled out in Chapter 3 for further discussion; this discussion also highlights why commercial banks have been a primary conduit for the transmission of monetary policy.

The values of the financial instruments that are made available by the financial system, such as deposits, bonds, and stocks, are based on the value of the cash flows that their owners receive. In Chapter 4, we develop a model calibrating the (present) value of these cash flows. The interest rate (the time value of money), importantly affected by the central bank's monetary policy, is key to determining this value. In practice, at any moment in time, there are many different interest rates, but they are linked together. In Chapter 5, we discuss how such things as differences in credit risk, liquidity, and taxation affect these rates. Also, the yield curve relating interest rates on instruments of different maturities—the term structure of interest rates—is an important factor behind differences in interest rates. Indeed, an understanding of the term structure of interest rates is key to understanding how central banks go about setting in motion the forces that influence private spending decisions. In practice, holders of financial assets—be they individuals or financial institutions—have objectives that can be met by building portfolios of assets, the subject of Chapter 6. The question of whether you can expect to beat market returns through sagacious selection of stocks and other assets is also explored in Chapter 6.

With this background and the tools developed, we can dig into the major markets, such as the money market, bond market, mortgage market, and equity (stock) market, the subjects of Chapters 7 through 11. Included among them is the relatively recent process of securitization and the creation of securitized assets, which involves the combination of ordinary loans or other instruments into huge portfolios of assets from which pieces are sliced off and sold to various investors.

As noted, the values of financial instruments depend greatly on central banks and their influence on interest rates. In turn, central banks rely on financial markets, commercial banks, and other financial institutions to transmit their policies to the economy. Chapters 12 and 13 look at the evolution and basic features of central banks and how they go about setting and implementing monetary policy. In Chapter 14, we examine the challenges faced by central banks that often interfere with the achievement of their goals. Enhancing the effectiveness of monetary policy is stability of the financial system, and central banks in recent years have elevated the pursuit of policies that will foster financial stability—and avoid financial crises. In Chapter 15, we look at the causes and consequences of financial crises, and the kinds of policy measures that central banks have been developing to prevent them.

Exchange rates and the foreign exchange market increasingly play a role in the financial system and in the transmission of monetary policy, the subject of Chapter 16.

The major financial institutions—commercial banks and other depository institutions, mutual funds, hedge funds and other alternative investments, and pension funds and life insurance companies—are examined in Chapters 17 through 20.

Before proceeding, it is worth noting that the term *investment* or *investor* is used in this book to mean two different things, as is common elsewhere. In the first, investment refers to spending on such things as structures, equipment, software, or research and development that will add to the profits of a business in the future. This type of investment adds to the capital stock of the economy. In the second, investment refers to a financial investment such as a bond, a stock, or a deposit in a bank. It should be clear from the context which meaning to apply.

CONTRIBUTIONS MADE BY THE FINANCIAL SYSTEM

How does the financial system contribute to economic well-being or create economic value? We can list several:

- It transfers resources from surplus to deficit spending units (from those earning more than they spend to those spending more than they earn).
- A well-developed financial system provides both suppliers of funds (investors) and users of funds with a variety of financial instruments that meet their objectives.
- The variety of instruments available in financial markets enable investors and users of funds to readjust their financial positions when conditions change, requiring a different asset or funding mix to meet their objectives.
- A well-developed financial system provides a payment system that offers inexpensive and reliable ways of making payments for transactions that contribute to a higher standard of living.
- It reallocates risk from those least able to manage risk to those more able.
- It can impose discipline on business managers to focus on expanding revenue and curbing costs.

Let's look at each of these in more detail.

Transfers of Resources from Surplus to Deficit Units

In looking at this role of the financial system, it is useful to break down economic units into four different sectors: households, businesses, governments, and external (foreign). Some tend to be surplus units, others deficit units, and others predominantly neither. Let us look at each sector.

> *Households* are important providers of funds to financial markets—surplus units. However, not all households at any one time are in such a position. Households follow a so-called life-cycle pattern in which many spend more than they earn early in their post–high school years (they are dis-savers). They then move into years in which their incomes rise more rapidly than their spending and they become surplus units (savers). This is followed by their later years when their earnings drop off and at some point again fall below spending and they draw down accumulated saving (dis-savers). This is illustrated by the age, earnings, and spending profile presented in Figure 1.1. In the early years, many people are attending college or other training that will improve their earnings capacity in the future, and are not working full time. As a consequence, they are forgoing income. The earnings that they make, if any, fall short of their spending. Once they get a regular job, their

Introduction

earnings rise rapidly and begin to surpass spending, as illustrated by point *a* in the diagram. Later on, earnings grow more slowly and tend to level off.

Meanwhile, spending grows, but less rapidly than income for a number of years. The excess of income over spending—saving—is used to repay any debt accumulated in the early years and to build assets for future goals—home purchase, education of children, retirement, and bequests. At some time later in life, point *b* in the diagram, earnings drop below spending and the household becomes a dis-saver again. However, during much of the household's adult years, it saves, and over its entire life the household is a net saver. Thus, the household sector as a whole is a surplus unit, supplying funds to the financial system.

The amount that households will be willing to save will depend, among other things, on the level of interest rates. When interest rates rise, it will be attractive to save more—cut back on spending—and when interest rates fall, it becomes less attractive to save—or more attractive to expand spending.

Similarly, for those households that may be contemplating borrowing to finance consumption spending, a rise in interest rates will make such debt-financed spending less attractive, and they will forgo some spending. Conversely, a decline in interest rates encourages more spending financed by borrowing

Businesses seek to make profits for their owners, and, in the course of doing so, are users of funds—deficit units. Business managers can make profits by looking for investment projects that have rates of return that exceed the cost of financing. The greater the project's rate of return over financing costs, the greater will be the contribution of the project to future profits. The cost of financing can be thought of as the interest rate that must be paid to borrow funds in the market.[2]

Businesses receive earnings in the form of profits, but some of those profits are paid to owners in the form of dividends. Businesses also have funds for

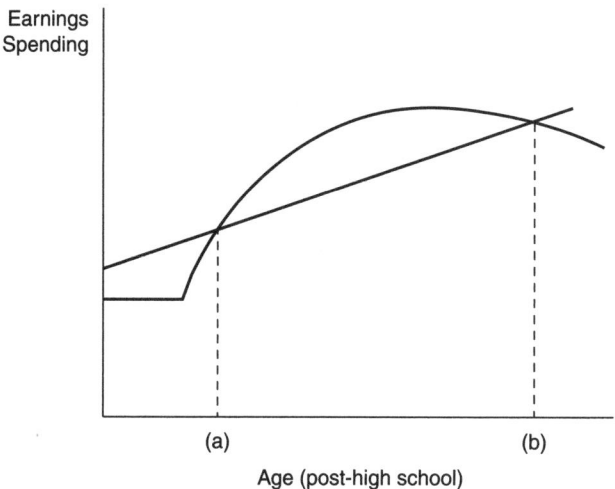

FIGURE 1.1   Age, Earnings, and Spending Profile

investment from depreciation allowances that are intended to replace worn-out or obsolete capital (previous investments). However, it is usually the case that the amount of new investments exceeds the amount of internal funds from retained earnings (profits after dividends) and depreciation—resulting in businesses being deficit units. To undertake all the investments that provide net profit to the owners—those having returns in excess of financing costs—businesses must acquire funds in the financial marketplace. It is worth noting that businesses acting in such a way are not only adding to shareholder profits, but the investments they undertake add to the level of aggregate output and enhance the productivity and (real) wages of workers.

One further issue worth mentioning at this point is the relationship between business investment and the cost of financing—the level of interest rates. We noted above that a business could make more profits for its shareholders by undertaking all projects that have returns that exceed financing costs. If we think of business managers as arraying all potential investment projects from those having the highest to the lowest returns, they will select all projects having returns that exceed the interest rate that they pay when they borrow and will forego those with returns below financing costs. However, if market conditions should change and financing costs—interest rates—decline, then some projects that previously were not pursued—unprofitable—now will become profitable. Thus, businesses will undertake more investment. Because central banks affect the level of interest rates, they play an important role in investment spending decisions.

Governments can in principle be either surplus or deficit units. In practice, in the United States, which category they fall into depends greatly on the level of the government. The *federal* government is a chronic deficit unit, spending well in excess of its receipts. Political leaders at the federal level seem to find it irresistible to favor large spending programs and, at the same time, favor lower taxes. *State and local* governments, in contrast, are usually constrained by constitutions or laws that require that they formulate balanced budgets. This means that in preparing their annual or biannual budgets, they must set spending in line with expected receipts. In practice, they almost never actually achieve balanced budgets—tending to have shortfalls in receipts when their tax receipts are weakening along with their economies or excesses of receipts over spending when their economies are showing unexpected strength. But, over longer periods, their budgets tend to be in balance. That is, state and local governments are neither surplus or deficit units.

The foreign sector can also in principle be either a surplus unit supplying funds to the U.S. financial system or a deficit unit drawing funds from the U.S. financial system. In practice, the foreign or external sector has been a long-time supplier of funds to the U.S. financial system. The reason for this involves a complicated relationship between business investment and government deficits relative to saving. The supply of funds from abroad comes into the U.S. market through our external trade deficit—exports falling short of imports. Suffice it to say that the forces underlying our trade position are unlikely to cause the external sector to shift any time soon from being a surplus unit for the U.S. financial system to a deficit unit.

Putting it together, we can use a diagram to illustrate the transfers of resources from surplus to deficit units. In Figure 1.2, the column on the right contains the amount of funds that surplus units—in practice, households and foreign participants—wish to supply. The column on the left contains the amount of funds demanded by deficit units. And the horizontal bar in the center moving from right to left is the channel through which the financial system makes this transfer. In the next chapter, we will refine this to include different channels representing different parts of the financial system. Note that in this diagram the size of the two bars is the same—that is, the amount that surplus units want to supply equals the amount that deficit units demand. This constitutes an equilibrium situation.

Actually, the supply of funds by surplus units need not equal the amount demanded by deficit units at all times. When disequilibrium occurs, an economic process will be set in motion that brings supply and demand back into balance. This is illustrated in Figure 1.3. In this case, supply has fallen short of demand. In these circumstances, not all deficit units will be able to get as much funds as they desire. As a consequence, those deficit units coming up short will compete with others to get more funds by offering better terms—higher interest rates.[3] As interest rates rise, surplus units are induced to supply more funds, and deficit units begin to trim their demand for funds as returns on some projects have now fallen below the new higher level of interest rates. This process of yields rising will continue until the supply of and demand for funds are matched. This is illustrated by broken lines in both columns and the arrows for each column pointing to the direction of movement. The supply expands (moves up) and the demand contracts (moves down). Interest

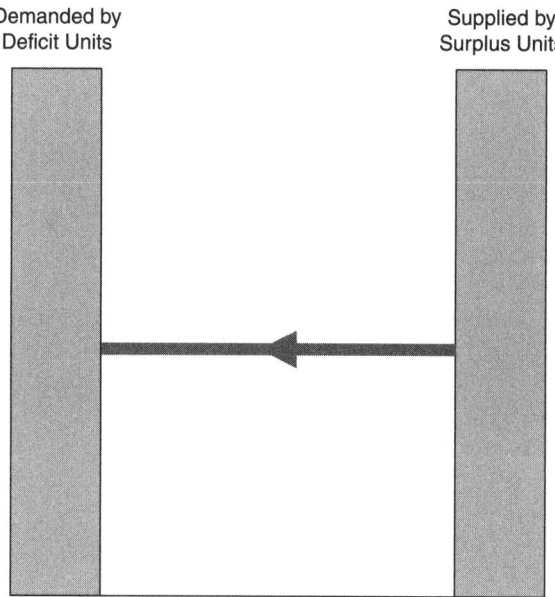

FIGURE 1.2 Transfer of Funds from Surplus to Deficit Units

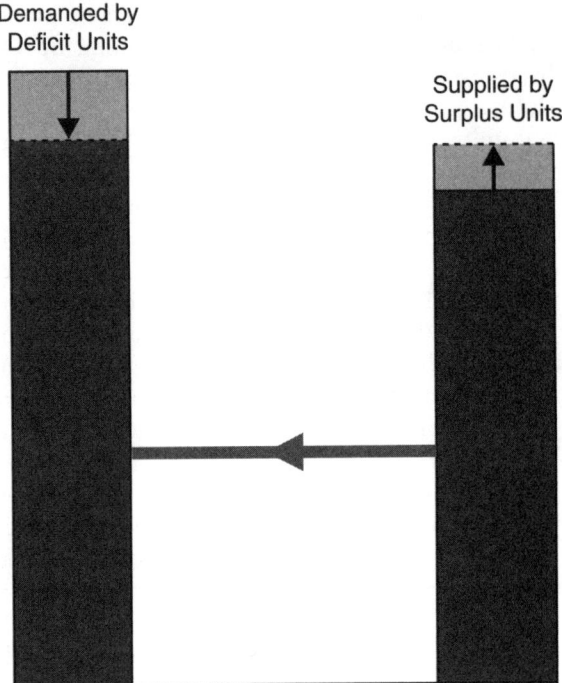

FIGURE 1.3 Shortfall of Funds Supplied (Interest Rates Rise)

rates stop rising when the two bars again have the same height—a new equilibrium is achieved.

A similar situation occurs when the supply of funds exceeds demand, illustrated in Figure 1.4. This could occur, for example, if households wish to save more, perhaps because they become more cautious or because they want to set aside more for retirement or for their heirs. Or perhaps foreign participants want to place more funds in the U.S. market. In either case, some suppliers of funds would become frustrated because they cannot place their funds—demand is less than supply—and would be willing to accept a lower yield to be able to get their funds placed. That is, interest rates would be declining. This would induce some demanders of funds to want more and some suppliers of funds to cut back on their supply. The process ends when supply again matches demand and interest rates stabilize at their new lower level.[4]

It is worth noting that the competitive process of reaching an equilibrium results in the amount of surplus funds being allocated to the highest-valued uses. That is, price rationing ensures that the highest-valued uses will get funded. This leads to a higher overall level of output and growth over time.

Other Contributions

Earlier in this chapter, we listed some *other* important contributions that are made by an effective financial system. Let's discuss them in more detail.

Introduction 9

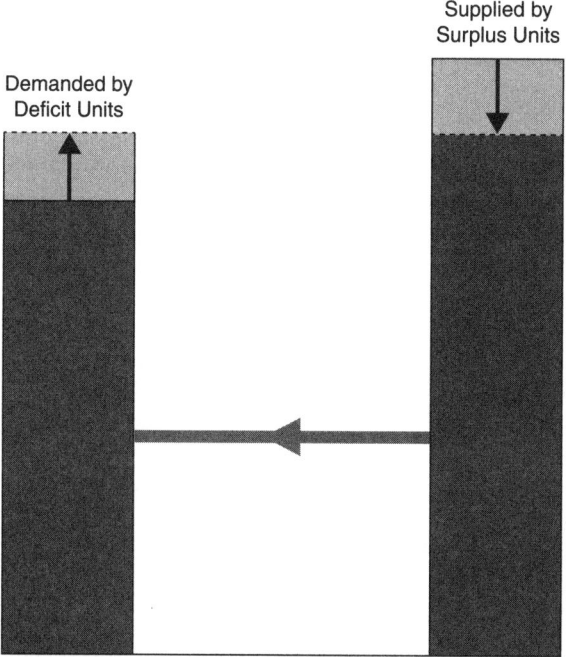

FIGURE 1.4 Surplus of Funds Supplied (Interest Rates Fall)

A variety of financial instruments available to channel funds from surplus to deficit units permits both suppliers and demanders of funds to select those instruments that best suit their objectives. Surplus units are heterogeneous in their objectives and their preferences and the same can be said of deficit units. For example, an investor—surplus unit—may want to place funds for three years, at which point those funds may be needed to meet an obligation, perhaps to pay a tuition bill. The availability of financial instruments that pay back the investor in three years—say, a three-year deposit—will match this saver's needs well, avoiding other difficulties. Similarly, a user of funds may expect to receive a large payment in 10 years, at which time this user can repay the surplus unit. A financial instrument that enables this deficit unit to get funds for a 10-year period will match its needs well and avoid other difficulties. In both situations, the economic unit achieved its preferred situation and avoided the complications that would have resulted if the 3-year or the 10-year instrument were not available—economic value was thereby created. The financial system fosters a matching of interests from within heterogeneous surplus units to counterparts within heterogeneous deficit units.

This variety of financial instruments also enables economic units to readjust financial positions when circumstances change. For example, many investors have intolerance for much risk. In the event that the instrument that the investor had acquired has now become more risky and the investor wants to get out of it for something safer, a secondary market for this instrument and for the safer one will allow the investor to readjust investments and get into a more comfortable position. We will see in Chapter 4 that some investors have responsibilities to meet payments at specific dates in the future and seek financial instruments that provide them with cash at those times. However, changes in the level of interest rates can cause the pattern of those cash flows to change in ways that diverge from their requirements. In these circumstances, a variety of financial instruments will permit them to readjust—rebalance—their investment portfolios. A large share of trading in financial markets reflects such readjustments of portfolios.

A reliable and efficient payment system fosters transactions that might not otherwise take place. We often take for granted our payment system—that is, the means that we use to make payments for goods, services, and financial assets. We buy something online and use our credit card to pay the vendor who sold us the item. Or you stop by a nearby grocery store to replenish your pantry and pay with your debit card. In both instances, you are able to get what you want and the seller can count on getting payment. Moreover, the costs of making these payments are usually negligible and the transfer of funds from buyer to seller is reliable. In some parts of the world, payments have to be made in cash—sometimes suitcases full. Indeed, if you are buying something from a location far away, you must transport the cash to that location—which can be very risky, even life threatening. A cumbersome or unreliable (risky) payment system reduces the number of transactions that people are willing to make. In contrast, our system does not impose those kinds of barriers to economically worthwhile transactions. Low transactions costs and reliability of our system encourage specialization and division of labor, which promotes higher levels of economic well-being. As we will see in Chapter 3, the banking system provides much of the backbone of our advanced payment system.

The financial system facilitates a reallocation of risk from those unwilling and unable to bear it to those with better ability to manage and more appetite for risk. Some investors wish to avoid risk while others are more willing and better suited to absorb it. For example, investing in long-term mortgages, as we will see, can be very risky for commercial banks that rely on much shorter maturity deposits. Yet commercial banks are well positioned for interfacing with homebuyers and making (originating) such loans. Financial markets have developed to the point where some institutions, such as banks, originate these loans and then sell them—either directly or indirectly—to pension funds and insurance companies that have locked in funds for longer periods and are seeking longer-term investment outlets for such funds. Also, complicated financial instruments have been created using ordinary loans—including auto and credit card loans—in which a large pool of such loans is assembled. Then, the pool is structured in such a way that some investors can be assured of getting repaid in full while others are exposed to more risk of not being fully repaid in return for more yield. The former can be acquired by investors with a high degree of aversion to risk while the latter can be acquired by those better positioned for taking on large amounts of risk.

The financial system imposes discipline on business managers pursuing unwise business strategies. For example, if a business manager needing to raise funds in financial markets is pursuing a new product line that is destined to fail, that firm will be unable to get many investors to part with their funds, or it will need to pay them painfully high interest costs. Also, if the company has stock trading in the marketplace, the price of that stock will drop so low that investors holding the stock—the company's owners—will be motivated to take action against the manager's plan. In such ways, managers are redirected to pursue more promising strategies. Should management, instead, prove to be stubborn in making the needed changes, the low price of the company's shares will induce activist investors or private equity firms to step in and buy up shares, thereby gaining more leverage to force the changes.

RECURRING THEMES IN THE CHAPTERS AHEAD

There are a few themes regarding our financial system today that will recur in the chapters ahead.

- Financial markets are forward looking and are continually repricing financial assets based on new assessments of the outlook for the issuer of the instrument and of the broader economy. The prices of financial instruments that trade throughout the day are continually changing. This is affected by news about the issuer, which alters assessments of the financial health of the issuer and its prospects going forward. Similarly, news bearing on the economy will affect the prospects for a wide range of issuers and market prices more broadly.
- Financial markets dislike uncertainty and risk, and the prices of financial assets fall when uncertainty and risk rise. Another way to view this is that investors must be compensated to take on risk. The more risk, the larger must be the compensation—meaning that the price of the financial asset must be cheaper to attract buyers. Frequently, the entire financial and economic landscape seems to be riskier, and financial markets will respond by selling off assets with risk embedded in them.
- Yields on U.S. Treasury securities tend to be benchmarks for the pricing of other financial instruments, and, as a result, the market for Treasury securities is one of the most closely watched financial markets in the world. In this market, there is price discovery—changes in underlying factors affecting the pricing of credit show through in this market promptly and then are echoed in other markets. Moreover, as we will see, it is through this market that the Federal Reserve seeks to influence credit conditions throughout the economy and thereby spending decisions and output, employment, and the prices of goods and services.
- Financial institutions, such as commercial banks, must have capital (funds placed by owners) to protect creditors, such as depositors. Capital provides a cushion for declines in the value of an institution's assets to be absorbed by its owners before bleeding over to its creditors. The greater the risk profile of the institution, the more capital will creditors insist upon as protection. However, when creditors perceive that the government will protect them from losses, they will not insist on as much capital for protection. Under such circumstances, their

insensitivity to the risk profile of the institution will encourage managers of the institution to pursue more risky strategies on behalf of the shareholders (owners). As we will see in Chapter 2, this creates a moral hazard problem.
- The financial system has increasingly become globalized. Investors seeking diversification and higher returns are reaching across borders. Similarly, those seeking to raise funds are looking for the lowest cost source, be it at home or abroad. Moreover, commercial banks have been following their business customers into new markets and have been seeking new customers abroad. As a consequence, asset prices and the financial condition of major financial institutions are becoming more responsive to developments in other parts of the world.

RESOURCES

You will get the most out of this book if you follow developments in the financial sector and the economy and monetary policy on a regular basis. To assist you are a number of very good resources. These include:

Bloomberg news service www.bloomberg.com

Federal Reserve Board www.federalreserve.gov

Federal Reserve Bank of New York www.newyorkfed.org

St. Louis Fed database (FRED) http://research.stlouisfed.org/fred2?

Federal Deposit Insurance Corporation www.fdic.gov/

Securities and Exchange Commission www.sec.gov/

Wall Street Journal www.wsj.com

Financial Times www.ft.com

The public website of Bloomberg has a vast amount of information posted on a timely basis. This includes stories about the economy, financial markets, and a wide array of financial data covering the stock market, bond market, and the foreign exchange market.

The Federal Board's website has speeches and testimonies of Board members and reports on monetary policy, banking and financial policy, and other policies; a substantial amount of monetary, financial, and economic data; and research papers on these issues. Similarly, the website of the Federal Reserve Bank of New York (FRBNY) contains timely monetary and financial data along with other useful information. The FRED database contains over 35,000 monetary, financial, and economic data series, along with charting software that can be used to produce customized graphs and spreadsheets.

The Federal Deposit Insurance Corporation's (FDIC's) website has a vast amount of banking data, as well as research and policy statements on banking issues. The Securities and Exchange Commission's (SEC's) website contains information on publicly traded companies and securities markets, policy statements, and research on financial markets.

The *Wall Street Journal* is probably the best-known source of information and analysis of economic, financial, policy, and business developments. The *Financial Times* covers these same areas, but with more of a global emphasis.

In this and later chapters, you will be given assignments that utilize these sources, especially Bloomberg, the Board, and FRED. In addition, accompanying this text is a website that contains timely issues relating to financial markets and institutions and monetary policy, with links to individual chapters in the text. This is intended to help you keep up to date on current issues and to better learn how to apply the principles developed in this book to a rapidly changing world.

SUMMARY

1. The financial system underpins and is closely connected to the economy. A well-developed and sound financial system fosters a higher standard of living and better overall economic performance.
2. By the financial system we mean markets for financial instruments, such as stocks and bonds, and financial institutions, such as commercial banks, pension funds, and hedge funds, along with the payment system.
3. A major function of the financial system is to transfer resources from surplus units to deficit units. In practice, households and the foreign sectors are suppliers of resources through the U.S. financial system—surplus units—while businesses and the federal government are demanders of these funds—deficit units.
4. When the supply of funds does not match demand, an economic adjustment occurs in which interest rates change—rising when demand exceeds supply and falling when supply exceeds demand. The equilibrating process ensures that the most worthwhile projects get funded.
5. Other important functions performed by the financial system (creating economic value) are providing a variety of financial instruments that better match the objectives of financial market participants; providing a reliable and efficient payment system that encourages more worthwhile economic and financial transactions; providing a means by which risk can be shifted from those less willing and able to bear risk to those with more capacity and appetite for bearing and managing risk; and applying discipline on managers of resources.
6. The financial system is forward looking and continually responding to new information bearing on the value of financial assets; dislikes uncertainty and risk, requiring compensation for greater amounts of risk; is focused on the market for Treasury debt, using interest rates on such debt as benchmarks for pricing other financial instruments; requires that financial institutions hold capital to protect creditors; is increasingly integrated into the global financial system and affected by developments outside the United States.

QUESTIONS

1. How do you think a well-functioning financial system serves to improve economic well-being?
2. How does the life cycle of earnings and spending result in the household sector's being a net supplier—or surplus unit—of funds to the financial system? Are all households suppliers of funds at any given time? Which typically are not?

3. How does the profit maximization condition imply that business investment will move inversely with the level of interest rates?
4. How would a balanced budget amendment to the U.S. Constitution affect the demand for funds by deficit spending units? What would happen to the level of interest rates in the United States?
5. If the amount of savings outside the United States were to shrink, how would this affect conditions in the U.S. financial system? Interest rates in the United States?
6. How does a reliable, efficient payment system affect the level of economic well-being in the United States?
7. What is the current slope of the Treasury yield curve—flat, upward sloping, or downward sloping?
8. What is the current value of the British pound? Euro? Japanese yen? (All measured against the U.S. dollar.)
9. What is the price/earnings (trailing) for Cisco Systems?
10. What was the amount of securities held outright by the Federal Reserve in the most recent week?
11. What was the volume of securities lent by the Federal Reserve in the most recent week?
12. What is the level of the yield on the three-month Treasury bill? The 10-year Treasury note?
13. Chart the level of the 10-year Treasury note from January 1970 to the current period. (Hint: Use the FRED database.) What has been the recent trend? Identify the period of the highest levels of this interest rate? The lowest.
14. What was the most recent interest rate on 10-year interest rate swaps?
15. What is the actual level of the federal funds rate? The target level?

NOTES

1. Central banks are public policy institutions charged with monetary policy and, in many parts of the world, with regulating commercial banks and other parts of the financial system.
2. In practice, the cost of financing can include the cost of raising equity funds, which is usually higher than the cost of borrowing. This will be discussed further in Chapter 8.
3. As we will see in subsequent chapters, not all funds that transfer from surplus to deficit units carry interest rates. Indeed, equity (stocks or shares) is a financial instrument that provides its owner dividends, which are paid out of the business's profits. We will also see in later chapters that a decline in yields—be it in the form of lower interest rates on credit instruments or dividend yields on stocks—results in higher prices on shares or credit instruments. This adds to the value of assets and wealth of household investors, which will induce more spending and less saving.
4. On occasion in recent years, funds coming from investors abroad have been an important influence on U.S. financial markets and the U.S. economy, along the lines of the analysis underlying Figure 1.4. In the early part of the decade of the 2000s, a bulge in saving in other parts of the world—importantly,

Asia—worked its way into the U.S. financial system. In other words, this augmented the amount of surplus funds supplied to the U.S. financial system from other sources and put downward pressure on U.S. interest rates, encouraging more spending by U.S. deficit units. This has been referred to as the *global saving glut*. Ample amounts of funds supplied and the accompanying low interest rates are thought to have been an important contributor to the housing bubble and other financial excesses that developed during that period. The bursting of the bubble was a catalyst for the financial crisis and the economic downturn later in the decade. See Ben S. Bernanke, "The Global Saving Glut and the U.S. Current Account Deficit," Board of Governors of the Federal Reserve System, March 10, 2005.

CHAPTER 2

Overview of the Financial System

WHAT YOU WILL LEARN IN THIS CHAPTER

- Critical features of an effective financial system.
- A framework for understanding the various parts of a financial system.
- Direct versus indirect forms of finance.
- Debt versus equity.
- Money markets versus capital markets.
- The concepts of asymmetric information, moral hazard, and adverse selection.
- Primary- versus secondary-market trading.
- Different types of trading platforms.
- The role of brokers.

INTRODUCTION

Without a road map, the financial system can be a bewildering maze. There are bonds and stocks, underwriters, and commercial banks and other depository institutions, not to mention finance companies, insurance companies, pension funds, mutual funds, hedge funds, and private equity funds. Further, there are brokers and dealers, exchanges, and over-the-counter markets. Each handles huge amounts of funds that are entrusted to them. What are these pieces of the financial system, and what is it about what they do that makes them distinctive and a contributor to our economic well-being?

In this chapter, we develop a framework that will place these various parts of the financial system in perspective and answer these questions. Before we start, though, we examine some often overlooked features of a successful financial system.

FEATURES OF AN EFFECTIVE FINANCIAL SYSTEM

There are three features of a financial system that are critical for its success. First, the financial system is a *fiduciary* system—that is, it is based on trust. Financial transactions typically are very large and involve money being surrendered for a promise—for some specified stream of payments in the future or a claim on some uncertain future cash flows. The investor who is giving up the substantial sum today must be able to trust the recipient of those funds or the investor will walk away from the deal—meaning that an economically worthwhile transaction may fall through. If you go to a clothing store and buy a pair of socks for $10, you have given up $10 but you have gotten the socks. In contrast, with a $10,000 investment in a certificate of deposit (CD) at a local bank, you have given the bank $10,000 and have gotten only a promise along with a paper or electronic confirmation of your investment. To be sure, you had to trust the store owner who sold you the socks that your socks were made with the materials listed on the label, had no serious defects, and were not contaminated with something harmful, but that does not come close to the stretch required to invest in the CD.

To assure customers that they can be trusted, many financial institutions build solid-looking structures based on classic architectural lines, implying that they are strong and can be trusted to be around for a long time. Or they take on names such as Fidelity or Prudential (and its Rock of Gibraltar logo), which are intended to exude integrity and reliability. Often, the institution will advertise the date it was founded to convince you that it has been around a long time and will be around a lot longer to honor the investment agreement it made with you. Think of it this way: you may be inclined to stop at a roadside stand where fresh tomatoes are being sold, but you would pass by a similar roadside stand selling large financial investments fearing that once they have your money there is nothing to prevent them from vanishing.

The second important feature of a successful financial system is a *strong legal infrastructure*. This means a set of transparent laws that both parties to a financial transaction regard as fair and protective of their interests. On top of this is an impartial adjudication mechanism—a court system and legal advocates for both parties—that can be relied upon to address a dispute and deliver a fair and just outcome. The parties will have confidence that political influence or corruption will not alter the judgment. Beneath such a legal system is a stable political system for which there is a broad consensus supporting the rule of law underlying private contracts. In other words, participants can have confidence that the laws governing financial contracts will not be changed in capricious ways that would jeopardize their interests. The evidence across countries clearly indicates that those with such legal infrastructures have better developed financial systems and better economic performance.[1]

A third feature of a well-performing financial system is a *safe, reliable, and efficient payment system*. Participants can make contractual payments and be assured that the funds get transferred to the right place on time and at a relatively low cost. We discussed the importance of good payment systems in the previous chapter and will explore the role of commercial banks in the payment system in the next chapter.

Again, it is easy for us in the United States to take all of these features for granted. We have had sound financial institutions, a strong legal infrastructure, and a robust payment system for a very long time. They have served us well, and largely because they work so nicely, we do not pay much attention to them. Nonetheless, they are all very important to the success of our financial system, which in turn supports our economy.

DIRECT METHODS OF FINANCE

Resources are transferred from surplus to deficit units in two basic ways—direct or indirect. With *direct* finance, the resources get transferred directly from the surplus to the deficit unit without the use of an intermediary. This is usually done

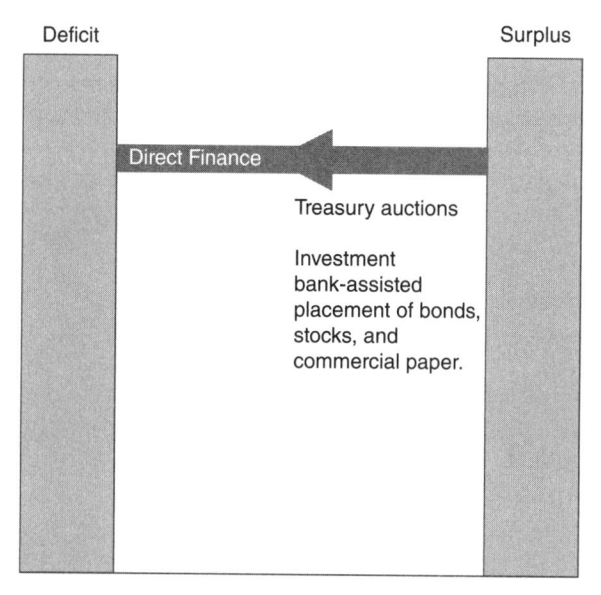

FIGURE 2.1 Direct Channel of Finance

when a security—stock or bond—is placed (sold) directly to the investor. It is illustrated in Figure 2.1. The funds transfer directly from the investors (surplus units) on the right to deficit units on the left. An example of direct finance is the U.S. Treasury's use of regular auctions to sell newly issued securities to investors. The Treasury announces each auction publicly—the amount and type of the security, the day it will be auctioned, and instructions for submitting bids. Interested investors can then submit bids directly to the Treasury, and if their bids are successful, they will be awarded the securities for which they submitted bids (the auction process for Treasury securities is described in more detail in Chapters 7 and 8).

Investment Banks

Corporate and municipal (state and local government) bonds, corporate stocks, and commercial paper typically are placed with investors using the assistance of an *investment bank* (or underwriter). The issuing business or government may be well known among investors but does not find it efficient to place the securities by itself. The investment bank, in contrast, has good connections with potential investors and knowledge of how to market the securities.[2] That is, there is an underlying information gap between issuers and interested investors, and the investment bank specializes in overcoming this by acquiring information about potential investors that enables an effective matching of sellers with buyers. Often, the size of an underwriting will exceed the capacity of a single underwriter, and a consortium (syndicate) of underwriters will be assembled that brings together their collective underwriting capacities and their networks of potential buyers (investors).

Debt versus Equity

There are two basic types of financial instruments issued—debt and equity. Debt instruments involve a commitment on the part of the issuer to pay a specific stream of cash flows (or to use a specific formula to determine cash flows) to the investor over a period until maturity, when the obligation is discharged. This commonly takes the form of bonds issued by corporations, the Treasury, or state or local governments that carry an interest rate to be paid to the investor and a specified sum of funds to be paid at maturity—the bond's principal or par value. For example, the bond may have a principal of $1 million and an obligation to pay an interest rate of 5 percent each year on the principal—$50,000 annually—over the next 10 years and the $1 million principal at maturity, in 10 years. Treasury bills and commercial paper, issued by corporations for short-term cash needs, have shorter maturities, up to a year, and typically promise to pay the investor a specific sum, say, $1 million at maturity.[3]

With common equity, the investor is entitled to receive what is left over after all other obligations have been paid. The investor is an owner of the corporation.[4] If there is a lot left over, the shareholder has done well; if not, the shareholder has done poorly. In other words, the shareholder is exposed to more risk than others.

A NOTE ON CORPORATIONS AND CORPORATE GOVERNANCE

In the United States and elsewhere, the corporate form of business organization plays a dominant role in the private economy. It is worth spending a moment going over what this means from the standpoint of governance, as we will be alluding to governance issues at various points in the book.

With a sole proprietorship, such as a local restaurant, the owner is typically also the manager of the business. The owner develops the business plan and makes the day-to-day decisions regarding the business—there is no separation between owners and managers. All efforts are focused on improving the bottom line.

However, with corporations there are a vast number of owners (equity holders or shareholders) and there is no practical way for them to be involved in the regular business decisions of the firm. Instead, they select a board of directors to represent their interests—to ensure that profits are being maximized or the value of their shares (ownership position) is maximized. It is the responsibility of the board, in turn, to hire managers to assist in developing the business plan of the organization and to make day-to-day decisions in keeping with the plan. In the event the managers are not acting in the interests of the shareholder owners, it is the responsibility of the board to address this problem by refocusing or replacing management. Thus, in making financial decisions, the managers are to be acting in the interests of the shareholders, which can be in conflict with the interests of others having a financial interest in the firm—such as bondholders or those making loans to the firm. We will see in some later chapters—especially Chapter 8—that tensions arise in these relationships and need to be addressed in a manner that ultimately is in the interests of the shareholders.

Money versus Capital Markets

By convention, we label financial instruments with maturities of one year or less as *money market instruments*. Treasury bills and commercial paper are among money market instruments. We label instruments with longer maturities as *capital market instruments*. Included here are bonds, stocks, and mortgages.[5] In volume, the capital market is dominant, although, as we will see, the money market plays a key role in the functioning of our financial system and in the transmission of monetary policy. We address the money market in Chapter 7, and the bond, mortgage, and stock markets—all components of the capital market—in Chapters 8, 10, and 11, respectively. In Chapter 9, we discuss how ordinary loans made by commercial banks and other financial instruments are transformed into securities—mostly capital market instruments—through the process of securitization.

Asymmetric Information

Investors will not be interested in directly placed securities if they do not know the issuer (borrower) well. If the investor has scant, if any, information about the borrower and what the prospects are for being repaid, we characterize this as *asymmetric information*—the borrower knows a lot more than the investor. Asymmetric information plays a very important role in the structure of finance, as we will see throughout this book. Let us look at an example. Suppose that you have inherited $10,000 and are looking for a good investment. You get a solicitation from someone you have never heard of in Alaska who wants to set up a network of dry cleaning shops and claims to have impressive business management acumen and to have done considerable research on where to locate them. He is looking for investors willing to make a minimum investment of $10,000 in bonds and is promising a yield of 10 percent. Shortly afterward, you get a solicitation from Apple Corporation. They are seeking funds for developing and marketing a new product line. They offer you bonds with a promised yield of 10 percent. You happen to own an iPod, iPhone, and iPad and are impressed with Apple's ingenuity and the quality of their products. Which will you choose? Clearly, you know much more about Apple—and can access volumes of publicly available information at the touch of your keyboard—and no doubt would discard the Alaskan dry cleaner's solicitation. We would say that the Alaskan dry cleaning situation is characterized by substantial asymmetric information. With Apple, there is not much of an asymmetric information problem.

Adverse Selection

An issue related to asymmetric information is the problem of *adverse selection*. When one party to a transaction finds it difficult to get necessary information about the other, the first party can be exposed to adverse selection. This is especially important when there are varying risk attributes among persons or businesses appearing in the second category. In these circumstances, a disproportionate number of higher-risk units will be interested in arranging a transaction. A helpful illustration of this principle is health insurance. People vary considerably in terms of health and the risk they pose to health insurers. However, getting the information about a person's health and the risks he poses is costly to the insurer—but typically known to the individual. In practice, people with poorer health will be more inclined to seek health insurance and those in better health will forgo insurance. Thus, from the perspective of the insurer, the applicants for health insurance will be disproportionately of poorer health. Moving over to the financial world, persons applying for personal loans will tend to be disproportionately higher-risk borrowers. Lenders to individuals—or health insurers—must take this tendency into account when setting the terms on a loan or the premium on health insurance.

Moral Hazard

Related to these concepts is the problem of *moral hazard*. This occurs when one party to a transaction does not act in good faith and may provide misleading information to the other party or may take on more risk than the other party deems to be acceptable. In financial arrangements, moral hazard typically takes the form of the recipient of the funds—borrower—pursuing an excessively risky strategy. This happens when the recipient enjoys all the gains from taking on more risk, but is not exposed to all the losses and shares them with the provider of the funds. We will be focusing on moral hazard problems resulting from incentives in financial contracts that induce one party to take on excessive risk. Moral hazard played an important role in the big build-up of risk in the U.S. financial system that preceded the financial crisis of 2008 and in the savings and loan debacle of a couple decades earlier. The potential for moral hazard occurs in various ways in everyday financial contracting and is typically addressed through contract provisions that limit risk taking, as we will see in later chapters.[6]

Getting back to asymmetric information, the presence of significant asymmetric information will discourage direct forms of finance. For example, our Alaskan dry cleaner above will find very few investors willing to take the leap—there is too much uncertainty about this deficit unit. Instead, this unit will likely turn to indirect forms of finance.

INDIRECT METHODS OF FINANCE

Those unable to access direct methods of finance can turn to *indirect* forms, which involve an intermediary standing between the surplus unit and the deficit unit. This is illustrated in Figure 2.2. The diagram shows funds going from surplus units to a financial intermediary and from the intermediary to deficit units. In most cases, there is a transformation of claims that occurs when the intermediary is involved. That is, the claim the surplus unit receives from the intermediary when it places funds with the intermediary differs from the claim that the intermediary receives when it advances the funds to the deficit unit. Financial intermediaries that perform indirect methods of finance fall into four general categories: depository institutions, finance companies, contractual saving institutions, and collective investment schemes. We will discuss each of these in turn.

> *Depository institutions* receive funds mostly in the form of deposits and use these primarily to make loans. The foremost among depository institutions are *commercial banks*. Commercial banks have a wide range of customers who place funds with them—businesses, households, nonprofit organizations, and governments. They make loans primarily to businesses and households.

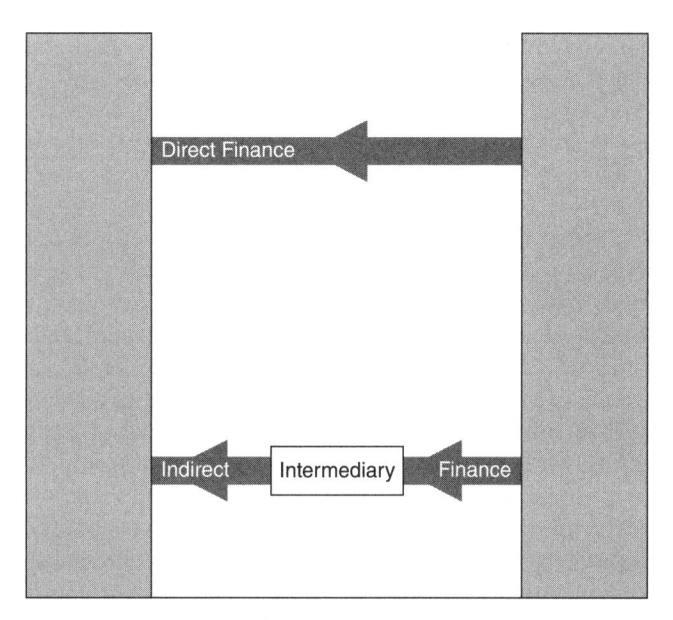

FIGURE 2.2 Direct and Indirect Channels of Finance

Other depository institutions are *savings institutions* and *credit unions*. Their customers—both deposit and loan customers—are mostly individuals, so-called retail customers. Savings institutions developed more than a century ago to collect deposits (savings) of lower-income households and to pool these funds to make mortgage loans to many of these same households at a time when commercial banks focused more on businesses and wealthier individuals. The savings institutions industry—largely consisting of savings and loans—went through a major crisis in the late 1980s and early 1990s, which led to a vast number of failures and absorptions by commercial banks. Since that time, this has been a fairly stagnant sector. Credit unions are cooperative institutions requiring membership, which typically takes the form of employees of a particular organization or residents of a community; credit union members are the owners of the credit union. These two types of institutions are much smaller than commercial banks. Combined, they are only a seventh the size of commercial banks.

As noted, depository institutions make loans to customers not having access to direct forms of finance because of substantial information asymmetries. They specialize in acquiring information from the customer and from other sources. They then process this information, and make a judgment about whether to lend to the customer and on what terms. Doing so involves costly human and other resources, which must ultimately be paid for by the credit customers of the institution. Payment takes the form of fees and interest rates charged to borrowers that exceed those paid by borrowers with access to direct finance.[7]

Though the intermediary passes funds from surplus to deficit units, the claim the surplus unit receives differs considerably from the one issued by the deficit unit. For example, you may deposit $1,000 in your account in a commercial bank and your $1,000 may be used to make a loan to a local business. You will receive a deposit claim on your bank and your bank receives a loan claim on the local business. In the event the local business defaults on its loan, you will still be entitled to the funds promised to you by your bank. Thus, there is a transformation of claims through this intermediation process.

Depository institutions have also engaged in maturity transformation—getting funds from their deposit customers at shorter maturities than the loans they make or the securities they purchase with depositor funds. For example, there was a time when savings institutions received deposits in maturities of a couple of years or less and turned around and used these funds to make 30-year mortgages. Such maturity transformation can be very risky. When short-term interest rates rise, the institution finds its deposit costs rising while its interest earnings from mortgages are little changed. If short-term interest rates rise by much, losses can be severe.

Furthermore, commercial banks—and, to a lesser extent, other depository institutions—provide liquidity to other parts of the economy.

We will discuss the functions provided by commercial banks in more detail in the next chapter and public policy issues involving commercial banks and other depository institutions in Chapter 17.

Finance companies are more specialized institutions. Some are so-called *captives,* meaning they are dedicated to financing the products of a particular firm and usually are owned by that firm. For example, IBM Global Financing is owned by IBM Corporation and is dedicated to financing IBM products as a means of promoting IBM sales. Major motor vehicle companies also use captives to promote sales. In addition to making loans to finance such purchases, captives typically also offer a leasing option in which the customer can enter into a long-term lease instead of purchasing the product with a loan. While leasing may seem very different than purchasing, they are not all that different. The customer usually must make an up-front payment in both situations and make regular payments for a specified period of time—be they loan or lease payments. Leases and loans differ at the end of the contract when either the equipment becomes fully owned by the buyer choosing the loan or reverts to the leasing company (providing that company with some residual value).

Other types of finance companies specialize in providing financing for small businesses and individuals typically lacking access to credit from depository institutions. For businesses, this includes providing financing for accounts receivable or inventories—usually for short periods. For individuals, this takes the form of personal loans, which can be for short or intermediate periods; sometimes these loans are backed by collateral.

Finance companies get the funds they need for making loans or leases by issuing bonds or commercial paper in the market, or by getting loans from commercial banks.[8]

Contractual savings institutions are *pension funds* and *life insurance companies.* Pension funds are of two basic varieties—*defined benefit* and *defined contribution.*[9] Many employers offer pension plans as a form of compensation to their employees. Typically, the employee makes a contribution to the plan each pay period. In return, under a defined benefit (DB) plan, the employee is entitled to pension benefits upon retirement, which are based on a formula involving the employee's tenure with the employer and the employee's earnings. The employer becomes the sponsor of the plan and is responsible for using the contributions to make and manage investments to ensure that there will be sufficient funds available to pay retirement benefits to employees. Nonetheless, regardless of how those investments perform, the employer is responsible for paying its employees the benefits promised, even if they need to dip into the firm's profits. In other words, the employer (sponsor) bears the investment risk of the plan—having to tap profits when returns on investment are low and being able to reduce its contributions to the plan when returns are high. A plan that does not have enough assets to meet its pension liabilities is said to be underfunded. DB plans tend to be structured in such a way that they encourage employees to stay with the employer until retirement. DB plans have been offered to a greater extent by older, established employers and have been declining as a share of retirement plans.

Growing in importance have been defined contribution (DC) plans. Contributions to DC plans (commonly supplemented by a matching contribution from the employer) go into individualized accounts—one for each employee. The employee usually has a choice in how the contributions will be invested, and a professional investment management firm typically is hired by the employer to manage employee accounts. Investment risk is borne by the employee. If the investments earn high returns, the employee will have more at retirement and vice versa. The employer has no obligation to provide a specific level of pension benefits at retirement, as under a DB plan. The popularity of DC plans owes both to employer and employee preferences. Employers wish to avoid investment risk, which they face under DB plans, and focus on their core business. Employees have come to like these plans because they are reluctant to lock themselves into a single employer until retirement, as in a DB plan. After a specified period of contributions, usually only a few years, the assets belong to the employee, regardless of whether the employee remains with the firm. This becomes more attractive to employees the more they are inclined to switch employers over their careers—something more appealing to younger generations of workers.

Because of the vast numbers of employees covered by pension plans, the pension industry has accumulated substantial amounts of assets and plays a major role in financial markets.[10]

Life insurance companies, in addition to providing life insurance, provide savings plans for individuals, usually commingled with insurance. Insurance companies specialize in assessing the likelihood of death for individuals at various ages, relying on their actuarial expertise. The life insurance that they offer takes two basic forms—term and permanent. With term insurance, a premium is paid for insurance coverage for a single period, usually a year. The insurance lapses after that period and there is no saving component. With permanent policies, which take various forms, the policy is in force for the life of the individual and it includes a saving component. Of course, with the saving component, the premiums will be higher for permanent policies, to cover both insurance and saving, especially in the early years of the policy. Like pension funds, life insurance companies are able to invest the savings component in securities such as stocks and bonds.

Life insurance companies also offer annuities to individuals for which the individual will be guaranteed a specific regular payment—often monthly or quarterly—for the rest of his or her life. The person either can pay a lump sum up front for this stream of payments, or he or she can contribute over time to a fund—usually during working years—that gets converted at retirement to regular annuity payments. Clearly, the actuarial expertise that life insurance companies need for pricing life insurance can be applied to pricing annuities, because a key component of annuity pricing will be gauging how long the annuitant will live and collect annuity payments. For example, knowing a person's life expectancy will be key to knowing how much that person will need to pay up front for a guarantee of, say, $20,000 per year. Depending on age, the amount of the fund needed for this annuity might be $200,000 or more.

Pension funds and life insurance companies are discussed in more detail in Chapter 20.

Collective investment schemes take four basic forms: mutual funds (investment companies), hedge funds, private equity funds, and venture capital funds. They involve investors acquiring shares or participations in portfolios of assets. This entitles the investor to a proportionate share—corresponding to the investor's ownership share of the entire portfolio—of the returns on the entire portfolio, less a management fee that goes to the managers of the portfolio.

Mutual funds build portfolios of marketable assets.[11] These funds are offered and managed by large complexes that provide a variety of funds and allow easy conversion from one fund to another. In these complexes are money market funds that invest in short-term assets and provide convenient withdrawals, various types of domestic and international stock funds, and various types of domestic and international bond funds. Under federal law, mutual funds must be registered and regulated by the Securities and Exchange Commission (SEC). A large portion of the customer base of mutual funds is made up of individuals, and the SEC seeks to ensure that the funds disclose sufficient and accurate information to potential shareholders for them to make well-informed investment decisions. Mutual funds are very large in size, second only to commercial banks. Especially popular in recent years have been exchange-traded funds (ETFs). ETFs typically replicate the composition of a commonly followed index of asset prices, such as the Standard & Poor's (S&P) 500 index of share prices. We will discuss ETFs and other types of mutual funds in more detail in Chapter 18.

Hedge funds have many similarities to mutual funds. They offer investments in professionally managed portfolios and focus largely on marketable instruments. Basically, they pursue strategies that seek to profit from expected movements in asset prices—either up or down. They are offered to investors with large sums to commit and are structured to avoid registration with the SEC and the need to disclose their proprietary strategies. To avoid SEC registration, they are restricted in numbers of investors—not being allowed to have more than 99 or, in some cases, more than 499 investors. Moreover, their investors must meet certain conditions—have substantial assets that can be put at risk and be well informed. Hedge funds are typically organized as limited partnerships. We will discuss hedge funds in more detail in Chapter 19.

Private equity funds are organized like hedge funds but have very different investment objectives. They look for established corporations that are not performing up to their potential, acquire them, and take them private. That is, they acquire the existing publicly traded shares in the target firm and convert to private ownership. Once private, the firm no longer needs to be registered with the SEC and the new (private equity) management has full control over the firm. Typically, several of these firms are placed in an investment pool (fund), and participations in the pool are sold to large investors in the form of shares in the private equity fund. Specialists are contracted by the pool's managers to restructure the firms in the pool in order to realize their potential. This often involves replacing the firm's management, enhancing and streamlining product lines, upgrading production methods, or all of the above. It usually takes several years to turn the firms in the pool around, and thus investments in private equity funds tend to be longer term in nature. Private equity funds will also be discussed in Chapter 19.

Venture capital (VC) funds are organized similar to hedge and private equity funds, but are focused on investing in and assisting firms in the early stage of development, commonly in the high-tech and biotech sectors of the economy. Firms in the early stage of development tend to be very risky and often require the assistance of professional business managers. The VC firm will provide much-needed capital for product development and expansion to the early stage firm in return for an ownership interest and the right to exercise considerable control over the business plan and management of the firm. A number of such early stage firms are put into a pool and participations in the pool are sold to large investors. VC funds, like hedge and private equity funds, are usually limited partnerships structured to avoid SEC regulation. VC firms are discussed in more detail in Chapter 19. VC, private equity, and hedge funds are frequently referred to as alternative investments.

PRIMARY VERSUS SECONDARY MARKETS

Primary-Market Transactions

When deficit units issue new securities to raise funds from surplus units, these securities are said to be issued in the *primary market*. If they issue a security that has not been previously issued, this new security is called an *initial public offering* (IPO). If, instead, the security has already been issued and more of that security is being issued to raise funds, this offering is called a *seasoned issue*. For example, if a firm is issuing stock for the first time, this offering is an IPO, but if the firm were issuing more stock in the market, it would be regarded as a seasoned offering.

Businesses typically raise considerably more funds from their existing shareholders in the form of retained earnings than they do from offerings in the primary market. To see how this occurs, keep in mind that the earnings from a share of stock, in principle, belong to the owner of that stock. They could be paid fully to the shareholder owner. In this case, if the firm requires more funds to finance worthwhile investments, it could raise those funds by selling new shares in the primary market. Alternatively, the managers of the firm and the shareholders may agree that the interests of the shareholders are better served by plowing some of the shareholders' earnings back into the firm—that is, the returns to the shareholder will be higher than if the earnings were paid in full to the shareholder and the shareholder had to find another place to invest those funds. The shareholder's return on the retained earnings takes the form of appreciation in the price of the share. In essence, the shareholder can be thought of as increasing his or her equity investment in the firm by the amount of retained earnings—or even more if the rate of return on the internally invested retained earnings is high.

Secondary-Market Transactions

When securities that have already been issued exchange hands, this is said to be a *secondary-market* transaction. Such a transaction does not involve the transfer of resources from surplus to deficit units, as does a primary-market transaction. For example, if you buy a hundred shares of Merck stock from a classmate, this transaction involves shares that already exist and no funds get transferred to Merck. In many closely watched markets, such as the stock market or the market for Treasury securities, the volume of transactions in the secondary market greatly exceeds the volume in the primary market.

In practice, a well-functioning secondary market adds to the attractiveness of the primary market. Investors will be more inclined to purchase securities in the primary market if they are confident that they can sell them in the secondary market and are not stuck with holding the security in the event they no longer want to own the security. A well-functioning secondary market enhances the liquidity of the security and its value in the marketplace—an issue we will discuss more fully in Chapter 5.

COMPLICATIONS IN THE DIRECTION OF FUNDS FROM SURPLUS TO DEFICIT UNITS

In practice, the process of indirect finance is often more complicated than that depicted in Figure 2.2. For example, a stock mutual fund may acquire funds from a surplus unit and use the proceeds to acquire shares through an IPO, or a commercial bank may use the proceeds from a customer's deposit to buy Treasury securities in a regular Treasury auction. In these cases, the intermediary has obtained funds in an indirect form and has passed those funds on to a deficit unit issuing the securities to the intermediary rather than to the surplus unit directly. In such a case, one can envision a channel of funds in Figure 2.2 going from the financial intermediary to the deficit unit.

Things get even more complicated when the mutual fund acquires shares or the bank acquires Treasury securities in the secondary market. Perhaps a business sold Treasury securities to the bank or its holdings of equity shares to the mutual fund to raise funds to finance investment outlays. In this case, funds from the surplus unit will be transferred to the deficit unit through the intermediary via a secondary-market transaction. They get even more complicated when the intermediary acquires the shares or Treasury securities from a business or household selling the securities to buy other securities. Indeed, there may be a chain of such transactions before the funds finally end up in the hands of the deficit unit. Nonetheless, the result will be the same: The financial system will serve to transfer funds from surplus to deficit units, regardless of the number of steps that may be involved.

Trading Platforms

There are different types of *trading platforms* for trading financial instruments in the secondary market. One of the most common platforms is the *over-the-counter* (*OTC*) system. For example, U.S. Treasury securities and stocks appearing in the closely followed Nasdaq index are traded over the counter. In an OTC market, competing *dealers* stand ready to buy or sell the financial instrument at their so-called bid or asked prices. The bid price is the price that they are willing to pay to acquire the instrument from the investor and the asked price is the price the investor must pay to acquire the instrument from the dealer. The investor can shop around among the dealers for the lowest purchase or highest selling price.[12] Dealers hold an inventory of the instruments that they are making a market in. For example, dealers in Treasury notes have an inventory of notes that are available for making sales when an investor wants to "hit" the dealers asked price. The dealer's inventory grows when an investor sells a note by hitting the dealer's bid price. As a result of their market-making activities, dealers' inventories fluctuate a great deal.[13]

A second type of platform is the *specialist* system. The most notable user of the specialist system is the New York Stock Exchange (formally known as NYSE Euronext). In the specialist system, the exchange listing and trading the security assigns a specialist to that security. When orders are submitted to buy or sell the security on the exchange, they go to the designated specialist. The specialist has the responsibility for balancing buy and sell orders—so-called crossing these orders—which frequently requires raising the price when buying interest exceeds selling interest or lowering the price when the reverse occurs. The specialist also holds an inventory of the security, which can be drawn down to meet an upturn in demand that cannot be met fully through available sell orders. Conversely, the inventory will grow when an upturn in sell orders cannot be readily matched through available buy orders.

A third platform, one that has been growing in importance, is the *electronic communications network* (*ECN*). ECNs have characteristics of both the OTC and specialist systems. The operator of the ECN tries to cross buy and sell orders, like the specialist system, but the various ECNs compete among themselves, as with the OTC platform. ECNs are used for making after-hours trades, after exchanges have closed for the day, and have become popular for making large block trades among institutional investors. The amount of trading on ECNs has been growing over time relative to the other platforms, in part because costs tend to be lower, and many analysts expect this trend to continue.

Brokers

Trading in the secondary market is commonly done through *brokers*. Brokers serve the customer by executing the trade for the customer. That is, the customer submits an order to the broker and the broker is responsible for finding the trading platform(s) where the instrument is traded and for getting the best terms for the customer. These days, the broker uses high-speed electronic systems to execute the trade, which is low cost as well as fast and reliable. In turn, customers of brokers are increasingly using electronic brokerage systems to submit their orders to their brokers.[14]

SUMMARY

1. Financial systems are fiduciary—they are necessarily based on trust.
2. A sound legal infrastructure underpins an effective financial system. This entails well-developed and fair laws, a competent and impartial adjudication mechanism to deal with disputes, and a stable political system to support the legal system. In addition, a safe, reliable, and efficient payment system is an important part of the infrastructure of an effective financial system.
3. Direct methods of finance transfer resources from surplus to deficit units directly, through issuance of securities such as bonds, stocks, and commercial paper. The securities can be distributed through auctions, as with U.S. Treasury securities, or through the services of an investment bank (underwriter).
4. Such financial instruments with maturities of one year or less are called money market instruments, and those with longer maturities are called capital market instruments.
5. Indirect methods of finance involve intermediaries positioned between surplus and deficit units. The intermediary receives funds from surplus units and places those funds with deficit units, typically transforming the claim that surplus units receive in the process. Intermediaries take the form of depository institutions, finance companies, contractual savings institutions (private pensions and life insurance companies), and collective investment schemes (mutual funds, hedge funds, private equity funds, and venture capital funds).
6. Asymmetric information plays a key role in whether transfers of funds take the direct or indirect route, with the presence of substantial asymmetric information leading to the latter. Related to asymmetric information is the process of adverse selection and moral hazard. Moral hazard induces excessive risk taking in the financial system.
7. Securities created in the process of transferring resources from surplus to deficit units are said to be issued in the primary market. Once issued, any trades of those securities take place in the secondary market—and do not result in any resources being transferred from surplus to deficit units. Trading in the secondary market takes place on various platforms—OTC, specialist, and ECN platforms.
8. In practice, firms raise substantial amounts of funds from shareholders by retaining earnings.
9. Orders directed to secondary markets are placed through securities brokers, increasingly through electronic systems.

QUESTIONS

1. What is meant by a fiduciary institution? In this regard, is a sporting goods store comparable to a financial institution? Is Bernard Madoff a good example of a fiduciary?
2. What is the significance of the legal and payments infrastructure for the functioning of the financial system? The economy?
3. List and describe three financial instruments that are issued in direct forms of finance. How are each of these placed with investors?

4. Look for a recent IPO of stock. Who was the underwriter? What was the pricing of the shares? How did they fare in subsequent (secondary market) trading?
5. List and describe three types of financial institutions that provide indirect forms of finance. How does each intermediary transform claims?
6. Do both primary and secondary markets transfer resources from surplus to deficit units? Why or why not? Money and capital markets? Why or why not?
7. What are the implications of asymmetric information for direct or indirect forms of finance?
8. What is moral hazard? How does it relate to asymmetric information? How does adverse selection relate to asymmetric information?
9. Look for recent stories in the financial press about private equity funds or hedge funds. Explain the transactions that are being discussed and how this relates to the basic objective of the fund.
10. What is the difference between mutual funds and hedge funds? Are the investors in each the same?
11. Contrast the economic function of hedge funds, private equity funds, and venture capital funds. In other words, how does each create economic value added and how does this differ from the others?
12. Explain the relationships among corporate shareholders, boards of directors, and managers? Why has such a system of governance proven to be essential for efficiency?
13. Explain what happens to an order to buy shares of stock in an OTC system. A specialist system. An electronic communications system. What is the role of the broker in this transaction?
14. What is the difference between a securities dealer and a securities broker? How do they differ from a securities underwriter?

NOTES

1. See David A. Grigorian and Albert Martinez, "Industrial Growth and the Quality of Institutions: What Do Transition Economies Have to Gain from the Rule of Law?" *World Bank*. Policy Research Working Paper 2475. November 2000.
2. The investment bank can actually buy all the securities from the issuer and then resell them to investors, hoping to make a profit on the differential between the price it buys and the price it sells. In such cases, the investment bank is said to have underwritten the securities. Alternatively, the investment bank and the issuer can agree to have the investment bank sell the securities to investors under a consignment agreement on a so-called best-efforts basis in return for a fee.
3. Bonds, stock, and commercial paper are generally structured to be securities—they contain certain legal features, notably specifying property rights and making them easily transferable. That is, they can be sold and transferred to another investor easily. Securities can take physical—certificate—form or they can take electronic form, which has become increasingly dominant. Commercial paper is a security typically issued by a corporation (including financial institutions) that contains a promise to pay a specified sum in up to 270 days. The term *financial instrument* refers to these and other financial assets, such as deposits, foreign currencies, and ordinary loans.

4. In practice, there are two kinds of equity—common and preferred. Common shareholders are entitled to the profits of the corporation. Preferred equity usually carries a specific dividend—calibrated as a percent of the principal of the stock—which is paid before the common shareholders get paid. More on this in Chapter 11.
5. Bonds with original maturities in excess of one year, but remaining maturities of less than one year are regarded as money market instruments. Thus, a 10-year Treasury note issued 9.5 years ago will typically be regarded in much the same way as a six-month Treasury bill.
6. Moral hazard also is present in areas other than finance, notably insurance. For example, you may be less careful in keeping potentially flammable rags around your house if your house is insured for loss in a fire (or you may drive less carefully if you have car insurance). To discourage you from behaving in more risky ways, insurance companies typically impose deductibles under which you (the insured) must pay for damages up to the amount of the deductible.
7. Interest rates received by depositors placing the funds for lending typically will be below those that can be earned in the market for directly issued financial instruments.
8. A finance company getting a loan from a commercial bank complicates our diagram a little. In Figure 2.2, we need to draw two boxes between surplus and deficit units. The first represents the commercial bank, which receives deposit funds from the public. The second, to the left of the commercial bank, represents the finance company, which receives funds from the commercial bank in the form of a loan and then places the funds with the deficit unit in the form of a loan or lease.
9. The pension plans discussed in the text exclude the national Social Security program. Social Security is structured as a defined benefit plan.
10. Pension plans invest heavily in bonds and stocks, which complicates our diagrams a bit. In other words, funds are received by pension plans from surplus units—employees—and are invested in bonds and stocks issued directly by deficit units instead of loans made to the deficit units (directly). See the feature box after the discussion of secondary-market transactions.
11. The discussion here is of open-end funds, the largest category of investment companies. Closed-end funds, as their name implies, limit the size of their investment portfolio and acquire assets that are less easily bought and sold in the marketplace. We will discuss closed-end funds in more detail in Chapter 18.
12. Usually, an algorithm is used to electronically search all the bid or asked prices to find the best available at that moment. Retail investors rely on brokers to perform this search on their behalf.
13. At times, a dealer may not have sufficient inventory to meet a customer's buy order. In this case, the dealer will need to borrow the security from another dealer or from an investor (that portion of the transaction that involves borrowed securities is referred to as a short sale). In the case of Treasury securities, some dealers are eligible to borrow securities from the Fed.
14. A clearing and settlement process follows after the transaction has been completed, which results in ownership of the security to the buyer and payment to the seller. This typically involves financial institutions serving as agents of the brokers of the buyer and seller matching the trade and then arranging for the transfer of funds from the buyer to the seller and the change in title to the asset. The payment system, discussed in the next chapter, handles the transfer of funds.

CHAPTER 3

The Special Role of Commercial Banks

WHAT YOU WILL LEARN IN THIS CHAPTER

- The key components of commercial bank balance sheets.
- The central role of commercial banks in the payment system and the evolution of payment media, including the variety of electronic payment methods available today.
- Important features of the payment system infrastructure.
- The difference between a debit card, credit card, and stored value card.
- The dominant role of commercial bank deposits in the money stock, which, in principle, can be used by the central bank for conducting monetary policy.
- How banks provide liquidity to the rest of the economy.
- How banks address asymmetric information and determine which deficit units will get funds in the form of loans—and on what terms.
- How banks transform shorter-term deposits into loans with longer maturities.
- Why banks are provided a government safety net and, in return, are subject to more regulation than most other sectors of the economy.

BACKGROUND

Chances are that it has been some time since you have been in the lobby of a commercial bank. Perhaps you have never been. This, however, should not be construed to be reflective of the importance of commercial banks to you and to our economy more broadly. How did you pay for your textbooks this semester or your last tank of gas? Unless you used cash, commercial banks handled the various steps that were involved in those transactions, which resulted in funds being transferred to the account of the seller—either directly from your checking account or from a loan made to you by your bank (if you used a credit card). Even if you paid cash, the cash probably came from an automated teller machine (ATM) operated by a bank. Moreover, there are high odds that the loan on your car was made by a commercial bank. Beyond this, every entity you deal with in the marketplace depends importantly on commercial banks for payment and credit services, some to a greater extent than others.

Historically, the most important type of financial institution around the globe has been commercial banks. In less developed economies today, commercial banks still dominate the financial system by providing the bulk of financing to businesses—and often to governments—and serve as the principal holders of the funds owned by households and businesses. As in more advanced economies, commercial banks in developing economies provide the backbone for payments other than those made with cash.

In lesser-developed financial systems, the other important source of financing for businesses is stock (equities). Only as the financial system develops do other types of financing, such as bonds and commercial paper, and other types of intermediaries, such as pension funds, mutual funds, and insurance companies, come to play an important role.

In the United States, commercial banks still are the largest financial institutions, despite the rapid growth of other institutions—such as mutual funds, hedge funds, and pension funds. In this chapter, we examine the special role played by commercial banks in the financial system. In particular, we examine their role as issuers of a major component of the nation's money stock—bank deposits. These deposits are used for making the bulk of economic and financial transactions. In this context, we will explore how the banking system is at the core of our payment system, providing much of the "plumbing"—or infrastructure—for our payments system. That payment system supports the billions of economically beneficial transactions that take place each day.

Related to this, commercial banks are major providers of liquidity to the economy and the rest of the financial system, which we will explore next. Commercial banks as major lenders address informational asymmetries, the next feature to be explored. This will be followed by a discussion of the way that commercial banks perform maturity transformation—transforming the shorter-term deposit funds received by businesses and households into longer-term loans and securities. We conclude this chapter by examining how the special economic functions performed by the banking system have resulted in the government providing a safety net for the banking system and, in return, supervise and regulate these institutions more heavily than most other types of businesses. But first, we will look at key features of commercial bank balance sheets.

COMMERCIAL BANK BALANCE SHEET

We can better understand the economic role of commercial banks by examining the basic features of commercial bank balance sheets. The balance sheet is based on the accounting identity: $A = L + NW$ or assets equal liabilities plus net worth. That is, a bank's assets must equal its liabilities plus the ownership interest of its shareholders. The following T-account illustrates this relationship.

Balance Sheet of the U.S. Banking System

Assets		Liabilities Plus Net Worth	
Cash and securities	5,435	Transaction deposits	1,252
Loans	6,271	Other retail deposits	6,919
Business	1,605	Wholesale deposits	1,576
Consumer	1,153	Other managed liabilities	1,570
Real estate	3,513	Other liabilities	1,136
Other assets	2,275	Net worth	1,528
Total assets	**13,981**	**Total liabilities and net worth**	**13,981**

Amounts in billions of U.S. dollars as of November 27, 2013.
Source: Board of Governors of the Federal Reserve System, *Assets and Liabilities of Commercial Banks in the United States* (H.8 release), December 6, 2013.

Assets

In the preceding T-account, major asset categories are presented on the left side and major liability categories and net worth are presented on the right. Amounts, in billions of dollars, are shown for the entire U.S. banking system.

In the assets column, the first category shown is cash and securities. Cash can be thought of as funds that are immediately accessible and can take the form of deposit balances with other commercial banks or with the central bank (the Federal Reserve in the United States). Securities are largely federal government securities (sovereign debt) that can be sold or purchased quickly. To better understand the role of this category of assets, it is worth noting that commercial banks are continually facing shocks to their balance sheets in the form of unexpected losses or inflows of funds. As noted later in this chapter, banks lose funds when they make loans to customers or customers draw down their deposits at the bank; they gain funds when customers deposit funds or repay loans. The cash and securities category can be thought of as the bank's liquid reserves that can be tapped to meet daily shocks that cause an unexpected loss of funds, or they can serve as a repository for holding unexpected inflows of funds. They can be drawn on when the bank finds itself in need of funds—that is, customer activity has resulted in an outflow from the bank—and added to when customer activity has resulted in unexpected cash inflows. Note that this category represents more than a third of all banking assets.

Historically, a primary business of commercial banks has been making loans, the next category. Banks make loans primarily to businesses, consumers, and to finance real estate (both household and business sector properties)—the three loan components listed.[1] Loans to businesses, sometimes labeled commercial and industrial loans, were the traditional focus of commercial bank lending. Lending to consumers has been a more recent line of activity. Loans backed by real estate—real estate loans or mortgages—have been made to businesses for some time (commercial real estate loans) while residential real estate loans (residential mortgages) came along later. These three loan categories, known as *core loans*, account for well more than half of all banking assets.

The other assets category includes certain other kinds of loans, bank premises and equipment, real estate owned, and miscellaneous other assets.

Liabilities

Turning to the other side of the T-account, the principal liabilities of banks are deposits—the first three categories on the right. Transaction deposits are those that can be used for making payment, sometimes called checking accounts.[2] They were the traditional form of deposit account offered by commercial banks. Holders are businesses and households (as well as nonprofit organizations and governments). Other retail deposits take the form of savings accounts (including money market deposits) and fixed-maturity time deposits (sometimes called certificates of deposits [CDs]). Households are the primary holders of other retail deposits. Transaction deposits and other retail accounts are commonly called *core deposits*. Core deposits account for roughly two-thirds of all liabilities of commercial banks. The balances in these accounts are not subject to much control by banks, at least over short periods. They are determined by customer decisions, which are hard to predict.

In contrast, wholesale deposits are placed by large businesses and institutions, which are careful shoppers. These deposits can be turned on or turned off by banks by offering more or less attractive terms. They are said to be *managed liabilities* in the sense that banks can control or manage them by varying the terms offered. Banks can also turn to managed liabilities other than deposits to raise funds. Such managed liabilities take the form primarily of borrowings from other banks—so-called federal funds and eurodollars—and repurchase agreements (RPs), which are arranged mostly with businesses.

Net Worth (Capital)

The difference between the bank's assets and its liabilities is what is left over for its shareholders: net worth or equity. It is also called the bank's capital. The bank's creditors—the holders of its liabilities, including depositors—want the bank to have adequate amounts of capital to protect their financial interests. Capital acts as a cushion against losses in asset values. That is, the shareholders experience first losses when asset values decline. After that, some or all creditors will suffer losses. The more capital, the greater is the scope for losses of asset values to be absorbed by the bank's shareholders without creditors taking a hit.

In addition, government policies place the government as a potential creditor of the bank, and the government has a strong interest in ensuring that banks are sufficiently capitalized to protect the interest of taxpayers. Deposit insurance—under which the government insures balances in depositor accounts, usually up to some maximum—is a way in which the government can become a creditor to the bank. This happens when the Federal Deposit Insurance Corporation (FDIC) must step in to address a weak or failing bank to ensure that adequate funds are available to meet obligations to insured depositors. For these reasons, government regulatory agencies impose capital requirements on banks, mandating minimum levels of capital to buffer potential asset losses. They also attempt to restrict the amount of risk that banks are exposed to, to limit the size of potential losses.

Figure 3.1 shows the amount of owners' equity to assets. It shows that equity positions have nearly doubled since the 1980s.[3] This largely owes to the greater emphasis placed by federal bank regulators on bank capital for safety and soundness.

PAYMENT SYSTEM AND MONEY

Commercial Banks and the Payment System

Commercial banks are the largest providers of payment services. The bulk of payments in the United States and other advanced economies take place through commercial banks. Banks provide the accounts—transaction accounts—that hold

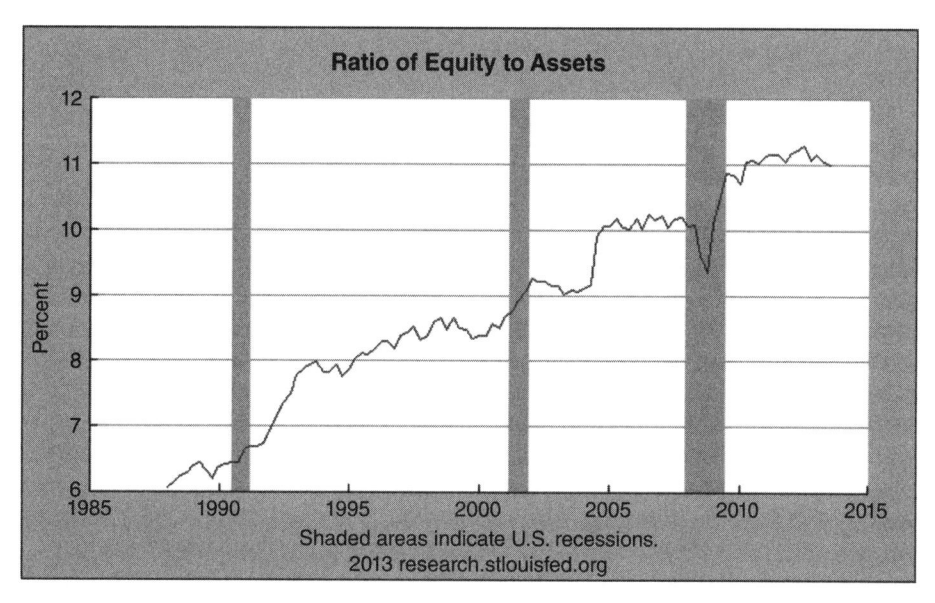

FIGURE 3.1 Total Equity/Total Assets (EQTA)
Source: Federal Financial Institutions Examination Council.

balances used for making payment. Based on payment instructions, funds are transferred from the account of the party making the payment (payer)—for goods or services or for financial transactions—to the account of the recipient party (payee)—the seller. These days, payment instructions take a variety of forms.

Traditionally, payment instructions have taken the form of the paper check, which is a written instruction by the payer to the payer's bank to take funds out of the payer's account and transfer them to the payee's account. If you examine a standard check, you will notice that it states, "Pay to the order of," and this is followed by the payee's name. The check then denotes the amount to be paid and becomes a legal payment instrument when the order is dated and signed by a person authorized to make payment from the account.

With more inexpensive, faster, and reliable electronic means for submitting payment instructions, checks have been diminishing in importance rapidly.[4] Instead, the payer can now use point-of-sale (POS) terminals to submit payment instructions—the so-called debit card used in a wide variety of stores. In addition, Internet banking enables the payer to instruct payment using a dedicated Internet site operated by the bank. Mobile (phone) banking has become a more recent system for making payment. With mobile banking, the customer issues payment instructions using a cell phone. Interestingly, this means of payment has become very popular in parts of Africa and other developing areas, where other types of payment have not been available and cell phones have become widespread. Indeed, mobile payment systems have become very user friendly, even for illiterate people.

THE EVOLUTION OF MONEY

The monetary system in advanced economies today bears little resemblance to original forms of money. However, in many other parts of the world today, the type of money that is widely used is not greatly different from original types—the notable differences are that the physical features and the issuer have changed. Nonetheless, even in these areas, modern technology is bringing about radical change.

Evidence that humans were taking advantage of the economic gains from trade and specialization goes back to earliest historical accounts. Even in these very early times, instead of bartering one good for another, people found that it was more convenient—transactions costs were lower—when they used another common commodity as an exchange medium. This usually took the form of a familiar, durable metal, such as copper or gold (even shells, beads, and cattle have been used in some civilizations). The seller traded goods for this medium. Later, the seller could exchange the medium for the goods desired by the seller.

COINAGE

Still, there were complications that involved the pieces of metal not being of the same weight or purity, and these needed to be worked out. The lack of standardization of the pieces of metal caused inconvenience in the exchange process—it added to transactions costs and limited the exploitation of the gains from trade and specialization. In response, some well-recognized and respected merchants began to standardize the exchange medium by making coins of uniform weight and purity. They would authenticate the coins by affixing their seal to them. Parties to trade would recognize these coins and trust them as payment for the things that they sold. As a result, transactions costs were lowered by such coins, and this fostered more economically beneficial exchange. It also proved worthwhile for the producer of the coins.

It did not take long for governments to get into the act. Monarchs (including Caesars) realized that they could do the coining of metals themselves. This would afford them an opportunity to celebrate their reign by placing favorable likenesses of themselves on the coins, and, more importantly, public coinage could fatten the public treasury in the process. Profit would come from the coins having greater monetary value than the metal they contained—so-called seigniorage. To ensure that their coins were favored in transactions and seigniorage was enlarged, these coins could be deemed legal tender. That is, they could be designated to be the only medium that could officially discharge obligations under the law of the land.

Over time, governments came to realize that they could boost seigniorage profits by substituting paper-type notes for precious metal coins.[a] People

---

[a] Actually, these notes have not been made of paper, but commonly a substrate that includes cotton and other materials. In recent decades, notes in some parts of the world have been made instead from a polymer substrate, which tends to last longer. Durability of the note is important, as well as security features that can be embedded in the note to discourage counterfeiting.

valued the monetary medium primarily because of its utility in performing exchange, not so much for the commodity value of the medium. The authority issuing the notes needed to be mindful, though, of not overissuing them. When they were overissued, their value would decline in terms of what they could be exchanged for—inflation resulted. When inflation became serious, the public would substitute other mediums to perform their transactions and the government issuer's seigniorage would shrink.

BANK NOTES

Meanwhile, the practice of banking was emerging. People holding precious metals, such as gold, for transactions often found that they had more than they needed for their daily business activities. They began to place the excess with goldsmiths who held it in safekeeping and, by so doing, these goldsmiths could earn more income. In return for receiving gold, the goldsmith would issue warehouse receipts that could be redeemed for gold. In time, the receipts came to be used for some payments instead of the gold itself. Moreover, goldsmiths came to realize that they did not have to keep all the gold in their vaults, and they could lend some of it out for interest. In so doing, they could earn a fee for holding the gold in safekeeping and interest for lending some of it out. These became the forerunner of banks.

For a time, banks issued notes (in essence, warehouse receipts) that could be presented for gold—or some other precious metal. These notes were easier to manage than gold and were commonly accepted as transaction mediums. Today, these private bank notes have been supplanted by notes issued by central banks (currency); as we will see in Chapter 12, central banks are public institutions today.

DEPOSITS

Over time, banks also provided third-party payment services to their deposit customers. Instead of the customer coming to the bank to withdraw funds from an account and arranging for these funds to be delivered to the customer's counterparty for payment, banks would accept an order from the customer to pay a designated third party. This order could be done with a paper instruction—a check—as noted in the text. Also, as noted in the text, these payment orders have increasingly become digital, which is less costly, faster, and more reliable.

Looking ahead, it seems likely that the trend toward a digital means of making payment will continue. Payments from transaction accounts will increasingly be made using Internet, mobile phone, and POS instruction messages and no doubt other methods of submitting electronic payment instructions will emerge. Stored value cards and other mediums that enable persons to conveniently carry funds for making purchases may also largely supplant currency.[b]

---

[b] Actually, U.S. currency has been growing faster than many other balances used for making payment over the past few decades. This is primarily due to growing demand for dollars outside the United States, especially in trouble spots and other places where people have concerns about their local currency.

Payment System Infrastructure

Beneath the surface of the payment system is an extensive infrastructure. When both the payer and payee have accounts with the same commercial bank, the transfer from the payer to the payee is an in-house accounting operation.[5] However, when the parties to the transaction have different banks, there must be a system for transferring funds from the payer's bank to the payee's bank. This involves a so-called clearinghouse. Traditionally, banks located in the same region assemble each day at the clearinghouse and present checks drawn on other banks in that region. For example, Bank A might present $20 million in checks that it accumulated over the previous day from its depositors that are drawn on accounts at Bank B, and Bank B might have accumulated $23 million in checks that are drawn on Bank A.[6] Once they have exchanged checks—netted positions against each other—Bank A will owe Bank B $3 million. They must have a way to transfer good funds from Bank A to Bank B in the amount of the net balance—$3 million. This can be done if both banks have an account with a common third bank, say, Bank C—a so-called correspondent bank. In this case, Bank A can instruct Bank C to transfer $3 million from its account to Bank B's account. Alternatively, the two banks can make the transfer on the books of the central bank, because each will hold an account with the central bank to be used for various purposes, including for making these types of payments.

As the payment system has evolved, more advanced forms of the clearinghouse have been created. The bulk of payments now go through an automated clearinghouse (ACH). Commercial banks routinely over the course of the day send payment orders submitted by their customers electronically to the ACH. The ACH accumulates such payment instructions from all the banks in its network. At regular intervals, the ACH nets the (bilateral) interbank positions and arranges for transfers of funds to cover net interbank positions. Usually, this takes the form of a transfer of funds on the books of the central bank from those banks having a net negative position to those having a net positive position. To complete the process, all the information on the separate individual transactions processed by the ACH is sent to the banks so they can credit each customer's account at their bank.[7]

Credit and Stored Value Cards

We have not yet discussed *credit cards*, such as Visa and MasterCard, which are used widely for buying goods or services. A credit card transaction, as the name suggests, involves an extension of credit to pay for the good or service that is bought. The bank that issued the card to the buyer, when it electronically accepts the transaction, agrees to make payment to the seller in the amount of the purchase. It, in effect, is granting a loan in the amount of the purchase to its customer having the credit card. These loans are accumulated over a statement period—usually around a month—and the customer is billed this accumulated amount. The customer can pay the entire credit card bill by directing his or her bank to transfer the full amount from his or her account to the account of the bank issuing the credit card. Alternatively, the customer can pay a portion of the bill, thereby continuing to have a credit balance (loan) from the issuing bank.

Still another payment medium is the *stored value card* that entitles the holder to make purchases. Stored value cards take different forms but are similar in that they have a certain maximum amount that the holder can spend. For so-called closed-loop cards the card can be used only for a specified vendor, such as a restaurant chain or a home improvement store. In other cases, so-called open-loop cards, the balance can be used at a wide variety of stores, typically those that accept credit cards. The buyer of the card pays up front the value of the card (which could be given as a gift), and each time a purchase is made, the amount of the purchase is deducted from the card's balance. For many of these cards, the holder can add to the balance on the card by transferring more funds to the issuer.[8]

Payments Media in the Money Stock

Clearly, balances in transaction accounts are related to overall transaction activity in the economy, which in turn is related to the overall level of economic activity and employment. For this reason, economists have long regarded such accounts—and currency, also used for transactions—to be of special interest. Indeed, one measure of the nation's money stock—*M1*—is defined to include currency and transaction deposits.[9] Some have thought that M1 could be used as an indicator of the economy, because it typically expands when the economy expands and contracts when the economy contracts. That is, it can be used to assess the condition of the economy. Others have argued that the central bank can exercise control over the economy by controlling the stock of money—raising growth in the money stock when it wants the economy to expand faster and curbing the money stock when the economy is overheating and inflation becomes a worry.

Some economists have argued that not only are transaction deposits related to spending and the economy but certain other accounts, too. This is because funds can easily be moved from these other accounts to transaction accounts to cover purchases. Accordingly, they advocate a broader measure of the money stock—*M2*—that includes other retail deposits at commercial banks and other depository institutions.[10]

The magnitudes of M1 and M2 are shown next.

Money Stock Measure	Amount
M1	2,618
Currency	1,155
Transaction deposits	1,463
M2	10,935
M1	2,618
Other components of M2	8,317

Amounts in billions of U.S. dollars as of November 25, 2013.
Source: Board of Governors of the Federal Reserve System, *Money Stock Measures* (H.6 release), December 5, 2013.

M1 is roughly one-sixth the size of (nominal) gross domestic product (GDP), while M2 is approximately two-thirds the size of GDP.

Velocity (Turnover of Money)

Figure 3.2 illustrates the relationships between M1 and M2 and GDP. Shown are the velocities of M1 and M2—the ratios of GDP to the M1 and M2 measures of the money stock (top and bottom lines, respectively). It represents the number of times the money stock turns over each year for purchases of all final goods and services (GDP). If the velocity of money is stable—the public wishes to hold money in proportion to its spending and income—then a change in the money stock will translate into a proportionate change in GDP. To illustrate, if policy objectives call for a 3 percent increase in GDP, this could be achieved through a 3 percent increase in the money stock.[11] In contrast, if velocity varies a good bit and cannot be predicted easily, trying to stabilize the economy by controlling the money stock would prove counterproductive.

In practice, neither the M1 nor the M2 measure of the money stock have tracked overall spending or output very closely, especially over the past few decades. This can be seen by the variations in their respective velocities in Figure 3.2. The velocity of M1 has been especially volatile, although that of M2 has varied a good bit, too. And movements in both velocities have proven hard to predict. Because of serious slippages in these relationships over recent decades, the monetary authority of the United States—the Federal Reserve—has placed very little emphasis on measures of the money stock in its conduct of monetary policy. Not only have measures of the money stock proven to be unreliable guides to monetary policy in the United States, but other countries have had similar experiences. The conduct of monetary policy using alternative guides to the money stock is explored more fully in Chapter 14.

The deterioration of the relationship between the money stock and economic activity owes importantly to the evolution of the financial system. Over recent decades, financial institutions have provided the public with a wide array of financial

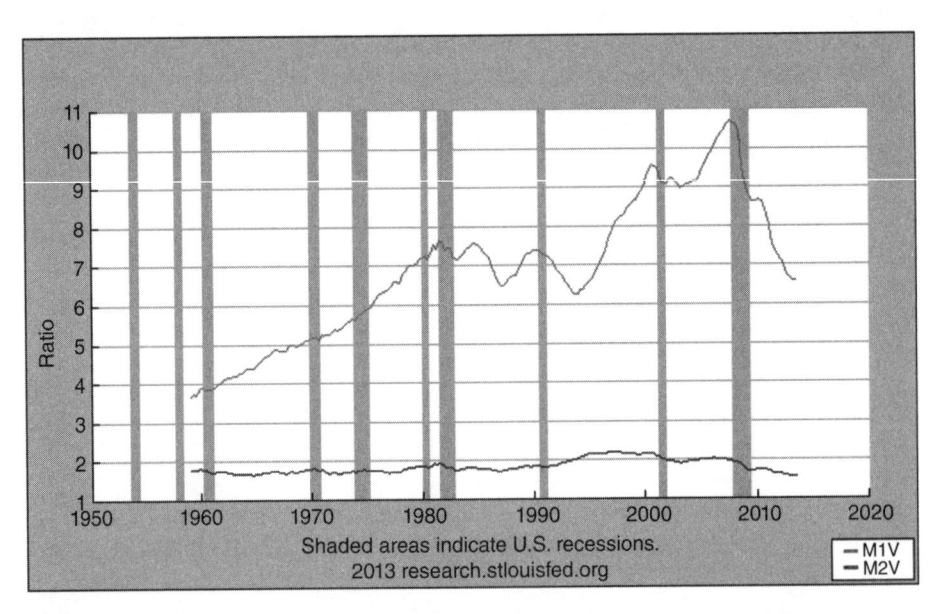

FIGURE 3.2 Velocity of M2 Money Stock (M2V)/Velocity of M1 Money Stock (M1V)
Source: Federal Reserve Board and Bureau of Economic Analysis.

MONEY DEMAND AND MONEY SUPPLY

For a couple centuries, economists have given the concept of the stock of money special attention. The stock of money has been viewed as something that tracks the economy closely and can be used to exercise control over the economy, as noted in the text. One can think of the stock of money as being determined by the supply of and demand for money. In other words, it represents equilibrium when demand equals supply. Money demand varies directly with the level of economic activity—expanding when the economy expands and contracting when the economy contracts. The demand for money also varies inversely with the level of interest rates, representing the opportunity cost of holding money balances. Thus, a rise in interest rates will reduce the quantity demanded of money and a decline in interest rates will increase the quantity demanded.

The manner in which this equilibrium is achieved has absorbed volumes of treatises. The consensus that evolved over time is that it depends on the monetary regime that is in place. Under a gold standard—or fixed exchange rate system discussed in Chapter 16—a nation's supply of money is largely determined by external considerations and the demand for money—its level of economic activity—must adjust to this amount. In other words, the supply of gold is fixed by international considerations and it is the demand for money and thereby the economy that must adjust to this amount. For example, if the supply of gold—and thus the supply of money—were to contract, a disequilibrium results in which the supply of money falls short of demand. If this new lower supply does not change, the economy must contract to lower the demand for money and reestablish equilibrium.

Over the course of the first 70 years of the twentieth century, fixed exchange rate regimes were modified (relaxed) and then abandoned. Fixed exchange rates were replaced by other monetary regimes, implying different ways in which the demand for money would be equated with the supply of money. Most of the time, the regime has allowed the supply of money to passively adjust to the public's demand for money.

The most notable exception occurred from October 1979 to October 1982 when the U.S. Federal Reserve sought to control the stock of money by setting the supply of bank reserves. In essence, the Fed was attempting to influence the level of economic activity through its ability to control the supply of bank reserves. Because banks need these reserves to meet legal reserve requirements, the supply of reserves can be set by the central bank to achieve an objective for the stock of money, which, in turn, is based on an objective for the level of economic activity. This can be seen as follows:

$$R = \delta \cdot MS$$

In this expression, R represents the amount of reserves supplied by the central bank, δ represents the required reserve ratio set by the central bank, and MS represents the amount of money stock deposits subject to this reserve requirement. This expression can be rearranged as follows:

$$MS = R/\delta$$

(continued)

In other words, the supply of money, MS, will be proportional to the amount of reserves set by the central bank, R. For example, if the required reserve ratio were 10 percent and the amount of reserves set by the central bank were $50 billion, the stock of money would be $500 billion—or $MS = \$50$ billion$/0.10 = \$500$ billion.[a] By setting the supply of money in this manner, the Fed was attempting to bring about monetary equilibrium by having the level of economic activity adjust to bring money demand into alignment with the Fed's target for the supply of money. Under the conditions of the time in which the U.S. economy was overheating and inflation was a serious problem, the Fed sought to cool off the economy by restricting the supply of reserves and thereby the supply of money. As noted in the text, such a system for controlling the stock of money is effective for achieving macroeconomic goals when the demand for money is related to the economy in a stable manner and is not subject to unpredictable shifts—something that has not been present for some time.

Currently, as we will see in Chapters 12 and 13, the Fed sets the interest rate on interbank loans of reserves—the federal funds rate—and, in these circumstances, the supply of money (and reserves) passively adjust to match the demand for money.[b] The Fed forgoes its ability to control the supply of reserves and the money stock in order to be able to use its ability to control the federal funds rate and set it in accord with its macroeconomic objectives for the economy, which it views to be achieved better through another approach—to be discussed in Chapters 13 and 14.

---

[a] The discussion here is a simplification of the actual process used by the Fed during this period. It ignores currency, which is issued by the Fed, and is also a component of the money stock together with money stock deposits. It further ignores banks' demands for excess reserves and the distinction between total reserves and nonborrowed reserves, discussed in Chapter 12. In practice, the Fed controlled the supply of nonborrowed reserves. The preceding expression can be modified to allow for these complications.

[b] Changing the supply of reserves will change the federal funds rate, and vice versa. For example, reducing the supply of reserves will cause the federal funds rate to increase. Thus, the central bank can either choose to control the supply of reserves or the interbank interest rate. It cannot control both.

---

instruments having features similar to those of components of the money stock. In response, the public has substituted other financial instruments for standard money balances, disrupting relationships between measures of money and GDP.

LIQUIDITY PROVISION

Commercial banks perform another important role in being a provider of liquidity to the rest of the financial system and to businesses and households. By liquidity, we mean providing readily available funds for making payment, often on little or no notice.[12] Financial institutions, ordinary businesses, and households occasionally find themselves in situations in which they need funds quickly to cover some unexpected outlay. For example, a corporation may find that some other business it has wanted to acquire has become available for purchase and the acquiring firm needs to marshal funds for the purchase quickly. Similarly, a household may find itself facing an unexpected bill that needs to be paid immediately. Or another financial institution may need to pay out a large sum quickly.

Absent liquidity provision by commercial banks, the business, the financial institution, or the household would need to hold large amounts of cash—in the form of currency or deposit balances—to be prepared for such contingencies. If not, it would have to forgo the business opportunity or possibly default on the payment with potentially serious consequences.

However, commercial banks are well positioned to meet such situations, whether the sums involved are very large or small. Typically, the bank extends access to such funds to its customer by a *line of credit*. The line of credit allows the bank's customer to tap the bank for funds, up to a limit, with little or no prior notice. Businesses and other financial institutions usually pay a fee for such a line based on the size of the line, regardless of whether the line is used. Often, these lines of credit are revolving lines. With a "revolver," the customer can borrow any amount up to the limit, in a single draw or in several draws, and can repay some or all of the borrowing at will. Bank credit cards offered to individuals have lines of credit and revolving features.

Businesses of all sizes rely on commercial bank lines of credit to cover a variety of contingencies. The lines can get very large, especially for businesses seeking to acquire another (large) business. In these cases, the line of credit could be $20 billion or more.

Clearly, commercial banks providing liquidity must manage their balance sheets carefully if they are going to be able to honor all customer demands for funds. It is hard for a bank to know from one day to the next what such demands for funds will be. This implies that it must hold balances with the central bank or other commercial banks or other liquid assets that can be tapped on a moment's notice. In the event these sources are not adequate, they also need to have arrangements with other banks that enable them to get funds from these banks on short notice. Often, this can take the form of a line of credit with another financial institution.

Going back to the balance sheet presented at the beginning of this chapter, the discussion above implies that many loan balances are determined by customer discretion and cannot be controlled or predicted by the bank. Much the same can be said of core deposits on the other side of the balance sheet. Depositors as a group on any particular day can, without warning, withdraw or deposit large sums. The bank must be in a position to meet such shocks—be they withdrawals or deposit inflows. To manage these balance sheet shocks requires state-of-the-art information and management systems as well as skilled managers.

In practice, what matters to the bank is the net between inflows (or outflows) of core deposits and loans made (or repaid). Some days, balance sheet shocks may take the form of deposit outflows or large amounts of loans taken down under lines of credit. In this situation, the bank will need to draw down its cash and liquid securities or turn to managed liabilities to meet the shortfall. On other days, it will be faced with large amounts of loan repayments or inflows to core deposits. On these days, it will need to place funds in liquid assets or pay down managed liabilities. Of course, there will be still other days when core deposit inflows roughly match outflows of funds for new loans. In this case, the bank's managers need to do very little.

DEALING WITH ASYMMETRIC INFORMATION

We noted in Chapter 2 that very few businesses and almost no individuals have access to direct forms of finance. This is because little is known about them—they are characterized by substantial informational asymmetries. These situations open up business opportunities for banks and other lenders that can acquire critical information about the borrower, process that information, and make a sound judgment about whether to lend to that party or not, and, if so, to fashion the terms of such a loan. Commercial banks—and other lending institutions—have invested considerable resources to develop the expertise to make such loans. In addition to making the loan, the bank will monitor the borrower to better ensure that the borrower is making decisions that will enhance prospects for repayment of the loan. In this way, the bank will be applying discipline on the borrower.

Usually, commercial banks prefer that the borrower also be a depositor or a user of other services, because those relationships can provide valuable missing information about the borrower. This is frequently referred to as *relationship banking*. The bank develops a relationship with the customer through various credit and deposit arrangements and this relationship enables the bank to acquire valuable information for assessing the customer's risk profile.

Once the bank has become comfortable with the customer's reliability and ability to repay obligations, it will be willing to provide guarantees or lines of credit for the customer. With a guarantee, the bank guarantees the obligation of a customer, supplementing the customer's promise to pay with its own. The bank is better known than the customer and, when the customer can get a respected bank to provide a guarantee, the customer's counterparty to a transaction will feel more confident about getting paid. Economically worthwhile transactions involving the bank's customer will be completed and these might otherwise not happen without such guarantees.

Guarantees take various forms. They can take the form of a back-up line of credit behind a firm's issuance of commercial paper—a direct form of finance. In this instance, the bank guarantees payment to the commercial paper investor in the event the issuer lacks funds when the instrument matures. Alternatively, they can take the form of letters of credit (L/Cs) under which a seller of goods to the bank's customer can get assurances of payment by the customer's bank. L/Cs are widely used in international trade, as we will see in Chapter 7. Banks usually charge their customers fees for providing such guarantees.

MATURITY TRANSFORMATION

Maturity transformation occurs when a bank receives funds in the form of deposits having one maturity and uses these funds to make loans or acquire investments having another maturity. Usually, it refers to banks taking in deposits that are relatively short in maturity and making loans that are longer in maturity. It is thought that depositors want their deposits to have short maturities, but loan customers want longer-maturity loans. Thus, the bank can make both sides happy by such a maturity transformation—that is, create economic value through such maturity transformation.

Such practices, however, are risky for the bank. The maturity mismatch exposes the bank to interest rate risk, as briefly noted in Chapter 2. If market interest rates rise, the bank will immediately begin to experience its interest costs on deposits rising, but it will take a very long time before it can replace its low-yielding loans with higher-yielding assets—that is, it needs to wait until its old low-yielding loans mature before they can be replaced with loans having higher interest rates better aligned with its now higher-rate deposits. As we will see in the next chapter, the rise in interest rates causes the value of those old longer-term loans to drop. Meanwhile, it is experiencing an adverse cash flow as its interest costs rise much faster than its interest receipts.

Because of such risk, commercial banks engage in only a limited amount of maturity transformation. They use their shorter-term deposits to make shorter-term loans or acquire marketable securities that do not have very long maturities. If a bank were to have a significant interest rate mismatch, it could cover its resulting interest rate risk exposure with financial futures or options contracts that provide compensation to the bank if longer-term interest rates rise, which can offset the impact of rising interest costs. Indeed, bank supervisors watch closely the maturity balance between assets and liabilities to prevent significant interest rate risk from developing. In contrast, several decades ago, savings institutions were allowed to incur large imbalances between their short-term deposits and long-term (mortgage) loans, until losses from a rise in interest rates nearly wiped out the entire industry. Today, savings institutions are restricted by regulatory policy from taking on too much interest rate risk.

THE SAFETY NET AND REGULATORY POLICY

Commercial banks and other depository institutions are among the most heavily regulated businesses in our economy. In part, this is because they are fiduciary institutions that hold much of the public's wealth, and there has been a long-standing desire to use public policy to protect their customers—especially retail customers—by ensuring that these institutions do not engage in fraudulent or excessively risky practices. In addition, it has long been recognized that difficulties faced by one bank can disrupt the payment system and in other ways spill over to other banks, and even disrupt the entire economy. Today, we call this *systemic risk*. Banking crises over our history—including the recent financial crisis and Great Recession—are testimony to the power of such spillovers.

To limit the scope for disruption, public policy over time has developed a so-called safety net for commercial banks. Since the 1930s in the United States, this has importantly involved *deposit insurance*, under which an agency of the federal government—the Federal Deposit Insurance Corporation—insures each deposit up to a maximum amount, currently, $250,000. The purpose behind deposit insurance has been not only to protect retail depositors from losses, but just as importantly to discourage them from running on their banks. If depositors came to fear that they might not be able to get all of their funds back, they would rush to withdraw their funds ahead of others and place unsustainable strains on their bank's liquidity.[13] This likely would lead to a broader panic among depositors that spreads to all banks and spills over to the economy. With federal deposit insurance, depositors can feel assured that they will have access to their funds and not face losses even if their bank fails. Financial crises are the topic of Chapter 15.

In addition, commercial banks have access to the *discount window* of the central bank—a second component of the safety net. This is intended to enable financially sound institutions that may be facing temporary liquidity shortages to be able to get funds instantly in the form of a loan from the central bank to avoid having to suspend payments to depositors and thereby trigger a broader financial panic.[14] The central bank's discount window is discussed more fully in Chapter 12.

Finally, the payment system, because of its critical role in the functioning of the financial system and broader economy, is deemed to be the equivalent of a public utility. As such, *access to the payment system*—another component of the safety net—is largely restricted to commercial banks.

Access to the safety net confers special privileges to commercial banks—and other depository institutions that are covered. They are viewed as having certain protections not available to other financial institutions. As a consequence, they can get funds from depositors and other creditors on more favorable terms. This can lead to a moral hazard situation. The bank is able to attract deposit and other funds on attractive terms, irrespective of the risk it undertakes. That is, the normal market discipline that would limit risk taking—depositors insisting on more compensation for the risk they are being subjected to or pulling out their funds—is largely absent. In these circumstances, bank managers will have a strong incentive to take on more risk than would otherwise be prudent. They—actually, their owners—enjoy all the upside gains to be had from more risk, but they are not exposed to all the losses to be incurred from more risk. This shifts incentives toward favoring excessive amounts of risk. The safety net backstop exposes the public sector—taxpayers—to some of the corresponding potential losses. There are numerous examples of commercial banks and other financial institutions exploiting their moral hazard situation, most recently leading to the financial crisis of 2008.

Because of the risk that some larger commercial banks pose to the financial system—and to the economy—observers have argued that large banks are too big to fail. That is, the failure of a large bank—highly intertwined with other important financial institutions—could bring down the entire financial system, and, as a result, federal authorities will step in to prevent this from happening. If market participants believe that the authorities will not allow large commercial banks to fail, these participants will be less diligent in their dealings with large banks. That is, they will not apply the same degree of market discipline to these banks as they would to less systemically important institutions, which encourages more risk taking by the managers of these banks having special protections.

To address this problem, bank regulators establish rules and procedures for curbing risk taking by commercial banks, especially the larger ones that are deemed to have stronger safety net protections and that expose the system to larger spillovers. Indeed, as risk positions at these institutions have become more complicated and risk management more advanced, regulatory approaches have had to adapt. Over recent decades, regulators from major financial centers around the globe have adopted a common approach to imposing prudential regulations on commercial banks—most recently, this has been called the Basel III approach to bank regulation. It has involved development of common guidelines for bank capital, liquidity, and other aspects of bank operations that pose serious risk to the safety net.

In addition, in the United States, it has become clear that some large nonbank financial institutions—part of the so-called shadow banking system (see box)—pose systemic risk concerns as well.[15] Under the landmark Wall Street Reform and Consumer Protection (Dodd-Frank) Act of 2010, federal regulatory authorities have been given the responsibility to designate such institutions to be systemically important financial institutions and to regulate them in much the same way that they regulate commercial banks. We will discuss regulation of commercial banks in more detail in Chapter 17.

THE SHADOW BANKING SYSTEM

The term *shadow banking* has been used a lot in recent years, but in various ways. It has generally been used to denote arrangements for intermediating credit outside traditional deposits and loans at commercial banks. Usually, the creditor (surplus unit) extends funds on a short-term basis, acquiring an instrument with some deposit-type features that is thought to have very little risk. The funds are then placed in instruments of longer maturity—resulting in maturity transformation. The creditor is able to earn a higher yield than available on standard bank deposits. Being outside traditional loans and deposits at commercial banks also has meant being outside the pale of banking regulation.

Examples of such arrangements outside the regular banking system are asset-backed commercial paper that were arranged to avoid being on commercial bank balance sheets (discussed in Chapter 7), money market mutual funds (discussed in Chapter 18), and investment banks (discussed in Chapter 2). Each was involved in intermediating credit in ways that proved vulnerable to disruption and grew very large prior to the onset of the financial crisis in 2007 (discussed in Chapter 15). As creditors became concerned about the safety of their funds, they headed for the exits and, in so doing, placed severe strains on these shadow-banking arrangements, which got transmitted to the financial system more broadly.

Going forward, it is not clear that the shadow banking system will pose the same concerns for the stability of the broader financial system. The Dodd-Frank bill of 2010 provides for federal authority to deal with financial arrangements that pose systemic risk that are outside the banking system. The SEC is addressing the weaknesses in money market mutual funds. And banking regulators are tightening the regulation of off-balance-sheet activity of commercial banks, while major investment banks have opted to come under the ambit of regulations applied to commercial banks in order to have access to the safety net.

SUMMARY

1. Commercial banks play a central role in the financial system and the economy more broadly. Their balance sheet contains the following principal asset categories: cash and securities and loans—to businesses, households, and for real estate. Principal liability categories are transaction deposits, other retail deposits, wholesale deposits, and other liabilities. Net worth represents bank owners' position—assets less liabilities.
2. The items that have been used for making payment have changed a lot over history. For some time, though, commercial banks have provided the public with transaction deposits that serve as payments media, augmenting coins and notes issued by governments and central banks.
3. Commercial banks play a pivotal role in the payment system—and thereby in facilitating the transactions that support the economy. Businesses and households keep transaction deposit balances with commercial banks (and other depository institutions) and they use a growing array of methods to instruct their banks to make payment to a third party on their behalf to complete the staggering number of transactions made each day.
4. These include written instructions in the form of paper checks and electronic instructions in the form of POS terminals, the Internet, and mobile phones. Payments by credit card involve the buyer's (cardholder's) bank advancing credit to the buyer to complete the transaction instead of transferring funds from the buyer's transaction account; however, the payment of the credit card bill must be made using a transfer from the buyer's transaction account. Stored value cards—relying on much the same electronic infrastructure as credit cards—have also become popular in recent years.
5. Because transaction activity expands and contracts with the economy, much attention has been given over the years to monetary aggregates that include transactions media—currency and transaction accounts. M1, which contains both, is a transactions measure of the money stock. Certain other balances—such as other retail deposits and money market mutual funds—are thought to be easily convertible into transactions media for making payment and are included in the broader measure of the money stock, M2. For some time, neither measure of the money stock has tracked the economy very closely and both have lost their roles as guides for monetary policy.
6. Somewhat related to the payment system, the banking system is an important provider of liquidity to the rest of the financial system and to the economy. This enables worthwhile deals to be completed that might not otherwise occur or unexpected obligations to be paid that might otherwise pose hardships. It also enables businesses, households, and other financial institutions to hold smaller amounts of liquid assets. Much of this liquidity is provided through lines of credit.
7. Commercial banks also address problems of asymmetric information. They devote resources to acquiring and evaluating information about prospective borrowers, and are able to make worthwhile loans that would otherwise not be made. They also provide important monitoring of borrowers.
8. Commercial banks further engage in maturity transformation, receiving shorter-term deposits and using the proceeds to make longer-term loans. However, these operations expose the bank to considerable risk when interest rates change. As a

consequence, bank regulators limit the amount of maturity transformation that banks are allowed to perform.
9. Because problems in parts of the banking sector can lead to serious disruptions to the financial sector more broadly and spill over to the economy, commercial banks (and other depository institutions) are provided with a safety net. This safety net tends to create a moral hazard situation, exposing taxpayers to large losses. To counter the risk posed by moral hazard, there is a considerable amount of federal regulation that is focused on limiting the risk profile of banks.

QUESTIONS

1. If a commercial bank were to face a loss on an asset (its value drops), what are the implications for shareholder net worth?
2. What distinguishes cash and securities on a bank's balance sheet from loans? Retail deposits from wholesale deposits?
3. What is meant by shocks hitting commercial bank balance sheets? How do banks deal with these?
4. How does a reliable, efficient, and low-cost payment system affect overall economic well-being?
5. How did coins lower transactions costs when they were first introduced?
6. What are the advantages to governments of issuing their own notes (typically through their central banks)? How is seigniorage earned?
7. What is meant by a payment instruction? How are they submitted to banks?
8. What does "netting" in the context of the payment system mean? What is the role of a clearinghouse? How are net balances settled between banks?
9. Why might a measure of aggregate transaction balances be regarded as useful for a central bank for monetary policy purposes? What is the label given to this measure? What is the label given to a broader measure that also includes deposits that are easily converted into standard transaction balances?
10. Using the FRED website (Chapter 1), chart the level of M1 and M2. Chart 12-month growth rates for each. What might you infer about the performance of the economy based on these growth rates?
11. What is meant by commercial banks providing liquidity to the financial system, businesses, and households? What role is played by lines of credit in this process? What is a line of credit offered by a commercial bank? Under a line of credit, who makes the decision of whether and how much to draw (borrow)? What is meant by a revolving line of credit?
12. How do commercial banks address the problem of asymmetric information? How do you suppose they get remunerated for their efforts?
13. How does maturity transformation pose risks for commercial banks? Does it make any difference whether the bank's assets have longer or shorter maturities than its liabilities? Is one more risky than the other?
14. What is the safety net provided to the commercial banking system? How might this be related to moral hazard? In this regard, what is the role of regulatory policy?
15. What is meant by "shadow banking"? How has it posed systemic risk concerns? Do regulatory authorities have authority to deal with problems caused by shadow banks?

NOTES

1. Commercial banks got their name from their traditional major customer—commercial (business) enterprises. They held the deposits of businesses and used the proceeds to make commercial (business) loans.
2. All transaction accounts are now permitted to pay interest to depositors. This has not always been the case. In the 1930s, a federal law prohibited the payment of interest on demand deposits, the only transaction account at the time. In the 1970s and 1980s, banks and other depository institutions were allowed to open a new type of interest-earning transaction account for households. These were referred to as negotiable order of withdrawal (NOW) accounts. The statutory prohibition on the payment of interest on demand deposits, held mostly by businesses, was removed in 2011.
3. The content of the measure of equity shown in the diagram differs from that in the table. The reason being that the measure of net worth in the table includes some types of debt that banks can count as capital, in addition to owners' equity (shown in the chart).
4. See "Federal Reserve Payments Study Offers Expanded View of U.S. Noncash Payment Trends," Federal Reserve Bank of Cleveland, December 19, 2013.
5. Even if the funds transfer is internal, it still requires a well-developed record-keeping system, especially if the bank has multiple offices or branches. In practice, commercial banks these days have very advanced software systems—so-called core banking systems—and their various offices are linked electronically through highly developed communications networks. This enables the bank to easily and reliably make the internal transfer from the payer's to the payee's account instantaneously.
6. Once the banks exchange checks, the banks making payment can use the checks to remove corresponding balances from payer customer accounts. In recent years, much of this is being performed by highly advanced check-imaging systems that can conduct these operations electronically.
7. Payments for some very large transactions do not go through an ACH. Instead, the bank of the payer submits instructions directly to the central bank to transfer funds from the payer's bank account to the account of another commercial bank—the payee's bank. The receiving bank in turn will credit these funds to the account of its customer receiving the payment (the payee). Transfers of this sort—often to settle large financial transactions—are said to involve real-time gross settlement (RTGS).
8. Underlying stored value cards is an infrastructure for open-loop cards comparable to that of credit cards. For closed-loop cards, the company offering the card must have a communications network that can validate the card and the amount stored on the card and then deduct the amount of the purchase from the card.
9. The transactions deposits in M1 also include those issued by other depository institutions—savings institutions and credit unions.
10. M2 also includes balances held with money market mutual funds, which can be used for making some payments or can be easily transferred to a transaction account at a commercial bank for making payment.

11. In practice, the velocity of money does not need to be unchanged, but predictable. For example, if predictions were for a 1 percent decline in velocity, the money stock would need to increase 4 percent to boost GDP 3 percent.
12. The term *liquidity* is used in different ways. In this context, we use the term to denote providing readily available funds; these funds can be used to make a purchase or to discharge an obligation. In a later chapter, we will refer to a financial instrument possessing liquidity as one that can be bought or sold easily at a price close to its fundamental economic value.
13. Recall from our discussion of the commercial bank balance sheet earlier in this chapter that banks use funds from deposits mostly to make loans, which are rather illiquid. They have relatively small amounts of cash to meet withdrawals. If many depositors become worried about their ability to get their funds, they will try to beat the next person to the bank's teller before the cash runs out—something akin to a stampede in a theater.
14. Central banks require such loans to be adequately collateralized, to limit their loss exposure.
15. Deemed to be part of the shadow banking industry were large investment banks that had not been part of banking organizations. Included in addition has been an affiliate of a large global insurance conglomerate.

CHAPTER 4

The Pricing of Financial Assets

WHAT YOU WILL LEARN IN THIS CHAPTER

- The time value of money and the distinction between future value and present value.
- The present value formula linking the value of an asset today (its present value) to the future cash flows that the owner expects to receive from the asset and the discount rate (interest rate).
- How to use this relationship for determining the value of an asset when the cash flows and the discount rate are known; the amount of payments on an amortized, fixed-payment loan when the amount of the loan and interest rate are known; and the yield to maturity when the current price of an asset and its future cash flows are known.
- The valuation of a perpetual stream of cash flows—a consol—and ways that this relationship can be used for shorthand approximations of value.
- The relationship between the sensitivity of asset prices to interest changes and maturity.
- Risks that result when an investor's holding period is longer or shorter than the maturity of the asset.
- The difference between yield and return.
- The concept of duration.
- The relationship between an asset's duration and its maturity.
- The difference between the real interest rate and the nominal interest rate.
- An appendix to this chapter illustrates how to perform some of the calculations performed in this chapter on a financial calculator.

BACKGROUND

Have you ever wondered how the price (value) of an apartment building or an office building—each of which provides its owner with flows of cash stretched out over a period of time—is determined? The pricing of such real estate is similar to that of a share of common stock, which gets its value from the cash payments (dividends) that will be paid to its owner at different points in the future. What these have in common is that the current value (price) of these assets is based on the payments of cash to the investor at different points over time. Did you know that the price or value of a financial asset is inversely related to the level of interest rates?

The valuation process is complicated by the fact that the cash flows paid to the owner of an asset contribute to the current value of that asset to different degrees, depending on when they are paid. That is, a certain amount of cash is worth more if it is paid next year than if it is paid in 20 years. Stated differently, in determining current (or present) value, a cash flow in the future is lowered (discounted) by a greater amount the farther into the future it is paid.

Although assets differ a great deal in the features of the asset and the cash flows they provide, their values are based on the same underlying principle: The current price of an asset is the present value of all the future cash flows to which the owner is entitled. For some assets, such as bonds, those cash flows are clearly specified. However, the prospects for actually receiving those cash flows can vary considerably depending on the issuer of the bond. The holder of a Treasury bond, for example, faces negligible risk of not getting paid interest or principal (known as default) in contrast to the holder of a lower-rated "junk" bond. In other cases, such as common stock or rental properties, the cash flows are not specified or known with certainty; in these cases, the investor must project the cash flows.

We have all seen how the power of compounding can transform a certain amount set aside today into a large multiple of that amount in the future. For example, $10,000 invested at an 8 percent interest rate today will accumulate to $100,627 in 30 years. The higher the interest rate, the more one will have at that later date. For example, this same $10,000 invested at a 12 percent return will result in nearly triple the amount in 30 years—$299,599. This is often referred to as *future value*.

Utilizing these same relationships, but in reverse, we come up with *present value*. For example, the value today of $100,627 in 30 years will be $10,000 if the interest rate—frequently called the *discount rate*—is currently 8 percent. The higher the interest rate, the lower the present value. For example, at a 12 percent interest rate, the $100,627 in 30 years is worth only $3,359 today.

This relationship between the value of a dollar today and the value of a dollar in the future is sometimes referred to as the *time value of money*. A dollar today is worth more than a dollar in the future. This is because of a complex interaction between the reluctance of people to save today—that is, a preference to consume now, sometimes called time preference or impatience—and the ability of businesses to put these saved funds to good use in generating future value. That is, resourceful businesses can put these funds to work in investments that generate positive returns—boosting future profits. In general, either greater reluctance by people to save today or higher returns earned by businesses on investments (putting these saved resources to work) results in higher interest rates (or discount rates).

PRESENT VALUE

We can spell out the precise relationship between the current price (present value) of an asset and the future cash flows produced by this asset using a formula that discounts and sums future cash flows—with the extent of the discount depending on when the cash flow is received. That formula is the following:

$$PV = \frac{CF_1}{(1+i)} + \frac{CF_2}{(1+i)^2} + \frac{CF_3}{(1+i)^3} + \cdots + \frac{CF_n}{(1+i)^n} = \sum_{j=1}^{n} \frac{CF_j}{(1+i)^j} \qquad (4\text{-}1)$$

The Pricing of Financial Assets 57

In this equation, CF_1 represents the cash flow received from the asset in year 1, CF_2 the cash flow in year 2, CF_n the cash flow in the final year of the investment (year n), and i denotes the interest rate (or discount rate). Notice that the interest rate term appears only in the denominator of each component, preceded by one, and it is raised to a higher and higher power the farther into the future the cash flow is received—hence the term *discounting* of cash flows. The term on the right of Equation (4-1) is a shorthand version of the long summation. The symbol Σ represents the summation across all the periods for which cash flows are received.

It is worth noting that this single equation has three classes of variables: *PV*, *CFs*, and *i*. But, it can be used to solve for only one unknown. The other two variables need to be specified. For example, the equation can be used to solve for *PV* if *CFs* and *i* are known. Or, under certain conditions, it can be used to solve for the cash flows, *CFs*. Finally, it can be used to solve for the interest rate—yield to maturity—if the cash flows and current price are known. In practice, it is a workhorse that is used heavily for all three purposes.

Value of a Single Future Payment

Some financial assets provide their owner with a single cash payment at some specific date in the future. Equation (4-1) can be used to determine the current or present value of that cash payment. That cash payment occurs in year n. In this instance, the present value of the single payment is given by

$$PV = \frac{CF_n}{(1+i)^n} \qquad (4\text{-}2)$$

For example, if a payment of $1,000 will be made in 2 years and the current interest rate is 5 percent,

$$PV = \frac{\$1,000}{(1.05)^2} = \frac{\$1,000}{1.1025} = \$907.03$$

In another example, the present value of $100,627 in 30 years at an 8 percent interest rate, as noted in the introduction, will be

$$PV = \frac{\$100,627}{(1.08)^{30}} = \frac{\$100,627}{10.627} = \$10,000$$

A particularly popular form of single-payment instrument is the *zero-coupon* security. These are commonly created from the components of U.S. Treasury notes or bonds, as will be discussed more fully in Chapter 8. At the time the note or bond is sold by the Treasury to its initial buyer, it contains semiannual interest payments for the life of the security and a payment of principal at maturity. Dealers acquire these securities and remove each payment of interest or principal. Each interest payment and the principal payment are then sold to investors separately as a zero-coupon security. Some investors favor zero-coupon securities over others because they foresee a need for cash in the future to be concentrated at a single time. For example, parents managing college portfolios for their children often want zero-coupon securities that mature at times they envision making tuition payments. Similarly, some institutional investors, such as pension funds, like to hold zero-coupon notes that mature when they anticipate making cash payments to retirees.[1]

This relationship can be used for a variety of other purposes. For example, suppose that you win the lottery and need to decide whether to take $600,000 today or $1 million in 10 years. At issue is which is larger in present value and this requires discounting the $1 million using an appropriate interest rate. Suppose the discount rate is 7 percent. The value of $1 million in 10 years then is

$$PV = \frac{\$1,000,000}{(1.07)^{10}} = \frac{\$1,000,000}{1.9672} = \$508,349.35$$

In this case, it would be advantageous to take the $600,000 today because it has present worth almost $92,000 more than the $1 million in 10 years. At lower interest rates, it would be better to take the $1 million in 10 years. For example, at a 3 percent discount rate, the present value of $1 million in 10 years would be $744,092.

Value of a Coupon Security

Most Treasury securities and corporate bonds provide their owners with coupon payments (twice) each year until maturity and then payment of principal at maturity. Equation (4-1) can be used to determine the value of such securities. The cash flows for those years prior to maturity are the CF_js and the cash flow in the final year, CF_n, is the coupon payment *plus* the payment of principal.[2] For example, the value of a corporate bond with a principal of $100,000, coupon payments of $6,000 per year, an interest rate of 8 percent, and a maturity of 5 years is shown by:

$$\begin{aligned}PV &= \frac{\$6,000}{(1.08)^1} + \frac{\$6,000}{(1.08)^2} + \frac{\$6,000}{(1.08)^3} + \frac{\$6,000}{(1.08)^4} + \frac{\$106,000}{(1.08)^5} \\ &= \frac{\$6,000}{(1.08)} + \frac{\$6,000}{1.1664} + \frac{\$6,000}{1.2597} + \frac{\$6,000}{1.3605} + \frac{\$106,000}{1.4693} \\ &= \$5,555.56 + \$5,144.03 + \$4,763.04 + \$4,410.14 + \$72,143.20 \\ &= \$92,015.97\end{aligned}$$

There are a couple things to note about this example. First, while the amount of each interest payment is the same—$6,000—its contribution to the value of this bond diminishes as the payment is made farther into the future. For example, the contribution of the interest payment in year 4 is $4,410.14, less than the $4,763.04 contribution in year 3. This is the discounting process showing that the present value of a particular amount of money will always be less the farther into the future that amount is received.

Second, the present value of this bond—$92,015.97—is less than its principal or par value—$100,000. This will not always be the case. It depends on whether the current interest rate used to discount the cash flows is higher or lower than the bond's *coupon rate,* which is its annual interest (coupon) payment—$6,000—divided by its principal or par value—$100,000. In this case, the current interest rate (yield

The Pricing of Financial Assets

to maturity)—8 percent—exceeds the coupon rate—6 percent. This results in the present value being below the par value. If the current interest rate were below the coupon rate, the present value of the bond would exceed its par value. As an exercise, you should confirm that this bond would have a value of $104,328.42—above its par value—if the interest rate is 5 percent. It follows that when the current interest rate is the same as the coupon rate, the present value of the bond will equal its par value.

Other Applications

The present value relationship can be used for a variety of other valuations than the pricing of securities. For example, you could use the equation for determining the price you would be willing to pay for an apartment building. Suppose that you determine that the apartment will provide cash flows of $100,000 per year after expenses, beginning in 5 years, and you will be able to sell the building for $1 million in 10 years. Using Equation (4-1), you would enter zeroes for the cash flows in years 1 through 4, $100,000 in years 5 through 9, and $1,100,000 in year 10 (representing both the net earnings from the property in that year and the expected sale price). You would not want to pay more than the amount derived below if interest rates are 6 percent:

$$\begin{aligned} PV &= \frac{\$100{,}000}{(1.06)^5} + \frac{\$100{,}000}{(1.06)^6} + \frac{\$100{,}000}{(1.06)^7} + \frac{\$100{,}000}{(1.06)^8} + \frac{\$100{,}000}{(1.06)^9} + \frac{\$1{,}100{,}000}{(1.06)^{10}} \\ &= \frac{\$100{,}000}{1.3382} + \frac{\$100{,}000}{1.4185} + \frac{\$100{,}000}{1.5036} + \frac{\$100{,}000}{1.5938} + \frac{\$100{,}000}{1.6895} + \frac{\$1{,}100{,}000}{1.7908} \\ &= \$74{,}727.25 + \$70{,}497{,}000 + \$66{,}507.05 + \$62{,}743.13 + \$59{,}189.11 \\ &\quad + \$614{,}250.61 \\ &= \$947{,}914.15 \end{aligned}$$

In other words, you would be willing to pay nearly $950,000 for this building.

Solving for Yield to Maturity

As noted earlier, Equation (4-1) contains three variables, including the interest rate or yield to maturity. Provided that the current price of an asset and the asset's cash flows are specified (known), the interest rate can be derived using this equation. For example, a 30-year bond may have a principal (par) value of $100 and interest payments of $4.25 per year.[3] The cash flows from this bond are $4.25 per year for 29 years and $104.25 in the 30th year (combining the coupon and principal payment in that year). Suppose that the price of this bond is known to be $92.875 from a recent trade. It is now possible to solve for the implied interest rate—the yield to maturity. The equation looks as follows:

$$\$92.875 = \frac{\$4.25}{(1+i)} + \frac{\$4.25}{(1+i)^2} + \frac{\$4.25}{(1+i)^3} + \cdots + \frac{\$104.25}{(1+i)^{30}}$$

The solution for the yield to maturity in this example is 4.70 percent. In practice, this is a very complicated exercise because the 1 plus the interest rate term in

Equation (4-1) is raised to a higher and higher power, up to the power of 30 in this example. Solutions require a very complicated algorithm, which usually requires a financial calculator or a computer.

Noteworthy about this result is that the current price of the bond, $92.875, is below its par value, $100. This implies that the current yield, 4.70 percent, must be above the bond's coupon rate of $\frac{\$4.25}{\$100}$ or 4.25 percent. Another way of looking at this is to recognize that if the cash flows in the preceding equation are discounted using the coupon rate of 4.25 percent, the present value of the bond would be $100. If, instead, a larger interest rate is used, such as 4.70 percent, the present value of those cash flows must be less than $100—indeed, $92.875. Alternatively, if the price of the bond is above par, the yield to maturity must be below the coupon rate of 4.25 percent.

Solving for Fixed Payments

Equation (4-1) can be used also to determine the cash flows that are required to pay off a loan with interest once the amount of the loan, its maturity, and its interest rate are known. This is the standard way in which auto and home loans are paid—the borrower makes the same monthly payment over the life of the loan. The last monthly payment discharges the full obligation. Loans of this sort that are scheduled to pay both interest and principal over the life of the loan are called *amortized* loans regardless of what they finance—real estate (a mortgage), a motor vehicle (car loan), or something else.

Suppose that you buy a used Honda Civic Hybrid that is a couple of years old for $19,000. You put down $3,000 by writing a check on your bank account and finance the rest—$16,000—for 5 years. The interest rate that you are being charged is 6 percent. Suppose further, for the sake of simplicity, that you make annual—not monthly—payments that cover both principal and interest. The first payment is in a year. Here is how Equation (4-1) can be used to solve for the amount that you will be paying each year for 5 years. Note that because the payments (*CF*s) are the same each year, this equation has been reduced to having only one unknown—*CF*.

$$\$16,000 = \frac{CF}{1.06} + \frac{CF}{(1.06)^2} + \frac{CF}{(1.06)^3} + \frac{CF}{(1.06)^4} + \frac{CF}{(1.06)^5}$$

$$= CF\left(\frac{1}{1.06} + \frac{1}{(1.06)^2} + \frac{1}{(1.06)^3} + \frac{1}{(1.06)^4} + \frac{1}{(1.06)^5}\right)$$

$$= CF(0.9434 + 0.8900 + 0.8403 + 0.7921 + 0.7473)$$

Or

$$CF = \frac{\$16,000}{4.2131} = \$3,798.68$$

Solving for *CF* in the preceding equation results in an annual payment of nearly $3,800 (or about $315 per month). In other words, you would be paying a cumulative $19,000 (approximate) over the next 5 years on a loan of $16,000.

The preceding approach can be used to calculate the amount of each payment when there are multiple payments during the year, such as monthly. Monthly payments are common for mortgage and auto loans.[4] The first appendix to this chapter illustrates how to calculate monthly payments on fixed-payment loans, as well as how to calculate the present value of coupon securities when coupons are paid semi-annually instead of annually.

The Special Case of a Consol

Since the early eighteenth century, the British have issued a bond that has no specified maturity—it has a perpetual coupon. Equation (4-1) can be used to determine the value of such a bond, if one regards the coupons to be paid for an unlimited period (mathematically speaking, to infinity). In other words, Equation (4-1) would become

$$PV = \sum_{j=1}^{\infty} \frac{CF}{(1+i)^j} \qquad (4\text{-}3)$$

In this expression, the cash flow each year is the same: CF.[5] While this may appear to result in a very complicated and unwieldy calculation, it converges to the following simple expression:

$$PV = \frac{CF}{i} \qquad (4\text{-}3)'$$

This can be a very useful expression for deriving quick approximations for values of assets that pay steady cash flows for very long periods of time. For example, a 30-year bond paying an annual coupon of \$4.375 per \$100 of par value would have an estimated value of \$4.375/4.32 = \$101.27 using (4-3)' close to the actual value of \$100.95. Alternatively, (4-3)' can be used to compute the approximate value of a commercial building that is fully leased out under a very long-term lease. Suppose that the building is expected to provide its owner \$500,000 per year (net of operating and maintenance expenses) and the current interest rate is 8 percent. A rough estimate of the value of the building is

$$\$500{,}000/0.08 = \$6{,}250{,}000 \text{ or } \$6.25 \text{ million}$$

MATURITY AND PRICE SENSITIVITY

The price of a financial instrument with a longer maturity will be more sensitive to a given-sized change in interest rates than the price of a shorter-term instrument. To illustrate, let us look at two instruments having different maturities—a 1-year and a 10-year instrument. The current interest rate is 5 percent for each instrument. The 1-year instrument will pay \$105 in a year, while the 10-year instrument is a 10-year note paying \$5 per year each year over the next 10 years plus \$100 at maturity. Both instruments have a current price of \$100. The price of the 1-year instrument is:

$$\frac{\$105}{1.05} = \$100$$

The price of the 10-year note is:[6]

$$\sum_{j=1}^{10} \frac{\$5}{(1.05)^j} + \frac{\$100}{(1.05)^{10}} = \$100$$

Should the interest rate increase to 10 percent, the decline in the price of the 10-year note would be considerably larger than that of the 1-year instrument. This can be shown as follows for the 1-year instrument:

$$\frac{\$105}{1.10} = \$95.45, \text{ a decline in price of about 4.50 percent}$$

For the 10-year instrument, the new price will be

$$\sum_{j=1}^{10} \frac{\$5}{(1.10)^j} + \frac{\$100}{(1.10)^{10}} = \$68.84, \text{ a decline of more than 31 percent}$$

The impact of the same increase in the interest rate on the price of a consol, with an indefinite maturity, would be even greater than that on a 10-year note. To illustrate, the price of a consol paying $5 per year would be the following at an interest rate of 5 percent:

$$\$5/0.05 = \$100$$

At an interest rate of 10 percent, the price declines to

$$\$5/0.10 = \$50, \text{ a decline of 50 percent}$$

Moreover, the impact of a change in interest rates will be larger for a zero-coupon security than for a coupon security of the same maturity. To illustrate, a single payment of $162.89 in 10 years would, at an interest rate of 5 percent, have a present value of

$$\frac{\$162.89}{(1.05)^{10}} = \$100, \text{ the same as the 10-year note above}$$

If the interest rate rises to 10 percent, the value of the zero-coupon security will drop to

$$\frac{\$162.89}{(1.10)^{10}} = \$62.80, \text{ a decline of 37 percent}$$

By contrast, the value of the 10-year coupon security fell by less, 31 percent. The reason for the larger drop in the price of the 10-year zero-coupon security is that all the cash flow occurs at the very end of the period when the discounting is most magnified. In contrast, cash flows from the coupon security are paid throughout the 10 years, starting in a year when the discounting is least magnified. That is, cash flows for all periods prior to the end are discounted less heavily than the final cash flow, corresponding to the cash flow on the zero-coupon, implying that the price of the coupon security will decline less than that of the zero-coupon security.[7]

HOLDING PERIODS VERSUS MATURITIES

An investor's holding period—the length of time before the investor expects to need the cash from the investment—need not be the same as the maturity of the investment. When the holding period and the maturity are not the same, the investor is exposed to a risk. If the holding period exceeds the maturity, then the investor will be exposed to *reinvestment* or *rollover risk*. Suppose that the investor's holding period is 5 years and the investor acquires an instrument with a 2-year maturity. In this example, the investor in 2 years will need to reinvest maturing funds at an interest rate that could be lower (or higher) than the one available at the present time. As a consequence, the investor could end up receiving less interest (or more) than if a 5-year investment were chosen.

Alternatively, the investor could have acquired an instrument with a maturity that exceeds the holding period, thereby becoming exposed to *price* (or *interest rate*) *risk*. In the example above, the investor may have purchased a 10-year note. In 5 years, the investor would be in need of the cash from the investment and would have to sell the instrument at the price prevailing at the time, which could be lower or higher than par depending on whether interest rates have risen or fallen. In sum, when the maturity of the investment exceeds the investor's holding period, the investor is exposed to price risk, and when the maturity is shorter than the holding period, the investor is exposed to reinvestment risk.

In sum, if M represents maturity and H the holding period:

$M > H$ Price (interest rate) risk

$M < H$ Rollover (reinvestment) risk

RETURN VERSUS YIELD

The return on an investment will be its yield to maturity if the instrument is held to maturity. However, if the investment is held for less than its maturity, the investor is likely to experience a capital gain or loss because interest rates are likely to be higher or lower than at the time of investment. For example, the investor may have acquired a 5-year instrument having a 4 percent yield to maturity. However, suppose that the investor sold the instrument after 3 years at a loss of 6 percent because interest rates had risen. In this example the investor would have received a yield of 4 percent each year on the amount invested, but that must be counterbalanced against the 6 percent loss that took place on the sale—2 percent per year when the loss is prorated over the 3 years. Thus, the investor's return on this investment would be 2 percent per year (the 4 percent annual yield netted against the 2 percent annual loss). Of course, interest rates could have fallen over this period and the investor could have experienced a capital gain. If the investor had experienced a 3 percent capital gain instead, the return on this investment would be 5 percent—the 4 percent yield to maturity plus the 1 percent prorated annual gain. Expressed formally,

$$\text{Return} = \text{Yield} + \frac{CG}{n}$$

In this expression, the return equals the annual yield on the asset plus the capital gain (CG) divided by the number of years that the asset is held (n). Note that if the investor experienced a capital loss, CG would be negative and the return would be less than the yield.

The concept of return can be applied to investments other than interest-earning (fixed-income) investments. Some, such as common stock, have a tendency to appreciate over time, and thus capital gains can be an important component of their investment returns.

DURATION

The concept of duration—sometimes called bond duration—is related to maturity. Indeed, it can be thought of as a weighted average of the maturities of the cash flows that the investor is scheduled to receive. Expressed algebraically,

$$D = w_1 \times t_1 + w_2 \times t_2 + w_3 \times t_3 + \cdots + w_n \times t_n = \sum_{j=1}^{n} w_j t_j \qquad (4\text{-}4)$$

In this expression, D represents the instrument's duration in years, w_1 represents the weight attached to the first cash flow provided by the instrument, t_1 represents the time into the future when the first cash flow is paid the investor (in years or fractions thereof), and the other terms have similar meaning for subsequent cash flows. In practice, the weights, w_js are the share of the price (present value) of the instrument accounted for the corresponding cash flow. In other words,

$$w_j = \frac{\dfrac{CF_j}{(1+i)^j}}{\sum_{j=1}^{n} \dfrac{CF_j}{(1+i)^j}}$$

Extending this to all the terms, Equation (4-4) becomes

$$D = \frac{\sum_{j=1}^{n} j \times \dfrac{CF_j}{(1+i)^j}}{\sum_{j=1}^{n} \dfrac{CF_j}{(1+i)^j}} \qquad (4\text{-}5)$$

An example might help. Suppose the instrument is a 5-year note that pays a coupon annually, beginning in a year. The coupon rate is 5 percent, the current interest rate is 4 percent, and the par value is $100.

Using Equation (4-1), the current price (present value) is

$$PV = \frac{\$5}{1.04} + \frac{\$5}{(1.04)^2} + \frac{\$5}{(1.04)^3} + \frac{\$5}{(1.04)^4} + \frac{\$5+\$100}{(1.04)^5}$$
$$= \$4.81 + \$4.62 + \$4.44 + \$4.27 + \$86.30 = \$104.44$$

The Pricing of Financial Assets

Observe that this note is selling above par—$104.44 versus $100 of par. This is because the current interest rate—4 percent—is below the coupon rate—5 percent. To derive the duration of this note, we plug the numbers above into Equation (4-5)

$$D = \frac{\$4.81}{\$104.44} \times 1 + \frac{\$4.62}{\$104.44} \times 2 + \frac{\$4.44}{\$104.44} \times 3 + \frac{\$4.27}{\$104.44} \times 4 + \frac{\$86.30}{\$104.44} \times 5$$
$$= 0.046 \times 1 + 0.044 \times 2 + 0.043 \times 3 + 0.041 \times 4 + 0.826 \times 5$$
$$= 0.046 + 0.088 + 0.128 + 0.164 + 4.132 = 4.56$$

The units are years and thus the duration of this instrument is 4.56 years.

Note that the maturity of this note is 5 years while its duration is less—about 4.5 years. This is because four of the six cash flows are received prior to maturity and the weight attached to the last cash flow associated with 5 years is less than 100 percent (less than 1.0). In the preceding example, the weight attached to the maturity of the last cash flow—5 years—is 0.826, implying a weight of 0.174 is attached to shorter maturities. Thus, the weighted maturity of the cash flows of the instrument is less than its maturity. The longer the maturity of an instrument, all else the same, the greater will be its duration.

In the case of a zero-coupon (or single-payment) instrument, there is only one cash flow and that is at maturity. As a consequence, the duration of a zero-coupon security will always be the same as its maturity. This can be seen by going back to Equation (4-4). If all the cash is received at maturity, t_n then the weights attached to all cash flows up to and including t_{n-1} will be zero. All of the weight will be attached to t_n. Thus, D will be the same as the maturity, t_n.

A second feature about duration worth knowing is that a change in interest rates will affect duration: higher interest rates will lower duration for all but zero-coupon (or single-payment) instruments and lower interest rates will increase duration.

An example might help. In the above calculation of the duration of the 5-year instrument, should the interest rate increase to 7 percent from 4 percent, the present value of the cash flows would decline to

$$PV = \frac{\$5}{1.07} + \frac{\$5}{(1.07)^2} + \frac{\$5}{(1.07)^3} + \frac{\$5}{(1.07)^4} + \frac{\$5 + \$100}{(1.07)^5}$$
$$= \$4.67 + \$4.37 + \$4.08 + \$3.81 + \$74.86 = \$91.79$$

Note that the new price has fallen below par, to $91.79.

The new duration is

$$D = \frac{\$4.67}{\$91.79} \times 1 + \frac{\$4.37}{\$91.79} \times 2 + \frac{\$4.08}{\$91.79} \times 3 + \frac{\$3.81}{\$91.79} \times 4 + \frac{\$74.86}{\$91.79} \times 5$$
$$= 0.051 + 0.096 + 0.132 + 0.164 + 4.04 = 4.52 \text{ years}$$

Note that duration has declined from 4.56 years to 4.52 years.

A third feature is that the longer the duration of an instrument, the more sensitive is its price to a change on interest rates.[8] This can be seen by comparing the 5-year coupon security above—having a duration of less than 5 years—with a 5-year zero-coupon security—having a duration of 5 years. In the above example, when the interest rate rose from 4 to 7 percent, the price of the instrument fell from $104.44

to $91.79—a drop of 12 percent. A zero-coupon payment of $127.08 in 5 years would have a current price of $104.44 at an interest rate of 4 percent—the same as for the 5-year coupon instrument above. If the interest rate were to rise to 7 percent, that payment in 5 years of $127.08 would have a new price of $90.60—a 13 percent decline.

A final feature worth noting is, the duration of a portfolio of instruments is equal to a weighted average of all the individual instruments making up the portfolio where the weights represent the shares of each instrument in the portfolio. For example, if the portfolio consisted of two securities—one with a duration of 5 years and the other with a duration of 10 years—then the duration of the portfolio would be 7.5 years if each instrument accounted for half the value of the entire portfolio. That is, the duration of the portfolio would be 0.5 × 5 years + 0.5 × 10 years = 7.5 years.

Some investors will have a target for the duration of their portfolio, sometimes called a "bogey." In such a case, a change in interest rates, by affecting the duration of the portfolio, will require a reallocation of instruments in the portfolio. For example, the manager of the portfolio above with two instruments may have a target duration of 7.5 years and if interest rates increase, the actual duration of the portfolio will decline, unless they are both zero coupon securities. If they are not zero coupons, the manager of the portfolio will need to buy more 10-year instruments and sell some 5-year instruments to return to the target. Thus, changes in the level of interest rates tend to result in transactions in security markets that are intended to rebalance portfolio durations.

The preceding discussion also illustrates why many portfolio managers like to hold zero-coupon (or single-payment) instruments. Their durations do not change when interest rates change, thus reducing the need for rebalancing portfolios as interest rates move around.

NOMINAL VERSUS REAL YIELDS

The interest rates that are most common—such as the interest rate on a mortgage or car loan or interest on a retail CD—are nominal interest rates. They do not have adjustments based on inflation. The actual return to the investor, in terms of the purchasing power of the interest payments, will depend on what happens to inflation. For example, if one invested funds at a 5 percent interest rate and inflation turned out to be 5 percent, the investor's interest payment would only cover the deterioration in the purchasing power of the principal. That is, an instrument with a $100 principal would lose $5 in purchasing power in a year and the interest payment of $5 would just cover that loss. The so-called real return or real interest rate would be zero. If, instead, inflation were to be 3 percent over the year, the real interest rate would be 2 percent—$3 of the $5 interest payment would cover the loss of purchasing power of the instrument's principal. This leaves $2 in purchasing power as a (real) return for the investor. Algebraically, this relationship between nominal and real yields can be expressed as follows:

$$i = r + \dot{P} \qquad (4\text{-}6)$$

In this equation, i represents the nominal interest rate, r the real interest rate, and $\dot{P}$ the rate of inflation. Subtracting the actual rate of inflation from the nominal interest rate results in the *ex post* real rate of interest.

In practice, markets are forward looking and investors will be seeking compensation for the loss of purchasing power based on their expectations of what inflation will be over the life of the financial instrument. We can denote expected inflation as $\dot{P}^e$. Thus, Equation (4-6) can be expressed as

$$i = r + \dot{P}^e \tag{4-7}$$

This says that the nominal interest rate will be equal to the real interest rate plus the expected rate of inflation. This is the expected or *ex ante* real rate of interest.

It is thought that saving and spending decisions are based more on real interest rates than nominal rates. For example, a business contemplating undertaking a capital investment will typically expect that its receipts—and thus its ability to service debt—will rise with inflation and will view its actual financing costs to be the nominal interest rate less its expectations of inflation. Similarly, a family considering the purchase of a home will tend to see its earnings rising with inflation and thus the actual strain of financing a new home would be that portion of the interest rate that exceeds expected inflation.

The U.S. Treasury has for some time been offering securities that compensate the investor explicitly for inflation. These are referred to as TIPS—Treasury Inflation Protected Securities. To compensate the investor for the effects of inflation, the Treasury adjusts the principal for actual inflation, based on the change in the Consumer Price Index (CPI). The interest payments are then based on the adjusted principal. To illustrate, suppose that the TIPS yield is 2 percent and the original principal is $100, implying an interest payment of $2. If the CPI were to increase 10 percent, the Treasury would adjust the security's principal to be $110, reflecting the measured erosion of purchasing power.[9] The interest payment going forward would then be based on this higher principal—2 percent of $110 or $2.20. In this example, the 2 percent interest rate is the real interest rate on this security.

The nominal yield on a Treasury security less this measure of the real yield for securities of the same maturity is referred to as *inflation compensation* (sometimes also referred to as the *break-even rate*). It will consist of compensation for expected inflation plus compensation for inflation risk. For example, a 10-year nominal Treasury note might have a yield of 4.50 percent and a 10-year TIPS note might have a yield of 2.25 percent. In this situation, inflation compensation would be 2.25 percent (4.50 − 2.25 = 2.25 percent). It is thought that the bulk of inflation compensation is inflation expectations and that movements in inflation compensation tend to be driven more by changes in expected inflation than inflation risk.

SUMMARY

1. Because of the time value of money, a certain amount of cash is worth more today than at any time in the future. The closer to the present, the greater will be present value of that cash.
2. Present value and future value are related. Going from present value to future value involves the process of compounding. Going from future value to present value involves discounting, the reverse of compounding. Key to both is the interest (discount) rate.
3. The present value formula relates the current value of an asset to its future cash flows, where each future cash flow is discounted before all are summed. The

higher the interest (discount) rate, the lower the present value of the asset, and vice versa.
4. The present value formula can be used to value a single payment in the future—a zero-coupon security—or to value an asset having a series of cash flows, such as a coupon security. It can also be used to solve for the regular—annual or monthly—payments on a loan if the amount of the loan and interest rate are known. Finally, it can be used to solve for the yield to maturity on an asset for which the current price and cash flows are known (the yield to maturity is the interest rate that equates the present value of those cash flows to the current price).
5. Longer maturity assets have prices that are more sensitive to changes in interest rates than shorter maturity assets. The holder is exposed to more price risk.
6. When an investor's holding period and the maturity of an asset are not the same, the investor is exposed to interest rate (price) risk or to rollover (or reinvestment) risk. The former occurs when the maturity exceeds the holding period and the latter occurs when the holding period exceeds the maturity of the asset.
7. The return on an asset can differ from its yield. The return is the asset's yield adjusted for capital gains or losses (expressed on an annual basis).
8. The duration of an asset is related to its maturity and is measured in the same units—years. Duration is the weighted average of the maturity of cash flows received on the asset, where the weights are the present value of each cash flow relative to the present value of the asset. For all but a single-payment (zero coupon) asset, duration will be shorter than maturity (some of the value of the asset is received prior to maturity).
9. A higher interest rate will shorten the duration of all but single payment assets. The longer the maturity of an asset, the longer will be its duration, all else the same. The longer the duration of an asset, the more sensitive is its price to a change in interest rates.
10. Most interest rates that we observe are nominal interest rates. But the real interest rate—the nominal interest rate adjusted for inflation—is thought to be more important for influencing business and household spending decisions. The *ex post* real interest rate is the nominal interest rate less the rate of inflation (average annual rate over the life of the security). The *ex ante* real interest rate is the nominal interest rate less the expected rate of inflation.
11. The present value formula can be adapted to allow for coupon securities paying coupons semiannually or for determining fixed monthly payments on loans (Appendix A).

QUESTIONS

1. A zero-coupon security pays $100,000 in 8 years. What is the current price of this security if the current interest rate is 4 percent? The current interest rate is 7 percent? What is the percent reduction in price caused by this 3-percentage-point increase in interest rates?
2. A 5-year Treasury note has a coupon rate of 2.50 percent. What price would you pay for such a security having a principal (par value) of $1 million if the current interest rate is 2.25 percent? The current interest rate is 3 percent? (To simplify

the calculations, assume that coupon payments are made once per year, starting a year from now.)

3. What is the current price of a security that pays its owner $1,000 per year into perpetuity if the interest rate is 5 percent? The interest rate is 8 percent? What is the percent change in its price when the interest rate goes from 5 to 8 percent?
4. What is the value of $1,000 in 1 year if the current interest rate is 5 percent? The current interest rate is 8 percent? What is the percent change in its price when the interest rate goes from 5 to 8 percent?
5. You negotiate the price of a new Toyota to be $26,062, including taxes and tags. You put $5,000 down and borrow the rest at an interest rate of 6 percent for 5 years. What will be your annual payment if this loan is fully amortized?
6. You win the $1 million lottery and must decide whether to take $1 million in 10 years or $500,000 today. Which would you choose if the interest rate is 5 percent? The interest rate is 10 percent? Explain.
7. A 10-year Treasury note has a coupon rate of 2.75 percent. The current price of this note is $102. Explain how you would go about calculating the yield to maturity on this note. Will the current yield be above or below 2.75 percent? Explain.
8. Using Bloomberg, what is the current price and yield on a 30-year Treasury bond? Is the bond selling above or below par? Is the yield to maturity (current yield) above or below the coupon rate? What is the relationship between yield to maturity and coupon rate, on the one hand, and current price versus par value, on the other?
9. Using Bloomberg, what is the current real interest rate on a 30-year Treasury bond? Inflation compensation?
10. Under what conditions is an investor exposed to interest rate (or price) risk? Reinvestment (rollover) risk?
11. What is the duration of a three-year Treasury note with a coupon rate of 3 percent if the note is selling for par? What is its duration if the current yield to maturity is 10 percent? (Assume only one coupon payment per year. Treat the security as having a par value of $100.) What is the duration of a three-year zero-coupon security at an interest rate of 3 percent? An interest rate of 10 percent?

APPENDIX A: VARIATIONS OF THE VALUATION RELATIONSHIP

As we noted in this chapter, most bonds pay coupons to the investor twice per year. Also, the vast majority of fixed payment (amortized) loans are paid monthly. In this appendix, we will adapt our present value relationship to allow for such situations.

Let us first look at a coupon security that pays interest (makes a coupon payment) twice yearly, the first in 6 months. We adapt Equation (4-1) to allow for semi-annual coupon payments as follows:

$$PV = \frac{CF_1}{(1+i/n)} + \frac{CF_2}{(1+i/2)^2} + \frac{CF_3}{(1+i/2)^3} + \cdots + \frac{CF_n}{(1+i/2)^n} = \sum_{j=1}^{n} \frac{CF_j}{(1+i/2)^j} \qquad (4\text{-}8)$$

In this expression, *PV* again is the price of the coupon security, CF_1 is the first coupon payment in 6 months (which is half the annual payment), CF_2 is the second payment in a year, CF_3 is the third payment in a year and a half, CF_n is the final payment amounting to the last coupon and the principal, and *i* is the annual interest rate. The annual interest rate is divided by two to get the discount rate to be applied to semiannual payments of coupons (and principal at maturity). For a 10-year note, *n* will be 20.

Equation (4-1) can be used to solve for monthly payments in a fixed-payment, amortized loan as follows:

$$PV = \frac{CF}{(1+i/12)} + \frac{CF}{(1+i/12)^2} + \frac{CF}{(1+i/12)^3} + \cdots + \frac{CF}{(1+i/12)^n} \tag{4-9}$$

In this expression, *PV* is the amount of the loan at the time it is granted, *CF* is the fixed monthly payment, and *i* is the annual interest rate on the mortgage. The number of months goes from 1 to *n*, the one in which the last payment is made. For a 5-year auto loan, *n* would be 60. For a 30-year home mortgage, *n* would be 360. The procedure for solving for *CF*, the monthly payment, would be the same as in the text for the annual payment on the loan to purchase a Honda Civic.

APPENDIX B: SOLUTIONS USING A FINANCIAL CALCULATOR

If you are familiar with a standard financial calculator, you can use it to solve for some of the numerical problems presented in the text. The examples below are based on a Texas Instruments financial calculator, but the steps are pretty much the same for an HP or other calculator.

Future Value

For starters, we can calculate the future value of $10,000 in 30 years, as discussed on page 56. To determine the value of this amount if invested at an 8 percent interest rate, take the following steps:

> The number of years, *n*, is 30—enter 30 and then *n*.
>
> The interest rate, *I/Y*, is 8—enter 8 and then *I/Y*.
>
> The beginning balance, *PV*, is $10,000 (this may require converting to a negative balance using the +/− key)—enter 10,000 +/− and *PV*.
>
> To compute the future value, press the *CPT* and *FV* keys to get $100,626.57.

Future Value—A Higher Interest Rate

Also on this page, we calculated the future value of $10,000 in 30 years at an interest rate of 12 percent. Follow the same steps as above except for the second step. Instead, replace the second step with

> The interest rate, *I/Y*, is 12—enter 12 and then *I/Y*.
>
> By following these steps, you will get $299,599.22.

The Pricing of Financial Assets

Present Value of Single Cash Flow

Next, on page 57, we calculated the present value of $1,000 in 2 years at an interest rate of 5 percent. This is performed as follows:

The number of years, n, is 2—enter 2 and then N.

The interest rate, I/Y, is 5—enter 5 and then I/Y.

The future value, FV, is $1,000—enter 1,000 and the FV key.

To compute the present value, press the CPT and PV keys to get $907.03.

Lottery Choice

In the text on page 58, you were asked to choose between taking $1 million in 10 years or $600,000 today if the interest rate is 7 percent. This decision depends on the present value of the $1 million. This is calculated as follows:

The number of years, n, is 10—enter 10 and then n.

The interest rate, I/Y, is 7—enter 7 and then I/Y.

The future value, FV, is $1 million—enter 1,000,000 and the FV key.

To get the present value press the CPT and PV keys to get $508,349.29, implying that the $600,000 today is the preferred choice.

Current Price of a Coupon Security

In the text on page 58, the current price (present value) of a coupon note was calculated. The principal (or par value) of the note was $100,000, the coupon rate was 6 percent, and the maturity was 5 years.

After clearing out previous work, press [2nd] [BOND].

Enter a settlement date, SDT; this can be the calculator's default option.

The coupon rate, CPN, to enter is 6.

The redemption date, RDT, is 5 years after the settlement date, SDT.

The redemption value is 100,000 (or you can stick with the default value of 100 and multiply the answer by 1,000).

For the yield, YLD, enter the current market yield to maturity of 8.

Select the price operation, PRI, and press CPT to get a price of $92,016.

Price of an Asset Providing Uneven Cash Flows

In the text on page 59, the current price of an apartment building was calculated. This apartment building was expected to provide its owners with the following cash flows: zero in years 1 through 5; $100,000 in years 6 through 9; and $1,100,000 in year 10 (net rental income of $100,000 plus the sale price of $1 million). The discount rate is 6 percent.

> After clearing out previous work, select the Cash Flow key [CF].
>
> Scroll down to get the first set of cash flows, CO1, which are zero (the default on the screen).
>
> Scroll down to get the number of periods, FO1, for which there are cash flows of zero, and place 4, followed by the ENTER key.
>
> Scroll down to get the second set of cash flows, CO2, and place $100,000.
>
> Scroll down to the number of periods for which there are these cash flows, FO2, and place 5, followed by the ENTER key.
>
> Scroll down to get the third set of cash flows, CO3, and place $1,100,000.
>
> Scroll down to get the number of periods for which there are these cash flows, FO3, and place 1, followed by the ENTER key.
>
> Having entered all the cash flows, select *NPV*.
>
> Select the interest (discount) rate, 6, followed by the ENTER key.
>
> Scroll down to NPV and press *CPT* and –$949,914.15 will appear (note the negative sign reflecting a current outlay).

Yield to Maturity

In the text on page 59, a coupon security had a current price of $92.875, cash flows of $4.25 per year for 30 years, plus a principal payment of $100 in 30 years. The task was to compute the yield to maturity on this instrument.

> Once cleared, press [2nd] [Bond].
>
> Scroll down to *CPN* and enter the coupon rate 4.25.
>
> Scroll down to the redemption date, *RDT*, which will be 30 years after the settlement date, *SDT*.
>
> Scroll down to the redemption (par) value, *RV*, and enter 100 (if it does not already appear in the display)
>
> Scroll down to the current price, *PRI*, and enter 92.875
>
> Scroll down to the yield, *YLD*, and press the compute button, *CPT* and the yield to maturity will appear, 4.70 percent.

NOTES

1. Various users of interest rate data—including researchers—prefer using interest rates derived from zero-coupon securities. Zero-coupon securities and coupon securities having the same maturity have different risk features; investors holding

coupon securities to maturity must reinvest their coupon payments at future interest rates that are unknown. A yield curve derived from adjacent maturities of zero-coupon securities is believed to present a cleaner measure of the underlying yield curve at any moment in time.

2. As noted, coupon securities pay coupons twice per year. As an approximation, the full annual coupon payment—the sum of both semiannual coupons—can be used for that year's cash flow. To be more precise, the present value formula can be modified to calculate the contribution from semiannual cash flows. This is done in Appendix A to this chapter.

3. Typically, the principal and coupon payments on bonds are considerably larger than those shown—commonly $1 million or more. However, it is conventional to express coupon payments and bond prices per $100 of principal, as shown in the text.

4. To calculate the monthly payment for the loan above, one would expand the formula to include 60 terms—one for each month. Instead of using an interest rate of 6 percent (the annual rate), one would use this rate divided by 12 or one-half percent—the corresponding monthly rate. Also, the superscripts in the denominators would start at one and increase by increments of one, ending at 60. Appendix A contains the formula for monthly payments.

5. In practice, British consols pay interest quarterly and not annually. However, the four quarterly coupon payments can be summed, and Equation (4-3)' can be used to calculate the present value using the annual interest rate or an actual quarterly coupon payment can be inserted into (4-3)' and one-fourth of the annual interest rate can be used in the denominator.

6. In the expression below, it is assumed that coupon payments are made only once per year, on anniversaries of this day. In practice, U.S. Treasury notes and bonds and most other bonds pay interest semiannually in an amount equal to half of the annual coupon.

7. Note that the decline in the 10-year zero-coupon security exceeded that of the perpetual consol. This seemingly anomalous result owes to the fact that the consol provides a number of cash payments before 10 years, and these get discounted less heavily than the cash flow in the 10th year (and beyond).

8. Indeed, an alternative measure of duration is called modified duration, which is the sensitivity of an instrument's price to a change in interest rates. Specifically, it is defined as the percent change in the value of an asset in response to a 1-percentage-point change in the interest rate. The larger the modified duration, the more sensitive is its price to a change in interest rates. In practice, modified duration and the measure that we have been using (sometimes called Macaulay duration) are very close, with modified duration converging to our measure of duration as the frequency of compounding increases.

9. In practice, the Treasury performs these adjustments semiannually, to conform to the semiannual payment of interest on the security.

CHAPTER 5

Factors Affecting Yields

WHAT YOU WILL LEARN IN THIS CHAPTER

- Interest rates at any point of time differ for various reasons.
- One important reason is the term to maturity.
- The yield curve or the term structure of interest rates.
- Yields at different points on the yield curve are based on an average of current and expected short-term interest rates.
- In addition, yields at different points on the yield curve embody a term premium reflecting price risk according to the term premium hypothesis.
- Central banks increasingly try to influence benchmark interest rates through forward guidance affecting expectations of future short-term interest rates.
- A second important reason why interest rates differ is credit risk—the risk of default.
- Credit rating agencies provide well-informed judgments of the likelihood of default in their letter-grade ratings of securities.
- A third reason why interest rates differ relates to differences in their liquidity and sovereign yields are typically the most liquid.
- A fourth reason why yields can differ is the tax treatment of the interest that they pay to their owner.
- A fifth reason has to do with whether they contain embedded options—some of which raise and some lower yields.

BACKGROUND

Ever wonder why interest rates at any point in time can vary so much? For example, the rate on a 30-year mortgage may be 5.5 percent, while the rate on a 10-year Treasury note is 3.5 percent and banks borrow from each other overnight at a 2 percent rate. Meanwhile, you just bought a car and financed it with a 6.5 percent loan and you read that a local business paid 9 percent on a bank loan. What can account for these vast differences in borrowing costs? Moreover, which interest rates are most important for spending decisions by businesses and households—and, thus, key to the success of monetary policy, which seeks to influence the economy through interest rates? Further, are these important interest rates set by the central bank (in the United States, the Federal Reserve)? If not, how can the central bank influence them?

In the previous chapter, we assumed that at any moment there was only one interest rate. But in practice, as noted above, yields on financial instruments vary widely at any point in time. They differ based on maturity, perceived credit risk, liquidity, taxation, and whether they contain embedded options such as allowing the borrower to pay down the credit balance prior to scheduled maturity. In addition, some instruments have interest rates that adjust over time at regular intervals, such as annually, depending on movements in a benchmark or reference interest rate, such as the yield on Treasury bills.

THE TERM STRUCTURE OF INTEREST RATES

An important factor causing differences in yields is maturity. The term structure of interest rates refers to the relationship among interest rates of different maturities. Usually, when analyzing the term structure, we deal with instruments having the same default (credit) risk so as not to confuse credit risk effects with term structure effects. Indeed, we most often deal with government (so-called sovereign) debt, such as yields on Treasury securities of different maturities. Doing so removes default risk from yields as government debt tends to be viewed as risk free.[1]

The yield curve connects interest rates of different maturities. Figure 5.1 illustrates a typical yield curve.

Presented on the vertical axis is the interest rate (measured as the yield to maturity) on the instrument and on the horizontal axis is the maturity of the instrument (measured in years). In this diagram, the yield curve has a small upward slope, which is fairly typical. However, the yield curve can slope downward or it can be flat.

In practice, when short-term interest rates are at historically low levels, the yield curve typically is upward sloping. In these circumstances, the slope will typically be steeper than that displayed in Figure 5.1. In contrast, when short-term interest rates are at historically high levels, the yield curve will typically be downward sloping.

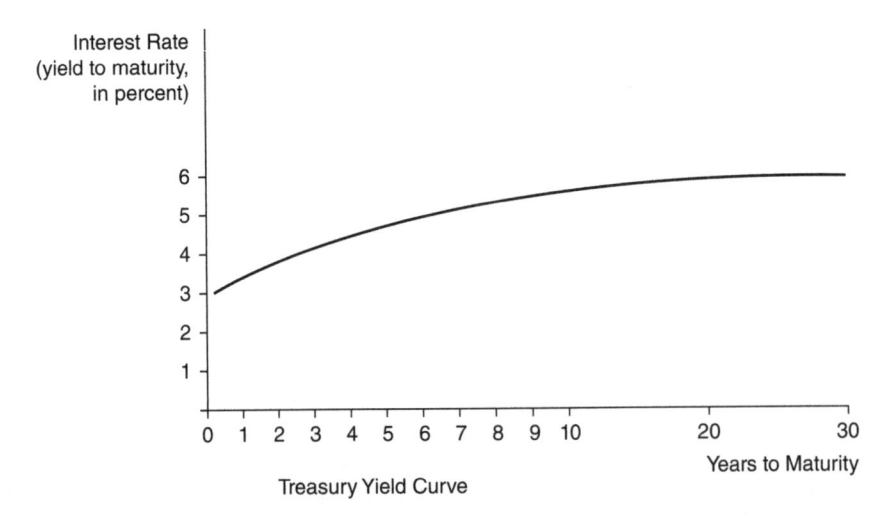

FIGURE 5.1 Treasury Yield Curve

We will now turn to reasons why the yield curve has the slope it does at any particular time. To do so, we will develop hypotheses of the term structure.

The Expectations Hypothesis

The foundation for term structure relationships is the *expectations hypothesis*. The expectations hypothesis argues that the yield on an instrument will be equal to an average of short-term interest rates expected to prevail over the life of that instrument. The reasoning is as follows: In deciding whether to invest in a short-term instrument and roll over the funds until the end of the holding period or invest in a longer-term instrument matching the investor's holding period, the investor will choose the path that provides the most funds at the end of the holding period. To make such a judgment requires the investor to form expectations of future short-term interest rates over the period to the end of the holding period. It is further argued that if other investors have the same expectations for future short-term interest rates, competitive forces will drive the longer-term interest rate into alignment with the average of expected short-term interest rates.

An illustration will help. Suppose the current short-term (one-year) interest rate is 3 percent and there are widespread expectations that the short-term rate in a year will be 5 percent. Under these conditions, the investor would expect to have the following amount of money accumulated at the end of two years if $100 were invested now:

$$\$100 \times (1.03) \times (1.05) = \$108.15$$

In the above, the amount that would be accumulated at the end of the first year would be $103. That would then be reinvested at an expected interest rate of 5 percent in the second year. The final amount would be $8 ($3 plus $5) on the original $100 investment plus $0.15 ($3 × 0.05) interest on the interest earned in the first year of the investment.

Under the expectations hypothesis, the interest rate on a two-year instrument (the long-term interest rate) would be such that the investor has the same amount at the end of two years. Thus, if i_2^l represents the two-year (long-term) interest rate and i_1 is the current short-term (one-year) interest rate and i_2^e the expected short-term interest rate a year from now, per dollar invested:

$$(1 + i_2^l)^2 = (1 + i_1)(1 + i_2^e)$$

or

$$1 + i_2^l = \sqrt{1 + i_1(1 + i_2^e)}$$

In our numerical example, $1 + i_2^l = \sqrt{1.0815} = 1.03995$ or $i_2^l = 0.03995$.

That is, the annual interest rate on the two-year instrument would be 3.995 percent. Note that this is very close to the 4 percent average of the 3 percent and 5 percent short-term interest rates.

More generally, the relationship between the long-term interest rate, i_n^l, and current and expected short-term interest rates, i_j^e, can be expressed as:

$$1 + i_n^l = \sqrt[n]{(1+i_1)(1+i_2^e)(1+i_3^e)\cdots(1+i_n^e)}$$

or (5-1)

$$i_n^l = \sqrt[n]{(1+i_1)(1+i_2^e)(1+i_3^e)\cdots(1+i_n^e)} - 1$$

In other words, the long-term interest rate will be a geometrically weighted average of the current and expected short-term interest rates over the life of the instrument. In practice, Equation (5-1) can be approximated by

$$i_n^l = \frac{\sum_{j=1}^{n} i_j^e}{n} \quad (5\text{-}2)$$

In other words, the long-term interest rate under the expectations hypothesis is *approximated* as an average of the current and expected short-term interest rates over the life of the instrument (to its maturity).

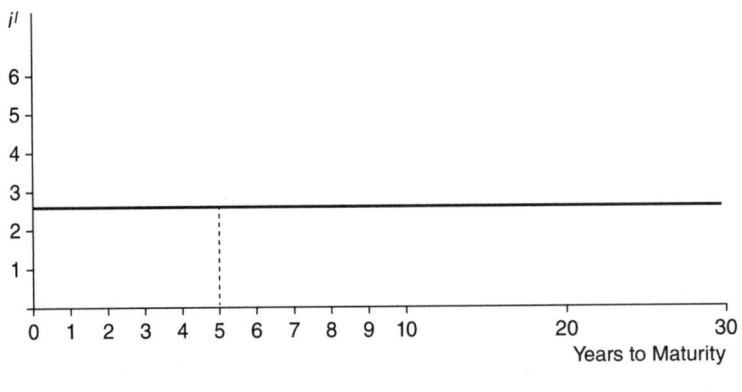

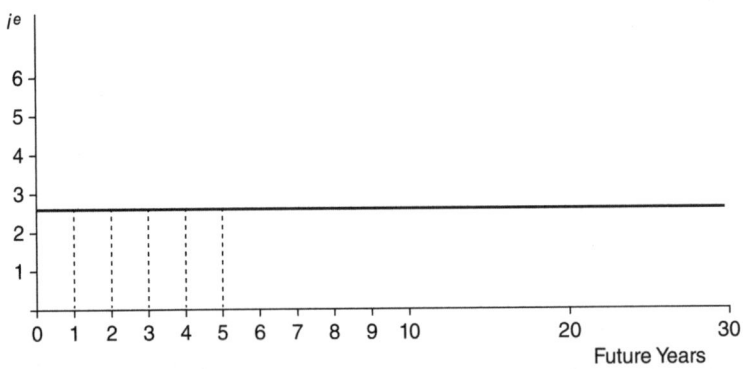

The relationship between long-term interest rates and the expected path of short-term interest rates can be illustrated in a two-panel diagram. Figure 5.2 displays this

FIGURE 5.2 Relationship between Long-Term Interest Rates and the Expected Path of Short-Term Interest Rates

Factors Affecting Yields 79

relationship. The upper panel shows the yield curve, the collection of interest rates on instruments of different maturities, long-term rates in Equation (5-1). The lower panel depicts the corresponding path of expected short-term interest rates. Thus, the interest rate on a five-year instrument in the upper panel, 3 percent, is the average of the current short-term interest rate, 3 percent, and the expected short-term rates over the next four years, also 3 percent. Because the path of short-term interest rates is expected to be flat for the foreseeable future, the yield curve in the upper panel will also be flat.

Typically, one goes from the path of expected short-term interest rates, the lower panel, to derive the yield curve in the upper panel. However, one can make inferences about the path of expected short-term interest rates, which is not directly observed, from the yield curve, which is directly observed.[2] Under the expectations hypothesis, an observed flat yield curve, as in the upper panel, must imply that the expected path of short-term rates, the lower panel, also is flat.

In Figure 5.2, the path of expected short-term rates is flat. This is usually not the case. Market participants most of the time assume that short-term rates will be rising or falling. We illustrate a situation in which short-term rates are expected to be rising in Figure 5.3. This can be seen in the upward-sloping line in the bottom panel. It produces an upward-sloping yield curve in the top panel. In other words, if the short-term rate is rising from one period to the next, the average of short-term rates will also be rising. Note that the upper panel has a shallower upward slope than the lower panel. This is because the upper panel is

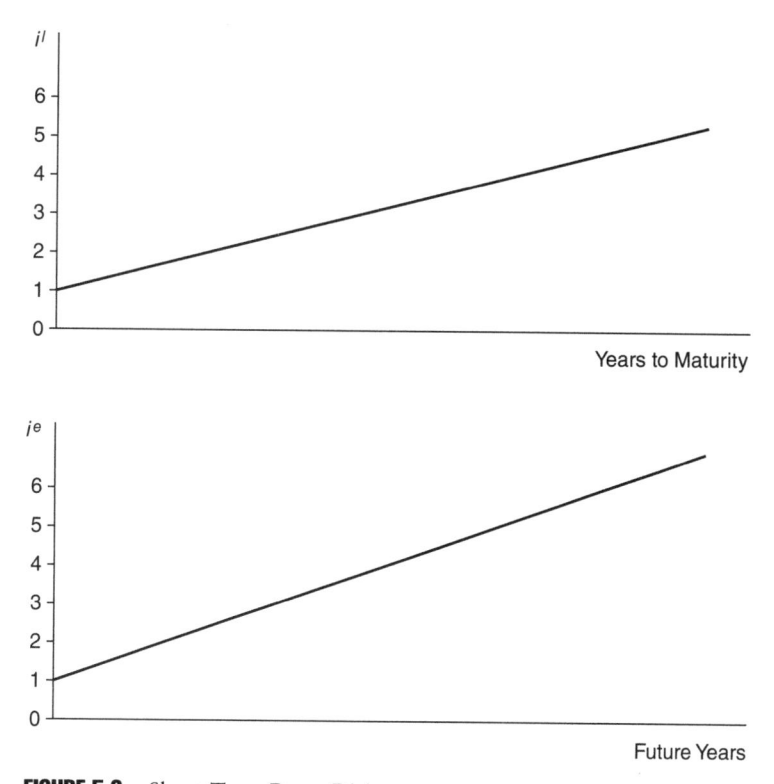

FIGURE 5.3   Short-Term Rates Rising

an *average* of all the short-term rates in the lower panel out to that maturity. As another year is added in the lower panel, that short-term rate is averaged with all the previous short-term rates. That means that long-term rates rise at a slower pace than short-term rates.[3]

Under the expectations hypothesis, a rising yield curve implies that market participants are expecting short-term interest rates to be rising. In other words, one can go from the upper panel to derive the lower panel, as in Figure 5.2. As we go from one point on the yield curve to the next point, the long-term interest rate can rise only if the expected short-term rate has risen. Indeed, the expected short-term rate (the marginal) will have risen by more than the long-term rate (the average).

Expectations of declining short-term interest rates will result in a negatively sloped yield curve under the expectations hypothesis. This is illustrated in Figure 5.4. The reasoning is analogous to that of expectations of rising short-term interest rates, as displayed in Figure 5.3. In the lower panel of Figure 5.4, the current short-term rate is 6 percent, and future rates are expected to be declining. As a result, long-term rates will also be declining, but at a slower pace because of the averaging process. Again, one can make inferences about market expectations for the path of short-term rates from the yield curve in the upper panel. If the yield curve is downward sloping, as in Figure 5.4, it must be true that market participants are expecting short-term rates to be falling and falling more rapidly than the yield curve.

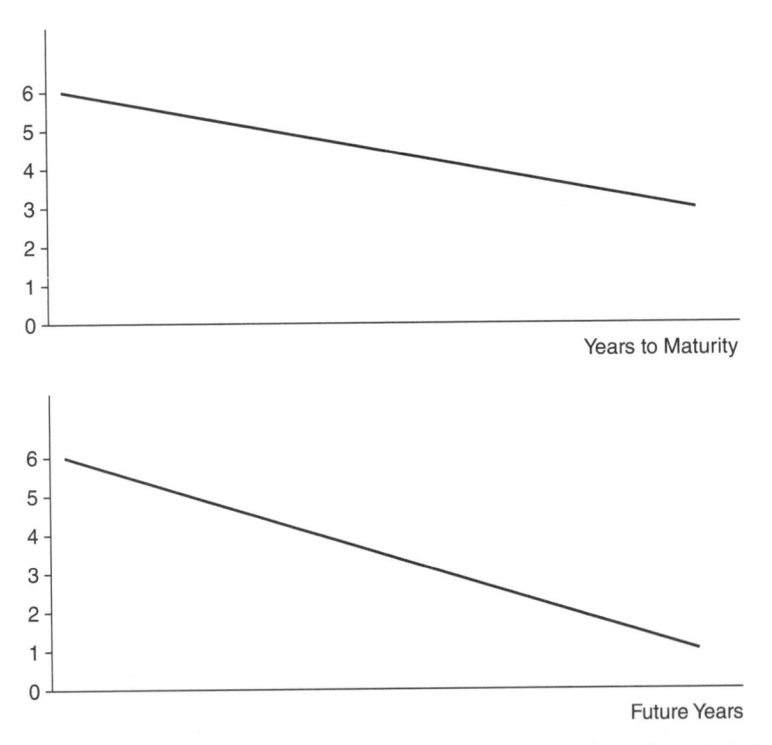

FIGURE 5.4 Curve Based on Expectations of Declining Short-Term Interest Rates

The Term Premium Hypothesis

An alternative explanation of the term structure of interest rates is provided by the *term premium hypothesis* or sometimes called the *liquidity premium hypothesis*. The term premium hypothesis starts from the expectations hypothesis and takes into account that longer-term interest rates are more vulnerable to interest rate movements—that is, they are subject to more price or interest rate risk. This is a point that we developed in Chapter 4.

Because holders of longer-term instruments are subject to more price risk, it is argued that these holders will need to be compensated for this risk. That is, they will insist on earning the average of expected short-term interest rates over the length of the long-term instrument *plus* a risk premium. Moreover, because price risk increases with maturity, the term premium will increase with maturity. Including a term premium, τ_n, in Equation (5-1) results in the following expression for the long-term interest rate:

$$i_n^l = \sqrt[n]{(1+i_1)(1+i_2^e)(1+i_3^e) \cdots (1+i_n^e)} + \tau_n - 1 \qquad (5\text{-}3)$$

The approximation to this rate (the counterpart to Equation (4-2)) can be expressed as

$$i_n^l = \frac{\sum_{j=1}^{n} i_j^e}{n} + \tau_n \qquad (5\text{-}4)$$

In these expressions, τ_n will increase as the maturity, n, increases.

The relationship between long-term interest rates and expected short-term rates under the term premium hypothesis can be illustrated using two paneled diagrams along the lines of Figures 5.2 through 5.4. Figure 5.5, corresponding to Figure 5.2 under the expectations hypothesis, depicts this relationship when expected short-term interest are flat at the current rate.

The lower panel illustrates the expectation of short-term interest rates remaining at 3 percent indefinitely. The lower (flat) line in the upper panel illustrates the translation of these expectations into long-term interest rates under the expectations hypothesis. The upper line represents actual long-term rates that include the term premium, τ. The term premium at a five-year maturity, τ_5, τ_5 equals b-a. Note that the difference between the upper and lower lines in the upper panel increases with maturity, reflecting the rising compensation for price risk because price risk rises with maturity.

Under the term premium hypothesis, one can make inferences about the expected path of short-term interest rates from the yield curve. However, it is more difficult than under the expectations hypothesis. Doing so requires knowledge of the term premium, which cannot be directly observed.[4] From the observed yield curve, the upper line in the upper panel, one would subtract the estimated liquidity premium at each maturity. This will result in the lower line in the upper panel, which corresponds to the estimated yield curve under the expectations hypothesis. From this, one can use the expectations hypothesis relationship between long and

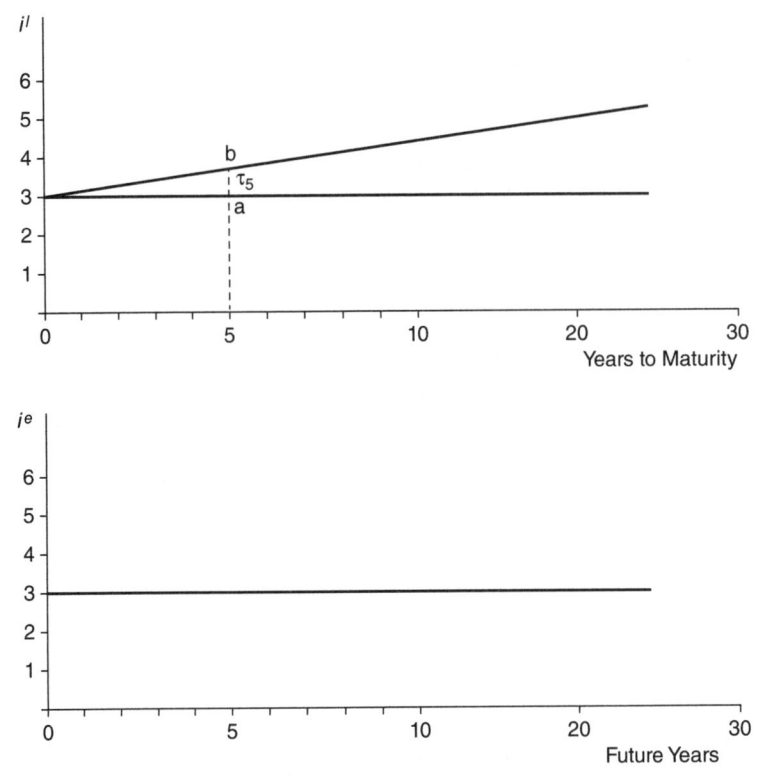

FIGURE 5.5 Curve When Expected Short-Term Interest Is Flat at the Current Rate

expected short-term interest rates to derive the expected path of short-term rates, the lower panel.

Under the term premium hypothesis, an upward-sloped yield curve, as in Figure 5.5, can have different implications for the direction of the path of expected short-term interest rates, depending on the size of the term premium. In Figure 5.5, the upward-sloped yield curve implied that the path of expected short-term rates is flat. However, if the term premium had been larger than that displayed, the implied path of expected short-term rates would have been downward. That is, subtracting a larger term premium from the upper line in the upper panel would have resulted in a negatively sloped adjusted yield curve (lower line in the upper panel). This would have resulted in a downward-sloping line in the lower panel, and thus market expectations of declining short-term interest rates.

In contrast, a flat or negatively sloped yield curve unambiguously implies that market expectations of short-term interest rates are declining. This is illustrated in Figure 5.6 for a flat yield curve. Adjusting the yield curve to remove the term premium, τ, results in a downward sloping adjusted yield curve, the lower line. From this can be derived an expected path for short-term rates, the lower panel. This will also be downward sloping, indicating that market participants expect short-term interest rates to be declining in the future. Note that the drop in expected short-term rates exceeds that of the drop in corresponding adjusted long-term rates in the upper panel as discussed above.

Factors Affecting Yields

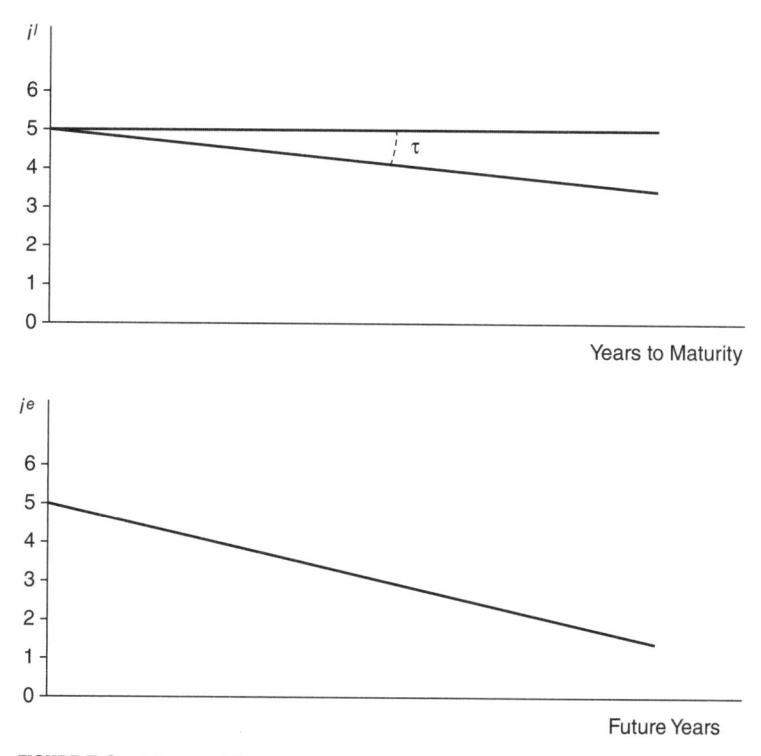

FIGURE 5.6 Flat Yield Curve

Market Segmentation Hypothesis

Some argue that there is another factor that can affect the yield curve, beyond expectations of short-term interest rates and compensation for price risk. It is argued that some investors may have such a strong preference for short- or long-term investments—a so-called preferred habitat—that they would be willing to sacrifice significant amounts of yield to be able to hold such instruments. For example, pension funds may want to hold very long-term bonds to match the duration of their pension liabilities. If there are many of these investors, they may bid up the price of very long-term bonds well beyond what would be suggested by the path of expected short-term rates and term premiums. Similarly, a reduction in the supply of very long-term bonds could result in a sizable increase in their price as such long-term bond investors bid aggressively to be able to get them. The reluctance on the part of these investors to substitute shorter maturity and higher-yielding bonds for these very long-term bonds causes the resulting pricing anomaly. This has been labeled the *market segmentation* or *preferred habitat hypothesis*. Basically, it says that shifts in relative supplies of securities with different maturities can have an effect on yields beyond changes in expected short-term rates and term premiums.

To a degree, central banks—especially the U.S. Federal Reserve—have relied on relative supply effects to compress term premiums and thereby lower the longer-term interest rates faced by private borrowers to boost aggregate demand. By buying up long-term securities, central banks were attempting to reduce the amount of such securities in the hands of investors and raise their price. In the United States, this has been done at a time when the scope to use the standard tool of monetary policy—the federal funds rate—had been exhausted once this rate had been lowered to near zero. The Fed has labeled these actions as Large-Scale Asset Purchases (LSAPs), while market participants have referred to this as quantitative easing (QE). More on this issue in Chapter 14.

Implicit Forward Rates

From the yield curve, we can extract *implicit forward rates* of interest, which will be related to the expectations by market participants of future short-term interest rates. The forward rate relates to terms of an agreement that is negotiated today for delivery at some future date. Forward markets are markets in which prices (or terms) are negotiated today for future delivery. Futures markets are a variety of forward markets in which standardized contracts are negotiated today for standard delivery times in the future. Forward prices (or interest rates) will be closely related to prices that are expected to prevail on the future delivery date.

The forward interest rate is the interest rate that is determined today for the delivery of funds at some specified date in the future. For example, you may be expecting to receive $1,000 in four years and may not anticipate needing those funds for another year. You may want to make a commitment today to invest those funds for a year—to lock in a yield for the fifth year. A forward market in funds would enable you to make that investment today. Actually, you could, in effect, make that investment easily if you currently owned a four-year Treasury note having a value of $1,000. You would do so by selling that note and by using the proceeds to buy a five-year note. What you have done by this transaction is essentially to have taken the proceeds that you were expecting in four years from the four-year note and committed them for another year by purchasing the five-year note. Suppose that the interest rate on a four-year note is 4.0 percent and that on a five-year note is 4.5 percent. The implicit interest rate that you will receive for the fifth year in this transaction is the following:

$$1 + i_4^f = \frac{(1+i_5^l)^5}{(1+i_4^l)^4} = \frac{(1+0.45)^5}{(1+.04)^4} = \frac{1.24618}{1.16986} = 1.065 \tag{5-5}$$

In this expression, i_4^f is the implicit forward interest rate on an investment to be made in four years with a one-year maturity and the other terms have the same meaning as above. This says that the implicit forward interest rate is 6.5 percent.

You will earn 6.5 percent interest on the one-year investment in four years that you agreed to today. Note that this rate is well above the 4.5 percent that is available on the five-year investment. In effect, it takes a 6.5 percent interest rate in the fifth year to pull the long-term interest rate from 4 percent for four years to 4.5 percent for five years.

The generalized formula for the implicit forward rate is the following:

$$i_n^f = \frac{(1+i_{n+1}^l)^{n+1}}{(1+i_n^l)} - 1 \tag{5-6}$$

Factors Affecting Yields

In this expression, i_n^f is the implicit forward interest rate on a one-year investment that is made today for delivery in *n* years. The other terms have the same meaning as above.[5]

The Role of the Term Structure

The term structure relationship will be playing a key role in subsequent chapters. In this regard, the term premium hypothesis will serve as the basis for future discussions of the term structure as it is generally best able to explain the actual behavior of interest rates.

The term structure relationship plays a central role in the monetary policy process. The current short-term interest rate and the expected path of short-term rates, together with term premiums, determine long-term interest rates. And long-term rates are the most important interest rates influencing spending decisions by businesses and households. As we will see in Chapter 12, central banks control short-term interest rates. This implies that market participants, interacting with each other in the setting of long-term interest rates, will not only be factoring in the current setting of short-term interest rates but, more important, will be forming expectations of where the central bank will be setting short-term interest rates in the future. Reflecting this, central banks increasingly make public statements aimed at shaping expectations of future short-term rates. This has come to be referred to as *forward guidance* and, in some respects, has become a tool of monetary policy, much like the setting of the current short-term rate itself. Forward guidance may also lower the risk that market participants attach to the path of future short-term interest rates and thereby reduce term premiums embedded in longer-term interest rates.

The preceding discussion viewed the short-term interest rate as a one-year interest rate. In practice, there are much shorter interest rates. Indeed, the most commonly followed short-term interest rate is an overnight rate—the federal funds rate in the United States. It is the interest rate at which banks lend reserve balances held at the Federal Reserve to each other. The Federal Reserve sets a target for this rate based on its monetary policy objectives. In practice, the Fed sets this rate at each Federal Open Market Committee meeting for about a six-week period—until its next meeting. The relationships that we have developed in this chapter can be adapted to situations in which the short-term interest rate prevails for shorter periods than a year. More will be said on this in Chapters 13 and 14.

CREDIT RISK

The discussion to this point has treated all financial instruments as having the same risk of default.[6] In practice, default or credit risk varies considerably among issuers. The U.S. Treasury has never defaulted on its debt in more than two centuries. As a consequence, Treasury debt has been regarded by market participants to be virtually default free. However, there are some very shaky debt instruments issued by private borrowers that either have defaulted or stand a very high chance of defaulting. Investors will be trying to identify the likelihood of default before making an investment decision and will require compensation for holding a financial instrument that has some likelihood of default. The higher that likelihood, the more will be the compensation.

Thus, the interest rate faced by a borrower can be thought of as having a risk-free interest rate component—represented by a sovereign debt benchmark—and a risk premium that compensates investors for the risk of default. Because there is a large amount of heterogeneity among borrowers, the situation is characterized by a considerable degree of asymmetric information, making it difficult for investors (lenders) to ascertain on their own the risk of default.

Credit Rating Agencies

In these circumstances, a market has developed for providing information about borrowers to investors. This takes place through private firms called credit agencies. In practice, there are three such agencies—Moody's, Standard & Poor's (S&P), and Fitch. These firms gather information and evaluate the information in forming a judgment about the risk of default. They then translate that into a letter grade for the instrument.

The chart in Figure 5.7 gives the ratings scale for each of the agencies. For each agency, there is a scale for ratings of long-term instruments, typically bonds, and a

Ratings Categories by Rating Agency

Moody's		S&P		Fitch		
Long Term	Short Term	Long Term	Short Term	Long Term	Short Term	
Aaa		AAA		AAA		Prime
Aa1		AA+	A-1+	AA+	F1+	High grade
Aa2	P-1	AA		AA		
Aa3		AA−		AA−		
A1		A+	A-1	A+	F1	Upper medium grade
A2		A		A		
A3	P-2	A−	A-2	A−	F2	Lower medium grade
Baa1		BBB+		BBB+		
Baa2		BBB	A-3	BBB	F3	
Baa3	P-3	BBB−		BBB−		
Ba1		BB+		BB+		Noninvestment grade speculative
Ba2		BB		BB		
Ba3		BB−	B	BB−	B	
B1		B+		B+		Highly speculative
B2		B		B		
B3		B−		B−		
Caa1	Not prime	CCC+				Substantial risks
Caa2		CCC	C	CCC	C	Extremely speculative
Caa3		CCC−				In default with little prospect for recovery
Ca		CC				
		C				
C		D	/	DDD	/	In default
/				DD		
/				D		

FIGURE 5.7 Ratings Scale for Agencies
Source: A.M. Best

scale for short-term instruments, typically commercial paper (each will be discussed in a later chapter). For long-term instruments, the top rating is a triple A—Aaa for Moody's and AAA for S&P and Fitch. Ratings go down to a single C on the Moody's scale and a single D on the S&P and Fitch scales—all represent instruments in default. Note the narrative in the right column that describes the different categories. Note, too, that for each letter rating there are three grades denoted by numbers 1 to 3 in the Moody's scale and pluses and minuses in the S&P and Fitch scales. These are subcategories of the letter grades.

Investment-Grade versus Below-Investment-Grade Debt

An important dividing line takes place between investment-grade and speculative-grade instruments. This occurs at the Baa3 level for Moody's and the BBB–level for S&P and Fitch. Anything at or above this grade is called *investment grade*. Anything below this level is deemed to be *speculative grade*—also called below-investment-grade, high-yield, or junk. Many investors are restricted in their ability to hold speculative-grade instruments. They may be prohibited by rules from holding any such bonds or limited to holding small portfolio shares. Thus, being able to get an investment-grade rating has the advantage of making your securities available to a wider range of investors.

The ratings agencies regularly review the instruments that they rate to determine whether that instrument still merits the same rating or whether a downgrade or upgrade is called for. Thus, the rating of an instrument may change over time. Usually, the ratings agencies will announce that an instrument has been placed under review for either an upgrade or downgrade before any action is taken. An instrument that has dropped from investment-grade to speculative-grade status is called a *fallen angel*. There was a time when the only way a security became speculative-grade was to become a fallen angel. In recent decades, however, many firms have issued securities that are below investment grade at the time of issuance.

In practice, the ratings agencies rate the financial instrument and not the issuer directly. A borrower may have issued more than one security to raise funds and these may differ with regard to the standing of the security's holder on the cash flows and assets of the issuer. Some debt is issued with a senior claim while some other is issued with a subordinated (junior) claim on the cash flows and assets of the issuer. The former is deemed to have less risk of default. As a consequence, the risk of default and the rating can differ even though the same borrower issues them.

Another issue relating to bond ratings involves the practice of the ratings agency being paid by the issuer of the bond (the borrower). It has been argued that such a system for compensating the ratings agencies creates a conflict of interest because the borrower will seek a better rating for the issue from the agency than it merits, threatening to go elsewhere for a better rating if the agency does not comply. Of course, should these threats be broadly effective in extracting better ratings, investors would come to recognize such "grade inflation" and would place less confidence in published ratings and would take the grade inflation into account in coming up with their own assessment of underlying credit risk.

Cyclical Behavior of Credit Risk and Spreads

In addition to ratings changing from time to time, credit (default) risk embedded in yields varies over time, based on the position of the business cycle. Figure 5.8 illustrates typical patterns for three categories of interest rates: risk-free (Treasury or benchmark, the bottom line) securities; high-tier, investment-grade bonds (Moody's Aaa corporate bond yields, the middle line); and speculative-grade bonds (Merrill Lynch high-yield Master II series, the top line). During expansions, risk-free yields tend to rise, and during contractions, they tend to fall. This is because in expansions the central bank is boosting short-term rates to avoid an overheating of the economy and unwanted inflation, while in contractions it is lowering short-term rates to boost spending, output, and employment. This works through the term structure relationship discussed in the previous section. During downturns, the central bank shifts to lowering the policy rate to counter the weakness in the economy and, through the term structure relationship, long-term benchmark yields decline. The reverse takes place in expansions. Because of the secular downturn in long-term yields since the early 1980s, as inflation has drifted lower, these patterns are more evident for downturns than upturns.

The situation for high-tier (Aaa) corporate bonds is similar, with yields tending to rise in expansions and decline in contractions. However, note that these yields generally do not rise as much as benchmark yields in the expansion nor decline as much in the contraction. This is because during an expansion, credit risk is seen to be diminishing because the economy is performing well. The risk spread, the difference between the high-investment grade and benchmark yields, thus drops. In a recession, the likelihood of default—while low for top-tier borrowers—nonetheless

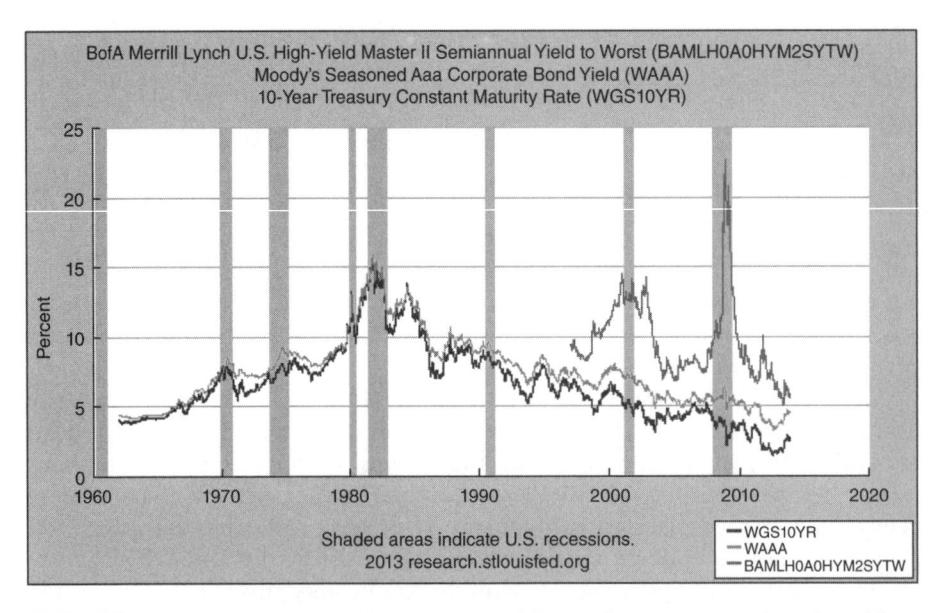

FIGURE 5.8 High Yield (top), Corporate Aaa (middle), and Treasury Benchmark Yields
Source: Merrill Lynch (high yield), Moody's (Aaa), and U.S. Treasury (Treasury benchmark).

Factors Affecting Yields 89

increases somewhat. This accounts for the yield falling less than that on risk-free instruments.

In contrast, yields on speculative-grade bonds tend to decline in expansions and rise in contractions. This is because risk premiums move more sharply over the business cycle—dropping markedly as the economy expands and the likelihood of default drops a lot and rising markedly as the economy weakens and default becomes a more serious possibility. Indeed, movements in default risk spreads swamp movements in the benchmark yield over the cycle, leading to these contrary patterns.

Figure 5.9 illustrates the spread of the speculative-grade (high-yield) bond shown in Figure 5.8 over a comparable-maturity Treasury benchmark note.[7] This measure of the credit risk spread widens considerably around recessions—the shaded areas— and retraces those movements after expansions have taken hold.

Credit Default Swaps (CDSs)

A more recent measure of default prospects has been credit default swaps (CDSs). Such swaps are essentially an insurance policy against a default. In the event that the bond having a CDS defaults, the holder of the bond receives compensation from the writer of the swap. The premium on the CDS on a bond can be viewed as a market assessment of the likelihood of default, in much the same way that the premium on a driver's auto insurance policy reflects the likelihood that that driver will be in an accident. The higher the premium, the greater the likelihood of default (an auto accident).[8]

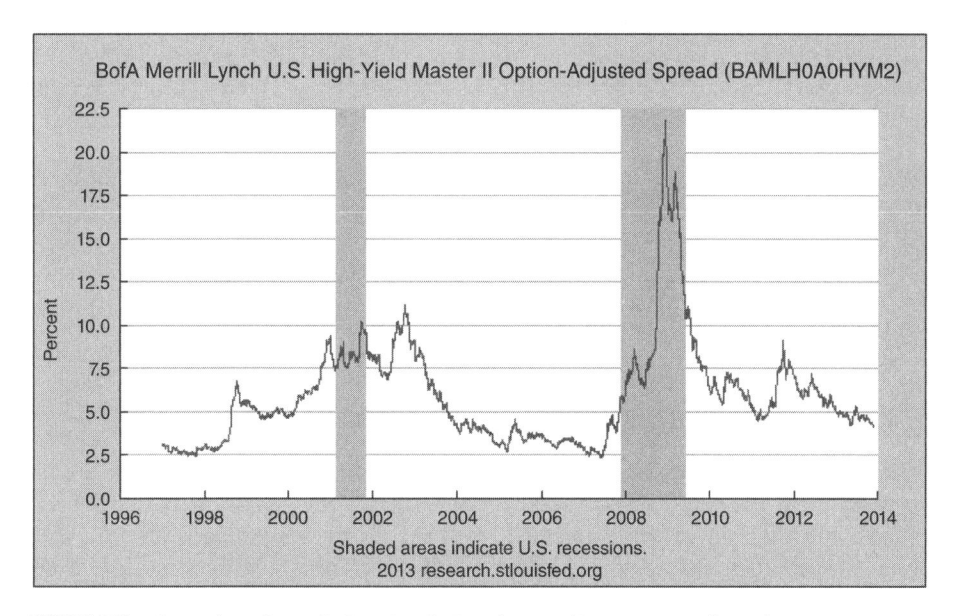

FIGURE 5.9 Spread on Speculative-Grade Bonds over Treasury Benchmark
Source: Merrill Lynch.

Changing Investor Tolerance for Risk

In addition to varying assessments of the likelihood of default over the business cycle, investors' tolerance for risk can change. If investors are less willing to hold risky instruments—they become more risk averse—they will insist on more compensation, and thus the risk spread will increase (or the premium on a CDS will increase). Of course, a greater tolerance for risk would lead to a decline in the risk spread (and CDS premiums). Often, investor tolerance for risk diminishes during a time of economic weakness and uncertainty about the outlook for the economy—coincident with a time when the actual likelihood of default is rising. This has been especially true of severe financial crises, the subject of Chapter 15.

LIQUIDITY

Securities can differ with regard to their liquidity and this, too, will lead to differences in yields. By liquidity, we mean the ease by which an asset can be sold (or purchased) and sold (or purchased) at a price near its fundamental value. A liquid instrument is one that can be sold quickly at a price reflective of its current value. An illiquid instrument is one that cannot be sold easily or its price must be discounted appreciably to attract a buyer. A common measure of the liquidity of a regularly traded security is the difference between the price at which a dealer will sell the security (its ask or asked price) and the price at which the dealer will buy the security (its bid price). The larger the bid-ask price difference, the less liquid the security.

Investors are willing to pay a higher price for a more liquid security, because if they want to sell it before maturity, they will find it easier to sell and will expect to get a better price. Thus, we could find two securities with the same maturity and comparable credit risk having different yields (prices) because of differing degrees of liquidity. The more liquid of the two will have a higher price—lower yield.

A good illustration of differences in liquidity can be found in the market for U.S. Treasury securities—the premium for so-called *on-the-run securities*. On-the-run Treasuries are the most recently auctioned security of each maturity. For example, the 30-year bond auctioned in May 2014 and scheduled to mature in May 2044 is the on-the-run 30-year bond once it is issued until the next auction in August 2014. During this period, some investors prefer holding this bond to off-the-run bonds, those issued before May 2014. As a result of investors deeming this to be the most desirable 30-year bond to hold and trade, this bond will command a higher price than other 30-year bonds. Stated differently, investors will be willing to accept a lower yield on an on-the-run bond than an off-the-run bond. The difference in yield between an off-the-run Treasury security and the on-the-run security of the same original maturity is sometimes referred to as the on-the-run spread. These spreads can be on the order of several basis points (a basis point is one-hundredth of a percentage point).

As might be expected, forward-looking market participants begin to act in advance of an on-the-run Treasury security going off-the-run. Its yield rises (price declines) as the next auction date approaches.

TAXATION

Financial assets are treated differently for tax purposes and these differences affect their yields. Most notably, securities issued by state and local governments—commonly referred to as *munis*—are exempt from federal income taxation.[9] As a result, investors subject to federal income taxation are willing to accept a lower yield on such securities than on taxable securities all else equal. For example, an investor in the 28 percent marginal tax bracket would be indifferent between earning 5 percent on a taxable security and 3.6 percent on a muni, if the two securities had comparable credit risk and liquidity. That is, this investor would receive 5 cents each year before tax for each dollar of principal of the taxable instrument, but would need to pay 1.4 cents in federal taxes (0.28 × 5). The after-tax return would be 3.6 percent (5 − 1.4). This can be expressed algebraically as

$$i_M = i_T(1-t) \tag{5-7}$$

In Equation (5-7), i_M represents the muni yield, i_T the Treasury yield, and t the marginal tax rate on interest income.

A muni with a 3.6 percent yield would provide the investor with the same after-tax interest because none of the interest would be subject to federal taxation. In these circumstances, investors will bid up the price of the state or local security until its tax advantage disappears. That is, arbitrage will result in after-tax yields being comparable.

In practice, munis do not have the same liquidity and credit risk as comparable maturity Treasury securities. Treasury securities have lower credit risk and are more liquid. As a result, there are crosscurrents affecting muni versus Treasury yields. The tax exemption acts to lower muni yields relative to Treasury securities, while greater credit risk and lower liquidity act to raise muni yields. Ordinarily, the tax exemption dominates higher credit risk and lower liquidity, leaving lower yields on munis relative to comparable maturity Treasuries. However, during times of financial turmoil or severe fiscal strains on state and local budgets, muni yields can exceed those on Treasuries. This was the case during the financial crisis and its aftermath when even very highly rated munis carried higher yields than similar maturity Treasury securities, despite their tax advantage.

EMBEDDED OPTIONS

Some securities have embedded options, often allowing the issuer (borrower) to repay the obligation prior to maturity. This is common for ordinary home mortgages. The borrower or homeowner typically can prepay a portion or the entire mortgage loan whenever the homeowner wants. Not only will the homeowner want to exercise this option when moving to another home, but also when mortgage rates have declined significantly and it has become attractive to refinance at the lower interest rate. This option has value to the homeowner but can lower the return to the investor, especially when the general level of interest rates has fallen and the investor will not be able to earn the same interest rate when reinvesting the repaid funds. As a consequence, the interaction of borrowers and lenders in this market will result in the mortgage interest rate being higher to reflect the value of the embedded option. The borrower may need to pay 6 percent on a mortgage when the interest rate on a comparable maturity Treasury security is 4 percent, the difference representing the embedded option as well (as more credit risk and less liquidity of the mortgage).

Similarly, corporate bonds can have embedded options that allow the issuer (borrower) to redeem the bond prior to maturity. These bonds are said to have a *call provision,* which allows the issuer to call (redeem) the bond on predetermined terms. Bonds with call provisions carry higher yields than others to compensate the investor for the possibility that the bond will be redeemed prior to maturity and the investor will be faced with finding another investment, most likely in an environment of lower interest rates on reinvestments. Bonds that cannot be called prior to maturity are said to have *call protection* and will carry a lower interest rate than a comparable callable bond.

Some bonds permit the owner to convert the bond into stock at some predetermined conversion rate. Typically, the amount of stock that the bondholder would get for the bond at the time of issuance will be worth a good bit less than the bond by itself—it is said to be "out of the money" at that point. However, should the value of the stock appreciate markedly, the option to convert the bond into equity shares will start to look attractive and at some point the investor will want to exercise the option to convert. Such an embedded option will lower the bond's yield as investors will be willing to pay a higher price for a bond with such upside potential.

FLIGHTS TO SAFETY

During times of turmoil, investors often seek the safety and liquidity of certain securities—most notably U.S. Treasury securities. At these times, prices of Treasury benchmarks are bid up, while prices of less safe assets drop. The turmoil could be triggered by events in the United States or they could take place elsewhere and be global in scope. When they involve investors outside the United States, the U.S dollar also tends to get bid higher in the foreign exchange market as investors holding securities denominated in other currencies sell those securities and use the proceeds to buy Treasuries, requiring that they first convert those proceeds to dollars and thereby bid up the value of the dollar.

Thus, one can see spreads between yields on securities other than Treasuries and Treasuries widening sharply during such a flight to safety, and the dollar strengthens. Once the crisis has passed, the process unwinds and yields on Treasuries begin to retrace their declines, and those on other securities begin to retrace their increases. If the crisis is international in scope, the dollar will also begin to reverse its rise.

SUMMARY

1. At any point in time, interest rates can differ for various reasons: differences in maturity, differences in credit risk, differences in liquidity, differences in taxation of interest, and differences in embedded options.
2. The term structure of interest rates refers to the relationship among interest rates at different maturities. The expectations hypothesis of the term structure

states that a long-term interest rate is a (geometric) average of current and expected short-term interest rates over the life of the instrument. The term (liquidity) premium hypothesis starts from the formulation of long-term interest rates under the expectations hypothesis, but takes into account that longer maturity instruments have more price (interest rate) risk; as a consequence, investors will require a premium to holder longer-term instruments, with that premium rising as maturity increases.

3. Under both hypotheses, there is a distinct relationship between the yield curve and the path of expected short-term interest rates. If short-term interest rates are expected to be increasing, for example, the yield curve will be upward sloping. Yield curves can be used to make inferences about the path of short-term interest rates expected by market participants.
4. An implicit forward rate of interest can be inferred from two adjacent points on the yield curve. This will be related to expectations by market participants of the path of short-term interest rates that is expected to unfold over that period.
5. The term structure relationship plays an important role in the monetary policy process. Monetary policy affects very short-term interest rates, but longer-term rates are more important for spending decisions. As a consequence, central banks attempt to shape the expected path of short-term interest rates—through forward guidance—so that associated long-term rates are better aligned with policy objectives.
6. Fixed-income instruments differ with regard to the likelihood that the borrower will default. As a consequence, investors must be compensated for being exposed to credit risk. This takes the form of a higher yield on riskier instruments. The difference between the yield on such an instrument and that of a risk-free instrument of comparable maturity and risk can be thought of as the credit risk premium.
7. Investors are assisted by credit rating agencies, which investigate each rated issue and assign a rating based on the agency's assessment of the likelihood of default. Securities rated Baa (BBB) or above are called investment-grade and those with lower ratings are called speculative-grade (also called below-investment-grade, high yield, or junk). Credit default swaps (CDSs) are also market measures of the likelihood of default.
8. Securities differ with regard to their liquidity—the ease with which they can be bought or sold (at a price reflective of underlying economic value). More liquid instruments will have lower yields (higher prices), owing to the value investors attach to liquidity.
9. Securities issued by state and local governments (munis) pay interest that is exempt from federal taxation, unlike Treasury or corporate bonds. As a consequence, investors subject to federal income tax will favor such securities and be willing to accept a lower yield (pay a higher price) than for a comparable taxable security.
10. Some fixed-income instruments have embedded options—usually the right of the borrower to repay the obligation prior to maturity. When such options are exercised, the investor receives payment before maturity, usually when interest rates have fallen and reinvestment opportunities have become less attractive. As a consequence, such securities (and loans) will have higher yields to compensate the investor (lender) for this risk.

11. At times, skittish investors seek the safety of Treasury securities. This involves an increase in the demand for Treasury securities and a reduction in the demand for more risky securities, causing Treasury yields to decline and these other yields to rise. Risk spreads thus increase. The dollar also often strengthens with prices of Treasury securities.

QUESTIONS

1. How will an increase in perceived credit risk on a risky bond affect its price? Its yield? How will it affect the price and yield of a riskless bond?
2. What is the role of credit rating agencies? What economic problem do they address? How does the yield on a C-rated bond differ from that of a Aaa-rated bond? Which is the highest and why?
3. How does the spread between a Caa-rated bond over a Aaa-rated bond vary over the business cycle? Why? A Aaa-rated bond over a comparable maturity Treasury security?
4. What is a speculative-grade bond? How does it differ from an investment-grade bond? What is a "fallen angel"?
5. What is a credit default swap (CDS)?
6. How does the yield on an on-the-run Treasury security change as it goes off the run? Why does this occur?
7. How would an increase in marginal federal income tax rates affect yields on muni securities? Treasury yields? Illustrate.
8. When short-term interest rates are very low, what is the slope of the yield curve? When short-term rates are high? Why do these patterns exist?
9. Under the expectations hypothesis of the term structure, what does a positively sloped yield curve imply for the expected path of short-term interest rates? A negatively sloped yield curve?
10. How would your answer to question 9 change under the term premium hypothesis?
11. Which of these two hypotheses can best explain the pattern of yields on different maturities? Explain.
12. Suppose that the current yield on a five-year Treasury note is 1.25 percent. What can you say about market expectations of short-term interest rates over the next five years?
13. Why has the Federal Reserve frequently mentioned that economic conditions are likely to warrant exceptionally low interest rates for an extended period? What are they trying to achieve through this statement?
14. What is a forward market?
15. Suppose that the current yield on a two-year Treasury note is 1.20 percent and the yield on a three-year note is 1.44 percent. What is the implicit one-year forward rate for two years ahead? Why is it higher than 1.44 percent?
16. Using Bloomberg, what is the shape of the Treasury yield curve? What can you infer about market expectations of the path of the federal funds rate over the next several years?
17. Using the St. Louis Fed website (FRED), chart the Merrill Lynch High-Yield (speculative grade) Master II option-adjusted corporate bond spread. How has it behaved over the business cycle?

NOTES

1. In recent years, though, some sovereign debt has come to be viewed as vulnerable to credit losses—be they from actual default or from being restructured. In a restructuring, the interest rate typically is reduced and the maturity of the debt frequently is extended, and the creditor must either accept the modified terms or sell the security at a loss. Risk of sovereign default has plagued some countries along Europe's southern rim, and rapidly growing debt of the U.S. Treasury has raised concerns that the United States may no longer be immune from a similar plight.
2. There are futures markets that are based on short-term interest rates, notably for federal funds and for eurodollar interest rates (LIBOR). The interest rates on such contracts are closely related to expectations of future interest rates. But they have limitations as indicators of expected short-term interest rates—either they do not go out very far into the future or trading is light and the implied interest rates may not be fully representative of expectations by market participants.
3. The arithmetic reason for this relationship between the long-term rate in the upper panel and the short-term rates in the lower panel is analogous to that of a marginal and average cost curve (beyond the point at which they intersect at the minimum point on the average cost curve). The rising marginal cost curve (comparable to the lower panel of Figure 5.3) pulls up the average cost curve (the upper panel). However, the average cost curve rises by less than the marginal cost curve.
4. There are various ways to estimate term premiums using indirect methods. However, these will yield approximations as each contains estimation errors. The situation is complicated further because it is believed that term premiums will change from time to time, reflecting changes in the volatility of interest rates and changes in investors' aversion to risk.
5. The implicit forward rate derived from adjacent points on the yield curve, as in Equation (5-6), will equal the expected short-term interest rate for that period plus a liquidity premium related to the liquidity premium in the term structure equation, Equation (5-4).
6. A default occurs when the borrower does not meet all the terms of the agreement. It usually involves missing an interest or principal payment on schedule. Sometimes, these missed payments are made up at a later time and the investor loses very little, if anything. In a few cases, these and other contractual payments are not made and the investor loses the entire investment. Typically, a default results in investor losses somewhere between these extremes. That is, the investor recovers a portion of the investment.
7. The measure of the speculative-grade yield is an average for a number of junk bonds (speculative-grade corporate bonds). It is also adjusted for options embedded in those bonds—notably the right of the issuer to call (retire) the bond before maturity (see the later section of this chapter on embedded options).
8. Both credit risk spreads and CDS for a particular security tend to move before ratings agencies take action, largely because the ratings agencies take a very deliberative approach to reviewing and changing ratings. This takes time. Market participants typically have at least some of the information being reviewed by the rating agency well before any announcement of a change and act on that

information promptly. Thus, if there were to be favorable news for an issuer of a bond that in time leads to a ratings agency upgrade, risk spreads and CDS premiums would have already fallen prior to the upgrade.
9. To be eligible for the federal tax exemption, the proceeds of the bond must be used for public and not private purposes; private purpose bonds issued by state or local government authorities are subject to federal taxation. Also, many states exempt bonds issued by governments in their jurisdictions from their state income taxes.

CHAPTER 6

Principles of Portfolio Selection and Efficient Markets

WHAT YOU WILL LEARN IN THIS CHAPTER

- Investors make investment decisions along two separate dimensions: expected return and risk.
- Measurement of expected return and risk have precise specifications.
- The desire to lower risk leads to the careful building of portfolios.
- Individual investments are viewed in terms of their ability to reduce the risk of the portfolio—or variability of the overall returns on the portfolio.
- An asset will be a good candidate for a portfolio if its returns move in a contrary fashion to the returns on the other assets in the portfolio.
- Some may be attractive for the portfolio even though, looked at just by themselves, they are highly risky.
- The principles of portfolio choice are not only utilized by portfolio managers, but also regulators of commercial banks and other financial institutions responsible for ensuring financial soundness of these institutions.
- The presence of savvy investors seeking high returns results in financial markets being *efficient* in the sense that current prices of financial assets tend to embody all relevant information bearing those assets' values.
- This implies that it is highly unlikely an investor can get above-market returns by seeking to pick winners in the market (if they, indeed, are winners, their prices already reflect this).
- For this reason, many investors choose to place their assets in a diversified portfolio that represents the market.
- These diversification principles imply going beyond equities in building a well-diversified portfolio—and also investing across borders.
- The presence of financial bubbles may or may not be consistent with efficient markets.

OVERVIEW

Have you ever wondered why investment advisers recommend that a portfolio of different securities be assembled for one seeking to build a nice little nest egg for the future? Why not just a single high-yielding security instead? What renders one security to be more suitable than another for a portfolio? Why is so much attention focused these days on index funds that attempt to replicate the performance of broad stock indexes rather than judiciously picking a handful of winners for a portfolio built to achieve long-term investment goals? Can I truly expect to make a lot from a "hot" investment tip?

To begin with, investors like to get high returns on their financial investments and they dislike risk—that is, they make portfolio decisions along two dimensions: return and risk. To achieve their investment goals of high return and low risk, they build portfolios of multiple assets rather than placing all their funds in a single asset. Thus, an asset will be a desirable candidate for the investor's portfolio if it adds to the portfolio's return or lowers the portfolio's risk. As we will see in this chapter, the contribution of a particular asset to the portfolio's return is fairly straightforward and not very complicated. However, gauging its contribution to the portfolio's risk is anything but simple.

UNCERTAINTY, EXPECTED RETURN, AND RISK

In the actual world of finance, the investor faces uncertainty. He or she cannot be certain about how an asset will perform. For some investments, there is a wide range of possible outcomes, and the probabilities of each of these outcomes might differ.

In such circumstances, the first order of business will be to calculate the expected return on an individual asset, R^e. Equation (6-1) addresses each possible outcome and relates the probability of that outcome to the return that would result from this outcome. Possible outcomes need to be arrayed from 1 to n.

$$R^e = p_1 R_1 + p_2 R_2 + p_3 R_3 + \cdots + p_n R_n \qquad (6\text{-}1)$$

In this expression, p_1 represents the probability attached to event 1's occurring and R_1 represents the return that corresponds to event 1's occurring. Similarly, for events 2, 3, ..., n. Let us illustrate with a simple example. Suppose there are only two possible outcomes, each having a 50 percent probability—note that the probabilities must always sum to one. In the first, the investor would get a return of 30 percent, and in the second a return of zero. The expected return in this case would be:

$$R^e = 0.5 \times 0.3 + 0.5 \times 0 = 0.15 + 0 = 0.15$$

That is, the expected return on this investment is 15 percent.

We turn now to measuring risk.[1] Risk relates to the dispersion of possible outcomes from owning this asset. The more dispersed these outcomes are, the greater the asset's risk. By convention, we use the statistical measure of the standard deviation of the asset's returns, σ, around its expected return, R^e. This is illustrated in Equation (6-2) below

$$\sigma = \sqrt{p_1(R_1 - R^e)^2 + p_2(R_2 - R^e)^2 + p_3(R_3 - R^e)^2 + \cdots + p_n(R_n - R^e)^2} \qquad (6\text{-}2)$$

The larger the deviation of the return associated with each event from the expected return—and the probabilities of those events occurring—the greater the measure of dispersion or risk, σ. Let us calculate the standard deviation for our numerical example with the expected return of 0.15 or 15 percent.

$$\sigma = \sqrt{0.5(0.3-0.15)^2 + 0.5(0-0.15)^2} = \sqrt{0.5(0.15)^2 + 0.5(-0.15)^2}$$
$$= \sqrt{0.5 \cdot 0.0225 + 0.5 \cdot 0.0225} = \sqrt{0.0225}$$
$$= 0.15$$

In this example, it happens to be the case that both the expected return and the measure of risk are 0.15 or 15 percent.[2] Suppose instead that an asset is believed to provide a return of 10 percent (0.10) under all circumstances. You should be able to verify that this asset would have an expected return of 0.10 and no risk—a σ equal to zero. In this case, expected return and risk differ.

SELECTING A PORTFOLIO

We are now ready to move on to selecting a portfolio of assets, all of which have returns that cannot be known with certainty and embody risk. We will label the assets under consideration asset 1, asset 2, asset 3, ..., asset n. Each will have an expected return, derived using the same methods as presented in the previous section.

Expected Return

We can express the expected return on the *portfolio*—in contrast to the expected return on a single asset (Equation (6-1))—as the following:

$$R_p^e = w_1 R_1^e + w_2 R_2^e + w_3 R_3^e + \cdots + w_n R_n^e = \sum_{i=1}^{n} w_i R_i^e \qquad (6\text{-}3)$$

In this equation, R_p^e is the expected return on the portfolio of assets, R_i^e is the expected return on asset i, and w_i is the (dollar) share of the portfolio held in asset i, or the weight of the portfolio assigned to asset i. It should be clear that if asset i is being considered for the portfolio and it has an expected return that exceeds the expected return on the existing assets in the portfolio, adding this asset to the portfolio will raise the expected return on the portfolio.

Risk

In contrast, determining whether this asset will raise or lower the risk of the portfolio is not as simple. Perhaps an illustration will help. Suppose that all of your assets are being held in Shell Oil (actually, Royal Dutch Shell, plc) and you are looking for ways to reduce your risk. You decide to sell half of your Shell holdings and use the proceeds to buy Exxon Mobil Corp. Do you think that you accomplished much by this action? To be sure, Shell and Exxon are two different companies that are managed differently and have other dissimilarities. However, their fortunes move closely together. The reason for diversifying is to avoid having the returns on one asset fall when those on another have also dropped. This will not be achieved with Shell and Exxon. Their returns tend to move too closely together. You did not achieve much risk reduction through this move.

Alternatively, suppose that you instead bought shares in Toyota Motor Corporation. In this case, if the price of motor fuel fell, returns on Shell, of course, would be hit. However, this would be good news for Toyota because people will be more willing to buy new cars—especially the more fuel-intensive models. This move likely would reduce the risk on your overall portfolio.

Note that what is important for risk reduction is the relationship between the returns of the different assets. If they move closely together, there is little to be gained by adding the asset to the portfolio. In contrast, if they are weakly correlated—or even negatively correlated—selecting that asset will often do the job of lowering the risk of the portfolio.

The formula for the variance of a portfolio's returns—the variance is the standard deviation squared—can be expressed as:

$$\sigma_p^2 = \sum_{i=1}^{n} w_i^2 \sigma_i^2 + \sum_{i=1}^{n} \sum_{j \neq 1}^{n} w_i w_j \sigma_i \sigma_j \rho_{ij} \tag{6-4}$$

In this expression, σ_p^2 is the variance of the returns on the portfolio, σ_i^2 is the variance of the returns on asset i, $\sigma_i \sigma_j$ is the product of the standard deviations of assets i and j (when they are different assets), and ρ_{ij} is the correlation coefficient between the returns on asset i and asset j. The Σs again represent summations. To calculate the standard deviation of the portfolio's returns, σ_p (the standard measure of risk), one takes the square root of the portfolio's variance in Equation (6-4), $\sqrt{\sigma_p^2}$.

Interpreting the Expression for Risk

For most, Equation (6-4) is a very intimidating expression. To get its meaning, it is helpful to break it down. The first term on the right side of the equation says that the portfolio's risk σ_p^2 will vary directly with the risk of the individual asset, σ_i^2. Of course, if the asset is a risky one, the contribution of that asset to the portfolio's risk will vary directly with the share of that asset in the portfolio, w_i. The more of the portfolio invested in that risky asset, the greater the portfolio's risk. The term on the right of the plus sign embodies the relationship among returns of the various assets in the portfolio. Key to the benefits from diversification is the correlation coefficient, ρ_{ij}, between the return on asset i and the return on asset j. The smaller this correlation is, the greater the contribution of diversification to risk reduction. That is, if an asset is selected for the portfolio that has returns that are weakly with those of other assets in the portfolio, the addition of this asset to the portfolio will lower the risk of the portfolio. Indeed, when there is a negative correlation between the return on this asset and those on other assets—that is, when a decline in the return on this asset is accompanied by an increase in the returns on other assets—the selection of this asset will have an even greater impact on reducing portfolio risk.

As ironic as it may seem, it is possible to reduce the risk of a portfolio by selecting an asset that is risky by itself—has a large σ_i^2—but is weakly correlated or negatively correlated with other assets in the portfolio—has a low or negative ρ_{ij}.

Adding an asset with a lot of risk increases the term on the left side of the plus sign in Equation (6-4). However, if that asset has returns that are weakly or negatively correlated with other assets in the portfolio, it will lower the contribution from the term on the right side of the plus sign. If the latter contribution exceeds the former, the asset will actually reduce portfolio risk.

An Illustration

We can work through an example, initially involving two assets, assets 1 and 2. We can then consider adding a third asset to our portfolio. In these circumstances, Equation (6-3) becomes

$$R_p^e = w_1 R_1^e + w_2 R_2^e + w_3 R_3^e \qquad (6\text{-}5)$$

Also, Equation (6-4) becomes

$$\sigma_p^2 = w_1^2 \sigma_1^2 + w_2^2 \sigma_2^2 + w_3^2 \sigma_3^2 + 2 w_1 w_2 \sigma_1 \sigma_2 \rho_{12} + 2 w_1 w_3 \sigma_1 \sigma_3 \rho_{13} + 2 w_2 w_3 \sigma_2 \sigma_3 \rho_{23} \qquad (6\text{-}6)$$

In calculating the expected return and risk of the portfolio of two assets, we will assign zero to the terms that include asset 3.

Let us start with a portfolio consisting of assets 1 and 2. Suppose that the expected returns on assets 1 and 2 are 0.10 and 0.12, respectively—or 10 and 12 percent. Suppose further that half of the portfolio is invested in each asset. Finally, assume the standard deviation of returns is 0.08 for asset 1 and 0.10 for asset 2 and the correlation coefficient of the returns of assets 1 and 2 is 0.3. Note that asset 2 has a higher expected return than asset 1, but it has more risk. The expected return on the portfolio and the variance of the portfolio's returns (the standard deviation squared) are derived as follows:

$$R_p^e = 0.5 \cdot 0.10 + 0.5 \cdot 0.12 = 0.11$$
$$\sigma_p^2 = (0.5)^2 (0.08)^2 + (0.5)^2 (0.10)^2 + 2(0.5)(0.5)(0.08)(0.10)(0.3)$$
$$= 0.0016 + 0.0025 + 0.0012 = 0.0053$$

If σ_p^2 equals 0.0053, then σ_p must equal the square root of 0.0053—or 0.073. In other words, the expected return on the portfolio is 0.11, and the standard deviation of returns is 0.073, below that of either asset. This means that the addition of asset 2 to the portfolio, with more risk than asset 1, has raised the expected return on the portfolio and lowered the risk of the portfolio—the work of diversification.

We will now try to decide whether to add a third asset to the portfolio, asset 3. Suppose that asset 3 is a good bit more risky by itself than assets 1 and 2. The standard deviation of its returns is 0.20—double that of asset 2. Suppose that it has an expected return of 0.11, the same as the above portfolio of assets 1 and 2. The correlation of asset 3's returns with those of asset 1, however, is −0.5—that is, they are negatively correlated. The correlation of asset 3's returns with those of asset 2 is 0.1—rather low. Finally, to make room for asset 3, we have lowered the share of the portfolio invested in assets 1 and 2 to 40 percent each, implying that asset 3 accounts for 20 percent. Let us now see if asset 3 would be a good choice for our portfolio, even though it is quite risky.

$$R_p^e = 0.4 \cdot 0.10 + 0.4 \cdot 0.12 + 0.2 \cdot 0.11 = 0.11$$

$$\begin{aligned}\sigma_p^2 &= (0.4)^2 (0.08)^2 + (0.4)^2 (0.10)^2 + (0.2)^2 (0.20)^2 \\ &\quad + 2(0.4)(0.4)(0.08)(0.10)(0.3) + 2(0.4)(0.2)(0.08)(0.20)(-0.5) \\ &\quad + 2(0.4)(0.2)(0.10)(0.20)(0.1) \\ &= 0.001024 + 0.0016 + 0.0016 + 0.000768 - 0.00128 + 0.00032 \\ &= 0.004032\end{aligned}$$

The standard deviation of this portfolio's returns is the square root of 0.004032 or 0.0635. In other words, the addition of risky asset 3 to the portfolio did not change the expected return on the portfolio—it stays at 0.11—but actually lowered risk by about 12 percent, from 0.073 to 0.0635—even more dramatic evidence of how diversification can lower risk.

These Principles in Practice

These principles are widely followed in the financial world. For example, investors in stocks seek to lower risk through diversification by acquiring a broad mix of common stocks, often attempting to get a basket of shares that replicate the entire stock market. Investors seeking to get a high level of diversification often attempt to buy the market—that is, buy into a portfolio of stocks that is representative of the market. It is thought that by buying the market one achieves the most risk reduction through diversification.

A popular such portfolio is based on the Standard & Poor's (S&P) 500 index of equity prices. The S&P 500 index (containing the 500 largest U.S. corporations) accounts for about three-fourths of the value of the stock market, and the index is calculated almost continuously throughout the business day for those wanting to track the value of their portfolio. More will be said about measures of stock prices in Chapter 11.

An interesting question for investors is what constitutes the market for diversification purposes? Is it only domestic stocks, or should it include stocks in foreign countries? Companies in foreign countries will tend to have returns that move in different ways than domestic companies. Moreover, the returns, measured in dollars, will vary with the exchange value of the dollar. For example, a U.S. investor holding shares in a German company will enjoy a higher return if the euro—the currency used in Germany—strengthens against the dollar. This is because the dividends earned in euros have more value to U.S. investors because a euro translates into more dollars as the euro appreciates.

Increasingly, investors around the globe are seeking to improve diversification of their portfolios by acquiring stocks in foreign companies. Investors who are reluctant to fully exploit risk reduction through opportunities for diversification abroad are said to have *home-country bias*. Such investors are forgoing reductions in risk through carefully selecting investments abroad. The principles applied to the selection of foreign assets will basically be the same as for selecting domestic assets. However, there are certain other risks that need to be factored into the process. These include various political risks, including the risk of expropriation, and exchange rate risk.

There is the further issue of whether the market consists only of stocks or whether it includes other assets, such as bonds—both domestic and foreign. Depending on correlations among returns, expanding the composition of portfolio assets to include bonds and other assets (including real assets, such as real estate) can also reduce portfolio risk. Increasingly, investor portfolios have been broadened to include a broader mix of assets for diversification purposes.

In addition, managers of financial institutions, such as commercial banks, attempt to lower the risk embedded in the loans they make—and the other assets they acquire—by diversifying across sectors of the economy and across different regions of the country. A bank making loans to a number of different companies in the same industry will be exposed to large losses if hard times fall on that industry, and many of those loans end up in default.

Bank regulators, too, pay close attention to diversification of the assets held by the banks they supervise. Indeed, they impose concentration limits on things such as the amount of loans made against real estate in a particular market. The reason for this is that, for example, a plant closing in a community or a natural disaster could cause a lot of mortgages—loans backed by real estate—to go sour, even though there are many separate borrowers. A bank holding a lot of these loans might find itself in peril.

EFFICIENT PORTFOLIOS AND RISK-RETURN TRADE-OFFS

An efficient portfolio is one in which, for a given expected return, risk cannot be lowered any further through diversification. A market portfolio, discussed in the previous section, is regarded as an efficient portfolio. Another way of looking at this is to regard an efficient portfolio as one that has achieved the highest expected return for a given level of risk.

Once achieved, the only way to lower portfolio risk is to accept a lower expected return. Investors, as we have noted elsewhere in this book, dislike risk. Once they have built an efficient portfolio, they must sacrifice yield to be exposed to less risk. Viewed differently, the only way that an investor will be able to achieve a higher yield will be to take on more risk after an efficient portfolio has been constructed.

A way to reduce portfolio risk is to hold a large portion of the portfolio in high-grade bonds or, even better, high-grade short-term instruments. But this will require a sacrifice of yield. Indeed, the lowest risk portfolio would involve holding only default-free instruments. U.S. Treasury securities have historically been thought of as the assets closest to being risk free.[3] A portfolio consisting only of Treasury securities would also have the lowest return. Conversely, higher returns can be achieved by increasing the share of assets held in an efficient portfolio of risky assets. In other words, an investor's overall portfolio can be thought of as consisting of two basic components: risk-free (Treasury) securities and an efficient portfolio of risky assets;

the share of the overall portfolio held in such risky assets can vary between zero and 100 percent.

Related to this is the pricing of a single risky asset when building an efficient portfolio of risky assets. The market will price this asset—that is, require an expected return on this asset—in keeping with the relationship between the return on that asset and the return on the market portfolio. This can be expressed as:

$$R_i^e = R_f + \beta_i(R_m^e - R_f) \qquad (6\text{-}7)$$

In this expression, R_i^e is the return on asset i required by the market—linked to the price of asset i. The term R_f refers to the return on the risk-free asset, such as the yield on Treasury securities, and R_m^e refers to the expected return on the portfolio of risky market assets. The remaining term, β_i, represents the relationship between the (expected) return on asset i and the (expected) return on assets that constitute a broad market portfolio (of risky assets). It equals $\rho_{im}\sigma_i / \sigma_m$ where ρ_{im} is the correlation coefficient between the return on asset i and the return on the market portfolio, σ_i is the standard deviation of the returns on asset i, and σ_m is the standard deviation of market returns. The more correlated the returns on asset i and the market—the larger the ρ_{im}—the more compensation will be required to get investors to hold asset i. This is because this asset is not helping to lower the overall risk of the portfolio.

However, the lower the correlation between asset i and the market, the smaller the compensation required to hold this asset because it is helping investors to achieve the goal of reducing the risk of their portfolios, and they will accept a lower return on this asset to achieve this result. This is the point we made earlier about how an asset that is risky by itself can actually lower portfolio risk if its returns are weakly correlated with other assets making up the portfolio. In addition, β_i depends on the variability of the returns on asset i. The greater the risk of asset i, relative to the risk on a portfolio of market assets, all else being the same, the larger the required compensation for holding this asset. Market participants often use βs to identify potential candidates for their investment portfolios.

The preceding analysis makes clear that asset prices are determined not just by their own risk but also by the way in which they affect portfolio risk. When they lower portfolio risk, investors will be willing to accept a lower return—that is, they will be willing to pay a higher price for the asset.

EFFICIENT MARKETS HYPOTHESIS

The *efficient markets hypothesis* relates to the pricing of financial assets, and has substantially transformed investment decisions over recent decades. The hypothesis maintains that the price of any financial asset reflects all available information bearing on that asset's value. In other words, the asset's price corresponds to its fundamental economic value, based on the information available at the time. An implication is that the returns on that asset cannot be expected to be higher or lower than that of any other asset, allowing for differences in risk.

One way of examining the logic behind this hypothesis is to look at what would happen if this were not true. For example, suppose that the price of Cisco Systems stock dropped 5 percent on the last day of each month and then recovered all of that loss the next day. This recurring pattern would provide an opportunity to make extraordinary returns by buying Cisco on the last day of each month and selling those shares the next day. This strategy would enable an investor to make 5 percent each month—excluding the cost of making these transactions—or a tidy 60 percent return each year on top of dividend and appreciation returns from holding Cisco shares. But others, also observing this pattern, would want to earn extraordinary returns by following the same strategy too. This means that investors would be bidding up the price of Cisco shares on the last day of the month until such time as the price of Cisco shares was typically the same on the last day of the month as the first day of the next month. No extraordinary returns would any longer be available.

Similarly, if information about the value of an asset were not fully priced into the shares, opportunities would be available to make exceptional returns. For example, suppose that the current price of Coca-Cola shares is $60 per share, but information widely available to investors suggests that prospects for Coca-Cola earnings translate into a fundamental value of each share of $80. This implies that an investor will be able to make extraordinary returns by purchasing Coke shares now. As more investors reach this same conclusion, the price of Coca-Cola shares would move upward toward $80 per share, and the potential for earning excess returns would disappear.

Of course, information bearing on the value of an asset is frequently changing and this implies that the price of assets such as stocks will change once new information becomes available. This could take the form of earnings announcements from the firms themselves, projections of earnings made by respected analysts, or news bearing on the economy—which will have implications for the earnings of all corporations.

Ensuring that prices remain in line with economic fundamentals will be the actions of highly skilled investors with substantial resources, such as hedge funds. They will be continually searching for assets that are mispriced and will be acting quickly to get ahead of others in exploiting these situations to earn extraordinary returns. This implies that any mispricing cannot persist for long. Similarly, they will attempt to acquire new information bearing on asset values, process this information, and act on it quickly and ahead of others to be able to eke out extra returns before prices fully reflect this information. Indeed, such investors are going to extremes to install equipment and systems that enable them to get information and submit orders faster than other investors.

All of this implies that the typical investor will find it very difficult to identify investment opportunities that will provide extraordinary returns. Opportunities will vanish quickly before the ordinary investor has time to exploit them. In these circumstances, higher returns can be expected only by taking on more risk.

An exception to this proposition can occur when that investor has inside information that has not been released to the market. This may be positive information that will result in the asset's price rising or negative information that will result in the asset's price falling, once released to the public. The only problem is that trading on inside information is illegal and could result in huge fines and even time in jail. Ask Ivan Boesky, Michael Milken, Martha Stewart, or Raj Rajaratnam of Galleon Group. All were convicted of trading on inside information and got to experience living behind bars.

Implications for a Random Walk

An implication of the efficient markets hypothesis is that asset prices will follow a *random walk*—that is, their next move is equally likely to be up or down. This is because the desire to earn extraordinary returns will remove any underlying patterns in asset prices or unexploited values. Price movements will reflect new information, which, by its very nature, will have random implications for prices.

Other Implications

The efficient markets hypothesis has other important implications. First, it implies that an investor performing careful research on companies for purposes of picking winners and losers will be wasting his or her time if he or she thinks that this will result in excess returns. They can expect to do as well selecting investments by blindfolding themselves and throwing darts at the stock listings in the *Wall Street Journal*.

Second, it suggests that when selecting an investment fund, such as a mutual fund, picking one that attempts to replicate the market will do at least as well as an actively managed one staffed by expensive asset managers. Such managers will be paid handsomely for researching potential investments and for routinely churning the portfolio by selling those expected to underperform and buying those expected to outperform. The efficient markets hypothesis argues that this strategy will not over time do any better than one based on a passive investment in a broad market fund. Indeed, gross returns should be the same for both over time, but the expenses incurred by the actively managed fund in hiring professional managers and frequently turning over the portfolio will lead to lower net returns to investors after expenses.

Third, technical analysis, which seeks to find patterns in asset prices and to trade on these, will not be able to provide returns that exceed the market. For example, it has been alleged that there has been a so-called January effect in share prices, with prices rising in the opening days of the new year. Another alleged pattern is a so-called head-and-shoulders pattern of share prices in which prices rise to a peak (shoulders) and retreat. This is followed by a new run-up to a higher peak (head), to be followed by another retreat. It is then followed by a third climb to a peak below the second (another shoulder). Still another alleged pattern is a price run that follows the mathematical Fibonacci series. A Fibonacci series is one in which the next item in a series is derived by adding the last two numbers. For example, if the series starts with the numbers 1 and 2, the third number will be their sum, or 3; the next number in the series would be 5, the sum of 2 and 3, and so forth. Under the expectations hypothesis, these patterns, if robust, would be identified by investors and then used to earn excess returns. Their actions would, in turn, remove the patterns and result in a random walk in their prices.

Asset Bubbles

Over the latter half of the 1990s, the stock market, especially tech stocks, soared to very high levels—levels that relative to earnings and other fundamentals were well above historical norms. This was followed in the mid-2000s by a surge in house prices that also went considerably beyond historical norms. These episodes are said to have been *asset bubbles* in which values were stretched beyond those that could be supported by economic fundamentals. Each was followed by a bursting of the bubble—that is, a plunge in prices. Many investors and homeowners suffered substantial losses as a result of the bursting of these bubbles. Indeed, the crash in home prices was a major contributor to the financial crisis of 2008 and the Great Recession.

To some, asset price bubbles are a contradiction of efficient market behavior. If prices are to always reflect fundamental economic values, how can such a seemingly sustained, large departure from fundamental values be explained?

To others, though, there can be a *rational bubble*. In these circumstances, market participants realize that prices have come unhinged from fundamentals, but they believe that the dynamics are such that there is likely to be more forward momentum. There may be a particular group of traders who are providing the upward momentum by aggressively buying shares in the belief that they can earn quick excess returns. Others seeing prices departing from fundamentals may believe that this departure will continue grow for a while. A widening departure of asset prices from fundamentals will provide them with the opportunity to earn excess returns by buying the asset. Heavy purchases by such speculators will add to the upward pressure of the price of this asset, which will be something of a self-fulfilling prophecy. The important thing from their perspective is to be able to know when the peak in prices is being reached and to be able to sell before the price bubble unwinds—that is, before others also rush to the exits.

Another explanation of how prices can depart from fundamentals has to do with there being groups of investors with very different assessments of the outlook for an asset—among them, super-optimists and pessimists. The optimists see prospects for cash flows from this investment to be very favorable while the pessimists see prospects to be fairly dismal. The super-optimists may dominate price movements at first, pushing prices higher, and more cautious investors—believing that prices have risen above fundamental values—may be reluctant to step in to counter this movement. Moreover, the optimists may see the run-up in prices as validating or even giving them reason to strengthen their outlook, emboldening them to be even more aggressive buyers. At some later date, the sentiment of the pessimists may begin to take over, driving prices back down. The truth regarding fundamental values may stand somewhere between these groups, implying that the movement of prices above fundamentals on the upswing may be followed by prices falling below fundamentals on the downswing.

Evidence

Evidence has been broadly consistent with financial markets behaving in a way consistent with the efficient markets hypothesis.[4] This is particularly the case if one considers the uncertainty about the values of assets and their fundamentals and the costs of conducting transactions when there seems to be mispricing. If there is a lot of uncertainty about the fundamental value of an asset, then, when its price rises above its fundamental value, there may be doubt about whether the asset is actually mispriced. Seeking to profit from a drop in its price by selling now—especially selling short, which requires that the security be borrowed for the sale—may not prove to be a surefire way to earn extraordinary returns. Moreover, when there are significant costs of conducting transactions that seek to take advantage of possible mispricing, this further reduces the incentive to step in when a price bubble has developed. In short, it has often proven hard to actually earn excess returns by trying to take advantage of perceived patterns in asset prices or other forms of mispricing.

Occasional bubble situations appear to be contradictions of the more restrictive version of the efficient markets hypothesis, although they can conform to a less restrictive rational bubble. Advocates of the efficient markets hypothesis argue that the hypothesis explains the vast bulk of asset pricing behavior and should not be disregarded solely because of some pricing aberrations.

SUMMARY

1. The return on most assets cannot be known with certainty and thus investors face risk regarding the return they will receive on such investments. The investor can be thought of as trying to select assets that have high (expected) yields, but low risk. The expected yield on an individual investment can be calculated once their probabilities of occurrence and the various possible outcomes for returns have been determined. This information can then be used to calculate the asset's risk—the standard deviation of its potential returns.
2. Investors choose portfolios of different assets to reduce the risk of their overall investment. An asset may increase or decrease the risk of a portfolio depending on both the variability of its returns and the correlation between its returns and those on other assets in the portfolio.
3. The weaker the correlation of the asset's returns with those of other assets in the portfolio, the greater the likelihood that this asset will lower the risk of the overall portfolio. Indeed, it is possible to add an asset that has a high degree of risk, when viewed by itself, but it lowers the risk of the portfolio because its returns have little correlation or perhaps even negative correlation with other assets in the portfolio.
4. Selecting a broad portfolio of assets—representing the market—is usually a strategy that will lower risk without sacrificing yield. At issue is how broad the market should be—only domestic stocks, also foreign stocks, bonds, or even other assets.
5. The market will price an asset—determine its yield—based on, among other things, its beta (β). Its beta relates its risk relative to the risk of assets comprising the market and the correlation between its yield and those of other assets constituting the market. The asset's beta will increase with the asset's risk and with the correlation between its returns and the returns on market assets. High betas reduce the appeal of the asset for a portfolio.
6. These principles imply that the more risk of an asset—measured in the context of its contribution to a portfolio's risk—will require that investors receive a higher return. That is, risk and return are related in a positive manner.
7. The efficient markets hypothesis maintains that the price of an asset embodies all information available at that moment that bears on it value. It implies that an investor cannot expect to earn returns that exceed the returns on the market, unless that investor is willing to take on more risk.
8. Trying to achieve extraordinary returns by carefully picking winners and losers, trading off of perceived patterns in asset prices, or investing in actively managed

Principles of Portfolio Selection and Efficient Markets

funds managed by high-priced specialists cannot provide better-than-market returns, according to the efficient markets hypothesis.
9. Asset bubbles can be inconsistent with the efficient markets hypothesis. However, it can be argued that a rational bubble could develop under certain circumstances, which would not contradict efficient markets.

QUESTIONS

1. If an investor were only concerned about maximizing expected return, would that person select a portfolio of assets or a single asset? If the latter, which asset would that be?
2. Why do investors hold portfolios of securities instead of a single security? Would a portfolio manager ever consider acquiring a security that, by itself, is very risky? Why or why not? What would have to be true of that security?
3. Calculate the expected return and risk (standard deviation of returns) on a portfolio consisting of two assets. Asset 1 has an expected return of 0.09 and a standard deviation of returns of 0.08. For asset 2, they are 0.13 and 0.14, respectively. The correlation coefficient of the returns on asset 1 and asset 2 is 0.5. The portfolio share of each asset is 50 percent.
4. Should asset 3 be selected for the portfolio discussed in question 3? Its expected return is 0.12 and its measure of risk is 0.20. The correlation between its returns and those of asset 1 is 0, and between its returns and those of asset 2 is −0.20. Portfolio shares are 35 percent for asset 1 and asset 2 and 30 percent for asset 3.
5. What is a security's beta? Does a high beta make a security attractive or unattractive for a portfolio? A low (or negative) beta? Why or why not?
6. What is an efficient financial market? A random walk? Does the evidence, on balance, favor market efficiency? Random walks?
7. Why do many investors seek to acquire an investment portfolio representative of the broad market, such as the S&P 500 index of stocks?
8. How do securities in foreign markets—stocks and bonds—figure into investment choice? What must be taken into account when considering such foreign assets for a portfolio?
9. How did Galleon Investment Group consistently achieve above-market returns?
10. Can you expect to earn extraordinary returns by picking "hot" stocks?
11. Your friend gives you a hot tip on a stock from a broker. What is the expected return on this stock? Will it exceed or fall short of market returns?
12. Why would you think that technical analysis could not predict security prices over time?
13. What is meant by an asset bubble? Is the presence of a bubble consistent with the efficient markets hypothesis?
14. There was a time when large mutual fund complexes touted the ability of their funds to post returns that beat the market. These days, they place more emphasis on the convenience of investing in their funds and their low costs. Some also will suggest that their funds can be counted on for achieving market returns. Why the change? Check out the web sites of Fidelity, Vanguard, or T Rowe Price to see how their equity funds are being promoted.

15. Mutual funds have a wide variety of investment strategies. And in a particular quarter or over a particular year, some will have substantially higher returns than others. Would you expect these same funds to outperform others on a consistent basis? Why or why not?

NOTES

1. The terms *risk* and *uncertainty* are often used interchangeably. However, in economic and statistical analysis, they have a somewhat different meaning. Risk is used to mean the range of possible outcomes when their respective probabilities are known with some certainty. Uncertainty, in this context, refers to a situation in which the probabilities associated with a range of outcomes are not known with much certainty.
2. Under standard statistical distributions, roughly two-thirds of all the returns are within one standard deviation of the expected return. The larger the standard deviation, the more spread out the returns—the greater the risk.
3. In recent years, concerns have grown about whether Treasury securities are truly default free. Outsized deficits and the accompanying mounting debt have raised doubts about whether the federal government will be able to service its debt down the road.
4. See Burton Malkiel, "The Efficient Market Hypothesis and Its Critics," *Journal of Economic Perspectives* 17, no. 1 (Winter 2003); 59–82.

CHAPTER 7

The Money Market

WHAT YOU WILL LEARN IN THIS CHAPTER

- Investors in the money market dislike risk—both price (interest rate) and credit risk.
- The money market is largely a wholesale market.
- Instruments are sold at a discount, and a straightforward formula can be used to compute annual yield.
- The Treasury auctions bills to meet shorter-term cash needs.
- Commercial paper is issued by large, well-known corporations and financial institutions to meet short-term financing needs.
- Asset-backed commercial paper (ABCP) had been used by large commercial banks to reduce the amount of costly regulatory capital they need to maintain, but regulators have tightened up on this subterfuge.
- The money market is of critical importance for commercial banks that daily must deal with mismatches between inflows of funds through core deposits and outflows through loans.
- Some banks use money market assets primarily to meet these imbalances while others use money market liabilities.
- Letters of credit (L/Cs) play a vital role in international trade, and commercial banks are at the heart of this market.
- L/Cs can become money market instruments in the form of bankers' acceptances.
- Monetary policy, working through the policy interest rate, affects other short-term interest rates.

BACKGROUND AND BASIC FEATURES OF THE MONEY MARKET

Why do investors want to hold money market instruments when they can typically get a higher return on longer-term investments? Why do issuers of money market instruments bother with issuing short-term (money market) instruments when they can access longer-term funds in the capital market? How do investors get a return on money market instruments when these instruments do not pay explicit interest? Why are commercial banks such big players in the money market? How can importers and exporters reach an agreement on a transaction when they don't know each other and they reside far from each other and are governed by different legal systems? Does monetary policy have any effect on this market? These are questions that will be addressed in this chapter.

As noted in Chapter 2, money market instruments have maturities that do not exceed one year. Moreover, maturities in the money market can be as short as overnight. In practice, much of the issuance of money market instruments is in maturities of three months or less.

The money market can be characterized as a wholesale market, inasmuch as denominations of money market instruments are very large—usually minimums of $1 million or more. Investors in the money market have a strong aversion to risk when it comes to their short-term assets. Investors typically hold funds in money market assets to meet a specific upcoming expenditure or to serve as a reserve for a contingency that can be quickly tapped. In these circumstances, experiencing a loss on these funds—be it from default or a rise in interest rates—would impose unwanted strains. As a consequence, the investor will be willing to sacrifice yield, if necessary, in order to avoid being exposed to loss.

Thus, only highly rated issuers are able to tap this market for funds. Of course, as we noted in Chapter 4, short-term instruments do not have much price or interest rate risk: a given change in interest rates has a trivial impact on the price of short-term instruments when compared to longer-term instruments.

The money market also is regarded as a liquid market. But its liquidity derives importantly from being short term, and thus the investor does not have to wait long before the money market instrument matures and cash is received. The secondary market for money market instruments is typically not as active or as deep as the market for some longer-term instruments, such as Treasury notes.[1] For Treasury money market instruments—Treasury bills—there is a secondary market where one can easily buy or sell bills, but for many other money market instruments there is not much of a secondary market. The investor who wants to sell before maturity may have to put the instrument back to the dealer who sold the instrument in the first place.

PRICING

Money market instruments do not pay the investor a coupon (interest) payment. Instead, they are sold at a discount and the investor receives a return in the form of price appreciation. This is illustrated in the following equation:

$$i = \frac{F-P}{P} \times \frac{365}{n} \qquad (7\text{-}1)$$

In this expression, i represents the annualized yield on the money market instrument, F the value of the instrument at maturity (face value), P the price paid for the instrument, and n the number of days to maturity. This expression can be broken down into two components. The first, $\frac{F-P}{P}$, represents the appreciation of the instrument (over a period that is less than a year). The second, $365/n$, represents an annualization factor. It converts the yield to an annual basis. This makes it comparable to other yields, which, as a standard matter, are expressed on an annual basis.

Let us look at an example. Suppose that we are dealing with a three-month (91-day) Treasury bill having a value of $1 million at maturity. Suppose the bill sells for $990,000. Translating these features into Equation (7-1) results in the following expression:

$$i = \frac{\$1,000,000 - \$990,000}{\$990,000} \times \frac{365}{91} = \frac{10,000}{990,000} \times \frac{365}{91} = 0.0101 \times 4.011 = 0.0405$$

or 4.05 percent. The appreciation component is 1.01 percent and the annualization component is 4.011. The preceding formula gives annual yield on a so-called *investment yield basis*. The annual yield is comparable to that of yields on longer-term instruments calculated in the manner described in Chapter 4.

There is another way to calculate money market yields. This is on a so-called *discount basis*. The formula for this calculation is the following:

$$i = \frac{F-P}{F} \times \frac{360}{n} \qquad (7\text{-}2)$$

In this expression, each term has the same meaning as in Equation (7-1). The only differences are that F instead of P appears in the denominator of the first component and the second component has 360 in its numerator instead of 365. The discount-basis calculation was developed as an approximation for the investment-yield basis at a time when calculators and computers were not available. This works especially conveniently if you round n to a multiple of 30.

Let us illustrate the calculation of discount-basis yield using our previous example.

$$i = \frac{\$1,000,000 - \$990,000}{\$1,000,000} \times \frac{360}{90} = \frac{10,000}{1,000,000} \times \frac{360}{90} = 0.01 \times 4 = 0.04$$

or 4.0 percent. Note that instead of using 91 days in the calculation, 90 days were used—a multiple of 30 days. This is a calculation that you can quickly perform in your head and does not require any long division or a calculator.

Note that the yield calculated on a discount basis, 4.0 percent, is lower than the yield calculated on an investment-yield basis, 4.05 percent. This will always be the case. Both the appreciation component and the annualization component are smaller on a discount basis. This is because $\frac{F-P}{F}$ is always smaller than $\frac{F-P}{P}$ owing to P always being larger than F. Also, the numerator in the annualization component is 365 on an investment-yield basis and only 360 on a discount basis. Obviously, when each number is smaller on a discount basis, their product will also be smaller. It should be recalled that the discount-basis calculation is only an approximation. In this day of high-speed machines, the discount-yield measure has become antiquated. Nonetheless, it is routinely provided on sources of financial information, such as Bloomberg.

Let us now look at each of the major components of the money market, starting with Treasury bills.

TREASURY BILLS

Auction Procedures

The Treasury issues bills in the following four maturities: 4 weeks (28 days), 13 weeks (91 days), 26 weeks (182 days), and 52 weeks (365 days). The Treasury sells each of these at regularly scheduled auctions, a form of direct finance. Auctions are announced a few days in advance, along with the amount that will be sold. An investor can submit a so-called competitive or noncompetitive bid. A noncompetitive bidder agrees to accept the rate determined by competitive bidders, and is limited to a maximum order of $1 million ($5 million in note and bond auctions). Both types of bidders must specify the amount that they will buy and the competitive bidders also specify the discount rate—the appreciation component of Equation (7-1) or 0.01 in the numerical example—corresponding to that amount. The discount rate received by all bidders will be determined by the highest successful discount rate submitted by competitive bidders. In effect, the Treasury relies on an algorithm that ranks discount rates on competitive bids from lowest to highest. It then subtracts the total amount of noncompetitive bids from the total amount it is selling. From there, it goes from the lowest discount rate bid to the next lowest and so on, until the point at which the total amount of bills is awarded. All get the *cutoff rate*—the highest accepted discount rate. It then announces the results of the auction—including the cut-off rate and minimum and maximum bid.

The Treasury has modified its auction procedures over the years. These procedures are widely believed to be transparent and fair. They are thought to attract a high level of investor interest and to result in the Treasury (taxpayers) being able to borrow at the lowest interest rate. This type of auction system works well for the Treasury because it is such a large and frequent borrower and it has a stellar reputation of repaying its creditors. Other issuers of money market instruments, as we will see, find it advantageous to use other means of issuing their debt.

The Role of Primary Dealers

Playing a key role in the market for Treasury bills—and notes and bonds—are so-called *primary dealers*. The designation of primary dealer status is done by the Federal Reserve. These are the dealers in Treasury securities that the Federal Reserve will use as its counterparties in its open market operations in Treasury securities in the secondary market, the principal means of implementing monetary policy. Large securities firms aspire to this status because such a designation is thought to connote a certain degree of financial soundness and integrity. To qualify as a primary dealer, a financial institution, in addition to meeting certain prudential criteria regarding its financial condition, must be a regular bidder in Treasury auctions and be active in making secondary markets in Treasury bills and coupons (notes and bonds). As we have seen, a good secondary market enhances the appeal of the primary market and tends to lower the interest rate that must be paid. There are about 20 major global commercial and investment banks that serve as primary dealers, more than half of which are owned by banks with head offices outside the United States.

Purpose for Issuing Bills

The Treasury uses its bill auctions largely to deal with seasonal swings in its cash flow. Treasury receipts tend to be very lumpy in comparison with outlays—bunching up on specific tax dates, such as the 15th of April, June, September, and January. Prior to these dates, cash inflows from other sources are not sufficient to cover expenses and the Treasury will issue bills to bridge the gap. The bulge in receipts on tax dates can then be used to pay down maturing bills. As a consequence, the amount of bills that the Treasury auctions varies a good bit over the course of the year—being extremely large in low spots and small in times when its cash position is flush.[2]

COMMERCIAL PAPER

Large corporations and financial institutions raise funds on a short-term basis in the commercial paper (CP) market. Corporations tap the commercial paper market to meet short-term financing needs, such as to cover a build-up of inventories or accounts receivable.

Credit Quality

Because investors in CP shun risk, issuers of CP either have strong credit ratings or the CP offerings are collateralized and structured in such a way that they can achieve a high rating. The former type of CP typically is not collateralized (unsecured) while certain types of assets back the latter. In addition, investors usually insist that the CP offering has a back-up line of credit from a well-regarded commercial bank. In this way, if the issuer is unable to find enough cash at maturity to repay the investors, it can draw on the back-up line.

Credit ratings agencies assign ratings to commercial paper based on their assessment of credit risk, following many of the same criteria that they use for corporate bonds. The classifications, however, differ from the scale used for bonds. Table 7.1 illustrates ratings categories assigned by the three major agencies that rate CP.

Because investors have a strong preference for low-risk CP, the bulk of CP issuance is in the top category—A1, P1, and F1. Indeed, the largest holder of CP—money market mutual funds—is restricted by the Securities and Exchange Commission (SEC) largely to that top tier.

TABLE 7.1 Rating Categories Assigned by the S&P, Moody's, and Fitch

S&P	Moody's	Fitch	Description	Counterpart Bond Rating
A1	P1	F1	Superior	AA (Aa) or above
A2	P2	F2	Satisfactory	A/BBB (Aa/Baa) or above
A3	P3	F3	Adequate	Lower-tier BBB (Baa)

Maturities

The SEC allows commercial paper to have maturities up to 270 days, but the bulk of issuance has original maturities of a month or less. Indeed, a substantial portion has maturities of a week or less. The receptivity of investors to longer maturities varies with economic and financial conditions. During times of considerable uncertainty and concern about the economy and the financial system, investors are reluctant to hold anything beyond very short maturities. In more tranquil times, they are willing to go farther out on the maturity spectrum.

Asset-Backed Commercial Paper (ABCP)

A number of years ago, asset-backed commercial paper (ABCP) developed into a large component of the CP market. Originators of loans, such as commercial banks, wishing to avoid holding regulatory capital against such loans have developed schemes that involve funding these loans through issuance of commercial paper. When commercial banks originate loans and keep them on their balance sheet, they must hold capital for regulatory purposes in proportion to these loans. Thus, moving such loans off their balance sheet can reduce the amount of costly capital for regulatory purposes. This is done by the bank establishing a legal entity—a so-called *special-purpose vehicle (SPV)*—that acquires ordinary loans from the balance sheet of the bank. These loans frequently are credit card receivables, student loans, or motor vehicle loans. The SPV then raises funds by issuing CP that is backed by these loan receivables. The bank (or other lending institution) becomes the sponsor of the SPV. The SPV structures its CP offerings in such a way that they receive a top CP rating from the rating agencies. This is achieved typically by overcollateralizing the SPV—putting in more loan receivables than the amount of paper issued against them.[3] In this way, the bank has shifted assets from its balance sheet to the SPV and thereby lowers assets on its books subject to capital requirements.

Retreat of the ABCP Market

The ABCP market had become overextended prior to the onset of the financial crisis in 2007. In particular, sponsors were placing longer maturity collateral in SPVs, much of it mortgage related, and investors willingly acquired the commercial paper used to finance these assets because it had a little higher yield than other short-term investments. In other words, maturity transformation through SPVs was compounded. At the time, these investors appeared to be complacent about the associated risk of this paper. However, when the crisis began to unfold, investors became nervous and pulled out of these investments. This posed strains on SPVs because the assets backing the paper were not maturing until well beyond the maturing of the commercial paper financing them. Moreover, the market for this collateral had dried up and it could not be sold easily to get the cash to pay commercial paper investors—at least for an acceptable price that would fetch sufficient cash to pay back the ABCP investors.

In these circumstances, the sponsors faced a dilemma—default on the paper or try to save their reputation as a fiduciary by injecting cash into the SPV to enable investors to be paid fully and on time. Many chose the latter, even though they were not legally obligated to do so. In other words, the sponsoring bank (or other financial institution, such as an investment bank) chose to suffer a loss related to its sponsorship of the SPV in order to preserve its reputation as a fiduciary. As a result, financial regulators have taken the approach that these off-balance-sheet vehicles actually do pose comparable risk to the lending institution as holding the loans on their balance sheet, and the regulators have become more aggressive in the application of capital requirements to off-balance-sheet positions. This has discouraged banks from using SPVs as a device to move loans off their balance sheet; indeed, ABCP outstanding has declined from a peak of nearly $1.2 trillion to less than one-fourth that amount. The role of funding vehicles—such as SPVs—in the financial crisis is discussed in more detail in Chapter 15.

Commercial Paper Placement

Commercial paper is placed with investors either by the issuer directly or through an investment bank. In the latter case, the investment bank typically buys the paper from the issuer and then places it with its network of investors.[4] Many large financial institutions that issue commercial paper do so in such volume that they find it worthwhile to develop their own system of direct placement. Many of these serve as investment banks for customers wanting to issue commercial paper or bonds, and have developed the infrastructure for placing assets directly, be they for their customers or for their own account. In practice, about half of CP is placed directly and the rest is placed by (other) dealers.

THE ROLE OF COMMERCIAL BANKS IN THE MONEY MARKET

We noted in Chapter 3 that commercial banks play a vital role in providing liquidity to the economy. To do so, they rely heavily on the money market. To illustrate, we will use a balance sheet or T-accounts similar to that developed in Chapter 3.

Assets	Liabilities and Net Worth
	Core deposits
Cash and securities	Wholesale deposits
Loans	Other managed liabilities
	Federal funds and repurchase agreements
	Eurodollars
	Net worth

    We have lumped together business, consumer, and real estate loans in the loan category on the asset (left) side of the balance sheet and transaction and other retail deposits together in the core deposit category on the liability (right) side of the balance sheet.
    There are a couple of categories—one on the asset side and the other on the liability side—that commercial banks have very little day-to-day control over. On the asset side, that category is loans. Many loans are taken down at the discretion of the borrower under a line of credit, similar to a credit line provided to credit card holders (and discussed in Chapter 3). Many businesses have such revolving credit lines—lines that permit the borrower to draw on the line or repay some or all of the

loan under the line at the borrower's discretion. Banks find it hard to predict how much will be demanded by these loan customers from one day to the next. On the liability side, core deposits fluctuate a great deal on a day-to-day basis in ways that similarly cannot be fully predicted. A business checking account customer may make a very large payment from its account, leading to a large unexpected outflow, or a lot more retail customers may respond to the bank's attractive rates posted on retail CDs than expected and open new accounts, leading a large unexpected inflow.

On any given day, the amount coming into core deposits may roughly match the amount going out through loans. However, this is going to be rare. On other days, there will be a mismatch between funds coming in and funds going out. Some days, more will come in than goes out, and on other days the reverse will occur. This is where money market instruments come in.

Commercial banks hold money market instruments—Treasury bills and other Treasury securities with short remaining maturities—and they place short-term federal funds with other commercial banks. These appear on the asset side of their balance sheets as cash and securities. They also can tap the wholesale deposit market—large CDs—for additional funds or they can tap other managed liabilities, federal funds, repurchase agreements (RPs), and eurodollars. These appear on the liability side of the balance sheet.

Smaller banks tend to rely on cash and securities to absorb variations in cash flow caused by core deposits not matching loans. In particular, overnight placements of federal funds with other commercial banks are a very flexible money market asset for these banks. These placements can be increased easily if core deposit inflows exceed loans, or they can be reduced if the opposite occurs. Buying or selling Treasury securities serve as a way of dealing with mismatches that are thought to last for longer periods of time than a day or two.

Larger banks rely more on managed liabilities. Wholesale time deposits—often called large certificates of deposit (CDs)—can be sold readily, either directly by large commercial banks that have direct placement capability or through a dealer. Typically, these CDs are negotiable, meaning that they can be sold easily to another investor. This enhances their appeal to investors and lowers borrowing cost to the bank.

Federal funds are unsecured funds received from another commercial bank.[5] Federal funds can have maturities of 30 days or more, but the bulk of federal funds are overnight. The bank receiving federal funds can attract more to cover a shortfall of core deposits from new loans by upping the interest rate that it pays, or it can reduce its federal funds borrowing by lowering the rate it pays in the event core deposit inflows exceed new loans. Commercial banks that lend federal funds to other commercial banks typically limit their risk exposure to those other banks by establishing a ceiling for the amount that they will place with them—a so-called *line* for that bank. Federal funds can be obtained directly from other commercial banks, usually respondent banks that have an ongoing relationship with the correspondent bank that borrows the funds; this correspondent relationship covers a variety of services that the correspondent bank provides to its respondent, such as check clearing.[6] In addition, federal funds placements can be arranged through a *federal funds broker*, which has contacts with a lot of commercial banks and matches borrowers with lenders.

RPs are a collateralized borrowing in which the collateral is a U.S. Treasury or federal agency security. Like federal funds, the maturity of RP borrowings is primarily overnight. Commercial banks raise RP funds from a variety of customers, including large corporations. To be able to raise funds using RPs, the bank must already have the collateral, meaning that it cannot get new funds if it must first acquire the collateral because the funds raised will be needed for the collateral. Overall, the RP market is huge, with government securities dealers playing a big role. They rely on RPs to finance inventories of securities that they use to make markets in Treasury and federal agency securities, and for them, RPs are not a managed liability in the same way as for ordinary commercial banks.

The last of the commercial bank-managed liabilities used by large banks to address mismatches between funds coming in and going out is eurodollar borrowings. Large commercial banks have a branch office in London, the center of the eurodollar market. Large banks from other parts of the world also have branches in London. Large global banks—U.S. and other banks—conduct a lot of business in U.S. dollars, both making loans and gathering deposits. The interbank market in London provides an opportunity for these banks to raise or place funds to address fluctuations in their cash flow in dollars. The interest rate on interbank transactions in London is called LIBOR—standing for the London Interbank Offered Rate. LIBOR has been used as a benchmark interest rate for pricing other loans in dollars, in the United States and elsewhere.[7] The interbank market in London was rocked by the financial crisis, as banks became very reluctant to be exposed to other banks because they feared that their counterparty banks might be holding vulnerable assets that could cause liquidity problems or even insolvency—leading to default. The market has also experienced hiccups associated with shifting concerns about European banks holding sovereign debt of European countries that may be in danger of defaulting.

LETTERS OF CREDIT AND BANKERS' ACCEPTANCES

Letters of credit play a vital role in international trade. They address the asymmetric information problem, which is even bigger when the parties live in different countries and have different customs and legal systems. To illustrate, suppose that you have a small business that specializes in decorative tiles for kitchens and baths. You try to distinguish your boutique from standard tile stores by selling extraordinary types of tile. You (an importer) learn that a tile maker in Croatia has a unique line of tiles and is trying to break into the global marketplace by offering very attractive prices. You visit the manufacturer located in a village outside Zagreb and become enthusiastic about adding this manufacturer's line to your offerings. You negotiate an order but reach a stumbling block when the seller (manufacturer) wants payment up front in the form of a wire transfer to his local bank because he fears that he may ship the tiles and never get paid. He does not know whether you are good for keeping your end of the bargain. From your perspective, you are concerned that if you pay before the tiles are shipped, the seller (exporter) may be unwilling to keep his end of the bargain. There is an impasse because of a major asymmetric information problem. An otherwise economically worthwhile transaction would not be completed.

The letter of credit (L/C) solves this problem. You have an ongoing business relationship with your local bank. Among the dimensions of this relationship is credit, which your bank advances to you fairly regularly. Under your banking relationship, you can ask your bank to issue a letter of credit on your behalf for this purchase.

Moreover, your bank may have a business relationship with the seller's local bank. Your bank, the so-called issuing bank, could then provide a promise to pay the seller's bank, the so-called confirming bank, if the terms of the agreement are met. In other words, if the seller ships the tiles as agreed in the contract, the seller's account at the seller's bank will be credited the amount of the transaction, often at a specified later date.[8] In effect, the deal gets completed because your bank is willing to substitute its promise to pay for yours. The seller is comfortable that he will get paid if the goods are shipped because his bank has provided assurances that payment will be made on that date. The seller's bank is comfortable making that assurance because your bank is guaranteeing payment. You are comfortable because you will not need to pay unless there is documentation that your tiles have been shipped. Your bank is trusting that you will have the funds to cover this transaction, but that is the nature of your ongoing business relationship with your bank.

A banker's acceptance could also be involved in this transaction. The terms of your agreement may call for the seller to get paid at or sometime after shipment. The seller could wait until that date to get paid. Or the seller could ask his bank for cash in advance of that date—in effect, discounting this promise by your bank. If his bank does not wish to hold this promise to the payment (maturity) date, it can stamp it "accepted" and sell it in the market. It then becomes a banker's acceptance, a money market instrument. The seller's bank is promising to pay the face value of your transaction at maturity, which has been guaranteed by your bank. The market for bankers' acceptances does not come close to the size of the other money markets that we have discussed in this chapter, and has not kept pace with the brisk growth of the market for L/Cs.

MONETARY POLICY EFFECTS ON THE MONEY MARKET

As we noted in Chapter 4, the central bank exercises a considerable amount of control over the policy interest rate—a very short-term interest rate (in practice, the federal funds rate on overnight interbank loans). As a consequence, money market interest rates (the prices of money market assets) are promptly and substantially affected by changes in the policy rate. This works through the term structure relationship and a change in the overnight interest rate will typically have a comparable effect on the expected overnight rate, translating the change in the policy rate fully to other money market interest rates. Indeed, even the expectation that the central bank will soon be changing its policy rate will have a pronounced impact on money market interest rates. Spending decisions by business and households that are sensitive to short-term interest rates will also thereby be affected.

SUMMARY

1. Money market instruments have maturities that do not exceed one year. They do not pay interest explicitly, but instead are sold to investors at a discount. Investors in money market instruments typically are very risk averse, not wanting to be exposed to much interest rate or credit risk. This means that only high-grade instruments are sold in this market.

2. The annualized yield on such an instrument can be expressed as the product of an appreciation component and an annualization component—its investment yield. An approximation to that yield—measured on a discount basis—can be derived from the same components as those used for calculating investment basis yield.
3. The Treasury is the largest issuer of money market instruments—Treasury bills. The Treasury sells bills using an auction system. It uses the bill market to bridge fluctuations in its seasonal cash flow.
4. Issuers of commercial paper (CP) are large, highly rated corporations and financial institutions. Corporations use CP to finance inventory and other short-term needs. Some CP is placed directly by the issuer and the rest by underwriters (dealers). CP can be unsecured or secured (collateralized). Asset-backed commercial paper (ABCP) was developed by large commercial banks as a means of avoiding regulatory capital requirements on loans they make; they use a special-purpose vehicle (SPV) to acquire the loans from the bank and pay for them with the proceeds of selling CP. The CP is backed by the loans from the bank.
5. Commercial banks rely on money market instruments to deal with daily mismatches between funds coming in and funds going out. On the asset side of their balance sheet, they have federal funds and short-term Treasury securities for this purpose. On the liabilities side, they have large CDs, federal funds and RPs, and eurodollars to raise or pay down funds arising from such mismatches.
6. Letters of credit are used extensively around the world to address asymmetric information problems arising in international trade. In these circumstances, the buyer's (importer's) bank substitutes its promise to pay for that of the buyer. The seller (exporter) will be much more willing to negotiate a transaction when payment is guaranteed by the buyer's bank. Letters of credit can be transformed into bankers acceptances—a money market instrument.
7. Changes—or even expected changes—in the central bank's policy interest rate will have a sizable impact on money market interest rates. Those types of spending that are sensitive to short-term interest rates will thereby be affected.

QUESTIONS

1. Are investors in the money market best characterized as having a strong appetite for risk or being highly risk averse? What evidence would you use to support your answer?
2. The auction price of 91-day commercial paper having a face (par) value of $1 million is $996,000. What is the quarterly yield on this bill (you can assume that there are 91 days in a quarter)? The annual yield? What is the yield on a discount basis?
3. How does the Treasury use the money market to meet its financing needs? That is, does it issue Treasury bills to meet longer-term financing needs or seasonal variations in its cash flow?
4. For commercial banks, what is meant by a managed liability? What role do liquid assets play on the balance sheet of commercial banks? What role do money market instruments play in the asset and liability management of large global banks? In other words, how do banks manage unexpected changes in loans or

core deposits? What roles do large CDs and eurodollars play? Liquid assets? What has happened to the eurodollar market during the recent financial turmoil?
5. What is meant by asset-backed commercial paper? SPVs? How have large commercial and investment banks used ABCP to reduce the amount of capital they need?
6. Which commercial paper credit rating is highest: A1 (P1), A2 (P2), or A3 (P3)? Lowest? How do these relate to corporate bond ratings?
7. Which type of institutional investor is the biggest investor in money market instruments?
8. Is a letter of credit (L/C) a money market or a capital market instrument? How do L/Cs deal with asymmetric information? What types of transactions are involved? What is the role of commercial banks in the market for letters of credit?
9. What is a banker's acceptance? Does it have any connection with L/Cs?
10. What is meant by the interbank eurodollar market? What role does it play in the global banking system? What is meant by the term *LIBOR*?
11. From Bloomberg, what is the current three-month Treasury bill rate? The one-year rate? What is three-month LIBOR?
12. From the Board's website, what is the level of the effective federal funds rate? The overnight RP rate? The one-month nonfinancial CP rate? The three-month CD rate? Can you explain why they differ?
13. Describe the steps by which a change in the central bank's policy interest rate affect the array of short-term interest rates.

NOTES

1. Treasury notes have maturities of 2 to 10 years and are the most actively traded securities in the world. The commonly used measure of liquidity is the bid-asked spread quoted by dealers. These spreads are typically smaller for notes than for Treasury bills—having maturities up to one year. Deep markets are those that can absorb large volumes of buy or sell orders without much impact on the asset's price.
2. The Treasury will also auction so-called cash management bills on short notice if it finds itself about to run out of cash before a major tax date. These typically have very odd maturities, timed to coincide with big tax inflows when the funds are plentiful for paying down these bills.
3. The bank or other lending institution takes a residual position in the SPV, meaning that it gets what is left over. If the loans in the pool perform well, then the lender (sponsor of the pool) will get back all of the excess collateral placed in the pool plus interest on its holdings in the pool.
4. The investment bank (dealer) makes a return by expecting to purchase the paper from the issuer at a lower price than it expects to receive when it sells the paper to its network of investors.
5. Federal funds are a source of funds to make loans for an individual bank, but not for the banking system. That is, they do not allow the commercial banking system to expand its lending because funds received by one bank, enabling it to lend more to its customers, come from another commercial bank, requiring it to lend less.

6. Many services can be characterized as having significant economies of scale, which are exploited by the correspondent. This enables the respondent to acquire the service at a lower cost than it would incur if it tried to produce it by itself.
7. The use of LIBOR has been tainted by revelations that bankers in London—who provided daily survey data on LIBOR interest rates that they were supposedly paying to other commercial banks to the British Bankers' Association, the compiler of LIBOR rates—had intentionally submitted false rates that they were paying other banks (rates that were more beneficial to their financial position than the actual rates they were paying). This has led to highly publicized prosecutions and fines for offenders.
8. Sometimes, still another bank may be involved in the transaction if the buyer's and seller's banks do not have a standard business relationship. This may be a bank that both the buyer's bank and the seller's bank have a correspondent relationship with. Also, in many instances, the seller wants to be paid in a currency—say, euros—different from the currency used by the buyer—say, dollars. In this case, the buyer may also be asking his or her bank for foreign exchange services—that is, to make payment in euros using the dollars deposited in its account.

CHAPTER 8

The Bond Market

WHAT YOU WILL LEARN IN THIS CHAPTER

- The importance of the bond market as a source of financing for businesses and governments at all levels.
- The reason why bonds are commonly called *coupon securities*.
- The importance of bond indentures and covenants.
- The distinction between Treasury notes and bonds.
- The Treasury's issuance of nominal yield and TIPS securities.
- The construction of Treasury STRIPS.
- What constitutes Treasury when-issued trading and a reopening of a security.
- The difference between Treasury on-the-run and off-the-run securities.
- The difference between the methods used to place securities in the primary market and to trade them in the secondary market.
- How government—or sovereign—debt markets play an important role in the functioning of other financial markets.
- Why only a small fraction of corporations have access to the bond market.
- How corporate bonds are placed in the primary market and traded in the secondary market.
- Why there is a conflict between corporate managers and bondholders.
- The various provisions that are commonly included in corporate indentures.
- Features of the below-investment-grade corporate bond market.
- The role played by private placements.
- The pricing of state and local government bond (munis).
- The difference between a general obligation and a revenue muni.
- Government-sponsored enterprises and the moral hazard problem they pose.
- Ways in which investors in bonds can be protected by insurance.
- How monetary policy works through the bond market.

BACKGROUND

Have you noticed that many analysts give more attention to the bond market than the stock market? Why, when we tend to gauge financial market developments by what is happening to the Dow? Why are the Treasury and other sovereign issuers able to borrow at a lower cost than corporations and state and local governments? Could this privileged position of national governments be jeopardized by chronic budget difficulties and a determined reluctance by political authorities to confront them? How does the outlook for inflation affect the pricing of bonds? Is there an inherent conflict between the interests of corporate bondholders and those of equity holders? In other words, why would a bond investor want to surrender funds if the corporate managers issuing the bonds represent the shareholders? How is this tension addressed in practice? How does moral hazard rear its ugly head in the bond market? How does monetary policy affect the bond market? These are questions that will be covered in this chapter.

The bond market is a major source of financing by the Treasury, corporations, and state and local governments. Indeed, for the federal government and state and local governments, the bond market is the only capital market that they tap. For corporations, the annual amount of funds raised in the bond market greatly exceeds the amount raised by issuing new equity.[1]

Bonds typically have a par value and pay their owners a semiannual coupon over the life of the security. The par value is the principal that gets paid when the bond matures. For example, a bond may have a par value of $100,000 and pay a semiannual coupon of $2,500 or $5,000 per year. We say this bond has a coupon rate of 5 percent—$5,000 (yearly)/$100,000. As we saw in Chapter 4, the actual yield to the investor will depend on the price paid for the bond, whether the price was par or not. If bought at par, the yield to maturity and coupon rate will be the same; if bought above (below) par, the yield to maturity will be below (above) the coupon rate.

Ordinarily, the coupon payment is fixed for the life of the bond. However, some bonds are issued with adjustable coupons. These tend to vary with movements in a benchmark interest rate—usually, a money market rate such as the Treasury bill rate or LIBOR.

Key to each bond is its *indenture*—the legal rights and responsibilities that are spelled out in the bond contract. The indenture includes such things as: the maturity of the security; the amount of the coupon and the dates on which it will be paid; embedded options such as a call feature or convertibility into stock or some other asset; the seniority of the bond; and covenants. *Covenants* can require the issuer to perform some action, usually to protect the interests of the bondholders, or they can restrict the issuer from undertaking certain actions, again to protect the interests of the bondholders. The seniority of the bond refers to its standing in relation to other debt holders—in the event all creditors cannot be paid, who stands at the head of the line to get paid first from the earnings and assets of the firm. In addition, the bond issue ordinarily has a bond trustee, which has responsibility to ensure that the issuer is meeting the terms of the indenture—protecting the interests of the bondholders. The decision about what provisions to include in the bond indenture is made on economic grounds (especially for corporate bonds), as we will see in this chapter.

TREASURY NOTES AND BONDS

Maturities

As noted in Chapter 2, the Treasury follows the practice of referring to its coupon securities with maturities of 2 to 10 years as notes and longer-term coupons as bonds. Its notes and bonds take two forms: *nominal* issues, which have principal and coupons that do not vary with inflation; and *inflation-protected* issues, which have principal and coupons that vary with inflation—so-called *TIPS* or *Treasury Inflation Protected Securities*. Nominal Treasuries are issued in maturities of 2-, 3-, 5-, 7-, and 10-year notes and 30-year bonds. TIPS are issued in maturities of 5- and 10-year notes and 30-year bonds. By far, the largest volume of issuance is in nominal securities.

Features of TIPS

The holder of a TIPS security receives a fixed rate of interest. However, the principal of that security adjusts with the Consumer Price Index (CPI), and the fixed interest rate is applied to the inflation-adjusted principal to determine the coupon payment. In this way, the investor receives a fixed real interest rate. As noted in Chapter 4, by comparing the nominal and real rates for a specific maturity, one can calculate the so-called break-even rate or inflation compensation required by market participants for holding nominal Treasury debt. For example, on March 19, 2014, the yield on a 10-year nominal note was 2.77 percent and the yield on a TIPS note was 0.60 percent. This implies that inflation compensation was 2.77 − 0.60 percent or 2.17 percent. *Inflation compensation* consists of an *expected inflation* component and an *inflation risk* component. The first is compensation for the expected erosion of the interest and principal payments from the inflation rate that is anticipated over the life of the security, and the second is compensation for the risk that inflation could be higher.

It is worth noting that, because the nominal market is more liquid, sometimes this measure of inflation compensation will be distorted by flights to safety, something we discussed in Chapter 5. In times of market turmoil, investors will flock to nominal Treasury securities more than to TIPS, driving up their prices and compressing their yields. The result will be a narrowing of the spread between the nominal and real yields, unrelated to inflation developments. This narrowing later unwinds once markets return to normal. During such flights to safety, the spread will not be an accurate measure of inflation expectations and inflation risk.

Placement

Like Treasury bills, the Treasury places new notes and bonds with investors through regularly scheduled auctions. Bidders can submit competitive or noncompetitive bids—the latter being subject to a $5 million upper limit. All bidders get the same interest rate—the yield that corresponds to the cutoff or the highest accepted interest rate that was bid. The Treasury auction process is described in more detail in the discussion of Treasury bills in Chapter 7.

When-Issued Trading

Once the Treasury has announced an auction, an investor can acquire a claim on a note or bond to be auctioned by the Treasury from a dealer in Treasury securities in the form of a so-called *when-issued security*. The dealer agrees to deliver that security to the investor after the auction has been held. It is a forward transaction in which the price (yield) is negotiated after the announcement of the auction for delivery after the auction. The when-issued rate is thought to be an unbiased predictor of the rate that will emerge from the auction and has proven to be a helpful guide to the Treasury as it prepares for the auction, as well as for dealers and other market participants.

STRIPS

Dealers in Treasury coupon securities acquire Treasury coupon securities to create zero-coupon securities, which they sell to investors seeking a single-payment investment. These are so-called *STRIPS—Separate Trading of Registered Interest and Principal of Securities*. The dealer creates STRIPS by removing—stripping—all the coupons and the principal from a coupon security and selling each of these payments of cash to investors as a zero-coupon security. Thus, a 10-year Treasury note can be transformed into 21 zero-coupon securities—corresponding to two coupons per year for 10 years and the principal. Because many investors prefer zero-coupon investments over coupon investments, the dealers can sell the 21 separate zero-coupon pieces for more than the price of the 10-year note, making it worthwhile for the dealer's bottom line.[2]

Secondary-Market Trading

In the secondary market, Treasury coupon securities are traded in an over-the-counter (OTC) market, with a large number of competing market makers. As with Treasury bills, primary dealers are the major market makers in Treasury coupons securities. Dealers rely heavily on repurchase agreements (RPs) to finance their inventories of Treasury coupons. They will also use reverse RPs (sometimes called matched sale purchases or MSPs) to acquire a particular Treasury security for making delivery to a customer when the security had been sold to the customer but was not actually held in the dealer's inventory at the time of the sale. Under a reverse RP, the dealer buys a security with an agreement to sell it back (or, more likely, one identical to it) at some later date—often a day or two later.

In the secondary market, a security that has been most recently auctioned is called the *on-the-run* security of that maturity. Active traders in the Treasury market prefer on-the-run issues because these are the most liquid of their maturity. This is a pattern that has evolved over time and reflects the desire of market players to have certain issues be more readily available for trading. As a result, the price will be higher and the yield lower for the on-the-run security. Indeed, yields are typically several basis points lower. Coupon securities that are outstanding but not the most recently auctioned are called *off-the-run* issues. Thus, an on-the-run issue goes off the run when an auction is completed for the next security of that maturity and a new on-the-run issue of that maturity takes its place. The yields that are commonly reported in the financial press are on-the-run yields.[3]

Reopening

From time to time, the Treasury will re-auction the on-the-run security. This is called a *reopening* of that issue. The reopened issue will have the same maturity date and coupon as the previously auctioned security. But if market conditions have changed since the previous auction, it will have a different price or yield to maturity. Sometimes the Treasury will reopen an issue when it is concerned about the adequacy of supply in the market as gauged by its price in relation to the prices of similar issues.

Purposes for Issuing Coupon Securities

The Treasury issues coupon securities to meet longer-term—permanent—financing needs, unlike bills, which, as noted in the previous chapter, are largely issued to meet intrayearly variations in cash flow. It chooses to issue a variety of maturities of coupon securities to meet these longer-term financing needs. The Treasury has a wide variety of investors with a range of preferred maturities and expects to get good terms by meeting those various demands. A positively sloped yield curve might suggest that the Treasury concentrate its offerings at shorter maturities to minimize interest cost. However, it is unlikely that this could be done without saturating this end of the market and pushing up those yields. A more uniform distribution of offerings by maturity is thought to keep overall interest costs low.

Credit Quality

Sovereign issuers of debt—such as the Treasury—typically enjoy easy access to credit markets and can borrow at some of the most favorable terms. For much of U.S. history, the Treasury has had a top-notch reputation among investors, with its securities seen to be virtually default free. The determination of the United States to be a gold-plated borrower can be traced back to Alexander Hamilton, the first Secretary of the Treasury.[4] Hamilton saw a strong credit standing contributing importantly to a nation's strength—enabling it to quickly access funds in global financial markets when needed, especially for war—and holding down budgetary costs. Other advanced industrial countries have enjoyed a similar reputation in global credit markets. However, over recent years, questions have emerged about the willingness and ability of many of these countries to service their debt in the face of sustained budgetary strains resulting from commitments to fund pension and health care entitlements that are mushrooming as their populations age. As a consequence, default on sovereign bonds is no longer regarded as an extremely remote possibility. Indeed, many countries have found their debt downgraded by credit ratings agencies, including the United States.

Because sovereign debt markets are large, well known, and liquid, they play an important role in the functioning of other credit markets. Sovereign markets are characterized by active trading and transparency of pricing, which means that this information can be used in the pricing of other credit. Indeed, sovereign yields tend to be regarded as benchmarks for the pricing of other credit. In this way, sovereign markets provide a price discovery function, and will usually be first affected by changes in market conditions. Issuers of other debt will thereby be able to key off developments in the market for sovereign debt as they make decisions on offering and pricing their securities.

CORPORATE BONDS

Only a small fraction of corporations have access to the bond market, largely owing to the asymmetric information problem. Moreover, to be able to access this market, the issuer must have its bonds rated by major rating agencies. Ratings were discussed in Chapter 5. As we noted in that chapter, bonds rated Baa (Moody's) or BBB (S&P) are called investment-grade and those below that rating are called below-investment grade (or speculative-grade, high-yield, or junk) bonds. Also, as we noted in that chapter, risk spreads on below-investment-grade bonds are particularly sensitive to the business cycle, widening sharply as the economy is thought to be softening, and retracing those movements as the economy is showing signs of solid growth.

Placements

Public offerings of corporate bonds typically are performed using the services of underwriters (investment banks). As with commercial paper, underwriters ordinarily buy the entire offering from the corporate issuer and then sell the bonds to investors. For large offerings, a consortium or syndicate of underwriters will join together to buy the offering, with one of them acting as lead manager. Underwriters get compensation for this service by buying the bonds from the corporate issuer at a lower price than they expect to get when they are sold to investors. Some of this compensation covers the risk that the underwriters are exposed to because market conditions may turn out to be less favorable than anticipated.[5] Large financial conglomerates that perform underwriting services will also issue their own bonds. They can do this exclusively by themselves or engaging other underwriters to join them in a syndicate.

Tension between Bond and Shareholders

Another important feature of the corporate bond market is the tension between the interests on bondholders and stockholders. A moral hazard situation exists because owners of the firm—shareholders—benefit from leverage and other higher risk strategies. This is because risk means that there are possibilities for high returns but also for low or even negative returns. When firms get financing from bonds (or other forms of debt), the bondholders do not share in the upside, but they do share in the downside; conversely, the shareholders benefit fully from upside gains and are able to share with bondholders the downside losses. This tilts managers' incentives toward more leverage and other forms of risk—a moral hazard problem—unless there are restrictions placed on managers.

The following example illustrates this tension:

	Low Leverage		High Leverage	
	Low Risk	High Risk	Low Risk	High Risk
Max.	20 (17.50)	30 (27.50)	60 (42.50)	90 (72.50)
Min.	10 (7.50)	3 (0.50)	20 (2.50)	0 (0)
Exp. value	12.50	14.00	22.50	36.25

In this example, equity is 100 in both the high- and low-leverage scenarios. However, debt is 50 in the low-leverage situation (a debt-to-equity ratio of 0.5) and 350 in the high-leverage scenario (a debt-to-equity ratio of 3.5). The interest rate on debt is 5 percent in both scenarios. This means that interest payments are 2.50 under the low-leverage scenario and 17.50 under the high-leverage scenario. Under both the low-leverage and the high-leverage scenarios, managers can pursue either a high-risk (apart from leverage) or low-risk strategy. The maximum returns and minimum returns are shown for each scenario. It is assumed that both are equally likely, as are every possibility in between. The return for each outcome is shown before paying debt holders and after paying them (in parentheses). The expected value of the return after paying debt holders is shown on the bottom line. In the first three scenarios, debt holders are paid in full, even if the minimum is earned. However, in the fourth scenario—high leverage and high risk—there are no earnings before interest. Thus, debt holders cannot be paid and the company must default on its debt.

Note that the expected returns to shareholders increase with risk and leverage. However, margins available to protect debt holders diminish as debt and risk increase. In the fourth case, there is no margin and debt holders are not paid. This example illustrates that corporate managers—acting on behalf of the shareholders—have an incentive to take on greater risk through leverage and other strategies. In the final scenario, some of the losses associated with the worst outcome are pushed onto debt holders. This illustrates the nature of the moral hazard problem and the underlying tension that exists between bond and equity investors.

Indentures and the Role of Covenants

In practice, this tension is addressed through covenants in the bond indenture. Among the covenants is a restriction on dividends paid to shareholders. Without such restrictions, managers could deplete asset cushions that protect bond investors by paying shareholders dividends in excess of earnings. In addition, covenants can limit the amount of new debt, especially more senior debt that would move above the current debt holders as claimants. Additional debt means more—competing—claims on the earnings and assets of the firm and issuance of more senior debt implies claims with a higher standing on the earnings and assets of the firm. Still another class of covenants relates to mergers and acquisitions. A merger with or acquisition of another firm with large amounts of debt would dilute the bondholder's claims on the earnings and assets of the firm in much the same way as issuing more debt.

A firm that chooses to leverage its balance sheet heavily, as in the high leverage scenario above, will find that it must pay bondholders more to compensate for the greater risk to them, thereby reducing its incentive to leverage. Indeed, one theorem—the Modigliani-Miller Theorem—argues, in effect, that the additional cost of financing completely negates all of the potential gains from more leverage.[6] Thus, market forces will act to limit firm leverage.

Beyond leverage restrictions, there are several components of bond agreements that can lower the interest cost of bonds to the corporate issuer. First, the issuer can agree to a *sinking fund* in which the corporation would regularly contribute funds out of earnings that would accumulate and go toward paying the bond's principal at maturity. Such a provision reduces the risk to the investor of not being paid the principal at maturity.[7] As a consequence, investors will be willing to accept a lower interest rate.

Second, the issuer can provide *convertibility*. A convertible bond is one that can be converted into shares of the company's stock—such as 30 shares of stock for one bond. They are structured in such a way that the value of the bond at the time of issue exceeds the value of the shares that can be acquired by the bond. However, if the share price rises significantly, the convertibility feature becomes more attractive. In essence, the bondholder receives an embedded option and options have value. Thus, the corporation can borrow at a lower cost than if the bonds were not convertible, reflecting the option value of the convertibility feature.

Third, the corporation could lower the cost of borrowing by *collateralizing* its bonds with assets having value and some liquidity. Think of the last time that you flew on a commercial airline. Who owned the aircraft that you rode on? If you mentioned the name of the airline—such as Jet Blue or Delta—you are probably wrong. An airline-leasing firm that you have never heard of likely owned the airplane and they leased it to Jet Blue or Delta. The leasing firm likely issued bonds to raise the bulk of the funds to purchase the aircraft, and if so, these bonds were collateralized by the aircraft itself—an asset that can be sold fairly easily in the event of default. Absent collateralization, the cost of borrowing to the leasing company would likely have been prohibitive.

Fourth, the bonds could be given *senior status*, giving them standing ahead of other bondholders and perhaps other creditors in the event of default. The senior bondholders will have a better claim on the earnings and assets of the firm and will be willing to accept a lower yield. But giving some bonds senior status implies that holders of other bonds, having claims now subordinated to holders of these senior bonds, will want more compensation in the form of higher yields for having lower claims.

Finally, the bondholders could be given *call protection*, meaning that the issuer will not be allowed to retire—call—the bonds prior to maturity. The reverse of this is *callability*. Callable bonds provide the issuer the right to redeem the bonds at par or often at a premium above par at the discretion of the issuer, typically following a period of time—called the lockout period—after issuance. With the callability feature, the issuer could redeem the bonds in the event interest rates decline significantly and the issuer can refinance at the lower level of interest rates. In these circumstances, the bondholder will end up with a pile of cash that can only be reinvested at a lower interest rate. This is an embedded option for the issuer and has value. Thus, the issuer typically pays for this option through a higher interest rate on the bonds.[8]

Credit Default Swaps (CDSs)

Investors can buy protection against default on corporate bonds through a credit default swap (CDS). Underwriters of CDSs will sell such protection on a particular bond—in effect, an insurance policy—for a premium that they perceive to be commensurate with the risk of default on that issue. CDS premiums can vary considerably over short periods of time to reflect shifting perceptions of the risk of default.[9] Many analysts of the credit process monitor CDS premiums carefully to determine whether credit has become tighter or easier.

Below-Investment-Grade Market

As we noted in Chapter 5, investment-grade bonds are those rated Baa (BBB) or above. Those rated below are called below-investment-grade, speculative-grade, high-yield, or junk bonds. Many investors have restrictions on whether they can hold below-investment-grade bonds or how much they can hold. Thus, moving below (or above) this threshold can significantly affect the pool of investors and have important implications for borrowing costs.

Major bond underwriters today are eager to assist in placing junk bonds as initial public offerings (IPOs), in contrast with earlier times when bonds only became junk bonds through downgrades of investment-grade bonds. Investors have come to realize that junk bonds can be a worthwhile component of a well-diversified portfolio. The spread of the yield on speculative-grade bonds over investment-grade corporate bonds or Treasuries—a measure of their risk premium—will vary over the course of the business cycle, as noted in Chapter 5.

Private Placements

Firms that are poorly known—characterized by substantial asymmetric information—have difficulty accessing the public bond market. Nonetheless, some are able to get bond financing from large institutional investors, such as insurance companies. These insurance companies find it worthwhile to have a staff of credit analysts that acquires and processes information on potentially promising investment opportunities in bonds, choosing those that are deemed to have good prospects for repayment. Typically, those firms selected will issue bonds in the form of *private placements*. As noted in Chapter 2, the Securities and Exchange Commission (SEC) exempts bonds from the public registration process if they are placed with a limited number of knowledgeable and well-healed (qualified) investors—the so-called *144(a) provision*. Because there are higher costs of acquiring and processing information on such issuers, the investors in these private placements receive a yield that compensates them for their additional costs.

Corporations with access to the public bond market will, from time to time, do a private offering. This usually is done when market conditions improve dramatically and the corporation's managers, fearing this may only be a temporary window, want to issue bonds quickly at the lower interest rates. Public offerings usually take time to meet all the requirements specified by the SEC. A private offering to qualified investors enables the firm to borrow at the fallen rates, usually while providing assurances to investors that the firm will register the bonds with the SEC and convert them to public status. Investors will be more willing to buy the bonds knowing that they will be able to sell them in the public market; even though they take the form of a private placement, borrowing costs will be lower with such an assurance than without.

Secondary-Market Trading

Corporate bonds trade in the secondary market on both specialist and over-the-counter platforms. The major specialist market is the New York Stock Exchange (NYSE), which conducts bond trades in much the same way as equities. The OTC market for corporate bonds tends to be less active than its counterpart for Treasury notes and bonds.

MUNIS

Bonds issued by state and local governments—*municipals* or *munis*—are typically used to finance capital projects, such as schools and roads. As noted in Chapter 2, such bonds are not taxed at the federal level. This makes them attractive to

U.S. investors subject to federal taxation—especially those in higher tax brackets. In practice, investors are mostly individuals and property and casualty insurance companies. Moreover, many states also exempt the interest from munis issued by jurisdictions within their state from income taxation; this makes such bonds even more attractive to investors located in these states.

Tax Considerations

Tax considerations suggest that muni yields should be lower than those for comparable maturity Treasuries. For example, the relationship between muni and Treasuries would be the following, if they were similar in every respect

$$i_M = (1-t)i_T$$

where i_M represents the yield on a muni, i_T represents the yield on a Treasury security of the same maturity, and t represents the marginal tax rate faced by muni investors. In other words, the yield on a muni should equal the yield on a Treasury after taxes have been paid to the federal government. For example, if the yield on a 10-year Treasury note were 4 percent and the marginal tax rate were 28 percent, then the yield on a 10-year muni, if they were otherwise the same, would be

$$i_M = 4 \cdot (1 - 0.28) = 4 \cdot 0.72 = 2.88 \text{ or } 2.88 \text{ percent}$$

Credit Risk and Liquidity Differences

However, in practice munis are different from Treasuries in other ways, too. These differences make them less attractive to investors and result in their yields being higher than the above formula would suggest. First, munis are generally perceived as having more credit risk, even higher-rated munis. Second, munis lack the liquidity of their Treasury counterparts.

Under normal circumstances, the yield on a muni will be below that of a comparable maturity Treasury security, but by a smaller amount than the above formula would suggest. For example, the muni yield might be 3.25 percent instead of 2.88 percent, in the example above. The 37 basis point difference between the actual and theoretical rates would reflect the lesser liquidity and greater credit risk of the muni. However, in the wake of the financial crisis, it has been common for muni yields to exceed those on comparable maturity Treasuries. Moreover, this excess has been accentuated during those times of market turmoil characterized by an intense flight to safety.

General Obligation versus Revenue Bonds

There are two basic types of munis—*general obligations* and *revenue bonds*. General obligations (GOs) are backed by the full faith and credit of the issuing government, implying that they are supported importantly by the taxing power of that jurisdiction. Revenue bonds are backed by the revenues from a particular project, such as a state university dormitory, a sports stadium, or a toll road. Typically, GOs are considered less risky because they are supported by the full faith and credit of the issuer and, as a result, have lower yields.

Placement

Issuers of tax-exempt securities use underwriters to assist in the sales of their bonds to investors, much as do corporations. The process followed is very similar for both types of issuers. However, their investor bases are very different, with munis being of interest to individuals subject to higher income tax rates.[10] The secondary market for munis takes the form of an OTC market in which dealers post bid and asked prices. It is not a very active market and those bid-asked spreads tend to be much larger than in the highly liquid Treasury market.

Indentures

Like corporate bonds, the indenture for tax-exempt bonds will have components that will affect the interest rate that the governmental unit will need to pay investors. If the bond includes a call provision, the unit will have the option of redeeming the bonds before maturity. However, it will need to pay investors more than if the bonds had call protection. Many state and local governments choose to issue *serial* bonds to lower interest cost. Serial offerings contain bonds of different maturities, such maturities of seven, eight, and nine years instead of all bonds having a single maturity date of eight years. In this way, the repayment of principal in any one of those three years will be a smaller claim on the finances of that government in that year than if all came due at the same time. Serial bonds perform a similar role as sinking funds, which are also used by state and local issuers.

Many state and local governments acquire insurance for the bonds they issue to lower their interest rate. To be able to achieve this, the insurer must have a credit standing—credit rating—that exceeds that of the state or local government. In essence, bonds that are insured take on the credit standing of the insurance company instead of the issuer.[11] Insurers usually insure the timely payment of interest and principal on the insured bonds.

Ratings

State and local government securities are typically rated by the major credit rating agencies, using a scale similar to the one used for corporate bonds. Again, the reason for relying on credit ratings has to do with asymmetric information. Investors may be familiar with the jurisdiction issuing the bonds, but they often are not very familiar with that unit's financial position and credit history. With insurance, they only need to look to the credit standing of the bond insurer.[12]

GOVERNMENT-SPONSORED ENTERPRISES (GSEs)

Government-sponsored enterprises (GSEs) are privately owned corporations that have a special relationship with the U.S. government. They have federal charters and a credit line from the Treasury, which has been viewed as a symbol of implicit federal support for these institutions. The major GSEs are Fannie Mae, Freddie Mac, and the Federal Home Loan Banks.[13] All three play an important role in the mortgage and housing sector.

Fannie Mae and Freddie Mac

Fannie Mae and Freddie Mac acquire residential mortgages from participating mortgage bankers and either hold them in their asset portfolio or put them into mortgage pools and sell participations in those pools to investors—they securitize them (the subject of the next chapter). When Fannie Mae and Freddie Mac elect to hold the mortgages in their portfolios, they must finance them. They typically finance such assets by issuing bonds. Because of their perceived connection with the federal government, they can borrow at lower interest rates. Such a perceived federal backstop leads to a moral hazard situation, encouraging excessive leveraging and risk taking. Indeed, Fannie and Freddie faced major losses from their risk exposure in 2008 and, in order to avoid a major disruption to the mortgage and housing markets, were rescued by the federal government and placed under a federal conservatorship.[14] In recent years, Congress has been looking into ways to reform Fannie Mae and Freddie Mac—to reprivatize them, but change risk bearing so that moral hazard incentives would be reduced.

Federal Home Loan Banks

Federal Home Loan Banks (FHLBs) are owned by member financial institutions—depository institutions involved in the mortgage market. Member institutions are eligible to borrow from FHLBs so long as they post acceptable collateral related to mortgage or other assets related to community development. To be able to fund these loans, the FHLBs issue bonds.

Features of GSE Bonds

GSE bonds can have many of the features of corporate bonds, such as callability, which will affect their yield. The preponderance of such securities have a fixed coupon, but some are issued as floating rate debt—so-called floaters—that have coupon payments that vary with some shorter-term benchmark yield, such as a Treasury bill yield or LIBOR. GSE debt is issued in a range of maturities corresponding to the financing requirements of these enterprises as well as investor interest.

GSEs typically use underwriters to place their bonds. In the secondary market, their debt is traded over the counter.

THE IMPACT OF MONETARY POLICY ON THE BOND MARKET

Monetary policy can have a large impact on bond rates and the bond market. Much depends on how big of an impact a change in the central bank's policy interest rate has on the expected path of short-term interest rates, as described in Chapter 5. The more the policy action—say, an increase in the policy rate—leads to the expected path of short-term rates moving in the same direction, the bigger the impact on bond rates. In contrast, if a change in the policy rate were seen by market participants as being reversed in the near future, the impact on bond rates would be hardly noticeable. Of course, the central bank can utilize forward guidance to have a more predictable effect of the path of expected short-term interest rates and thereby on bond rates. Those types of business and consumer spending that are longer-lived and sensitive to interest rates will be most affected by changes in bond rates. This includes business plant and equipment spending and household spending on big-ticket items.

SUMMARY

1. The bond market is a primary source of financing for corporations, governments at all levels, and GSEs.
2. The bond indenture contains the terms and responsibilities of the parties of the bond contract. Included are restrictive covenants, limiting the actions of the issuer.
3. The Treasury issues notes and bonds at auction in the capital market. It issues both nominal securities and inflation-protected securities (TIPS), with the former being much larger in volume. From nominal and TIPS yields can be derived inflation compensation, consisting of compensation for expected inflation and inflation risk. The Treasury—a sovereign issuer of debt—enjoys a very high credit standing, which goes back to the early days of the country. Prospective budget difficulties, though, threaten to undermine this standing.
4. Dealers in Treasury securities create zero-coupon securities—STRIPS—from the coupons and principal payments of notes and bonds. Dealers also enable investors to acquire about-to-be-auctioned coupon securities through when-issued securities.
5. On-the-run Treasuries are the most recently issued notes and bonds of each maturity and are the most liquid of each maturity. As a consequence, their yields are the lowest. When a new security with that maturity is issued, the on-the-run security goes off the run.
6. The Treasury uses the market for notes and bonds to meet its longer-term financing requirements.
7. The situation involving corporate bonds contains an inherent tension between bond and stockholders. Managers—representing shareholders—have an incentive to take on more risk than is in the interests of bondholders. Restrictive covenants are placed in indentures to curb these incentives, or else investors would insist on much higher yields to be willing to hold the bonds. Issuers of corporate bonds need to have them rated by credit rating agencies or buyers will be uninterested, owing to asymmetric information.
8. Some common features of bond indentures that affect the risk to investors and, therefore, their yield are a sinking fund, callability (or the reverse, call protection), convertibility, collateralization, and senior or junior status. Investors can acquire insurance against defaults by purchasing CDSs.
9. The corporate bond market has become receptive to below-investment-grade bonds, as for many investors the higher yields adequately compensate for risk.
10. Some firms without access to the public market for bonds are able to place bonds privately with investors, typically large institutional investors such as insurance companies. Sometimes, firms with access to public markets will, when borrowing costs drop, place a private offering to avoid the delays associated with public offerings.

11. Issuers in the public corporate bond market rely on underwriters to place their bonds with investors. The secondary market for corporate bonds is considerably less active than that for Treasury coupons and utilizes both OTC and specialist platforms.
12. State and local governments also use underwriters to place their bonds. Secondary markets for state and local bonds—munis—use the OTC platform and have thin trading. Munis need to be rated by the credit-rating agencies for the same reasons as corporates.
13. Munis take the form of GOs and revenue bonds. The absence of federal taxation of interest on these bonds makes them attractive to investors facing taxation on income.
14. Features that can affect muni yields are callability, serial offerings, and insurance.
15. Government-sponsored agencies—GSEs—are large issuers of bonds and have a special relationship with the federal government. The biggest—Fannie Mae, Freddie Mac, and the FHLBs—are involved in making funds available in the mortgage (and housing) market. They have been characterized by a moral hazard problem encouraging their managers to take on excessive amounts of risk. Their securities are typically placed through underwriters and they trade in an OTC secondary market.
16. The impact of monetary policy on bond rates depends importantly on whether market participants alter the path of expected short-term interest rates when the central bank changes its short-term policy interest rate. Forward guidance has come to play an important role in the transmission process.

QUESTIONS

1. Describe the method by which the following securities are distributed in the primary market: Treasury bills, notes, and bonds; corporate bonds; muni bonds; GSE bonds.
2. For the above securities, describe the secondary market in which they are traded.
3. In the Treasury market, what is: a when-issued security; a reopening; an on-the-run security; an off-the-run security?
4. What happens to the yield on an on-the-run Treasury security as a new auction date is approached? Explain. How would the yield be affected if the Treasury announced a reopening of that security? Explain.
5. As a first approximation, is leverage a zero-sum game between debt holders and shareholders? Why do shareholders benefit from more leverage? More risk? Is there a moral hazard problem?
6. What is the role of restrictive covenants in a bond indenture? What are some common covenants?
7. According to the Modigliani-Miller Theorem, does it benefit a firm's shareholders when more leverage is added to the firm's financial structure? Why or why not?
8. How do the following features of a corporate bond affect its yield: call option, convertibility, collateralization, sinking fund, and senior status.
9. In what respect does a privately placed bond resemble a loan made by a commercial bank? Why do firms with access to the public bond market sometimes issue privately placed bonds under Rule 144a?

10. Why are junk bonds riskier than investment-grade bonds? How do investors in junk bonds reduce their risk exposure?
11. What is a CDS? How can an investor use a CDS to reduce the risk of holding a corporate bond? Is there any residual risk to the investor?
12. Why would a muni issuer want to place a serial issue of bonds rather than a single maturity? A callable rather than call-protected bond?
13. If the yield on a 10-year Treasury note is 3.5 percent and the marginal tax rate facing an investor is 30 percent, what is the expected yield on a muni of that maturity if that security has the same liquidity and credit risk features of the Treasury?
14. Using the FRED database, plot the nominal yield on a 30-year Treasury bond and the yield on a 30-year TIPS bond. Do they move together? Next plot inflation compensation on the 30-year bond. Can you spot periods of flights to safety?
15. Using the FRED database, plot the yield on an investment-grade corporate bond. Next plot the yield on a junk bond. Do they move together? Next plot the risk premium on the junk bond. Can you identify business cycles from this premium?
16. Why are the GSEs said to be characterized by moral hazard? Any evidence that this is a serious problem?
17. How does monetary policy affect bond yields? How might forward guidance result in a more predictable impact on bond rates? What kinds of spending might be affected by such changes in bond rates?

NOTES

1. Corporations raise substantial amounts of funds from their shareholders through retained earnings. Recall that corporate profits belong to shareholders, each in proportion to their ownership share. When corporate management decides to retain some of these profits, they are essentially getting the assent of shareholders to use these funds to plow back into the firm. This is based on a presumption that the shareholders will earn a better return on these retained earnings invested in the firm than they could get by investing the funds elsewhere. The amount of corporate retained earnings greatly exceeds the amount of new stock issued, implying that retained earnings are the primary source of equity funds. Indeed, in 2012, nonfinancial corporations retained nearly $500 billion of profits after taxes, which was used for internal investment instead of dividends to shareholders. These corporations actually retired stock, net, as the amount of shares bought in the market and retired exceeded the amount of new shares issued by a sizable margin.
2. Occasionally, the reverse will occur—the value of the note or bond as a whole will be priced above that of each of the zero-coupon securities created from the coupon and principal payments. In this case, the dealer can profit from reconstituting the note or bond—acquiring each coupon and the principal and putting them back together as a regular coupon security for a sale.
3. One needs to be careful when following yields of a particular maturity around the time of a new auction. As the auction approaches and the on-the-run issue is about to go off the run, its yield tends to rise simply because market participants know

that it will no longer be the most liquid security at that maturity. When the new on-the-run issue replaces it, the reported yield will show a drop. This is because the reported yield now represents the yield on a new issue having the attractive liquidity properties previously possessed by the now first off-the-run issue.
4. Ron Chernow, *Alexander Hamilton* (New York: Penguin Books, 2004).
5. Underwriters also, from time to time, place bonds on a "best efforts" basis. Instead of buying them outright, the underwriter will try to line up buyers to acquire the securities directly from the corporate issuer at prices favorable to the issuer. The underwriter and the issuer in these circumstances will negotiate a fee to be paid to the underwriter for the service.
6. F. Modigliani and M. H. Miller, "The Cost of Capital, Corporate Finance and the Theory of Investment," *American Economic Review* 48, no. 3 (1958): 261–297. Modigliani and Miller make the case a little differently, maintaining that more leverage increases risk for shareholders—as the volatility of their earnings rises with leverage—and they must be compensated for this risk by receiving higher returns.
7. To better assure investors that they will be paid the funds placed in the sinking fund and the funds will not be tapped for other purposes, the bond trustee acting on behalf of the bondholders commonly controls the funds.
8. A less adverse situation for the bondholder occurs when the issuer's fortunes improve and its bonds are upgraded. This will lower the interest rate at which the firm can refinance, even though the general level of interest rates has not declined and the bondholder can reinvest at a similar yield.
9. Large commercial and investment banks act as the principal underwriters of CDSs. This line of business complements their other credit-related lines of business. AIG, a large multiline insurance company, had been a major underwriter of CDSs before the financial crisis and nearly failed as a result of heavy losses from grossly underpriced CDS products (mostly written on exotic mortgage-related securities).
10. Many investors in munis acquire them indirectly through tax-exempt mutual funds.
11. The insurance companies are sometimes called monoline insurers because they have historically specialized in insuring munis. They address the asymmetric information problem by investigating the governmental unit and assessing the likelihood that the bonds will be repaid, basing their premiums on that assessment. The monoline insurers got into some difficulty at the time of the financial crisis by writing insurance on a new type of financing, so-called auction rate securities in which longer-term holdings of securities were financed by very short-term borrowings (at rates determined by an auction). Investors got skittish during the crisis and pulled their short-term financing out, leaving the insurers with the need to replace that financing. Their prospective losses from their auction rate security business threatened their muni insurance business.
12. Interest rates on insured munis will often be lower than implied by the credit standing of the insurer. This is because, if the insurer should fail, there is some chance that the muni issuer will still have the capacity to pay investors.
13. In addition, there are some farm sector GSEs that issue bonds—notably, the Federal Agricultural Mortgage Corporation (Farmer Mac) and the Farm Credit Banks. However, they are much smaller issuers. In addition, there are federal

agencies that issue debt having the full faith and credit of the U.S. government to back them (the GSEs do not have such explicit backing). Principally, these are the Small Business Administration (SBA), Government National Mortgage Association (GNMA or Ginnie Mae), and the Tennessee Valley Authority (TVA). While the credit risk accompanying such federal agency debt is the same as for Treasury securities, the instruments that they issue are less liquid and thus carry higher yields.

14. A conservatorship allows the federal government to take control of the institutions and replace their management. The conservator can then continue to keep them open or liquidate them (sell off their assets). The federal government in 2008 wanted to keep them operating in order to support the mortgage market.

CHAPTER 9

Securitization

WHAT YOU WILL LEARN IN THIS CHAPTER

- The meaning of securitization.
- How unbundling of the standard loan product occurs as a result of securitization.
- Challenges caused by asymmetric information and adverse selection.
- What is meant by regulatory arbitrage.
- The alphabet soup of securitized products: MBSs, ABSs, CDOs, CLOs, CBOs, and CMBSs.
- The key role played by Fannie Mae and Freddie Mac in the MBS market and thereby the mortgage market.
- How the process of building structured securities involves parsing the cash flows from the underlying loans into separate types of securities.
- How the financial crisis set back many types of securitization.
- How securitization acts to integrate credit markets more tightly.
- How securitization creates value added.
- How monetary policy has become more effective as securitization has developed.

BACKGROUND

When people buy a home or refinance, what happens to the new mortgage (home loan) that gets made? Does the lender hold on to the mortgage—having to fund it for as long as the loan exists—or does another party acquire and fund the mortgage? What about ordinary credit card and auto loans? What happens to them? Does securitization play a role here? If so, what is meant by securitization? Is securitization the wave of the future or was it a flash in the pan that the financial crisis demonstrated to be seriously flawed?

Securitization refers to the process by which ordinary, illiquid loans are placed in a pool of other assets and converted into fairly liquid securities. By carefully pooling a number and variety of loans, securitization can reduce risk through diversification. Securitization also enables the separation of loan origination from funding. That is, securitization fosters specialization between the process of originating a loan—acquiring and processing information required for making a sound credit judgment—and the need to get the funds to permanently finance the loan.

When commercial banks (or other traditional lenders) must both originate and fund these loans, they can be exposed to interest rate risk that is difficult for them to manage. This can occur when the maturities of the loans are longer than the maturities of the deposits they rely on to fund them. To illustrate, for a long time savings institutions were the largest originators of home mortgages. They funded these very long-term loans—typically having 30-year maturities—with short-term deposits, exposing themselves to vast amounts of interest rate risk; in these situations, when the level of interest rates increases, deposit costs rise much faster than the interest received from loans, leading to a substantial erosion of earnings; looked at differently, the present value of their long-term loan assets falls by much more than the present value of their short-term deposit liabilities. In contrast, there are other institutional investors—such as pension funds and life insurance companies—that are in a better position to hold these long-term assets. For them, the interest rate risk is considerably less and may be close to zero because of their much longer holding periods. But they do not have the infrastructure to originate these types of loans. Securitization enables such loans to be funded by the institutional lenders that are better positioned to hold such assets with maturities much longer than would be prudent for savings institutions—or, for that matter, commercial banks.

This separation of origination from funding is sometimes called *unbundling*. Another aspect of the unbundling process is the sale of servicing rights to the loans that go into the pool to another party. Servicing involves getting the documentation for the collateral backing loans in the pool, collecting the regular payments on the loans in the pool, paying out the cash flows to the investors in the pool, keeping meticulous records of all payments and transactions, and addressing problems as they arise. Information technology—both hardware and software—has allowed this highly complex task to become manageable. In the process, it has given rise to significant economies of scale in the provision of servicing, which has led to a considerable degree of concentration in the servicing industry. Today, a handful of servicers perform the bulk of loan servicing.

OBSTACLES TO OVERCOME

Asymmetric Information and Adverse Selection

Securitization faces significant challenges, too. Not only do originators face an asymmetric information problem when they originate the loans that they place into pools; the borrowers are in a better position to judge the prospects that the loan will get repaid on schedule. However, investors buying participations in the pools of such loans face an even greater asymmetric information problem. They know nothing about the soundness of the loans going into the pool. Indeed, originators have an incentive to originate a lot of loans for sale because, typically, the amount they can earn on origination fees typically is based on volume, not on performance. This means that they may be willing to make a questionable loan or not exercise due diligence in learning more about a borrower. As a result, loans that they may not be willing to hold themselves can be off-loaded to a pool. This is a problem of adverse selection in which the originator will be more inclined to sell those loans that it originates and does not want to keep—also called a "lemons problem."

Investors, knowing these incentives, will be reluctant to acquire such securitized loan products, fearing that they may end up with more risk than they bargained for. Indeed, they will be suspicious that the originators have been engaging in adverse selection arising from asymmetric information by cherry picking the loans—keeping the good ones for their own portfolios and foisting the bad ones off on others. Without some standards or controls, few, if any, potentially worthwhile transactions involving the pooling of loans in the secondary market would occur.

Corrective Measures

Among the things that have been done to address these perverse incentives is the imposition of underwriting criteria that must be met before the securitized asset is offered to investors. These can include minimum credit scores and maximum loan-to-value ratios (a form of leverage limit) for each loan going into the pool. They can also include a requirement that the originator retains a certain portion of each loan sold to the pool to ensure that the originator has some "skin in the game," and will be exposed to losses in the event that the originator compromised sound underwriting standards in making the loans. The reputation of the originator as a reputable business counterparty will also play an important role in these circumstances. Beyond such underwriting measures, the investment bank forming the pool can seek to achieve diversification of the loans being placed into the pool, to further limit risk. Often, too, credit rating agencies are retained to evaluate the pool and assign it a credit rating; this, of course, is a standard way of dealing with the asymmetric information problem, by relying on the assessment of a third-party specialist.

Regulatory Capital on Ordinary Loans

Another reason why securitization has become popular is that commercial banks and investment banks have used securitization to avoid regulatory capital charges, in much the same way that they have developed asset-backed commercial paper programs discussed in Chapter 7. With securitization, they can continue to originate loans, but they can avoid having to hold them on their balance sheet as assets. Because regulatory capital is based on the bank's assets, they avoid these capital charges by selling them to a special-purpose vehicle (SPV) set up to create the security made up of the pool of loans.[1] This became known as *regulatory arbitrage,* in which the bank is able to continue to originate loans and collect fees in the process but is not subject to regulatory capital as it would be by holding the loan as an asset. However, after many banks incurred substantial losses from their involvement in the securitization process during the financial crisis—through the SPVs they set up and the loans they sold to the SPV—regulators have become more stringent in applying capital requirements and banks have cut back their reliance on securitization for regulatory arbitrage purposes.

To place this issue in perspective, the securitization process got ahead of itself prior to the financial crisis of 2008. Underwriters formed pools of mortgages—and structured investments made from these pools—that had risk properties that were poorly understood. Their calibrations of the risk properties of these securities were based on very limited historical experience that proved to be highly misleading and proved to grossly underestimate the true amount of risk. Moreover, ratings agencies often assigned ratings that were based on similar methodologies, and they, too, proved to be too generous. As a result, massive amounts were lost, and this has set back the evolution of the securitization process. The weaknesses in this process are being addressed by market participants. It is likely that the adaptations being made with the benefit of the knowledge of the weaknesses that were revealed during the crisis will enable securitization to move ahead on a more solid footing.

BEGINNINGS OF SECURITIZATION—MBSs

Ginnie Mae

Securitization started in the early 1970s with the creation of the Government National Mortgage Association—GNMA or Ginnie Mae. In an effort to broaden the array of investors interested in holding mortgages, and thereby increase the amount of funds available to finance home purchases, Ginnie Mae was established to guarantee timely payment of interest and principal on *mortgage-backed securities* (*MBSs*). These took the form of pools of mortgages in which investors were sold participations—that is, investors were able to buy a slice of the cash flows from the underlying mortgages in the pool. Ginnie Mae is an agency of the U.S. government, and the MBSs it insures are backed by the full faith and credit of the U.S. government, much like Treasury securities. The underlying mortgages must be federally insured or guaranteed mortgages—primarily Federal Housing Administration (FHA) or U.S. Department of Veterans Affairs (VA) loans.

MBSs are sometimes referred to as *pass-throughs*. All of the cash flows from the underlying mortgages go into the pool and are passed through to investors, less fees to cover the administrative costs of managing the pool and payment of a franchise fee to Ginnie Mae. The issuer of the GNMA pass-through acquires the underlying qualified mortgages, places them into a pool of mortgages, and transforms the pool into a security. Participations—shares—of that security are then sold to investors. The issuer must also provide for the servicing of the pass-through. This involves collecting the monthly payments from the mortgage borrowers, maintaining payment records, and passing payments through to investors; it also includes covering missed payments by mortgage borrowers until those missed payments can be recovered from the borrower or Ginnie Mae. Investors in Ginnie Mae pass-throughs receive monthly payments, in contrast to the semiannual payments that get paid on ordinary bonds.

Illustration of the Process

This process is illustrated in Figure 9.1. On the right are shown the originators of the mortgage loans. They screen loan applications, decide which qualify, close the loans, get the documentation for the collateral, and sell the loans to the issuer of the pool. The issuer, also shown, selects the loans that go into the pool, ensures that they meet the criteria established by Ginnie Mae, and sells participations (shares) in the pool to investors. The issuer also selects a qualified servicer for the pool and sells to them the servicing rights. Through this process, a number of ordinary home mortgages (sometimes called *whole loans*) have been transformed into a security that may be acquired by a large institutional investor, domestic or foreign.

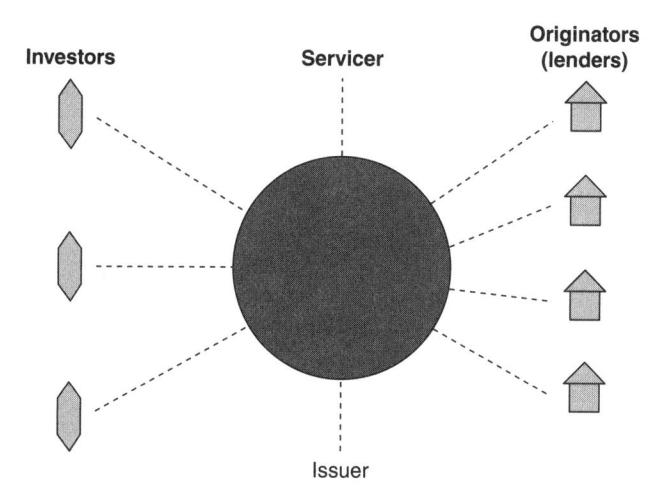

FIGURE 9.1 Standard MBS Pass-Through

Fannie Mae and Freddie Mac

Following in the footsteps of Ginnie Mae were Fannie Mae and Freddie Mac.[2] Unlike Ginnie Mae, both are private corporations. However, unlike other private financial institutions, Fannie Mae and Freddie Mac have federal charters and a line of credit to the U.S. Treasury (discussed in the previous chapter). They are classified as government-sponsored enterprises (GSEs). Whereas Ginnie Mae deals only with federally insured or guaranteed mortgages, Fannie Mae and Freddie Mac guarantee MBSs containing conventional mortgages. These mortgages must meet certain requirements to qualify for being eligible for a Fannie Mae or a Freddie Mac pool; the requirements include borrower income, credit score, maximum loan-to-value, and a maximum mortgage size. Those loans that satisfy these criteria are called *conforming* (or *conventional*) *mortgages*.

Because Fannie Mae and Freddie Mac have been government-sponsored agencies and not actual agencies of the federal government, they did not have the formal backing of the U.S. government. However, many investors regarded their special relationship with the federal government to imply an implicit guarantee, which added to the attractiveness to investors of MBSs guaranteed by the GSEs. Indeed, this contributed to the size of conforming MBS pools substantially exceeding the size of Ginnie Mae pools.

In the cases of all three types of MBSs—Ginnie Mae, Fannie Mae, and Freddie Mac—investors need not be concerned about the quality of the loans in the portfolio because the timely payment of principal and interest has been guaranteed by a federal agency or a GSE. In other words, the major asymmetric information problem noted earlier in this chapter is not a concern for investors in these pools. The promise of the agency or GSE to make regular payments has substituted for that of the homeowner. The asymmetric information problem is shifted onto the agency or GSE.

In late summer 2008, Fannie Mae and Freddie Mac were about to default on their debt and MBS guarantee obligations. To avoid more disruption to the mortgage and housing markets when the financial crisis and economic downturn were intensifying, Fannie Mae and Freddie Mac were taken over by the federal government under a legal arrangement called a conservatorship. Absent such action, they would have been unable to support new mortgage lending at a time when the financial markets were in disarray and the economy—especially the housing sector—was on the verge of collapse. The Treasury has announced that it intends to come forth with a proposal to restructure Fannie Mae and Freddie Mac, likely returning them to private status. Meanwhile, members of Congress have been developing their own plan.

Secondary-Market Trading

Secondary trading of MBSs is done over the counter. The secondary market for these securities is not nearly as active or as liquid as that of Treasury securities. As a consequence, bid-ask prices are larger.

Other Mortgage Pools

The securitization of mortgages later was extended beyond pools of loans insured or guaranteed by the federal government or pools of conforming mortgages guaranteed by the GSEs. These came to be known as *private-label pools*, because they did not involve agencies of the U.S. government or the GSEs. Issuers of private-label pools found that they needed to have their pools rated by credit ratings agencies or investors would lack interest—the asymmetric information problem again.

Private underwriters formed pools of mortgages that met all the standards for being conforming mortgages, except that they exceeded the maximum size.[3] These loans came to be called *jumbos*. In addition, pools were formed for mortgages that did not meet all of the conforming mortgage underwriting criteria—so-called *Alt-A mortgages*. Finally, pools were formed of considerably higher risk mortgages that fell well short of meeting the criteria for conforming status. These were *subprime mortgages*.

Issuers tried to add to the appeal of pools of nonconforming mortgages or private-label pools—containing jumbos, Alt-A, or subprime mortgages—by overcollateralizing the pools. That is, they backed the pool with mortgages having greater market value than the securities they back. Alternatively, they required that mortgages going into the pool have private insurance against default losses—in effect, substituting the credit standing of the insurer for that of the homeowner. They also had the ratings agencies assign ratings to the pools—often attractive ratings.

Nonetheless, it was pools containing subprime mortgages that played a major role in the financial crisis. Many of the pools that inflicted heavy losses on investors had been rated highly by the rating agencies, which has proved to be a blemish on the agencies' standing in the financial world. It also prompted Congress to put these agencies under federal regulation. Since the onset of the financial crisis, all of these forms of private-label pools have faced intense investor resistance and, as a result, have been slow to emerge from being dormant.

OTHER SECURITIZED LOANS—CONSUMER ABSs

Auto ABSs

The success of MBSs led to the extension of the concept of securitization to other kinds of assets—*asset-backed securities* (*ABSs*). In the mid-1980s, lenders for autos began to pool some of their motor vehicle loans into pools, following the model of the MBS pools. At first, this was done by commercial banks. But it was quickly followed by the captive auto finance companies. Indeed, during the early 1990s, when these captive finance companies faced serious financial difficulties and were having to pay very high risk premium to attract funds from investors to finance motor vehicle loans, they turned to ABSs to avoid high interest costs while still providing customer financing. That is, they would place virtually all of their production of these collateralized loans into a pool and sell participations to investors to avoid booking and financing these loans. At this time, investors regarded owning shares in the pool assembled by a finance company to be less risky than acquiring bonds issued by the finance company (which would have been used to fund the loans on the balance sheet of the finance company).

Credit Card ABSs

About the same time, commercial banks began to assemble ABSs using credit card receivables—credit card loan balances under ordinary revolving credit card lines of credit. This proved to be more challenging because such balances can increase or decrease at the discretion of card holders. Also, credit card loans, unlike auto loans, are unsecured. The issuers addressed this challenge by various means. In some cases, the issuer replaced the accounts that were being paid down or expanding too quickly with others. In other cases, classes or tranches of securities were created under which more predictable cash flows or prioritized claims on the cash flows were separated from others; in other words, the cash flows from the underlying credit card receivables were parsed into different categories, including the timing of when they would be received, and separate securities were created that assigned each stream of cash flows to the owners of that security tranche. The last tranche was a residual tranche—sometimes called the "Z tranche"—and the owners of this tranche would get whatever was left over, which constituted the riskiest tranche. At one point, more than half of all credit provided to households through credit cards was being provided though ABSs.

Other Consumer ABSs

Beyond credit cards and autos, lenders have securitized a variety of other loans. These have included student loans, loans for manufactured homes, and home equity loans.

Common Features

There are several common features of ABSs worth noting. First, they usually involve creation of a trust to receive the loans from the lender and to issue the securities backed by the loans. The trust is also responsible for servicing the loans and making payments to investors—usually, outsourced to a specialized servicing firm. Second, they frequently contain credit enhancements. These can take the form of backing by insurance or a standby letter of credit from another commercial bank, a structuring into senior and subordinated tranches, or overcollateralization of the pool. Third, the pools are rated by credit rating agencies. In doing so, they review the underwriting criteria for the loans in the pool, the structure of the security, the credit enhancements, and they form an opinion (rating) on the prospects for payment.

The Effects of the Financial Crisis

The ABS market was shaken dramatically by the financial crisis of 2008. Because securitized loans involving subprime mortgages had been at the center of the financial storm, investors feared that there may be inherent flaws in other securitizations and pulled back from nearly all securitized investments. This prompted the Federal Reserve to introduce a program to support the ABS market—the Term Asset-Backed Loan Facility (TALF) program. Recognizing the major role that ABSs had come to perform in providing financing for motor vehicle and credit card purchases and for student and small business loans, the Fed introduced a loan program to provide support for these types of ABSs. This program appears to have been successful in encouraging investors to overcome their reluctance to hold ABSs and fostered a turnaround in this market. As the market has normalized, the TALF program has been wound down. More recently, the market for various types of securitized assets has been recovering

ABSs INVOLVING BUSINESS CREDIT—CDOs AND STRUCTURED SECURITIES

The concept of securitization has been applied to other types of loans and debt. These fall under the general heading of *collateralized debt obligations* (CDOs).

Standard Types of Pools—CLOs, CBOs, and CMBSs

In some cases, these are straightforward pools of loans that follow the model of MBSs. Investors buy participations in a pool of such loans and get their proportionate share of the pool's cash flows. Standard business loans are pooled into a pass-through security called a *collateralized loan obligation* (CLO). Some of these consist of smaller loans guaranteed by the Small Business Administration (SBA), an agency of the federal government. Similar to the CLO is the *collateralized bond obligation* (CBO). A CBO is typically a pool of below-investment-grade corporate bonds. Still another form of standard MBS-type securitization involves commercial real estate loans. It is called a *commercial mortgage-backed security* (CMBS).

CMBSs, CBOs, and CLOs provide risk reduction through diversification. Indeed, rating agencies generally give the pool a better rating than they would give the underlying loans or bonds because the investor benefits from diversification.

Structured Securities

In other cases, so-called *structured securities* are created. Structured securities are built from a pool of loans or securities. The claims to the cash flows from these are transformed into different tranches, and securities are issued against the cash flows associated with each tranche. The cash flows can be ordered by maturity or by seniority (the priority of the claim on the cash flow).

The process of creating structured securities is illustrated in Figure 9.2. On the right are the assets that go into the pool. These can be loans, securities, or both. The securities can take the form of bonds—usually junk bonds—and securitized assets, such as MBSs and ABSs. Once the assets have been put in the pool, an underwriter creates different claims on the cash flows of assets in the pool—tranches—as shown

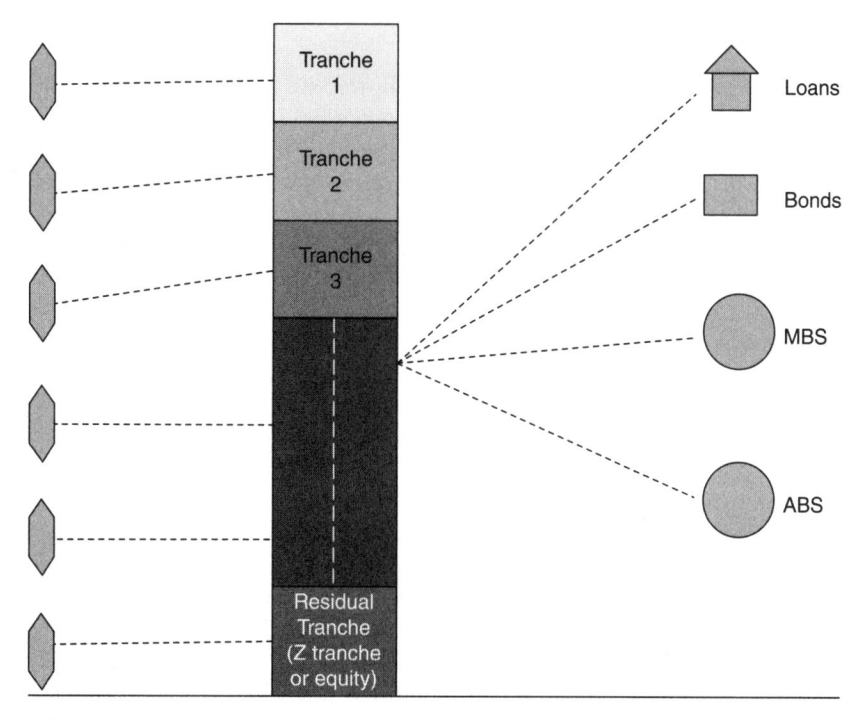

FIGURE 9.2 Structured Security

by the components of the column in the middle. These are then sold to investors having different preferences for the maturities or risk tolerances for the cash flows, shown on the left. The final tranche—residual or Z tranche—provides the owner with what is left over after all the previous claims have been met. Clearly, it is the riskiest tranche. Underwriters ordinarily will hold some or all of the residual tranche to improve the appeal to investors. By doing so, they can demonstrate to investors that they have "skin in the game" and confidence that the prior tranches will perform well. Typically, investors will receive higher yields on the longer maturity and the more distant priority claims on the cash flows in the pool. The return on the Z tranche will usually be highest, reflecting its higher risk.

CMOs

A *collateralized mortgage obligation* (CMO) is built from pools of MBSs. It typically arrays cash flows by maturity. The first tranche will be a short-term security. The second tranche is a little longer maturity security, and so forth, and later tranches become longer-term securities. As previously noted, a residual or *Z tranche* (also called the equity tranche) captures what is left over and embodies considerably more risk regarding when the investor will be paid. CMOs appeal to investors with very different preferred maturities, but also seeking a little higher yield than available on comparable maturities of many other assets. In so parsing tranches of cash flows from a pool of securities, value is created as investors in the separate tranches are willing to pay more for the sum of the tranches than they are willing to pay for the untransformed pool.

Senior-Subordinated Securities

Other structured securities rely on senior-subordinated tranches. Indeed, these are commonly divided into super-senior, senior, mezzanine, and equity tranches—ranging from the highest- to lowest-priority claim on the cash flows from the underlying securities. They are structured so that the super-senior and senior tranches receive top credit ratings. Of course, the yield will vary by tranche, with the lowest tranches providing the highest yield to reflect their greater risk. These structured products may be created from a hodge-podge of underlying assets in the pool, such as private-label MBSs, corporate bonds, and ordinary business loans. They can create economic value to investors by diversifying risk and by having separate tranches that appeal to investors with vastly different maturity preference and tolerances for risk.

Effects of the Financial Crisis

The structured product market grew very rapidly prior to the financial crisis. To a great extent, these products had highly complex risk properties that were poorly understood—not only by investors but also by the investment banks that designed them and the credit ratings agencies that rated them. Investors in these products and the investment banks putting them together suffered huge losses and secondary market trading in the various tranches came to an abrupt halt. As a result, the market for new issues of structured securities all but dried up. The market for these exotic securities developed at a rapid pace that was imprudent and did not allow for them to be tested under a variety of circumstances. It is slowly coming back, with the new structured products being more carefully designed and built.

SECURITIZATION AND THE INTEGRATION OF CREDIT MARKETS

The securitization process has fostered an integration of credit markets and a closer alignment of interest rates on ordinary loans with those on benchmark securities. In earlier times, interest rates on various consumer and business loans were slow to adjust to movements in market interest rates. It often took some time before a sizable change in market interest rates would start to be reflected in rates on these regular types of loans. With securitization, in contrast, loan originators intending to securitize these loans must pay close attention to market conditions and set the interest rate that they charge on their loans in line with prevailing market conditions. If not, they may not be able to get a price for the loan commensurate with the principal of the loan. For example, if the lender charges an interest rate on the loan that has not increased with a general increase in market interest rates and it seeks to sell the loan in the secondary market to an assembler of a pool, it will be disappointed to discover that no one will be willing to pay a price close to its face value. The lender would experience a loss on that loan.

MONETARY POLICY AND SECURITIZATION

With changes in interest rates being transmitted to loan markets more quickly, monetary policy—working through interest rates—will be able to influence spending decisions more quickly and more pervasively. This increases the effectiveness of monetary policy. In addition, when borrowers throughout the economy are facing loan rates linked to market benchmarks, resources are allocated more efficiently. The available amount of credit will be allocated to borrowers who value it most highly, which implies that the things getting financed will be those making the largest contribution to overall output and well-being.

SUMMARY

1. Securitization involves the transformation of ordinary loans originated by commercial banks and other lenders into securities that resemble bonds. This enables the function of loan origination as well as loan servicing to be separated (unbundled) from funding. Commonly, the acquirers (funders) of securitized assets are large institutional investors, such as insurance companies and pension funds. They are well positioned to hold investments that fund these loans.
2. The servicing of the loans placed in pools—which requires keeping numerous and very detailed records—is typically sold to a specialized servicer, another form of unbundling. Information technology has greatly facilitated such unbundling and the pooling of many loans into a security.
3. The securitization process faces some important obstacles stemming from asymmetric information and adverse selection. To overcome these, investors usually insist that originators use objective minimum underwriting standards and that originators retain some ownership in the loans they originate. They also resist investing in pools that have not been rated by credit rating agencies.
4. Securitization began with mortgage pools—pass-throughs—involving Ginnie Mae and later GSEs, primarily Fannie Mae and Freddie Mac. Investors acquired participations in these MBS pools—getting a proportionate share of the cash flows generated by the mortgages in the pool. Adding to the attractiveness to investors, the Ginnie Mae pools had a federal guarantee or federal insurance and the GSE pools had a GSE guarantee.
5. The concept of securitization was extended to consumer loans (receivables), such as pools of auto loans, student loans, and credit card balances. These are known as (consumer) ABSs. To make them attractive to investors, these pools typically build in credit enhancements—such as overcollateralization.
6. CLOs, CMBSs, and CBOs are pools of credit that have been extended to businesses—business loans, commercial real estate loans, and corporate bonds. They fall under the label collateralized debt obligations—CDOs.
7. Structured securities are typically created from various types of loan pools, sometimes with corporate bonds thrown in, too. The cash flows from the underlying assets are assigned to tranches. These can be based on the maturity of payments—resulting in tranches of different maturities—or the priority of the investor's claim—resulting in tranches with different credit risk. Sorting cash flows in these ways can broaden the base of investors and better customize securities to the tastes of investors.
8. Securitization has led to a closer integration of loan markets into national securities markets, resulting in more efficiency in the allocation of credit resources.
9. It has also led to a prompter transmission of monetary policy actions into borrowing costs for a wide array of borrowers, and thereby into their spending decisions.

QUESTIONS

1. What is meant by unbundling? How might this lead to more economic efficiency and less risk in the financial system? How do economies of scale fit in?
2. Why might investors be cautious about buying participations in a securitized pool of loans? How is this related to adverse selection? How might they be assured about the underlying quality of assets in the pool?
3. What is meant by *regulatory arbitrage?* How are banks able to lower regulatory capital through securitization? How have the regulators responded?
4. What are the differences between Ginnie Mae MBSs and those of Fannie Mae and Freddie Mac? Which might be regarded as having the lowest credit risk for investors?
5. How do pools of nonconforming mortgages differ from those of Ginnie, Fannie, and Freddie? In forming these pools, what do issuers have to do to make them attractive to investors?
6. Compare consumer ABSs with Fannie and Freddie MBSs. Which have longer maturities? More credit risk to the investor? What about nonconforming MBSs?
7. Describe the various types of securitizations involving business credits. How do their risk properties compare with consumer ABSs?
8. What are regarded to be structured securities? How do these utilize pass-throughs? What distinguishes the different tranches in a structured security? What is meant by the Z or equity tranche? How does a CMO differ from other structured securities?
9. How can structured securities create value?
10. How has securitization been affected by the financial crisis? How do you think it has affected the role of Fannie Mae and Freddie Mac in the mortgage market—their market share?
11. Why did structured securities do so poorly during the financial crisis? Would you regard their risk attributes as having been transparent or opaque?
12. Explain how securitization helps to integrate individual loan markets into national money and capital markets? Economic efficiency?
13. How does this improve the effectiveness of monetary policy?
14. How do you think the securitization process might evolve in coming years? Do you think that each of the component sectors will develop at the same pace? Why or why not?

NOTES

1. To qualify as an outright sale and to be able to not count the loan as an asset, there had to be no legal recourse back to the bank in the event of default.
2. Fannie Mae was originally named the Federal National Mortgage Association, or FNMA, and nicknamed Fannie Mae. Freddie Mac was originally named the Federal Home Loan Mortgage Corporation, or FHLMC, which somehow took on the nickname of Freddie Mac.
3. The maximum size for conforming mortgages is set by Congress and varies by local markets depending on home values.

CHAPTER 10

The Mortgage Market

WHAT YOU WILL LEARN IN THIS CHAPTER

- The connection between the availability of mortgage finance and home ownership rates.
- The difference between residential and commercial mortgages.
- The massive size of this market.
- Why mortgages tend to have long maturities and are amortized.
- Why home buyers tend to prefer FRMs over ARMs.
- The advantage to the home buyer of qualifying for a conforming (conventional) mortgage.
- The difference between first and second mortgages and how they are used and priced.
- How the prepayment option embedded in most home mortgages affects cash flows from mortgages and how it gets priced into mortgage interest rates.
- Why commercial mortgages have shorter maturities and are priced differently than home mortgages.
- How monetary policy gets transmitted through the mortgage market and onto residential and nonresidential investment.

BACKGROUND

Have you wondered why people tend to own their homes in the United States but rent in many other parts of the world? Might the availability of credit to finance home purchases play a part? Why do homeowners typically make monthly mortgage payments, instead of semiannual or annual payments? Why do mortgage payments cover both interest and principal, whereas bond coupon payments cover only interest? Why would a homeowner want a fixed-rate mortgage when payments are often lower on an adjustable-rate mortgage? Why are there so many mortgage refinancings—"refis"—especially when interest rates drop? How does the mortgage market compare in size with the gargantuan market for Treasury securities? Are there differences between mortgages used for buying homes and those for non-residential income properties? These and other issues are addressed in this chapter.

The United States has one of the highest home ownership rates in the world. The availability of mortgage credit for buying homes has contributed to this high ownership rate. Moreover, mortgages get favorable tax treatment—notably, the deductibility of mortgage interest from income for income tax purposes. To be sure, there are other public policies that also have contributed to the high ownership rate, but those related to housing finance have tended to be the most important.

Mortgages are loans secured by real estate—owner-occupied homes, multifamily income properties, and commercial properties (generating other kinds of income).[1] The mortgage market is the largest credit market in the United States, surpassing even the Treasury market. The biggest component is the residential (owner-occupied) mortgage segment. Perhaps this is not completely surprising, considering that the most valuable asset of households is residential real estate—homes. The mortgage market—involving both residential and nonresidential properties—was dealt a major setback by the financial crisis. It has been recovering, but slowly.

Mortgages are typically longer-maturity instruments, reflecting the long life of the asset being financed. The most common home mortgage has an original maturity of 30 years. Commercial mortgages tend to have shorter maturities. Mortgages can have fixed interest rates (fixed-rate mortgages, or FRMs)—the interest rate is fixed for the life of the mortgage. Or they can have adjustable rates (adjustable-rate mortgages, or ARMs)—adjusting on the basis of movements in a reference interest rate, such as the T-bill rate, the commercial bank prime rate, or the London Interbank Offered Rate (LIBOR). Mortgages, especially home mortgages, commonly are amortized—the payments made by the borrower include both interest and principal. Mortgages can differ with regard to the claim that the holder has on the property in the event of default—senior (first mortgages) or junior (second or lower mortgages). Home mortgages typically carry an option for the borrower to prepay any or all of the remaining balance at the discretion of the borrower, while commercial mortgages typically have penalties for prepayment. Both home and commercial mortgages have become securitized, as we discussed in the previous chapter. Two-thirds of home mortgages have been placed in mortgage pools or are held in the portfolios of the GSEs.[2] In contrast, only about a fifth of commercial mortgages have been securitized. Investors in mortgage securitizations tend to be large institutional investors, such as pension funds, and many come from foreign lands.

In this chapter, we will first discuss the market for home mortgages. This will involve a discussion of the key features of home mortgages and the economic rationale for each of them. We will next discuss the market for commercial mortgages.

HOME MORTGAGES

Home mortgages in the aggregate are substantially larger in value than commercial mortgages—more than three times larger. The total amount of home mortgages is roughly 60 percent of the value of the housing stock.[3] Expressed differently, homeowners' equity in their homes is around 40 percent of the value of their homes.

Homeowner Choices

In arranging a mortgage, the home buyer will need to make several choices.

Maturity First is the maturity of the loan. Maturities can vary from a short period, such as a year, to 30 years. The most commonly selected maturity, as previously noted, is 30 years, with 15 years also being popular. Because home mortgages typically are amortized, the longer the maturity, the smaller will be the size of the regular—monthly—payment.

FRM or ARM Second, the home buyer will need to choose between a fixed or variable interest rate—FRM or ARM. The FRM has the same interest rate for the life of the loan, but ARMs come in many different forms. They differ with regard to the benchmark interest rate that they are linked to and to the spread over that benchmark. Common benchmarks have been a T-bill rate (commonly a one-year rate), LIBOR, or the commercial bank prime rate.[4] Spreads can vary a good bit, in part owing to the lender's assessment of the credit risk of the borrower.

Another feature of ARMs is that they can have an initial interest rate—sometimes called a "teaser"—that is different than the rate implied by the benchmark and spread formula. In such cases, the initial rate is typically below the rate implied by the formula. After the initial period, the interest rate on the loan resets in line with the formula. In addition, ARMs can have caps or floors. The cap can take the form of a maximum upward adjustment to the interest rate on the loan in a year or over the life of the loan. The limit on the upward adjustment helps to avoid serious strains on household budgets when (short-term) benchmark rates rise sharply. The floor works in the same way on the downside, and conversely protects the lender from a large drop in interest earnings when benchmark rates plunge.

Because the typical shape of the yield curve is upward sloping, mortgages linked to short-term interest rates (ARMs) will commonly have lower interest costs over their lives than those linked to long-term rates (FRMs). Nonetheless, most households prefer having predictable, fixed payments and wish to avoid the risk that interest payments could end up being much higher on an ARM because short-term rates have gone up more than contemplated at the time the loan was taken out. For these reasons, FRMs have dominated home buyer choice. Homeowners who choose an FRM are still exposed to the risk that the general level of interest rates will drop and stay lower, implying that the homeowner will be stuck with higher interest payments, unless there is an option to refinance. In contrast, homeowners having ARMs will find their mortgage interest payments declining automatically once they enter a reset period.

Somewhere between an FRM and standard ARM is a *hybrid ARM*. Hybrids commonly have fixed interest rates for periods of 5, 7, or 10 years, at which point the mortgage converts to a standard ARM with regular resets based on movements in the benchmark short-term rate.

Conforming or Nonconforming Third, borrowers can seek to qualify for a *conforming* mortgage. A conforming mortgage is one that qualifies for purchase by Freddie Mac and Fannie Mae or to be placed into one of their mortgage pools. To be eligible for conforming status, the borrower needs to have a credit score from major credit scoring firms that exceeds a threshold; the amount of the loan must not exceed a specified portion of the value of the home (loan-to-value, or LTV, usually must not exceed 80 percent); the borrower's mortgage payment is not to exceed a certain percentage of family income; the home must be appraised by a qualified appraiser; and the loan must not exceed a maximum amount. The size of the latter varies by region—according to regional property values—and is adjusted annually based on changes in home prices. As noted in the previous chapter, loans that do not qualify for conforming mortgage status are either labeled jumbos (their size exceeds the conforming ceiling) or Alt-A or subprime (with both, the borrower does not meet the other criteria).

The advantage of qualifying for conforming status is that the mortgage rate is lower to the homeowner. This is because mortgages that qualify can be sold more easily in the secondary market—they have more liquidity—and they can be acquired by Fannie Mae or Freddie Mac or placed in their pools having investor protections. This has been especially important since the financial crisis, as investors have been very reluctant to develop exposure to mortgage investments that are not insured by the Federal Housing Administration (FHA) or guaranteed by Fannie Mae or Freddie Mac.

Home buyers who do not qualify for a conforming mortgage—often because they want a loan in excess of the maximum LTV—can improve their borrowing prospects by purchasing private mortgage insurance (PMI). With such insurance, the private insurer guarantees timely payment of mortgage principal and interest. In essence, the insurer is substituting its promise to pay for that of the homeowner. Such insurance can make a big difference if the insurer has a strong credit standing. However, the financial crisis left some major private insurers in a seriously weakened condition, and the option of PMI has not been utilized as much since.

Points Fourth, the borrower frequently must choose whether to pay *points* to get a lower interest rate. Points can be thought of as prepaid interest on the loan. They effectively reduce the amount of the loan. For example, if the borrower elects to pay one point on a $200,000 loan, that borrower would get $198,000 toward the purchase of the house from the lender at closing ($200,000 less 1 percent of that amount). The interest rate, though, will be applied to the full $200,000 amount. Usually, the interest rate is lowered about one eighth of a percentage point (0.125 percent or 12.5 basis points) for each point on the loan. For the point option to be attractive for the borrower, the borrower will need to expect that he or she will not want to prepay the mortgage for a significant period of time—usually, seven years or more.

First versus Second Mortgages The preceding discussion relates to *first* or *senior mortgages*. A first mortgage gives the lender the senior claim (first lien) on the collateral in the event of default. Beyond the first mortgage are *second* or *junior mortgages*. Holders of second mortgages stand behind those holding first mortgages in a default and get paid after the holders of first mortgages. Second mortgages, clearly, have higher interest rates because of the greater credit risk to the lender and because the secondary market is not as good for junior mortgages and junior mortgages are not as liquid. Second mortgages typically have shorter maturities than first mortgages and can have fixed or adjustable interest rates.

Home Equity Lines A special, and once popular, type of second mortgage is the *home equity line of credit (HELOC)*. Under such an arrangement, the borrower is given a line of credit, much like a credit card line, linked to the amount of equity the buyer has in the home.[5] The borrower can then draw on this line or repay borrowings at will, paying interest on the amount of credit outstanding under the line. A fee may be assessed on the full amount of the line or on the unused portion.

HELOCs became very large prior to the bursting of the housing bubble after 2005. Many lenders were attracted to such lending by a belief that residential real estate prices do not fall and thus they can count on having sufficient collateral for the loans to cover both the senior loan exposure and their exposure. However, lenders have since that time pulled back substantially owing to the large losses that were sustained by defaults on properties that dropped sharply in value. Securitization of secondary mortgages—especially HELOCs—developed some traction prior to the financial crisis and attracted an investor base. However, this market, too, was hit hard by the crisis as the margin of home (collateral) values in excess of first mortgages shrank with the drop in real estate prices.

Interest Rate Specification The interest rate on home loans must, as a legal matter, be quoted on an *annual percentage rate* (APR) basis. This is the true annual yield to maturity that matches actual scheduled payments to the amount of cash the borrower gets at closing. The actual cash received by the borrower will be net of points and any service fees built into the loan. In addition, it allows for compounding. That is, it takes into account that a monthly interest rate carries with it a higher annual rate when monthly interest payments are compounded on an annual basis.

Standard Features of Home Mortgages

There are a couple of standard features of home mortgages that act to lower the cost to the borrower.

Monthly Payments First is the frequency of payments. Payments typically are scheduled to be monthly to coincide with the receipt of income by the homeowner. In this way, the borrower is more likely to be disciplined in allocating a portion of each income payment to cover the mortgage payment. Lenders see less risk of default when mortgage payments tend to match income receipts. Some borrowers choose to lower borrowing costs even more by scheduling mortgage payments to take place semimonthly. This can be attractive if they get paid semimonthly. Matching payment frequency to the timing of income flows on mortgages is similar to the role of serial bonds for muni offerings and sinking funds for corporate offerings, discussed in Chapter 8.

Amortization Closely related to this is a second standard feature, amortization, which, as noted in Chapter 4, involves regular payment of both interest and principal on the loan. The alternative for a household would be a fixed principal on the loan, with a substantial balloon payment at maturity. To be able to meet that payment, the household would either need to have a regular saving program to build assets that would match the loan balance at maturity, would need to expect to come up with assets that would match the loan balance by loan's maturity, perhaps through an inheritance, or would need to refinance. Amortization, instead, can be thought of as a disciplined saving program that pays down the mortgage principal out of income as it accrues over the time of the mortgage.

In the case of standard FRMs, the homeowner makes a constant payment for the life of the mortgage, discharging the last bit of the principal with the final payment. The mix of interest and principal over the life of the mortgage is illustrated in Figure 10.1 for a 30-year mortgage. Scheduled monthly payments in this example are $750. Early in the life of the mortgage, the principal is largest and the preponderance of the regular (monthly) payment is allocated to interest, the top segment of the figure. Only a small amount covers the paying down of principal, the bottom segment. With each payment, the principal balance is paid down—by more than the previous payment. At some point—around month 250 in the diagram—the monthly payment is evenly allocated between principal and interest. Beyond that point, the portion allocated to principal exceeds the amount of interest.

With an ARM, the amount of regular payments allocated to payment of principal usually follows a similar pattern to that shown in Figure 10.1, but the amount going to interest can vary with movements in the benchmark interest rate. This results in the size of monthly payments varying from one year to the next in association with the reset of the interest rate on the mortgage.

Escrow Account A third standard feature of home mortgages is an escrow account for property tax payments and insurance. If the borrower defaults and also fails to pay property taxes, the local government will have a prior claim on the property, ahead of even the first mortgage lender. Escrowing property tax payments assures the lender that it will have the top claim on the property should the borrower fail to keep up with mortgage payments. Similarly, a fire or natural hazard, such as a tornado or windstorm, could lead to a decline in the value of the property to the point at which it would fall short of the balance on the mortgage. In this case, the homeowner might be inclined to walk away, letting the lender take control of the property. Escrowing for insurance provides protection to the lender against such an event. It is for these reasons that lenders insist that home buyers agree to an escrow account to cover tax and insurance payments. Home buyers, in return, are able to get a lower mortgage interest rate to reflect the reduced risk to the lender. It should also be noted that the inclusion of property tax and insurance outlays in the monthly payment will cause monthly payments to change over the life of the mortgage, even under an FRM, because taxes and insurance premiums change from year to year (usually increase).

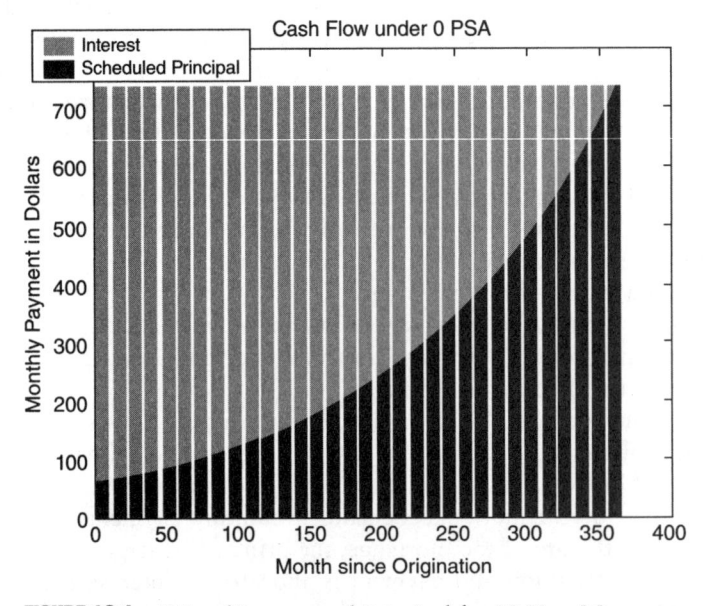

FIGURE 10.1 Mix of Interest and Principal for 30-Year Mortgage

The Prepayment Option   Another standard feature of home mortgages is the *prepayment option*. Home mortgages typically enable the borrower to prepay a portion or the entire remaining principal on the mortgage at will and without penalty.[6] This means that, from the perspective of the holder of the mortgage (lender or investor), cash flows are very uncertain. At any moment, the mortgage could be prepaid—the entire investment may be converted to cash. This feature enables homeowners who choose to move—in many cases for employment opportunities elsewhere—to be able to discharge this obligation and use their liquidated home equity for purchasing another home. For other homeowners, the prepayment option enables them to lower the claim on their income of mortgage payments by refinancing when mortgage interest rates drop. Indeed, this has come to be seen as an important channel of monetary policy: a decline in the general level of interest rates will provide households who refinance mortgages with more spendable funds after mortgage payments to purchase goods and services. This prepayment option on a mortgage is similar to a call option on a corporate or muni bond.

Because of the prepayment option, actual cash flows from mortgages follow a much different pattern from scheduled cash flows. A typical pattern is illustrated in Figure 10.2 for mortgages having the features of the one illustrated in Figure 10.1.

The middle segment represents interest payments and the bottom segment represents principal payments. The top segments of Figure 10.2 show prepayments. Actual cash flows—the sum of the three colored segments—tend to run above scheduled flows over the early years of the mortgage, reaching a peak around year four or so—that is, around month 50. After about 10 years—month 120—actual cash flows drop below scheduled flows because many mortgages have been prepaid and no longer provide monthly payments.

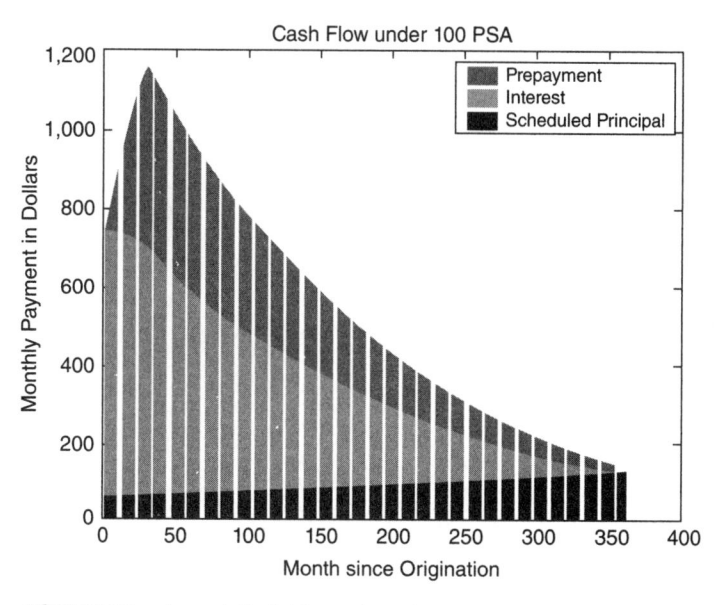

FIGURE 10.2   Actual Cash Flows from Mortgages

Prepayment Risk and Compensation From the perspective of investors, a pattern of this sort could be easily managed if they could be sure that cash flows from their holdings of mortgage assets would follow such a pattern. However, there is a great deal of uncertainty about what pattern actual cash flows will follow. In practice, cash flows will depend importantly on the path of interest rates in the future—rising when interest rates fall and refinancing picks up and falling when interest rates rise and refinancing drops off. Such swings in cash flows that are driven by movements in interest rates are not welcomed by investors because they provide investors with piles of cash that need to be reinvested at the worst possible time—when yields on other investments are also very low. Conversely, when interest rates are high—and yields available to investors on alternative investments are very attractive—prepayments slow to a trickle, and investors have less to reinvest at these higher yields. This pattern has a technical name—*negative convexity*. Advanced modeling methods have been developed for estimating the sensitivity of prepayments to movements in interest rates. These are then linked to measures of interest rate volatility to project the likelihood or risk of mortgage prepayments over the life of mortgages. Such information bearing on the risk of prepayment is taken into account by investors when they make their decision about holding mortgages or mortgage securities in their portfolios.

To be willing to absorb prepayment risk, investors require compensation, which takes the form of a higher interest rate on their mortgage investments. Figure 10.3 illustrates the spread of the rate on a 30-year conforming mortgage over a 10-year Treasury rate. This spread shows the compensation that investors require to hold such conventional mortgages instead of Treasury notes. It illustrates that compensation tends to average a little more than 1.5 percentage points but varies a good bit—between

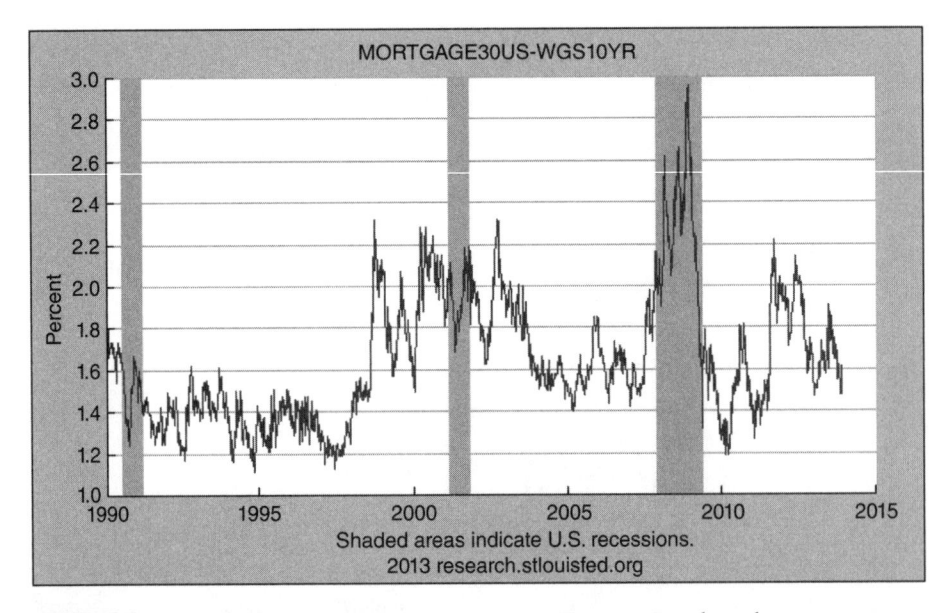

FIGURE 10.3 Spread of 30-Year Mortgage Rate over Treasury Benchmark
Source: Freddie Mac and U.S. Treasury.

1.25 and 3 percentage points. The high occurred during the financial crisis when investors were shunning all types of risk and sought the safety of Treasury securities.[7]

COMMERCIAL MORTGAGES

Commercial mortgages are used to finance a wide variety of real estate transactions other than buying a home. They include lending to real estate developers and buyers of commercial, office, and industrial properties. The borrower typically is a business of one type or another—corporation, partnership, or limited liability company (LLC). The properties being financed and serving as collateral generate cash flow, which provides the wherewithal for servicing the mortgage.

Like home mortgages, commercial mortgages can have either fixed or adjustable interest rates, with fixed rates being most common. Maturities can vary from only a couple years to as long as 30 years. Usually, commercial mortgages carry a balloon payment at around 10 years or earlier. The loan also has partial amortization, so the borrower makes regular (usually monthly) payments that cover both interest and principal. For example, the loan may be amortized over a 30-year period, but the borrower must pay off the balance in the form of a balloon payment at 10 years.[8] In many cases, the borrower will need to refinance the remaining mortgage balance at that point.

In underwriting commercial mortgages, lenders pay close attention to projected cash flow from the property being financed and require that there be a cushion between monthly cash flow and monthly debt service in the event there is an unexpected cash flow shortfall. In addition, lenders require a larger cushion between the appraised value of the property and the amount of the loan than is common for home mortgages—that is, a lower loan-to-value (LTV) ratio. Spreads of interest rates on commercial mortgages over Treasury benchmarks also typically exceed those on conforming residential mortgages. Higher spreads and lower LTVs on commercial properties owe to the absence of anything comparable to government-sponsored enterprise (GSE) pools for commercial mortgages, and the resulting lessened liquidity and greater credit risk on commercial mortgages.

Commercial banks, and to a lesser extent, life insurance companies are the primary lenders in the commercial real estate market. Together, they account for more than 60 percent of total credit for commercial real estate. As noted in an opening section of this chapter, securitization—commercial mortgage-backed securities (CMBSs)—accounts for another fifth of commercial real estate financing. This market, too, was dealt a big setback by the financial crisis and the ensuing recession. A drop-off in the demand for commercial space led to a glut in properties and downward pressures on rents and the prices of commercial properties. The recovery of commercial real estate lending, including securitization, has since been very slow.

THE MORTGAGE MARKET AND MONETARY POLICY

Both the residential and commercial mortgage markets play a key role in the transmission of monetary policy. Investment in residential and commercial structures typically accounts for around one-half of private fixed investment—nearly one-tenth of gross domestic product (GDP)—and is among the most sensitive components of aggregate spending to changes in interest rates. Changes in Treasury benchmark interest rates get passed through promptly to mortgage interest rates, for reasons noted in the previous chapter that are related to the integration of credit markets through securitization. As a consequence, construction spending decisions begin to be influenced quickly after a monetary policy action that gets transmitted to benchmark interest rates.

Moreover, as mentioned elsewhere in this chapter, reductions in mortgage interest rates encourage many homeowners to exercise their option to refinance at the lower rates. This frees up some income that can be spent on goods and services instead of mortgage interest, adding a lift to aggregate demand.

SUMMARY

1. Mortgages are loans that are secured by real estate, the property that is financed by the loan. The mortgage market is the largest credit market in the United States, with the home mortgage component considerably larger than the commercial real estate component.
2. The most common maturity of home mortgages is 30 years. The preponderance of home mortgages has fixed interest rates (FRMs) for the life of the mortgage. Homeowners prefer FRMs to ARMs, despite the latter's having lower expected interest costs over the life of the mortgage.
3. Being able to qualify for a conforming (conventional) mortgage is attractive for home buyers. Rates are lower on such loans owing to their eligibility for GSE pools and for GSE purchase. Ceilings exist on LTV ratios of conforming loans; mortgage payments must be below a specified fraction of household income; and borrowers must have solid credit scores.
4. The interest rate the borrower is able to get often depends on whether the borrower pays points up front—prepaid interest deducted from the amount of the mortgage. Points lower the stated interest rate on the loan.
5. Most home mortgages are first mortgages, meaning that this lender has the prior claim (first lien) on the collateral in the event of default. Other (junior or second) mortgages carry higher interest rates because the holders have a subordinate claim on the property and receive what is left over.
6. Standard features of home mortgages are monthly payments, amortization, and escrow accounts for property taxes and hazard insurance. Each serves to lower the interest cost to the borrower.
7. A notable feature of home mortgages is the prepayment option, enabling the homeowner to pay a portion or all of the remaining mortgage principal at will. This introduces prepayment risk for the investor (lender)—enlarged by negative convexity—and requires that compensation be paid to the investor in the form of a higher interest rate.
8. Commercial mortgages finance a wide variety of income properties of businesses. They tend to have shorter maturities and smaller LTVs, and carry higher interest rates than home mortgages. Like home mortgages, the bulk of commercial mortgages have fixed interest rates.

The Mortgage Market

9. Securitized commercial mortgages—CMBSs—are on a smaller scale than for home mortgages. Major commercial mortgage lenders are commercial banks and life insurance companies.
10. The mortgage market plays an important role in the transmission of monetary policy to aggregate demand.

QUESTIONS

1. Why do you suppose that lending for real estate purchases commonly takes the form of mortgages instead of unsecured loans? What are the advantages to the borrower?
2. Go to: www.fhfa.gov. What is the interest rate on a 30-year fixed-rate mortgage? What is the rate on a 15-year mortgage? Why is the first above the second? (Hint: Recall term structure patterns discussed in Chapter 4.)
3. Why would you expect the cumulative total of interest payments under an ARM to be less than those under an FRM of the same maturity? Compare the risks to the borrower.
4. Explain why and how the following features affect mortgage borrowing interest rates: monthly payments, amortization, an escrow account for taxes and hazard insurance.
5. Give reasons why interest rates on conforming mortgages are lower than those on other home mortgages?
6. Explain why the market for securitized HELOCs was battered more by the financial crisis (and bursting of the real estate bubble) than the market for GSE MBSs.
7. Describe how the pattern of actual cash flows from mortgages with prepayment options differs from scheduled payments. How would a drop in benchmark interest rates early in the life of such a cohort of mortgages affect this pattern? A rise in benchmark rates?
8. What is negative convexity? How does it affect interest rates on mortgages (with prepayment options)?
9. In the corporate bond market, what is the counterpart to the prepayment option on mortgages? Does it have the same impact on borrowing costs?
10. Apart from the collateral being financed, what are some of the other differences between commercial and residential mortgages?
11. Why do you think securitization of commercial mortgages is less developed than for home mortgages?
12. Describe the ways in which monetary policy works through the mortgage market—both residential and commercial.

NOTES

1. Mortgages are commonly used to finance the purchase of residential or commercial real estate. However, in some cases, the property owner may use a mortgage loan to finance the purchase of something else. For example, a homeowner may take out a mortgage to finance a vacation or a new car. Often, this will take the

form of a second mortgage (discussed later). The interest rate and other terms on such a secured mortgage loan will generally be more favorable than on an unsecured loan. Also, mortgage interest is tax deductible.
2. Prior to the financial crisis, the bulk of mortgages held by GSEs or placed in GSE pools took the form of the latter, GSE pools (MBSs). However, after the U.S government became the conservator of Fannie Mae and Freddie Mac in 2008, those proportions changed and the bulk is now held in the portfolios of the GSEs. In this way, the prepayment risk on the mortgages, discussed later in this chapter, is absorbed by the GSEs and they receive the compensation for such risk.
3. The ratio of mortgages to home values is up from around 40 percent before the bursting of the housing bubble and the onset of the financial crisis. This owes to the large drop in home values (the collateral for the mortgages), which has been unprecedented for the United States.
4. Because of the spike in LIBOR during the financial crisis, this benchmark has lost much of its luster. This is an interest rate on interbank loans, and during the financial crisis, lending banks became concerned about the health of their borrowing counterparties. As they pulled back from such lending, LIBOR rose sharply. Homeowners with loans linked to LIBOR found their mortgage rate rise at a time when Treasury yields were plunging (owing to the weakening economy and investors fleeing to the safety of Treasury securities).
5. Related to a HELOC is a home equity loan. Under a home equity loan, the borrower receives a fixed-sized loan and repays according to a fixed schedule.
6. Homeowners can opt for mortgages that do not allow prepayments, except at a penalty. Commonly, penalties apply for the first several years of the mortgage and can be waived if the borrower sells the property. Such mortgages carry lower interest rates because they lack the option.
7. Much of the compensation shown in Figure 10.3 reflects compensation for prepayment risk. However, some of it also owes to the lesser liquidity of mortgages. Moreover, some has been due to perceptions of credit risk. Prior to the federal takeover of the GSEs in 2008, investors could not be completely sure that the federal government would step in to prevent GSE losses from being passed along to holders of GSE debt or MBSs.
8. From Figure 10.1, we can see that at month 120 about 80 percent of the monthly payment covers interest, implying that only about 20 percent of the principal has been paid down at 10 years.

CHAPTER 11

The Equity Market

WHAT YOU WILL LEARN IN THIS CHAPTER

- The ways in which firms raise funds from shareholders—new issuance or retained earnings.
- The features of preferred shares and some reasons why they are issued.
- The ways in which shares are issued in the primary and traded in the secondary markets.
- How a present value model is adapted to determine the price of a share of stock.
- How price depends on the share's dividends and a discount factor that embodies a risk (or equity) premium over and above a risk-free interest rate to account for the greater risk of owning stock, and how higher discount rates lower the price of a share, while higher dividends raise the price.
- How the model can be adapted to account for prospective growth in dividends; and how more growth in expected dividends raises the price of a share.
- How the model can be transformed into one that relates the price of a share to earnings instead of dividends; how this form of the model highlights the importance of a firm's dividend (or retained earnings) policy.
- How to use this version of the model to determine the price-earnings (P-E) ratio of a firm's stock and why these vary across firms at any one time.
- How to view factors affecting the stock market as a whole and why the stock market is so sensitive to news on the economy
- How the stock market acts as a key channel of monetary policy.
- The key features of indexes of share prices, such as the Dow Jones and S&P.

BACKGROUND

Are you tempted to stop and look at the TV screen each time there is an update on the stock market? Have you tried to sort out what kinds of things drive movements in stock prices, such as earnings reports and statements by Fed officials, and why? Why do stocks over longer periods of time have significantly higher returns than Treasury bonds? Have you wondered why stock prices are so volatile? Why do companies coming to the stock market for the first time attract so much public attention? How important is the stock market for financing the activities of corporate America? These issues and others will be explored in this chapter.

The most closely watched market in the United States is the equity market. Many follow stock prices throughout the day. News reports on radio and TV routinely update their audiences on the stock market. This may not be surprising, given that, next to homes, equities are the largest asset in household portfolios. Moreover, this fascination with the stock market is not confined to the United States. In Hong Kong, for example, elevators in commercial buildings typically have tickers showing stock prices on a real-time basis.

EQUITIES AS A SOURCE OF CORPORATE FINANCE

In view of all the attention that is paid to the stock market, businesses do not raise significant amounts of funds through new stock offerings. Indeed, new issuance of equities is paltry and is greatly exceeded by share retirements—by corporations making outright purchases of their own shares or through corporate acquisitions of other firms and retiring their shares. In other words, net equity issuance is negative.

In effect, one can think of firms raising new funds from their existing shareholders through retained earnings. As owners of the firm, the shareholders are entitled to all the earnings of the firm. In practice, they receive only a portion. In many cases, they receive none. One can view this as an implicit contract between owners and managers under which owners agree to receive only a portion of their earnings as dividends. Managers, in turn, agree to use the retained funds to make internal investments in plants, equipment, and software in the firm having returns higher than what the owner could receive by investing the retained earnings elsewhere in the market. Looked at differently, owners could receive all the firm's earnings as dividends and then use those funds to make other financial investments. The managers might undertake the same investments in the firm, but would need to raise more of the funds externally in the credit market and likely at more costly terms. If internal returns on these investments exceed those available in the market, the shareholder will be better off by leaving some earnings in the firm. The returns from such policies will be in the form of higher share prices, because these actions raise future earnings and the potential for future dividends.[1]

PREFERRED VERSUS COMMON SHARES

Equity holders stand at the bottom of the food chain as claimants on the earnings and assets of a corporation. They get paid last. If the firm does poorly, they may get nothing. However, if the firm does well, they stand to receive huge returns.

In practice, equity holdings take two forms—*preferred* and *common shares*. Preferred shareholders stand ahead of common shareholders, but usually are not given voting rights. Typically, owners of preferred shares are paid a regular dividend that is specified as a percent of the par value of the shares, usually the price paid per share by the investor when the shares were first issued.[2] In this respect, preferred shares are similar to corporate bonds. Also like corporate bonds, preferred shares commonly are rated by the credit rating agencies. Indeed, preferred shares can be viewed as a hybrid between debt and common equity.

Types of Preferred

There are different types of preferred stock. Among them is *prior preferred,* which, as its name suggests, provides owners with the highest claim of preferred shareholders. *Convertible preferred,* as its name implies, can be converted into common stock at terms specified in the indenture.

Preferred shares occasionally are used for specific purposes, including by the federal government. During the financial crisis, the federal government launched a program—the Troubled Asset Relief Program (TARP)—under which it injected capital into large commercial banks and investment banks to raise the margin of protection against insolvency and to limit the need of these institutions to cut back on lending to their customers. These investments took the form of prior preferred shares, which placed taxpayers ahead of common shareholders. The FDIC, when it injects funds into a commercial bank as the bank approaches or becomes insolvent, acquires preferred shares for the same reasons.[3] In the private arena, venture capital and private equity firms typically acquire preferred equity positions in the firms that they become involved with, as we will discuss more fully in Chapter 19.

PRIMARY AND SECONDARY MARKETS

As noted in Chapter 2, new shares are placed in the primary market by investment banks acting as underwriters. Those offered by firms with no shares outstanding are referred to as *initial public offerings (IPOs).*[4] Those offered by firms with shares outstanding are referred to as *seasoned offerings.*

The pricing of IPOs has gotten a lot of attention. Typically, the underwriter underprices them, and their share price rises in the secondary market, often dramatically, immediately after the offering is sold to subscribers. Looked at differently, there is an intended excess demand for the shares at the price set by the underwriter (with concurrence from the issuer), and nonprice methods of rationing must be utilized to allocate shares to subscribers. Some argue that this underpricing causes issuers to get less funds than they could have if prices had been set more in line with market fundamentals. Also, it allows the underwriter to play favorites with who gets the shares. Others argue that, with uncertainty about the market value of the shares, it is better to err on the side of underpricing than overpricing the IPO; if the offering is overpriced, the subsequent drop in price may lead investors to conclude that the company is a dog and should be avoided in the future. Moreover, the media attention given to underpriced shares as their price soars is thought to stimulate interest on the part of potential investors in the firm, and perhaps to draw more customer interest (essentially, to improve its marketing efforts).

Turning to the secondary market, trading in the secondary market takes place on a couple of platforms, as discussed in Chapter 2. These include the specialist system (the traditional platform of the New York Stock Exchange [NYSE] Euronext), the over-the-counter (OTC) system (used by Nasdaq), and electronic communications networks (ECNs). Because ECNs have many attractive features—such as around-the-clock availability, good execution, and low transaction costs—their market share has been increasing steadily.

VALUATION OF INDIVIDUAL SHARES

Basic Model

The valuation model that we developed in Chapter 4 (Equation (4-1)) can serve as a starting point for valuing a share of common stock. The cash flows that the investor receives are dividends. They are received for an indefinite period, the uncertain life of the firm. This can be illustrated as follows:

$$P = \sum_{j=1}^{n} \frac{D_j}{(1+k)^j} \qquad (11\text{-}1)$$

In this equation, P represents the price of a share of stock, D_j represents the dividend expected in period j, and k represents the discount factor applied to the expected dividend stream from the share. It is made up by a risk-free interest rate (Treasury benchmark) component and a risk premium component. The risk premium reflects the compensation that investors require to hold a share of this company's stock over and above the yield they can get on a benchmark Treasury security—sometimes this difference is called the *equity premium*.

If dividends are expected to be constant and to be paid for an extremely long (in the limit, infinite) period, we can use the expression for a consol (Equation (4-3)′) to derive the following expression for the price of a share:

$$P = \frac{D}{k} \qquad (11\text{-}2)$$

For example, if the stock is expected to pay a dividend of $1 per year into perpetuity, the yield on a benchmark Treasury security is 4 percent, and compensation for holding this risky security is 5 percent, the price of a share would be

$$P = \frac{1}{0.04 + 0.05} = \frac{1}{0.09} = 11.11.$$

The price of the share would be $11.11. A higher benchmark yield or larger equity premium would result in a lower price for the share; in other words, in these circumstances, the share price would need to decline to make investors willing to hold this share having the same stream of dividends of $1 per year.

Dividend Growth

In practice, dividends can be expected to grow over time. Should dividends grow at an annual rate of g, Equation (11-1) can be used as follows: (11-3)

$$P = \sum_{j=1}^{\infty} \frac{D_0(1+g)^j}{(1+k)^j} \qquad (11\text{-}3)$$

This collapses to the following, using the same procedures used to derive Equation (4-3)′ in Chapter 4

$$P = \frac{D_0(1+g)}{k-g} = \frac{D_1}{k-g} \qquad (11\text{-}3)′$$

In this expression, D_0 is the current dividend, and D_1 is the dividend expected in year one, the year ahead.[5]

Let us check out Equation (11-3)' to determine if the expression makes sense. First, higher dividends result in a higher share price. Indeed, the price will rise by a multiple of the dividend increase—the multiple being the reciprocal of $k - g$. Because the term $k - g$ will be a number less than 1, its reciprocal will be a number greater than one. Second, a higher discount factor, k, results in a lower price. With a higher discount factor, the investor will not pay as much to get the same flow of dividends. This works in the same way as with bonds. Third, faster dividend growth, g, implies a higher share price. Algebraically, the term g appears in the denominator and is preceded by a minus sign. This means that as g gets bigger, the denominator gets smaller, causing the price to rise. Note that k must be greater than g or the expression will have no economic meaning. Thus, we can conclude that the terms in the model make sense.

A numerical example may help. Drawing on the values above—a dividend of $1, a benchmark rate of 4 percent, and an equity premium of 5 percent—we also need a value for the growth rate of dividends. Suppose that dividends are projected to grow at a 3 percent annual rate. In this case,

$$P = \frac{1}{0.09 - 0.03} = \frac{1}{0.06} = 16.67$$

In other words, the price of the share would be $16.67. Expected dividend growth of 3 percent per year results, in this example, in a 50 percent increase in the share's price, from $11.11 to $16.67. Not bad!

PRICE-EARNINGS

The above model expresses the price of a share of common stock in terms of the expected path of dividends. Analysts tend to favor price-earnings ratios, or so-called multiples, in assessing the value of a company's stock. The above relationships can be transformed into a price-earnings (P-E) ratio. To do so requires that we have an expression for the relationship between dividends and earnings. This is shown below:

$$D_1 = E_1 \times \Theta \tag{11-4}$$

In this expression, E_1 represents earnings in period 1, and Θ is the fraction of earnings that is paid out as dividends—the so-called dividend-payout ratio.

Next, we need to relate the growth rate of earnings to the rate of return on equity, ρ. This is shown as

$$g = (1 - \Theta) \times \rho \tag{11-5}$$

This equation specifies that the rate of growth of earnings will equal the share of earnings that is retained by the firm and invested internally—$(1 - \Theta)$—multiplied by the rate of return on those retained earnings, ρ. Either a higher retention rate of earnings for internal investment (smaller Θ) or a higher rate of return on internal investment of retained earnings (higher ρ) will increase the growth rate, g.

Inserting Equations (11-4) and (11-5) into Equation (11-3)′ produces the following:

$$\frac{P}{E_1} = \frac{\Theta}{k - \rho(1 - \Theta)} \qquad (11\text{-}6)$$

In this expression, the discount factor, k, has the expected impact on the P-E. A higher discount factor will lower the price of a share relative to earnings. In contrast, a higher rate of return on internal investment, ρ, raises the price of a share relative to earnings. To understand why this is so, keep in mind that a higher return on retained earnings invested in the firm will result in faster growth of earnings—and dividends—in the future. In effect, the higher earnings in the future are being built into the price of a share today and raising the share's price relative to current (or more appropriately, next period's) earnings.

A little more complicated is the impact of an increase in the dividend-payout rate, Θ. This term appears both in the numerator and the denominator of Equation (11-6). A higher Θ increases the size of the numerator and reduces the $\rho(1 - \Theta)$ term in the denominator. The former results in a higher P-E. But since $\rho(1 - \Theta)$ in the denominator is preceded by a minus sign, a higher Θ means that the denominator is larger—leading to a smaller P-E. The net result depends on which impact is largest, the numerator effect or the denominator effect. This depends on whether ρ is larger or smaller than k. If ρ is larger—that is, the return on internal investments exceeds the required return of shareholders—then retaining more earnings (a smaller Θ) will boost the company's P-E. In contrast, if k exceeds ρ, then shareholders, in essence, place a higher value on earnings paid out as dividends than retained for more earnings in the future. In this case, a higher dividend payout will raise the company's P-E. The bottom line is that managers of the firm need to carefully weigh the return on internal investments against the returns that their shareholders can get elsewhere in the market, related to k.

Some Implications

The preceding model has some interesting implications. Before exploring these, we can convert the expression for the P-E ratio, Equation (11-6), into a share price valuation relationship simply by multiplying both sides of this equation by E_1.

$$P = \frac{E_1 \Theta}{k - \rho(1 - \Theta)} \qquad (11\text{-}7)$$

First, when firms do not have attractive internal investment opportunities, ρ is small. The model implies that in these cases managers should be paying out earnings as dividends instead of retaining them, as this will raise the price of shares and shareholder wealth. Often, when managers are continuing to invest earnings in internal projects with low returns, shareholders will seek to redirect managers away from those investments and toward larger dividend payouts or, if that does not work, they will seek to remove the managers. Also, firms pursuing such ill-advised strategies frequently become targets for takeovers.

In other cases, managers realize that they do not have worthwhile internal investment opportunities and they use the retained earnings to build up holdings of cash. In some cases, managers, perhaps in response to pressures from shareholders, will raise the dividend payout or pay a one-off special dividend to shareholders to return this cash to shareholders. If they do not, then the firm likely will become a takeover target for others eyeing the cash (and having higher ρs).

Second, the model for P-Es can be useful when comparing P-E ratios for different firms. The model says that: if investors have the same required return for each firm (k); prospective growth rates, g, are the same (that is, rates of return on internal investments (ρ) and dividend-payout ratios (Θ) are the same for each firm); then P-Es will be the same.[6] In practice, P-Es can vary considerably, even in the same sector of the economy. For example, the P-E for Dollar General, a low-end retailing firm, was 17.0 at the same time that the P-E for Walmart was 12.6. This could imply that investors perceive there to be more risk in holding Wal-Mart shares—the k for Walmart is higher—or that prospective earnings (dividends) growth—$(1 - \Theta)\rho$—is better for Dollar General. Similarly, Hewlett-Packard (HP) had a P-E of 6.4 at the same time that Apple had a P-E of 10.6. Again, this difference can reflect a greater risk premium for HP, better earnings prospects for Apple, or both.

Because risk premiums can vary across firms, it is useful to break down the risk premium for firm j, k_j, as follows:

$$k_j = i_T + \phi_M + \phi_j \qquad (11\text{-}8)$$

In this expression, i_T represents the yield on the benchmark (risk-free) security, ϕ_M represents the risk premium that investors require to hold a basket of stocks representing the market, and ϕ_j represents the additional risk premium that investors require to hold shares in company j.[7] This latter term, ϕ_j, will be related to the share's beta as discussed in Chapter 6. The shares of all firms will have in common the same i_T and ϕ_M at any point in time. They differ with regard to specific or idiosyncratic risk, their respective ϕ_j terms.

EXTENDING THESE PRINCIPLES TO THE STOCK MARKET

We can use the model developed above to look at the valuation of the overall stock market. Combining Equations (11-7) and (11-8) yields the following:

$$P_M = \frac{E_1 \Theta}{i_T + \phi_M - \rho(1 - \Theta)} \qquad (11\text{-}9)$$

In this equation, P_M represents the valuation of the entire market, E_1 is aggregate corporate earnings, Θ is the economy-wide dividend pay-out ratio, ϕ_M is the risk premium (equity premium) required to compensate investors for holding the market, and ρ is the rate of return on new investments across the economy.[8] Instead of P_M representing the entire dollar value of shares, it can instead be used to represent an index of the price of shares, to be discussed in the next section.

The model shown in Equation (11-9) is useful for understanding the forces that act on the stock market. Basically, this equation tells us that the level of the stock market will be determined by the level of earnings, the level of the (real) benchmark interest rate, the equity premium, and expected earnings growth.

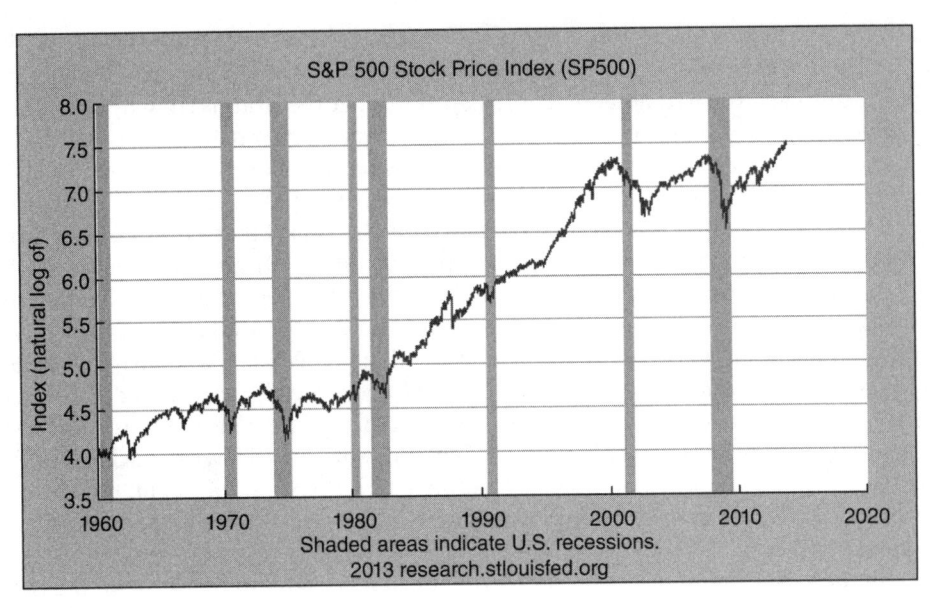

FIGURE 11.1 S&P 500 Stock Prices
Source: Standard & Poor's.

It implies that the market will be very forward looking. Figure 11.1 illustrates the Standard & Poor's (S&P) 500 index, to be discussed in the next section, over a fairly lengthy period.[9] There are a couple of things to observe about this index. First, stock prices have risen markedly over time. While some of this owes to the general rise in the price level over this period, most of the increase reflects growth in earnings (and dividends). Second, stock prices have a very distinct cyclical behavior. They drop in recessions—the shaded areas—and recover in expansions (actually, even before the expansions begin, owing to forward-looking behavior). Third, stock prices are highly volatile on a short-term basis. Whether this volatility can be fully explained by the fundamentals—the terms appearing in Equation (11-9)—has been the subject of ongoing research and considerable debate among financial economists.

One factor affecting share prices worth noting is the risk premium that investors require to hold stocks, ϕ_M—the equity premium. The equity premium can vary considerably. Over longer periods, it has varied between a level of 7 percent or higher at the upper end and only 1 percent at the lower end.[10] Over shorter periods, it can fluctuate markedly in view of changing perceptions of risk. There are times when the overall economic and financial environment has become extremely uncertain and the equity premium has increased sharply, driving down share prices.[11] A good example was during the financial crisis and Great Recession of 2008 and 2009, the last downturn shown in the chart. The entire landscape became exceptionally uncertain and risky, and investors sought to rid themselves of all types of risky assets, including stocks. This was a period characterized by an extreme flight to safety. As the outlook came to be seen as less threatening, the risk premium began to unwind.

The Equity Market **175**

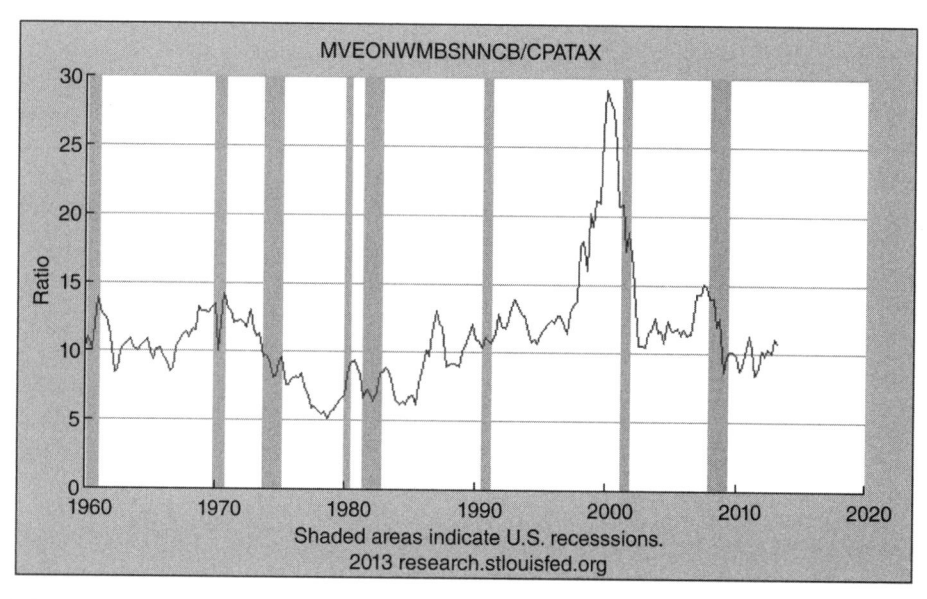

FIGURE 11.2 Aggregate P-E Ratio
Source: Federal Reserve Board, Flow of Funds Accounts.

These influences are also evident in a measure of the aggregate P-E ratio, shown in Figure 11.2. Periods of high P-Es are periods of relatively low equity premiums and vice versa. Note how high prices got in relation to earnings in the late 1990s during the so-called tech bubble. To some extent, investors had become very optimistic about the prospect for earnings growth during this period (the g term), but much of the high P-E owed to a sharp drop in the equity premium (φ_M). That premium rose sharply as prices plunged in 2000. The rise in the equity premium during the Great Recession can be seen in the decline in the P-E ratio to a very low level.

A proxy for forces that likely move with the equity premium is shown in Figure 11.3. The chart shows a market measure of the prospective volatility of the S&P 500 over the coming 30 days, the so-called VIX Index. It is derived from premiums on options on the S&P 500, which vary directly with investor perceptions of prospective volatility. As can be seen, perceived risk spiked during the Great Recession, which, along with concerns about earnings and prospects for growth in earnings, drove share prices down. The subsequent jumps in volatility in 2010 and 2011 reflected concerns about the European sovereign debt crisis, and illustrates that events abroad can raise uncertainty in the United States and place downward pressure on the U.S. stock market.

Our model can be used to illustrate how news about the economy and monetary policy can have a significant effect on the stock market. Overall profits are very sensitive to the economy. They rise sharply in economic expansions and fall in contractions. Thus, when, say, an encouragingly strong jobs report is released, stock prices typically will rally. Conversely, stock prices drop on bad news on the economy.

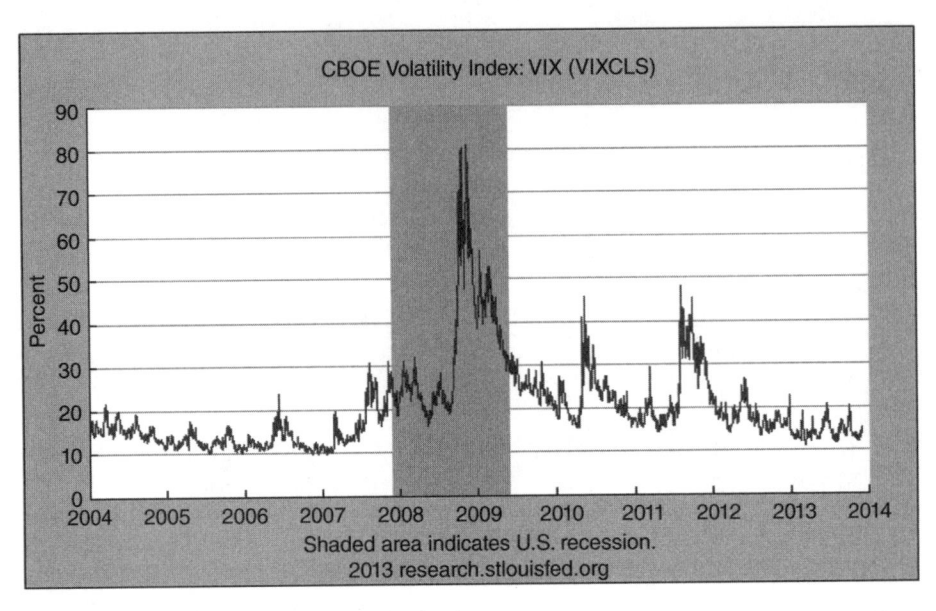

FIGURE 11.3 Prospective Stock Price Volatility
Source: Chicago Board Options Exchange (VIX).

ROLE OF THE EQUITY MARKET IN DISCIPLINING MANAGEMENT

As noted in Chapter 1, financial markets apply discipline on corporate management to pursue the interests of shareholders by taking actions that maximize the value of shares. Based on the discussion in this chapter, this will be achieved when managers seek to maximize the present value of current and expected dividends or, alternatively, earnings per share. Clearly, when managers take actions that are not in keeping with the interests of shareholders, share values suffer. Beyond equity values, the value of marketable debt—notably, the price of traded bonds—will be adversely affected, too, because actions that hurt the corporation's bottom line will also jeopardize its ability to service its debt. But, it is the shareholders who are affected most when the firm is not performing up to its potential.

It is worth noting that a certain fundamental tension exists between managers and shareholders. Managers will want more compensation than required for top corporate performance and they may not be diligent in pursuing corporate goals that would benefit shareholders. Moreover, when there are a large number of shareholders, it often is difficult to ensure that managers are routinely pursuing shareholder interests. Indeed, when ownership is highly diffuse, the benefits to be reaped by any single shareholder from taking measures to improve corporate performance will be small for that shareholder in relation to the total benefits. In these circumstances, there is said to be a *free-rider* problem—most of the benefits from monitoring and disciplining management accrue to other shareholders. Absent one or more shareholders with substantial ownership who can gain a large portion of the benefits from disciplining management, subpar performance could persist for some time. Of course, it is the responsibility of the corporation's board to represent shareholder interests, but the board may be more inclined to side with management in these situations of highly diffuse ownership and lax monitoring of performance.

Nevertheless, there are several ways in which underperforming corporate performance and accompanying low share prices can trigger corrective action. First, slumping share prices can serve as a wake-up call for managers, warning them that something has gone awry. Managers may respond by initiating measures to get the corporation back on track, if, for no other reason than to avoid unpleasant calls from irritated corporate directors and shareholders, and possibly losing some year-end bonus payments. Second, should managers ignore the warnings and make no significant changes, disappointed shareholders may begin to pressure directors to get more involved in taking corrective action.

Third, should the board prove to be unresponsive, some more activist shareholders may seek the voting proxies of other shareholders so they can gather sufficient votes to replace some or all board members with new members who will pursue an agenda that is aligned with shareholder interests. If this proves successful, the new board likely will replace management with a team more inclined to act on behalf of shareholders.

Fourth, another company may see an opportunity to turn this underperforming firm around by acquiring it through a merger or acquisition. If the board of the target firm is agreeable to the terms of a merger, they can recommend that shareholders vote in favor of the offer. If not, the acquiring firm may go directly to the voting shareholders with a tender offer for their shares. This often is referred to as a *hostile takeover*.[a] In both cases, the price offered for shares in the target firm will be a premium over the price it had been trading at in the market, in effect passing along some of the potential gains from restructuring the firm to these current owners as a way to induce them to surrender their shares. Often, a takeover will be financed by credit—the acquirer will pay for the target company's shares with the proceeds of bonds or loans—and more leverage will be the result. Such leveraged takeovers are referred to as *leveraged buyouts* (*LBOs*).

The acquirer may be a private equity firm, discussed in more detail in Chapter 19. In this case, the buyout firm will take the target firm private by retiring its publicly traded shares. It will then deploy a team of turnaround specialists to revamp the target firm, and these new managers will have free reign—unimpeded by the requirements of publicly traded firms—to restructure the firm over a period of several years. After this time, the buyout firm will look

---

[a] The management and directors of some firms may initiate defensive measures to fend off such a hostile bid. Common are so-called poison pills, which enable current shareholders to buy additional shares at cut-rate prices. This, effectively, dilutes the earnings of a prospective acquirer and reduces the potential gain from the acquisition.

(*continued*)

for ways to exit from this investment, either by selling the restructured firm to another firm or through an IPO. Access to credit at favorable terms plays an important role in this process, as the leverage enables the return to private equity investors to be magnified when these efforts prove to be successful (of course, they are exposed to magnified losses if the turnaround proves unsuccessful).

In any event, when a firm is chronically underperforming—not utilizing its assets effectively—valuations in the equity market prompt initiatives to improve returns from those assets by utilizing them more effectively. That is, they lead to corrective discipline.[b] Beyond this, when underperformance spills over to the bond market, the drop in bond prices and higher financing costs underscores the underperformance problem and compounds the subpar earnings problem by lowering earnings through higher interest costs.

[b] The various measures discussed above are sometimes referred to as the market for corporate control. They represent ways in which the assets of a firm can be transformed to provide better returns—and resource allocation to be improved.

MONETARY POLICY AND THE STOCK MARKET

Turning to monetary policy, should the central bank signal, for example, that it will soon be raising its policy interest rate, the i_T term in Equation (11-9) would increase, causing stocks to fall in price. Such a development might also lead investors to expect earnings, E_1, to be weaker for a while because of this prospective action, which, in turn, would add to the downward pressure on share prices. The stock market acts as an important channel of monetary policy. Stock holdings are a sizable component of household wealth, and changes in household wealth have a demonstrable impact on consumer spending. Moreover, stock prices affect financing costs and the attractiveness of undertaking new investment by businesses. Thus, a drop in share prices brought about by tighter monetary policy will result in softer household and business spending, while a rise in share prices contributes to stronger spending.

INDEXES OF STOCK PRICES

We follow developments in the stock market by keeping tabs on indexes of share prices. The most closely watched are the Dow Jones Industrial Average (DJIA), the S&P 500, and the Nasdaq indexes. But there are many others, such as the Wilshire 5000 and the Russell 2000 for the United States, and the Bovespa (Brazil), FTSE (United Kingdom), CAC (France), DAX (Germany), and Nikkei (Japan). Each measures something different, and the methodology used to construct them can vary.

The most closely followed of these indexes in the United States is the DJIA. It consists of shares of 30 of the largest firms in the United States. It includes manufacturing firms (such as Caterpillar and Boeing), technology firms (such as Cisco and Intel), retailing firms (such as Walmart and McDonald's), and financial service firms (such as Goldman Sachs and Travelers). The total market capital of these firms—the value of their shares outstanding—is about a fourth that of the entire U.S. stock market. The DJIA is a so-called price-weighted index. This means that it is, crudely, a simple average of the prices of the shares of the 30 firms in the index. Actually, it is the average of those prices relative to the average in a base period.[12] What this means is that a dollar movement in the price of any share in the index will have the same impact on the index, regardless of the level of the price or the relative size (capitalization) of the firm. A $1 increase in the price of a $200 share (0.5 percent) will have the same impact on the index as a $1 increase in the price of a $10 share (10 percent). Moreover, the total capitalization—price of the share multiplied by the number of shares—of the first firm may be only a fraction of that of the second firm.[13] The price-weighted methodology and limited coverage of the Dow are considered to be shortcomings of the index.

The S&P 500 index is made up of a larger number of major firms—500—and is a capitalization-weighted index. This index represents about three-fourths of the total value of shares traded in the United States. By being a cap-weighted index, a 10 percent increase in the price of a share of a company that has the largest capitalization will have a much larger impact on the S&P 500 than a 10 percent increase in the firm with the smallest capitalization. For example, the largest firm in this index (ExxonMobil) has a weight of about 3.5 percent of the total and the smallest (*New York Times*) has a weight of about 0.04 percent of the total. A 20 percent increase in the former will increase the S&P 500 index about 0.7 percent, whereas a 20 percent increase in the latter will barely move the needle (raise it by less than one-hundredth of a percentage point).

The S&P 500, because of its inclusiveness and methodology, is often regarded to be representative of the overall stock market. For this reason, many attempt to select a portfolio that has the composition of the S&P 500 index. Indeed, each major mutual fund complex offers investors an S&P 500-type fund and there is an S&P 500-type fund trading as an exchange-traded fund (ETF).

The Nasdaq index is a capitalization-weighted index of the nearly 3,000 companies listed on Nasdaq. The value of these shares makes up about 15 percent or so of the value of all shares traded in the United States. The companies listed on Nasdaq are disproportionately tech and biotech companies, and thus the Nasdaq is widely viewed to be a measure of the health of the tech sector of the economy.

The Russell 2000 index is a cap-weighted index of 2,000 smaller-capitalization firms, representing less than 10 percent of the overall value of shares traded in the United States. Whereas the S&P 500 represents large-cap companies, the Russell 2000 represents small- and medium-sized corporations.

The Wilshire 5000 contains the prices of all shares that trade in markets for which there are systems for providing up-to-date measures of prices. It, actually, has the prices of shares in more than 7,000 corporations, and, essentially, is the market. It is a cap-weighted index.

SUMMARY

1. Despite the attention given to the stock market, firms do not raise much capital by issuing new shares. Indeed, the number of share retirements greatly surpasses

the number of new issuances. However, investors do build their equity positions through firms' retaining earnings.
2. Preferred stock is to be contrasted with common stock. Preferred equity has features of both equity and debt. Holders typically earn a fixed dividend and have a claim that stands above that of common shareholders. Preferred shares will often be issued for specific purposes, such as when the federal government takes an equity position in a firm and wants a claim that is senior to common shareholders.
3. Shares are issued in the primary market in the form of IPOs or seasoned offerings, using the services of investment bank underwriters. Shares are traded in the secondary market on different platforms—specialist systems, over-the-counter markets, and electronic matching systems (ECNs). The latter platform continues to increase its market share, owing to its around-the-clock availability, good execution, and low cost.
4. The price of a share of common stock will be the present value of the flow of dividends. An important factor affecting share prices is the discount rate, consisting of a risk-free (real) interest rate and a risk premium. The risk premium will be made up of a premium required by investors to hold common stock in general, and a specific (idiosyncratic) premium for the share in question (which can be positive or negative). The higher the discount rate, the lower the price of a share.
5. The model can be extended to allow for growth in dividends. The faster dividends grow, the higher the price of a share.
6. Dividend policy—the portion of earnings paid out as dividends—will affect the growth of dividends (or earnings). The larger the portion of earnings that is paid to shareholders, the lower the growth of earnings.
7. The model can be used to show the P-E ratio of a firm. Price-earnings ratios facilitate comparisons of performance among firms. The P-E will be directly related to the rate of return on internal investment and inversely related to the discount factor.
8. The model can be used to value the stock market overall (or the average price of a share of stock). Affecting the price of the market will be the risk-free (Treasury) rate, the equity premium (the compensation that investors require to hold the market), and the overall rate of return on investment.
9. News on the economy affects the stock market. This is because corporate earnings are highly pro-cyclical, ramping up in an expansion and turning down in a contraction.
10. The model illustrates that monetary policy can have an important effect on share prices through its effect on the risk-free rate and expectations of earnings. Variations in stock prices, in turn, affect household wealth, which affects consumer spending. Movements in share prices also affect the cost of financing for businesses and business investment. Thus, the stock market is a major channel through which monetary policy affects the economy.
11. When considerable uncertainty develops regarding the prospects for the economy or the financial system, the equity premium rises and share prices fall.
12. Indexes of share prices are used to measure the overall market or segments of the market. Most are capitalization-weighted indexes, in which the weight attached to the price of each share is that of the firm's share of total capitalization of all

firms in the index. The notable exception is the DJIA, which is a price-weighted index. The S&P 500 index represents the price of a basket of shares in large-capitalization firms and accounts for a large portion of the value of all firms with stocks that trade.
13. Many regard the S&P 500 to be representative of the market as a whole, and mutual fund complexes offer investors funds that replicate the S&P 500.

QUESTIONS

1. Why is it said that preferred stock is a hybrid between debt (bonds) and equity? Why would investors want to hold preferred shares over equity?
2. What are the reasons for issuing preferred stock? Why does the federal government usually acquire preferred shares when it takes an equity position in a firm?
3. Why do you think that electronic communications networks (ECNs) are gaining market share over other platforms? What are the economic forces favoring them?
4. In any given year, the corporate sector retires more shares (in value terms) than it issues in new stock. Still, the value of the stock market increases over time. What can account for this increase in market value?
5. Explain how an increase in the risk-free interest rate affects share prices, the equity premium, and the rate of return on internal investments.
6. What determines whether an increase in the share of retained earnings increases or decreases share prices?
7. If a firm does not pay dividends, how do investors earn their returns? Why might personal tax considerations favor retaining earnings and not paying dividends?
8. What do you suppose accounts for the P-E for J. P. Morgan exceeding that of Bank of America?
9. The stock market is highly volatile. What accounts for this?
10. Explain how a major disturbance affecting financial markets in Europe and the European economy can have a big impact on share prices in the United States.
11. What are the shortcomings of the DJIA as a measure of the stock market? Which index is a better representation of the stock market? Why?
12. Why do you suppose that all major mutual fund complexes offer investors a fund that replicates the S&P 500? Why would investors be interested in such a fund if they were seeking to buy the market?

NOTES

1. There are other reasons for not paying out all earnings to shareholders as dividends, including tax reasons. When returns to the investor take the form of capital gains, as happens when earnings are retained, taxes on them can be deferred until the gains are realized (the asset is sold). As a result, investors are able to reduce the present value of their tax liabilities.
2. Dividends on preferred shares can be missed, and the terms of the shareholder agreement can differ on what happens when this occurs. In the case of *cumulative preferred shares*, the missed dividends must be made up, but with *noncumulative*

shares, they need not be. Also, under some provisions, missed dividends result in preferred shareholders getting voting rights, enabling them to have a voice in the direction of the firm.

3. The government tends to acquire warrants in the firm as well as preferred shares. These place taxpayers in a position to share in the upside if the firm recovers and does well. The government, in this case, will exercise the warrants and sell the shares at a high price.
4. With some frequency, firms with publicly traded shares are acquired and taken private—their shares are retired—and later the private owners of the firm seek to sell their ownership in the firm through a public offering of stock. In these instances, the firm is said to have an IPO, even though its stock had traded publicly before the shares were retired.
5. This variant of the model is sometimes referred to as the Gordon growth model. See Myron J. Gordon, *The Investment, Financing, and Valuation of the Corporation* (Homewood, IL: Irwin, 1962).
6. The P-E ratio allows earnings to differ among firms. It expresses the price per dollar of earnings.
7. The benchmark interest rate, i_T, should be a real interest rate. This is because inflation will increase earnings by the amount of the rise in the price level and therefore the price of the share of common stock by this same percent amount. In other words, the price of a share of stock can be thought of as a real price that will adjust in nominal terms with the price level.
8. In practice, the dividend payout ratio tends to be around 0.6. Because corporate earnings have tended be a steady share of GDP over a very long period of time, one can surmise that g is roughly the same as that of real GDP; currently, growth in potential real GDP is around 2.5 percent per year or less, likely headed lower as growth in the labor force continues to slow.
9. Stock prices are plotted as the natural logarithm of the S&P index, rather than the actual level. This is done to better illustrate variations in the earlier period that would otherwise be muted by the vast difference in the level of the index between the early and late periods.
10. See Ravi Jagannathan, Ellen McGrattan, and Anna Scherbina, "The Declining U.S. Equity Premium," Federal Reserve Bank of Minneapolis, *Quarterly Review* 24, no. 4 (Fall 2000): 3–19.
11. The risk premium increases in these situations because, not only has the perception of risk increased, but also investors tend to be more risk averse during these times. Both factors act to enlarge the equity premium.
12. The denominator of the index—the base period value—is actually adjusted for stock splits and some other events.
13. The Dow Jones index was introduced in 1896, long before modern information technology. It originally included twelve firms, and the index was relatively simple to calculate manually and could be updated during the day fairly easily.

CHAPTER 12

Central Banking and the Federal Reserve

WHAT YOU WILL LEARN IN THIS CHAPTER

- What central banks are and how they came about.
- Where the U.S. central bank—the Fed—fits into our structure of government.
- How the Fed is a blend of a federal agency and privately owned Reserve Banks.
- Who are the key officials in the Fed.
- What central banks do and why they have become extremely important policy-making organizations.
- What gives the Fed more independence than other governmental entities and why.
- The importance of accountability and transparency for independent central banks in democratic systems.
- The basic instruments available for implementing monetary policy.
- How the central bank uses all of these instruments to set a short-term interest rate.
- How the financial crisis has changed the way in which monetary policy is implemented.

BACKGROUND

What are central banks and why do they get so much attention these days? Indeed, why do observers hang on every word and its intonation by key central bankers? Are they part of the government? If so, why are they so different than other parts of the government and do they coordinate their policies with those of the rest of the government? Do their responsibilities go beyond monetary policy? How are these powerful figures selected?

Central banks around the globe are among the most important and have become the most closely watched policymaking institutions. They typically have primary responsibility for achieving macroeconomic objectives through their monetary policy. Central banks also are the principal line of defense against financial disturbances and turmoil in the financial system. Unlike other public institutions, central banks are able to create unlimited amounts of money—either by issuing currency or, more important, by crediting accounts held with them by commercial banks. Such accounts with central banks (discussed in Chapter 3) serve as the lifeblood of the financial system, providing final settlement for the bulk of the massive scale of transactions—financial and nonfinancial—that occur each day.

Beyond these responsibilities, many central banks supervise commercial banks and certain other important financial institutions. Moreover, central banks provide a variety of financial services to commercial banks, governments, and sometimes other central banks.

ORIGINS OF CENTRAL BANKS

The first central bank—the Riksbank of Sweden—was established in 1668. Not long afterward, the most prominent of the early central banks—the Bank of England—was established. This bank—known as the Old Lady of Threadneedle Street—was chartered in 1694 as a private bank to serve as the government's bank and to assist the government with its financing, especially during times of war. In time, it came to be a bankers' bank—a bank to other banks. Other commercial banks held balances with the Bank of England and the Bank provided liquidity to them during times of stress. This latter function came to be known as the lender of last resort function.[1]

Monetary policy, as we think of it today, was not fully contemplated during this period and came to be added to the list of central bank responsibilities much later. During the early days of central banking, the monetary regime was a commodity—gold—standard. The amount of money in circulation and interest rates were governed by the workings of the gold standard. There was limited scope for a monetary authority (central bank) to pursue a goal apart from the stability of the value of its currency in relation to gold. Pursuing the goals of central banks today—price stability and, in some cases, high levels of employment—was not fully envisioned, and would have required leaving this fixed-exchange rate regime. This will be seen when we explore the topic of exchange rate regimes in Chapter 15.

Meanwhile, central banks were introduced in other countries around the globe. For example, the Banque de France was chartered in 1800 and the Bank of Japan in 1882. Central banks were found to be useful for holding the government's funds, and for assisting the government in issuing and servicing its debt. The United States, however, was a latecomer to central banking. The Federal Reserve—the Fed—was not established until 1913 and did not open its doors until 1914. Nonetheless, the Fed has become the dominant central bank in the world over the century since its founding.

In this chapter, we examine developments leading to the creation of the Federal Reserve System by an act of Congress in 1913. We will look at the current structure and responsibilities of the Fed, and how they compare with other modern central banks. We will finish by examining the way in which central banks go about conducting monetary operations in setting their policy interest rate.

CONSTITUTIONAL FOUNDATIONS

Like our other public policy institutions, the basis for a central bank in the United States is rooted in the Constitution. Article 1, section 8 of the Constitution clearly assigns responsibility for monetary policy to Congress by stating "The Congress shall have Power . . . To coin Money, regulate Value thereof, and of foreign Coin . . ." In our tri-partite government, with its checks and balances, Congress was selected largely by default because the alternatives were deemed less desirable.

The executive branch was seen to be more risky, based on foreign experience.[2] Up until that time, in other parts of the world, the executive (the monarch) had responsibility for monetary matters, but this responsibility was often abused egregiously—precious metal coins issued by the executive were debased. This was done when the government was facing a hard budget constraint—outlays were running well above receipts—and the executive turned to money creation to finance the budget shortfall, often during times of unpopular wars. The result was inflation. That is, the greater amount of money resulting from stretching the country's gold stock into more coins (debasement) was chasing the same amount of goods and pushing prices higher. While Congress was not ideally suited for this responsibility, it was deemed to be better than the alternatives. Interestingly, in recent decades, many other jurisdictions around the globe have followed the U.S. precedent, owing largely to the success of central banking in the United States in the postwar period.

THE CENTURY AND A QUARTER WITHOUT A CENTRAL BANK

So why did it take a century and a quarter for Congress to create a central bank in the United States and to delegate its monetary policy responsibility to that bank? To appreciate why, it is helpful to keep in mind that this new country attracted people who had a deep suspicion of centralized authority, especially in the financial sphere. Thus, if commercial banks and other financial institutions were necessary for development of the economy, it was deemed that it would be best if they were smaller, local entities. Indeed, the chartering of banks, like other businesses, was thought to be the proper responsibility of the states.

There were a couple of attempts to establish a bank that would be national in scope and have some of the features of a central bank. The first of these was the (First) Bank of the United States, which was granted a 20-year federal charter in 1791. The major proponent of the bank was Alexander Hamilton, the nation's first secretary of the Treasury. Hamilton sought to establish a bank that was cast in the mold of the Bank of England and could assist the federal government in raising funds, especially in times of a national emergency.[3] The bill that authorized the charter of the bank was very controversial and was nearly not signed by President Washington. The bank was headquartered in Philadelphia and had several branches around the country. It was partially (20 percent) owned by the federal government and served as the federal government's bank. It also issued notes and deposits to the public—similar to those issued by private, state-chartered banks. But unlike other banks, it applied discipline to the banking practices of other commercial banks by presenting their bank notes to them to keep them from overissuing those notes. That is, the Bank of the United States would from time to time take the notes drawn on other banks that it had accumulated through deposits of its customers and present them for specie (gold); with the threat of such presentments looming over them, managers of other private banks felt compelled to issue fewer bank notes and to hold more gold as backing, which better preserved the value of state-chartered bank notes and fostered stability of the banking system (in those days, banks were the bulk of the financial system). Because of opposition from the state-chartered banks and concerns about the constitutionality of the bank, the charter of the Bank of the United States was allowed to expire in 1811.

The next few years did not go very well. The absence of the Bank of the United States added to the federal government's difficulties in financing the War of 1812. Moreover, its absence reduced the discipline that was being applied to the banking practices of other commercial banks. Turbulence in the banking system ensued. As a consequence, sentiment mounted for a new Bank of the United States. In response, a new (Second) Bank of the United States was chartered for 20 years in 1816. It, too, was headquartered in Philadelphia and had about 25 branches around the country. It got off to a rocky start but came to match the performance of the First Bank under its third president, Nicholas Biddle. A conflict developed between Biddle and President Andrew Jackson—who was very suspicious of banks, especially large ones—and took on a very high profile. President Jackson flamboyantly vetoed a bill to renew the charter of the Second Bank of the United States in 1832. He then proceeded to withdraw the federal government's deposits from the bank, which led to the slow demise of the Bank.

The period following the closure of the Second Bank was one of considerable confusion in the banking system. Many state banks overissued bank note liabilities and did not have sufficient amounts of specie to redeem the notes when presented. As a consequence, these notes were exchanged at discounts that varied from bank to bank and over time. Market participants had to carry books that provided the market exchange value of each bank's notes to avoid being stuck with worthless or near-worthless notes. Needless to say, transactions costs involving bank notes were high, which acted to depress trade and economic activity.

During the Civil War, the National Banking Act of 1863 was passed, which addressed the chaos in the banking sector. It created a new class of federal charters for commercial banks, and national banks having these charters were authorized to issue national bank notes. These were standardized—uniformly printed and backed by U.S. government debt.[4] A tax was then imposed on bank notes issued by state-chartered banks, which was effective in driving them out of existence. A new office in the Treasury Department was established—the Office of the Comptroller of the Currency (OCC)—to charter and regulate national banks. By standardizing and strengthening note issuance, stability was restored to the payment system.

However, the United States still lacked a central bank to serve as a lender of last resort in times of banking panics, of which there were several severe ones in the latter part of the nineteenth century (see Chapter 15). Meanwhile, other countries that had central banks experienced much smaller financial disruptions. The contrasting experiences between the United States and elsewhere led to growing support for a central bank in the United States. It was thought that such a central bank would have as its primary responsibilities the issuance of currency, serving as a lender of last resort in times of a banking panic, and the smoothing of seasonal variations in credit.[5]

CREATION OF THE FEDERAL RESERVE

By the early twentieth century, there was widespread agreement that the creation of something akin to a central bank could not be delayed much longer. However, two very different models emerged for a U.S. central bank. One, spearheaded by interests in the Northeast wanted a bank along the lines of the Bank of England—a privately owned bank that would be highly centralized and located in the financial hub, New York City; it would have branches in other banking centers. The other,

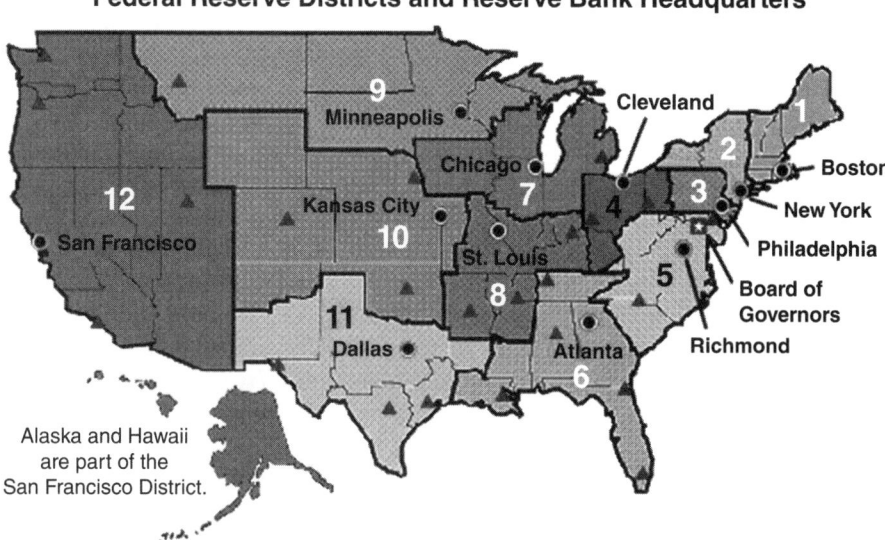

Federal Reserve Districts and Reserve Bank Headquarters

FIGURE 12.1 Map of Districts and Their Headquarters
Source: Board of Governors of the Federal Reserve System.

led by progressives (successors of the earlier populists) from the South and West, regarded this model to be an anathema. They were convinced that Eastern bankers would dominate the central bank and would use their influence to exploit rural interests in the rest of the country. They favored a decentralized central bank having a federal government component. In the end, President Wilson fashioned something of a compromise that had a distinct resemblance to the progressives' proposal. The president signed the Federal Reserve Act on December 23, 1913, which created the Federal Reserve System. The System began operations the following year.

While the Act authorized from 8 to 12 Reserve Banks to be established, it did not take long for the panel empowered to make decisions regarding the number of districts, their geographic boundaries, and the headquarters of each to determine that there would be twelve. The districts and the locations of their headquarters are shown in the map in Figure 12.1.[6] Roughly speaking, each district was to be of the same financial size as of 1914. Since that time, there has been substantial migration of the population and business activity westward and southward.

In addition to the 12 Federal Reserve Banks, the Federal Reserve Act created the Federal Reserve Board, a federal agency located in Washington, DC. It was to be a coordinating body for the System and to establish by-laws and procedures to standardize the operations of the Reserve Banks.

There are some notable features of the System created by the Federal Reserve Act:

- The Reserve Banks were private institutions owned by member banks. All nationally chartered commercial banks were required to be members of the Federal Reserve System and state-chartered banks could opt to become member banks. Member banks were required to invest 6 percent of their capital in shares in their district Reserve Bank and, in return, earned a statutory dividend of 6 percent on their invested funds.

- The Reserve Banks were to have a board with nine directors—three Class A, three Class B, and three Class C directors. Class A and B directors (representing member banks and agriculture, commerce, and industry, respectively) were to be selected by district member banks, while Class C directors—selected by the Board in Washington—were to represent the public more broadly. The chair and vice chair were to be selected by the Board from Class C directors.
- The chief executive officer (CEO) of each Reserve Bank was given the title governor, the traditional title of the (sole) head of other central banks. The Bank's governor was selected by the Bank's board of directors.
- The Board in Washington, DC, had seven members. Five were nominated by the president and confirmed by the Senate. One of these was assigned the title of governor and another the title of vice governor. The other two members of the Board were *ex officio* members—the Secretary of the Treasury and Comptroller of the Currency (subordinate to the Secretary of the Treasury).

The Federal Reserve System thus began with 13 primary units—12 private Reserve Banks and a Board, which was a federal agency. Each unit had a considerable amount of autonomy, satisfying the progressives who feared domination by any one unit (especially New York). Indeed, the System had 13 persons with the title governor, in contrast to other central banks having only one. The executive branch had two *ex officio* members on the Board and a good bit of influence on that body; indeed, the early Federal Reserve Board had its offices in the Main Treasury Building in Washington, DC, next to the White House. The early Fed was to provide for a new form of currency (Federal Reserve notes), to counter seasonal variations in credit markets, and to cushion disturbances to the banking system. The latter two were to be accomplished by providing funds to member banks through the discount window.[7] Seasonal stresses were alleviated by Reserve Banks discounting eligible ("self-liquidating") collateral posted by member banks seeking funds to lend, importantly to the agricultural sector. During times of stress on the banking system—banking panics—member banks were to be able to get funds from their Reserve Bank through discounts to replace the deposit balances being pulled out by their customers.

As noted at the beginning of this chapter, monetary policy, as we think of it today, was not contemplated at the time.[8] The United States was on a gold standard—a system of fixed exchange rates—and the level of interest rates and money stock were largely determined by the workings of this global system. The Fed had limited scope to influence these. As we will see in Chapter 16, fixed exchange rates imply that the principal objective of the central bank must be to ensure that its currency remains fixed in value in terms of gold (or another currency). If this means that employment or stable prices must be sacrificed to keep the currency pegged to gold, that is the way it must be.

EARLY YEARS OF THE FEDERAL RESERVE

During the first decade and a half of the Federal Reserve, the System functioned in a generally acceptable manner. This period included the First World War and large swings in the business cycle, but no major banking panics developed. Leadership in the System came importantly from the Federal Reserve Bank of New York, despite deep concerns by progressives at the time the System was designed. During this time, the Reserve Banks came to develop open market operations—the purchase of Treasury securities in the marketplace—mainly to improve their earnings by earning the interest from the securities acquired. Over time, they came to realize that they could influence the amount of liquidity in the banking system through such purchases—or sales. The growing realization that such operations by one Reserve Bank spilled over to other districts led to efforts to coordinate open market actions among the Reserve Banks.[9]

The generally favorable performance of the Fed over the early years gave way to serious problems in the latter part of the 1920s. Open market purchases by Reserve Banks helped to fuel speculation in the stock market and a bubble in stock prices. Then, the Board hiked the discount rate to curb the run-up in share prices, which helped trigger the stock market crash in 1929. Banking panics followed, but the Fed was reluctant to use the discount window to address them. Overall, the System did not cover itself with glory.[10] Moreover, the diffuse and fragmented governance structure made it difficult to assign responsibility and accountability for the System's mistakes.

REFORMS OF THE 1930s

The disappointing performance of the Fed during the worst banking panic in the nation's panic-riddled history led to a major restructuring of the System, one that centralized governance of the U.S. central bank. The Board in Washington was given primary responsibility for policymaking.[11] Indeed, the title of the Board was changed to the Board of Governors of the Federal Reserve System to convey that each of the seven members of the Board had the title governor. Board members continued to be nominated by the president and confirmed by the Senate. The title of the heads of Reserve Banks, in contrast, was changed to president. Thus, the number of persons in the Federal Reserve System with the title governor shrank nearly in half, but not to one, as was customary in other parts of the world.

Within the Board, one member was nominated by the president to serve as chair, and another was nominated to be vice chair—each for a four-year term. The Senate was to approve these nominations, too.

Essentially, the Board was given responsibility for all policymaking, with one exception. The exception was open market operations. The Federal Open Market Committee (FOMC) was created to set policy for conducting the System's open market operations, which has become the Fed's primary instrument for implementing monetary policy. It was given 12 voting members—all 7 Board members plus 5 presidents of Reserve Banks. Thus, the Board, while sharing this responsibility with Reserve Banks, still was given a majority of votes on the FOMC. The voting presidents of the Reserve Banks were established as follows: the president of the Federal Reserve Bank of New York was given a permanent vote and the other four votes were rotated among the other 11 Reserve Bank presidents.[12]

In addition to having a majority of votes on the FOMC, the Board can set reserve requirements on deposits within a range—another instrument of monetary policy. The Board further was given primary responsibility for discount window policy, the third instrument of monetary policy. It sets the rules governing access to such credit and determines the interest rate on such loans—the discount rate—based on proposals submitted by the Reserve Banks.[13]

Furthermore, the Board was given primary responsibility for setting the policies and procedures for regulating and supervising the financial institutions assigned to the System, though it delegates much of this responsibility to the Reserve Banks. The Federal Reserve has statutory responsibility for supervising all state-chartered commercial banks that are members of the Federal Reserve System and all large financial services holding companies. The Board also has been given responsibility for consumer financial regulation and for setting margin requirements on securities—the maximum amount that can be borrowed on purchases of stock and certain other financial assets.

While the president and other senior officers of Reserve Banks are selected by the Bank's board of directors, they must be approved by the Board of Governors. The same process must be followed for determining the compensation of the president and senior officers of each Reserve Bank. The Board in Washington, DC, was further given responsibility for oversight of the Reserve Banks to ensure that the System's policies and procedures were being followed properly and uniformly. The major changes made to the Fed in the mid-1930s persist to this day.

FED INDEPENDENCE

At the same time, the Fed was given a considerable amount of *independence* within the government. This was achieved by removing members of the executive branch—the Secretary of the Treasury and the Comptroller of the Currency—from the Board. Board members were not to have other employment or represent other interests. In addition, members of the Board were given 14-year terms, not to be removed except for cause.[14] Because Fed monetary policy does not affect the economy immediately and because public policy goals may at times require that the Fed deliver bitter medicine, these long terms of Board members better enable policymakers to look beyond the moment and focus instead on that point in the future when their actions today will have their effect. Related to these, the Fed is prohibited by law from financing the government by extending funds—either directly by crediting the Treasury's account or by allowing the Treasury to overdraw its account at the Fed—or by extending credit in the form of a loan or by purchasing Treasury newly issued debt directly from the Treasury. As we will see later in this chapter, the Fed does purchase Treasury debt, but does this in the secondary market.[15]

Beyond these, Fed independence is enhanced by the System's being outside the appropriations process of the federal government. As such, the Fed does not need to seek an allocation from Congress for the funds needed to perform its job. The appropriations process typically involves appearances before Congressional subcommittees. These subcommittees commonly have members who have special reasons for being on the oversight committee and may not be representative of Congress as a whole or the broader public. That is, they may want the Fed to pursue policies that are not congruent with the broader public interest. Exempting the Fed from such pressures can keep it from compromising public policy goals, much like the 14-year terms of Board members. In case you are wondering how the Fed is able to fund its day-to-day operations, keep in mind that the Fed owns a massive portfolio of interest-earning assets; the earnings from these assets are more than sufficient to cover expenses.[16]

In addition, the Fed's monetary policy function has been exempted from General Accountability Office (GAO) audits. This means that the GAO is not allowed to review the decision-making process and offer opinions on monetary policy actions taken by the Fed. The concern has been that such reviews, if permitted, could raise questions in markets about whether the Fed may feel pressured by GAO audits to alter its policy stance away from its best professional judgment, which could compromise the achievement of policy goals.[17] Indeed, the Fed has expressed concern that GAO audits could create the impression among market participants that the Fed might be pushed off course in its pursuit of price stability, which, as we will see in coming chapters, can affect the public's inflation expectations and thereby achievement of price stability.

There are limits to the independence of the Fed and to most other central banks in democratic nations. The final goals of monetary policy are believed to fall in the realm of responsibility of elected leaders, and not the central bank. As we will see in coming chapters, the Fed pursues a statutory dual mandate of maximum employment and stable prices while the Bank of England, the Bank of Japan, and the European Central Bank pursue the final goal of price stability established by their respective political processes. Central banks then have independence to use the instruments at their disposal to achieve these goals. Sometimes this is referred to as *instrument independence* in contrast to *goal independence*. Elected officials and not the central bank determine the central bank's ultimate policy goals. In addition, in the United States and in many other countries exchange rate policy (discussed in Chapter 16) is determined by the government (in the United States, by the U.S. Treasury), and not by the central bank. Beyond these, it is widely believed that independence does not extend to central bank policies other than monetary policy, such as supervisory and regulatory policy, discussion of which follows.

CENTRAL BANK ACCOUNTABILITY AND TRANSPARENCY

The centralization of Federal Reserve System responsibilities in the Board went a long way toward improving accountability. The Board has primary responsibility for System policy and actions. However, this, as noted earlier in this chapter, has run against the grain of longstanding American suspicions about the centralization of power, especially in the financial realm. Moreover, the Fed has been granted more independence than other agencies of the federal government. This has resulted in a major tension.

This tension has been addressed importantly by increasing accountability through transparency.[18] The Board opens many of its meetings to the public. It submits numerous reports to Congress—which, of course, has delegated its constitutional responsibilities to the Fed—and routinely testifies before Congress on its policies and operations. The Fed publishes the System's balance sheet weekly, and subjects itself to public audit. In the monetary policy sphere, its meetings—including those of the FOMC—are not open to the public, but minutes of meetings are published three weeks after each meeting and a verbatim transcript of FOMC meetings is made public after a delay of five years. Nonetheless, concerns remain about whether the Fed has become too powerful, and suspicions are frequently voiced about whether the Fed has a hidden agenda that does not serve the public interest and may be taking actions outside of public view.

CENTRAL BANK NET WORTH AND INDEPENDENCE

An issue of importance for central banks is their net worth status, particularly as it affects their net earnings. This, in turn, has implications for their *de facto* independence in conducting monetary policy. Central banks' asset holdings take the form largely of marketable securities issued by their government, interest-earning assets held in foreign currencies (mostly securities issued by foreign governments), and, to a much lesser extent, (discount window) loans made to domestic banks. On these assets, they receive interest earnings in their local currency on holdings of domestic government debt and on the loans they make and interest earnings in foreign currencies on their holdings of foreign securities. The liabilities side of their balance sheets consists primarily of the amount of local currency that they have issued and the balances (mostly deposits deemed to be reserves) held with them by domestic banks and the balances held by their government. Of these, they do not pay interest on local currency that they have issued and many central banks do not pay interest on the balances held with them by banks and the domestic government.

The difference between the central bank's assets and its liabilities is its net worth. Compared to the commercial banks that they supervise, central banks have small ratios of net worth to assets (capitalization ratios). For example, the Fed has net worth relative to assets of only about 1.5 percent, while U.S commercial banks have ratios averaging 11 percent. The norm for major central banks is a net worth ratio on the order of 0.5 to 3 percent, of which the Fed is around the middle. Many central banks have minimum statutory net worth (capitalization) ratios, and, should the central bank fall below that minimum, it is the responsibility of the government to recapitalize the central bank by putting assets into the central bank to raise its net worth to the minimum.[a] Economists have debated the issue of whether a central bank needs to have much, if any, net worth to perform its duties, given its ability to create money to cover any shortfalls.

In many respects, of more importance is the issue of whether the central bank has adequate earnings from its assets (and the fee-based services that it provides to depository institutions) to cover its interest outlays and its operating expenses (employee compensation and other expenses). In cases in which there

---

[a] In return, the central bank typically is expected to remit any excess of earnings over expenses to the government (finance ministry). Governments commonly scrutinize the expenses of their central bank, with an eye toward ensuring that the central bank is not engaging in extravagances at taxpayer expense (enjoying an improvement in lifestyle and thereby lowering the amount paid to the finance ministry, which, in turn, reduces funds available to the government).

is a shortfall of earnings—usually associated with a weak net worth position—the central bank may need to approach the government with cup in hand to be able to cover the shortfall.[b] In these circumstances, concerns develop about whether the independence of the central bank might be compromised, because the government might insist on a *quid quo pro* that conflicts with the central bank's statutory mandate. Over recent years, many central banks have suffered a reduction in interest income from their holdings of foreign currency reserves—primarily held in the form of U.S. dollars. With U.S. interest rates at historic lows, these central banks have lost substantial amounts of income. In many cases, the loss has been enough to cause a shortfall of earnings from expenses. As a consequence, some of these central banks have had their asset positions raised by the placement of interest-earning domestic government securities in the central bank—a recapitalization. When this has been done, it has eased concerns about loss of central bank independence.

The Fed has not been in such a position, even though it has thin net worth in relation to its assets. Its earnings have far exceeded its interest and operating expenses, enabling the Fed to transfer much of the excess to the Treasury. For example, in 2013, the Fed transferred nearly $80 billion to the Treasury. However, in coming years, it is likely that expenses of the Fed will rise more rapidly than interest earnings. This is because a move to normalization of monetary policy—returning interest rates toward more normal levels—likely will lead to higher interest rates paid on the massive amount of liabilities in the form of deposits (reserves) held at the Fed by commercial banks. Interest earnings on its asset holdings will rise more slowly, as these are based on the Fed's heavy concentration of longer-term assets, which will turn over slowly and thus will be replaced by higher-earning assets only gradually.

[b] Alternatively, it will need to draw down assets to cover the shortfall, further weakening its net worth.

CENTRAL BANK RESPONSIBILITIES

Central banks around the globe share a common set of responsibilities. These are shown for the Federal Reserve and for other central banks in Table 12.1.

Monetary policy—covered in the next two chapters—has until recently been regarded as the most important responsibility of the Fed and other central banks.[19] In the United States, the primary instrument of monetary policy is open market operations, the responsibility of the FOMC. As noted, the FOMC has 12 voting members—seven governors and five Reserve Bank presidents, although the seven nonvoting presidents fully participate in the policy discussion apart from voting.

Other economies have moved to a similar system in which a committee makes major monetary policy decisions. The Bank of England has a nine-member Monetary Policy Committee that is charged with monetary policy decisions, 4 of which are external to the bank. The European Central Bank has a Governing Council with

TABLE 12.1 Responsibilities of the Federal Reserve and Other Central Banks

Responsibility	Fed	Other Central Banks
Monetary policy	x	x
Financial stability	x	x
Fiscal agency	x	x
Payments system	x	x
Supervision	Partial	Mixed
Consumer protection	x	Mixed

23 members that has been given this responsibility—6 of the members constitute the Executive Board of the bank and the other 17 are governors of the component national central banks. The Bank of Japan has a 9-member Policy Board that is charged with monetary policy decisions, all of which are officials of the bank. Supporting policymaking by such committees is evidence showing that committees made up of competent persons typically make better decisions than any one member alone can make.

All central banks also are expected to be the first responders to financial crises, and achieving and preserving financial stability has risen in importance to a position comparable to that of monetary policy. This has come to be known as macroprudential supervision and will be discussed in more detail in Chapter 15.

A third common responsibility among central banks is serving as fiscal agent. This includes serving as the government's bank—receiving and holding the government's funds and making payment on behalf of the government. In addition, it involves helping the government finance its operations in credit markets by assisting the Treasury (or finance ministry) in selling its debt, making coupon payments on schedule to the investor of record, and paying the principal at maturity. The First and Second Banks of the United States did much of this in the late eighteenth and early nineteenth centuries. In addition, the Fed, through the Federal Reserve Bank of New York, serves as a fiscal agent for foreign central banks and international financial institutions. The U.S. dollar plays a key role in the international financial system, and, as a consequence, these foreign and international institutions acquire and sell dollars. They prefer to use their account with the Fed for these purposes, in many cases utilizing the services of the New York Fed to invest in U.S. Treasury or federal agency securities. In addition, the New York Fed will hold some or all of these institutions' monetary gold stock in its subterranean vault.

The Fed and other central banks further play an important role in a fourth area, payment systems. This includes the traditional function of supplying currency to the public through commercial banks and other depository institutions. The role of currency is being supplanted as a transactions medium over time and is being replaced by various means of transferring balances among commercial banks using digital methods. These were discussed in Chapter 3 and include Internet banking, point-of-sale (POS) systems, automated teller machines (ATMs), and stored value cards. They involve detailed netting systems among commercial banks, and, typically, the transfer of balances held at the central bank from banks having net customer outflows to those with net inflows. Smooth and uninterrupted functioning of these systems is essential to the functioning of business and commerce in the economy. Central banks establish standards for participation by financial institutions in national payment systems and they monitor performance of these systems to best assure that payment systems facilitate those broader economic goals and do not break down, disrupting a vast array of transactions in the economy.

Supervision of financial institutions has been another function performed by central banks.[20] This is intended to ensure that the institutions under their supervision are being operated in a safe and sound manner. Because commercial banks and similar institutions hold the wealth of many retail customers and they play a key role in the functioning of the financial system—as discussed in Chapter 3—these institutions have been singled out for special regulatory and supervisory attention. However, not all central banks have been given this responsibility. In many parts of the world, this responsibility has been given to a separate regulatory authority—a banking commission. In the United States, supervision of commercial banks and other depository institutions is shared among several federal agencies, as we note in Chapter 17. In the commercial banking arena, the Comptroller of the Currency supervises nationally chartered commercial banks and the Federal Deposit Insurance Corporation supervises state-chartered commercial banks that are not members of the Federal Reserve System. To ensure uniform treatment, these regulators must, by law, coordinate their actions.

The financial crisis has been changing the way that central banks are involved in supervising and regulating large commercial banks and other important financial institutions. In part, this has reflected the realization that there is a close relationship between the achievement of monetary policy goals and the condition of major financial institutions and the financial system more broadly. Having a hand in supervision can provide the monetary authority with important information about how the credit mechanism—a primary channel of monetary policy—is functioning, to better determine the appropriate stance of monetary policy. There has also developed a greater appreciation of the role of the central bank's discount window facility in both the implementation of monetary policy—as we will see a little later in this chapter—and in stabilizing the financial system at a time of severe stress. Having a hand in supervision enables the central bank to better ascertain when there is need for extending credit to such financial institutions and the adequacy of protections for the central bank—the collateral—for such loans. As a consequence, more countries are giving their central bank a greater role in supervision of so-called systemically important financial institutions (SIFIs). A SIFI is an institution that is deemed to pose a threat to the entire financial system in the event it gets into trouble. As noted, we will discuss financial crises in Chapter 15 and the regulation of financial institutions in Chapter 17.

Finally, some central banks, including the Fed, have been given responsibility for consumer protection in the financial sphere. This includes ensuring adequate disclosure of terms on deposit accounts and loans that are disclosed by financial institutions to consumers. Increasingly, central banks have also been providing information to consumers on principles of financial management to better enable them to make well-informed decisions regarding financial planning, especially retirement planning. This has become more important as defined contribution pension plans have been supplanting defined benefits plans. The Dodd-Frank financial reforms of 2010 have placed the bulk of consumer financial protections in the Consumer Finance Protection Bureau, a somewhat autonomous unit within the Board of Governors of the Federal Reserve System.

MONETARY OPERATIONS

In the next chapter, we will look at the way in which central banks formulate monetary policy to achieve statutory goals—which primarily involves the setting of *the policy interest rate*. The policy interest rate is a very short-term interest rate, applicable to interbank loans of balances held in accounts at central banks. In the United States, the policy rate is the *federal funds rate*.

The Demand for Reserves

The policy interest rate, like other prices, is determined by the interaction of supply and demand. In this case, it is the supply of and demand for reserves taking the form of balances held at the central bank. The demand for reserves is comprised of the demand for *required reserves* to satisfy reserve requirements and the demand for *excess reserves* to satisfy other purposes.[21] The Board has authority to set reserve requirements on certain deposits of commercial banks and other depository institutions. The requirements are set on the level of deposits and thus vary when deposits change. In practice, reserve requirements are set on transaction accounts—demand deposits and other deposits that are commonly used for making payments.[22] For example, a reserve requirement ratio of 10 percent would imply that a bank with $100 million in net transaction accounts would need to hold $10 million (10 percent) as balances with the Fed.[23]

We can illustrate the demand for reserves in Figure 12.2. On the horizontal axis is the quantity of reserves, R, and on the vertical axis is the interest rate—the federal funds rate or i_{ff}. The demand schedule—DD—is negatively sloped, mainly owing to the demand for excess reserves. The federal funds rate can be viewed as the opportunity cost of holding excess reserves, leading to excess reserves being more expensive as the federal funds rate increases.[24] This can be seen by the rise in the federal funds rate from i_{ff}^1 to i_{ff}^2. Each dollar of excess reserves now results in a loss of earnings of i_{ff}^2 instead of i_{ff}^1. As a result, bank reserve managers will want to manage their reserve holdings more actively and carefully, and direct more assets to the federal funds market.[25] Accordingly, the quantity of reserves demanded shrinks from R_1 to R_2.

The Supply of Reserves

The supply of reserves consists of *nonborrowed reserves* and *borrowed reserves*. Nonborrowed reserves are influenced by a wide variety factors, some outside the day-to-day control of the Fed. Most notably, Treasury deposits at the Fed and the public's holdings of currency can fluctuate widely and affect the quantity of nonborrowed reserves. For example, when the Treasury decides to transfer funds from its accounts at commercial banks—in which it collects a sizable share of its receipts in the form of individual withheld taxes and social insurance contributions, as well as corporate income tax payments—banks lose reserves. That is, when the Treasury directs that funds be transferred from collection accounts at commercial banks to its disbursement

Central Banking and the Federal Reserve 197

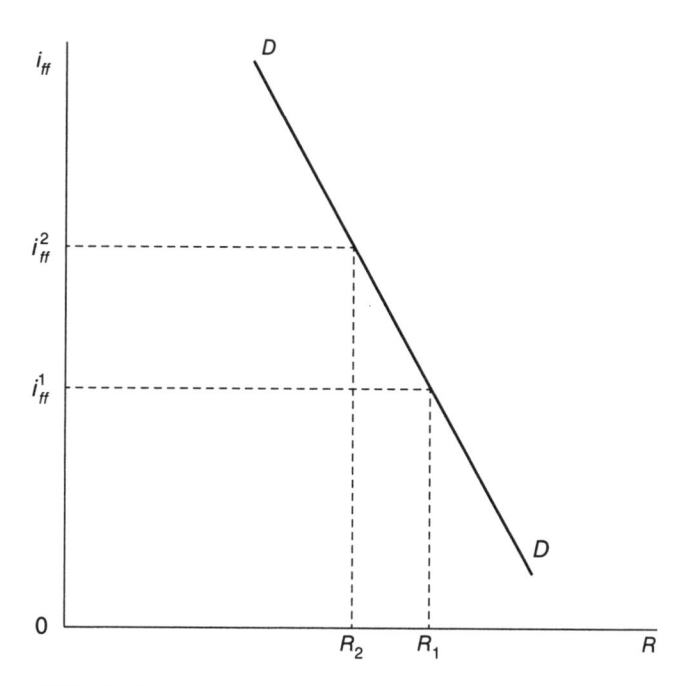

FIGURE 12.2 The Demand for Reserves

account at the Fed, the Fed transfers the funds from bank reserve accounts—which are reserves of the banking system—to the account of the Treasury, which does not get counted as reserves. Thus, day-to-day fluctuations in the Treasury's balance at the Fed result in day-to-day fluctuations in nonborrowed reserves.

Similarly, changes in currency in circulation result in changes in the supply of nonborrowed reserves. When the public wants more currency, they typically get it from their commercial banks—often from ATMs. Commercial banks, in turn, get currency from the Fed. They pay for it from their accounts at the Fed. In other words, they instruct the Fed to ship them currency and to pay for the shipment by taking it from their reserve account at the Fed. Thus, day-to-day fluctuations in currency also result in offsetting changes in the supply of nonborrowed reserves.[26]

Borrowed reserves are those obtained from the Fed's discount window. Banks make a choice to borrow, taking into account the terms on which they can borrow—including the discount rate, i_d. Commercial banks will not be inclined to tap the discount window for funds unless discount window credit is cheaper than borrowing from other banks in the federal funds market. As the federal funds rate rises above the discount rate, banks will want to increase their borrowing from the Fed. We can illustrate this in Figure 12.3, depicting the supply schedule of reserves. The vertical line at NBR_0 shows the quantity of nonborrowed reserves. This will be determined by the factors discussed above, as well as open market operations—which will be discussed shortly. The discount rate is shown by i_d^1. As the federal funds rate rises above the discount rate, banks turn to the discount window for reserves.[27] To illustrate, if the funds rate increases from i_{ff}^1 to i_{ff}^2 the amount of reserves will increase from R_1 to R_2. This increase in (total) reserves will come from an increase in borrowed reserves from $R_1 - NBR_0$ to $R_2 - NBR_0$.

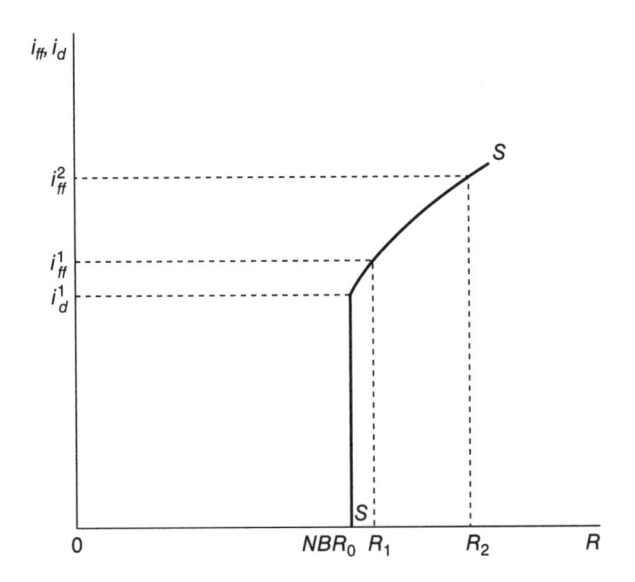

FIGURE 12.3 The Supply of Reserves

Market Equilibrium

We are now in a position to look at equilibrium in the market for reserves and the determination of the federal funds rate. Equilibrium occurs when the demand for and supply of reserves are the same, or

$$RR + ER = NBR + BR \qquad (12\text{-}1)$$

We illustrate in Figure 12.4. The intersection of DD_1 and SS_1 occurs at i_{ff}^1. Note that the intersection takes place at the quantity of reserves NBR_0 and that the federal funds rate is below the discount rate. Suppose now that the discount rate is lowered from i_d^1 to i_d^2. Note that the federal funds rate will also decline, but will now be above the discount rate. Banks will also be induced to borrow reserves from the discount window in the amount of $R_1 - NBR_0$.

Setting the Federal Funds Rate through Open Market Operations

Let us now look at the role of open market operations in setting the federal funds—or policy—interest rate. Figure 12.5 illustrates how this is done. The demand for reserves is given by D_1D_1. Suppose that the FOMC decides that i_{ff}^* is the level of the policy rate that will achieve the goals of monetary policy—to be discussed in more detail in the next chapter. The FOMC provides instructions to a group at the Federal Reserve Bank of New York called the Markets Group—traditionally called the open market "Desk"—to use open market transactions to hit this target. This means that the total supply of reserves must equal R_*R_* for demand to be satisfied at i^*. An amount less than this would result in the policy rate being above i^* and an amount greater would result in the funds rate being below i^*. Suppose that the supply of nonborrowed reserves is initially NBR_1, giving rise to supply schedule S_1S_1. Absent action by the Markets

Central Banking and the Federal Reserve

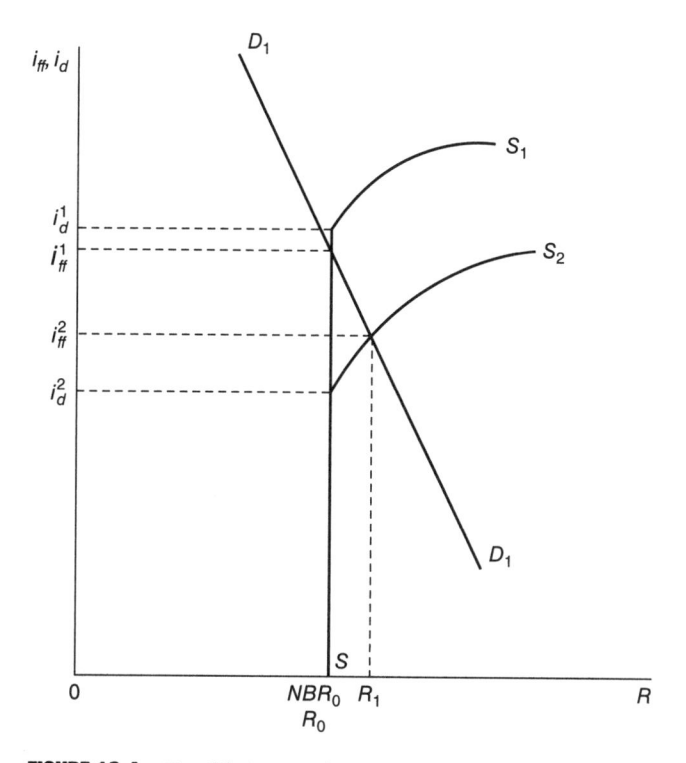

FIGURE 12.4 Equilibrium in the Market for Reserves

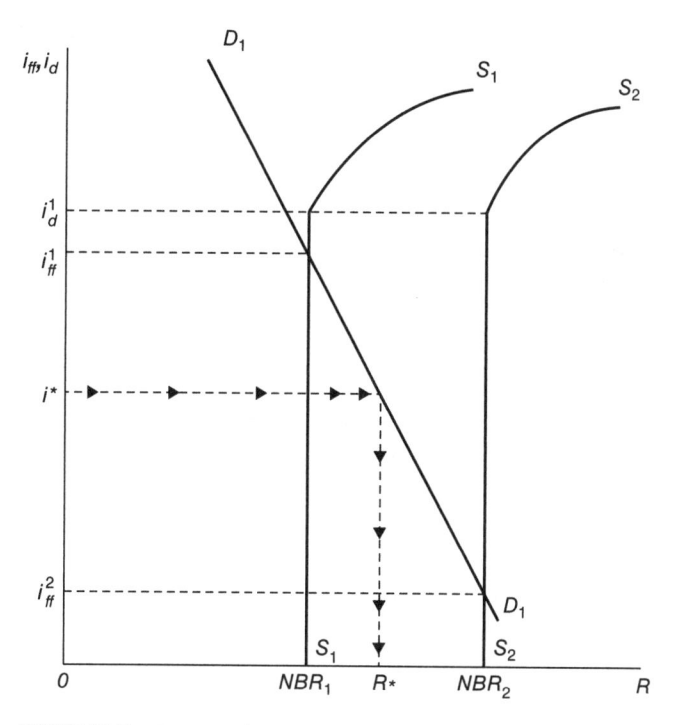

FIGURE 12.5 Hitting the FOMC's Target

Group, the federal funds rate would be $i_{\!f\!f}^1$, well above the target set by the FOMC.[28] By purchasing an asset in the open market, the Markets Group can increase the supply of reserves. In other words, the Markets Group will purchase the asset with newly created reserves. To hit the target, the Desk would need to buy assets in the amount of $R_*R_* - NBR_1$. This would increase the supply of reserves from NBR_1 to R_*R_*.

In principle, the Markets Group could purchase nearly any asset to achieve this result, including foreign currencies.[29] In practice, the Markets Group largely confines its transactions to U.S. Treasury securities. To an important extent, this is because the market for Treasury securities is large and deep enough to absorb transactions of the size that are performed by the Fed without causing dislocations in that market. Moreover, interest rates on Treasury securities serve as benchmarks for the pricing of credit throughout the economy and thus open market transactions get quickly transmitted to credit costs throughout the economy.[30] Thus, in the preceding case, the Markets Group would acquire $R_*R_* - NBR_1$ of Treasury securities.

Figure 12.5 also shows what would happen if the supply of nonborrowed reserves were to exceed R_*R_*. This is illustrated by supply schedule S_2S_2. Absent action by the Desk, the federal funds rate would be $i_{\!f\!f}^2$, well below the target, $i_{\!f\!f}^*$. To hit the target, the Desk would need to sell assets—Treasury securities. It would need to sell Treasury securities in the amount of $NBR_2 - R_*R_*$.

Permanent versus Temporary Transactions

When conducting open market transactions in Treasury securities, the Fed can perform *outright* (or *permanent*) transactions—purchases or sales—or it can perform *temporary* transactions.[31] With the former, it is conducting a standard transaction in which there is no obligation to subsequently reverse the transaction at a later date. With a temporary transaction, there is an obligation on the part of both counterparties to reverse the transaction at a specified later date. To add reserves with a temporary transaction, the Fed can conduct a *repurchase agreement* (*RP* or *repo*). Under an RP, the Fed buys a security from its counterparty and agrees to sell it back at a predetermined price at an agreed-upon date in the future—the difference between the initial transactions price and the price at which it gets reversed constitutes interest to the Fed. The Fed, in effect, is providing short-term collateralized financing to its counterparty. RPs can be performed for as short as overnight and commonly have maturities of 3 or 7 days—sometimes longer.

The Desk also conducts temporary transactions to absorb—remove—reserves. These transactions are called *reverse repurchase agreements* or *matched sale-purchase (MSP) agreements*. With a reverse repo, the Fed sells a Treasury security and agrees to buy it back at a predetermined date and price in the future, usually 1 to 7 days later.

In deciding whether to perform a temporary or permanent transaction in the open market, the Desk makes a judgment about whether the need to add or withdraw reserves is temporary or permanent. For example, if the situation depicted by NBR_1 in Figure 12.5 were deemed to be a persistent one, the Markets Group would likely conduct a permanent purchase of Treasury securities. In contrast, if the situation depicted by NBR_2 were deemed to be temporary, the Desk would arrange a reverse RP for a period to match the length of time that the extra reserves are expected to be in the market.

Payment of Interest on Excess Reserves

The preceding model of federal funds rate determination needs to be modified to allow for the Fed's newest instrument of monetary policy—the payment of interest on required and excess reserves. Since 2008, the Board has been authorized to set an interest rate that can be paid on both required and excess reserves. The payment of interest on reserves affects the demand schedule for reserves, as shown in Figure 12.6. Of particular significance is the interest rate that the Fed sets on excess reserves, i_{er}, as this will set a floor on the federal funds rate.[32] If the Fed sets the interest rate on excess reserves at i_{er}^1, then the demand for reserves will become flat at i_{er}^1. Commercial banks will not be willing to place excess reserve balances in the federal funds market if the federal funds rate falls below the interest rate paid on excess reserves because they will be able to earn more by keeping the funds in their account at the Fed.[33] Note that when the interest rate on excess reserves is i_{er}^1, the equilibrium federal funds rate, i_{ff}^1, is not affected by the interest rate on excess reserves. However, if the Board raises the interest rate on excess reserves to i_{er}^2, then the new equilibrium federal funds rate, i_{ff}^2, will be equal to the rate paid on excess reserves. Indeed, any further increases in the rate paid on excess reserves would be passed through to the equilibrium value of the federal funds rate basis point for basis point.

The Effect of the Financial Crisis on the Reserves Market

Since the financial crisis, the situation in the reserves market has taken on a very different form owing to the extraordinary measures taken by the Fed to address the financial crisis and the weakness in the economy. These resulted in a surge in the supply of reserves, as illustrated by Figure 12.7. In effect, the supply of nonborrowed reserves

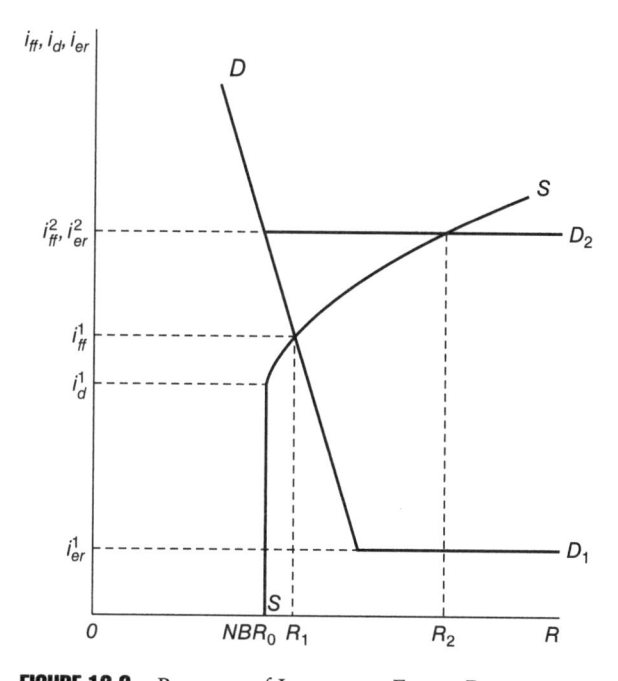

FIGURE 12.6 Payment of Interest on Excess Reserves

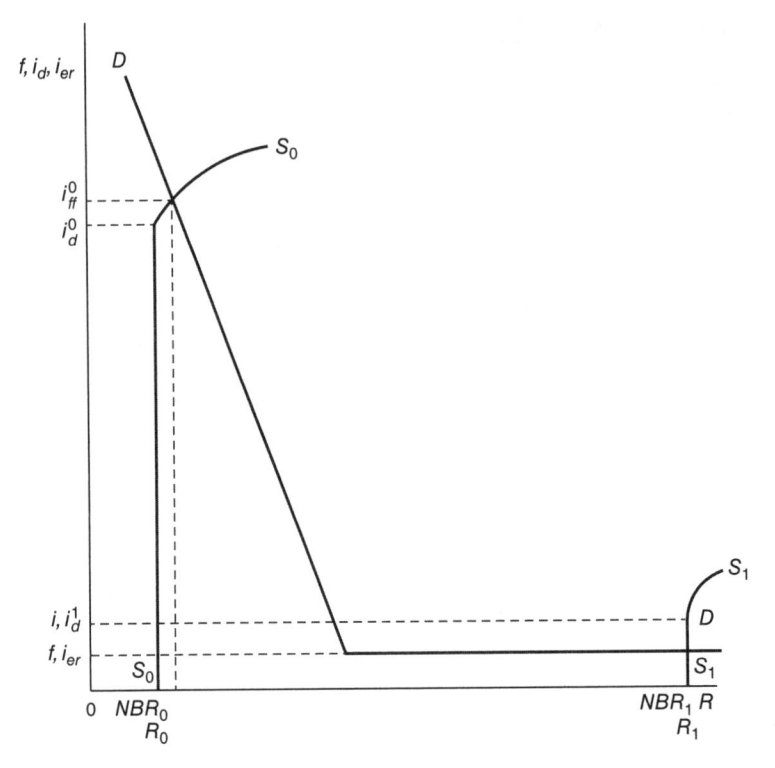

FIGURE 12.7 Reserves Market Following the Financial Crisis

rose from NBR_0 to NBR_1 and the supply schedule shifted from S_0S_0 to S_1S_1. Initially, this took the form of special replacement financing as regular sources of funding to large commercial banks dried up. As the financial system stabilized and regular sources returned, the Fed kept the supply of reserves high by purchasing massive amounts of securities—Treasury and GSE debt, and mortgage-backed securities. This took place at a time when the Fed lowered its target for the policy rate to rock bottom—0 to 25 basis points. The federal funds rate was determined by the intersection of the massive amount of nonborrowed reserves and the horizontal portion of the demand schedule determined by the interest rate established on excess reserves, which was 25 basis points. In response to concerns that were raised by the inflationary prospects of the huge amount of excess reserves in the banking system, the Fed noted that it would be able to raise its policy rate by increasing the interest rate that it pays on excess reserves. Alternatively, the Desk could sell a massive amount of securities from the System's portfolio. You can test your understanding of this model by examining whether increases in the interest rate on excess reserves, i_{er}, gets passed through fully to the policy rate.

Interaction of Policy Instruments in the Reserves Market

It is noteworthy that equilibrium in the market for reserves and determination of the federal funds—policy—rate depend on all the instruments of monetary policy. On the demand side, required reserve ratios—set by the Board—affect the position of the demand for reserves. A higher reserve ratio would cause the demand schedule to shift to the right.

Also affecting the demand for reserves is the payment of interest on reserves—set by the Board—which determines where on the demand schedule the discontinuity occurs and the demand schedule becomes flat. On the supply side, discount policy—determined by the Board—affects the point at which the supply schedule takes on a positive slope. Finally, open market operations—determined by the FOMC—affect the amount of non-borrowed reserves, and thus, the vertical segment of the reserve supply schedule.

SUMMARY

1. Central banks around the globe are major policymaking institutions. They began primarily to assist their governments in financing the budget, often in dealing with a surge in war-related expenses. Over time, they evolved into lenders of last resort that acted to contain financial disturbances. Monetary policy and other policymaking responsibilities came later.
2. In the United States, the Constitution assigns responsibility for monetary policy to Congress. It took a century and a quarter for the United States to establish a central bank, the Federal Reserve System (Fed). This owes importantly to longstanding concerns about the centralization of power in the financial system.
3. The original Federal Reserve, which began operations in 1914, was a decentralized central bank, with little accountability. The weaknesses in the System were revealed during the Great Depression, and Congress responded by centralizing responsibility in the Board—a federal agency. The area where responsibility for policymaking is shared with Reserve Banks is open market operations—governed by the FOMC and on which the Board has a majority of votes.
4. The Federal Reserve System contains the Board of Governors (a federal agency), privately owned Reserve Banks, and the FOMC.
5. The modern Fed has a considerable amount of independence—considered today to be international best practice. This enables the Fed to take the longer view regarding the consequences of its actions and insulates it from day-to-day political pressure. Such independence in a democratic political system creates a tension and requires a high degree of accountability and transparency.
6. The responsibilities of modern central banks are monetary policy, financial stability, fiscal agency, payments system, supervision of financial institutions, and consumer financial protection. Not all central banks perform all of these functions, especially supervision and consumer protection. The Fed is involved in them all, but shares supervision with other regulatory agencies.
7. The policy interest rate is determined by the interaction of the demand for and supply of reserves—balances held at the central bank. In the United States, the policy rate is the federal funds rate, an overnight interest rate on interbank loans involving balances held at the Fed.
8. The demand for reserves is comprised of required reserves and excess reserves. The former are determined by the product of the required reserve ratio (set by the Board) and the level of deposits subject to reserve requirements (selected by the public). The latter are determined by bank decisions to hold reserves in excess of requirements.

9. The supply of reserves consists of borrowed reserves and nonborrowed reserves. The former—discount window credit—is influenced by the policies established by the Board, including the discount rate. The latter is affected by a variety of factors, some of which fluctuate day to day, such as Treasury deposits at the Fed and currency in circulation. Open market operations, governed by the FOMC, affect the supply of nonborrowed reserves.
10. To hit the target for the federal funds rate, the demand for reserves must be satisfied at that interest rate. This means that open market purchases or sales of assets must be undertaken whenever the supply of reserves does not match demand at the interest rate target.
11. In practice, the Fed conducts open market operations primarily in U.S Treasury securities. It can do so through permanent transactions, outright purchases and sales, or temporary transactions, RPs or reverse RPs (MSPs). The decision of which to perform will depend on whether the need to add or withdraw reserves is permanent or temporary.
12. The payment of interest on excess reserves has given the Fed a new instrument for implementing monetary policy. The interest rate on excess reserves (set by the Board) affects the demand for reserves by creating a discontinuity in the demand for reserves at that interest rate. Changes in that interest rate can affect the federal funds rate, depending on whether that segment of the demand schedule intersects the supply schedule.
13. The financial crisis had a major impact on the market for reserves by increasing the supply of reserves substantially. In these circumstances, normalizing policy by raising the policy rate could be achieved by a huge absorption of reserves through open market sales or by raising the interest rate on excess reserves.

QUESTIONS

1. Which parts of the Federal Reserve System are private? Which is part of the federal government?
2. Who selects the boards of directors of Federal Reserve Banks? What are the principal responsibilities of those boards?
3. What does central bank independence mean? How does the Fed get its independence?
4. What is meant by fiscal agency? How might the Fed's role as fiscal agent differ from that of many other central banks?
5. Why do central banks perform a central role in the payment system for their economy? What are the aspects of this role?
6. What does a lender of last resort mean? How does this relate to the financial stability function of central banks?
7. What are the pros and cons of having the central bank playing a key role in the supervision of major financial institutions?
8. Who selects members of the Board of Governors? Does Congress play a role? Who selects the Board's chair and vice chair? Who selects senior officers of Reserve Banks?
9. How does the Fed get its independence? Why might central bank independence be beneficial for monetary policy? What is the tension created by an independent

central bank in a democratic political system? Why are transparency and accountability important?
10. In the market for reserves, what determines demand? What determines supply? How does an increase in the discount rate affect supply? An increase in Treasury deposits at the central bank? An open market purchase of securities? A purchase of foreign exchange? A reverse RP? A higher interest rate paid on excess reserves?
11. Illustrate how the Fed goes about setting the federal funds rate (policy rate) at its target using open market operations (assume initially that the Fed does not pay interest on excess reserves). Illustrate how the Fed can use its newly acquired authority to set the interest rate on excess reserves to raise the federal funds rate.
12. How did the Fed's response to the financial crisis affect the market for reserves? Illustrate.
13. Suppose that the FOMC decides to raise the target for the federal funds rate later this year. What tools are available to achieve this? Illustrate.
14. When the market for reserves is in equilibrium, what is the relationship between required reserves, excess reserves, on the one hand, nonborrowed reserves, and borrowed reserves, on the other?
15. How does an outright purchase of Treasury securities by the Desk relate to a repurchase agreement (RP)? An outright sale to a reverse RP (matched sale purchase)? What will determine whether the Desk executes an outright purchase or an RP? An outright sale or a reverse RP?

NOTES

1. Walter Bagehot introduced the classical notion of the role of a central bank as a lender of last resort in the nineteenth century. See Walter Bagehot, *Lombard Street, a Description of the Money Market* (London: Kegan Paul, 1873). Bagehot argued that the central bank—in his case, the Bank of England—should make credit freely available to solvent commercial banks facing liquidity problems at a penalty interest rate. In so doing, the loans would enable banks to meet runs caused by many depositors seeking to withdraw their funds, and thereby contain banking panics (financial crises). Such advances should be adequately collateralized—that is, the value of the collateral should be greater than the amount of the loan.
2. Assigning this responsibility to the third branch—the judiciary—was a nonstarter.
3. See Ron Chernow, *Alexander Hamilton* (New York, Penguin Books, 2005).
4. This provision of the act also helped the Union government finance its war effort.
5. The smoothing of seasonal variations in credit was of special interest to agrarian interests, because credit demands and interest rates varied with the agricultural cycle. This posed regular strains on farmers, in particular, as they were needing to raise funds from commercial banks during periods of peak activity before they could sell their output.
6. The territory covered by the districts has changed some since 1914. Most notably, Alaska and Hawaii were added to the territory of the Twelfth Federal Reserve District, headquartered in San Francisco.
7. The Reserve Banks could provide credit to member banks though *discounts*. With a discount, the Reserve Bank would purchase eligible instruments at a

discount—applying the Fed's discount rate—and often this transaction would be reversed—the member bank would buy the instrument back. Later, the Reserve Banks were given authority to make advances—loans secured by adequate collateral. Advances were easier to administer and became the favored means of providing funds to banks through the discount window.

8. See Ben S. Bernanke, "A Century of Central Banking in the United States: Goals, Frameworks, Accountability," speech given in Cambridge, Massachusetts, July 10, 2013.
9. An Open Market Investment Committee was created to coordinate open market transactions among Reserve Banks, following guidelines established by the Board. Individual Reserve Banks could opt out of participating in those coordinated actions. In addition to coordinating transactions involving credit instruments (such as commercial paper and Treasury securities), the Committee also coordinated transactions in foreign currencies and foreign investments. They agreed that the Board would need to approve the Committee's recommendations for actions in the open market.
10. Also contributing to the breakdown in the Fed's performance was the loss of an important leading presence in the System—Benjamin Strong, president of the Federal Reserve Bank of New York. Mr. Strong became ill and died in 1928, leaving a huge leadership vacuum.
11. The mid-1930s was a time of centralizing many of the functions of government in the United States in the federal government in Washington, D.C.
12. For more detail on the current structure of the Federal Reserve System, see Board of Governors of the Federal Reserve System, *The Federal Reserve System: Purposes and Functions*, 2005.
13. The role of the Reserve Banks' boards of directors in the setting of the discount rate has been controversial. These boards propose changes to their district's discount rates to the Board of Governors. Thus, bankers and businesspeople, who will be affected by such changes, are participants in the process. Defenders of this practice argue that directors are sworn to secrecy on such matters and agree not to perform transactions based on this information. Further, it is argued, the Board of Governors has the final say and can approve or reject proposed discount rate changes coming from Reserve Banks.
14. The term *cause* is a legal term and basically means that the officeholder has been found to be unfit for the job (by the president)—such as owing to demonstrated incompetence or having been convicted of a felony.
15. The Fed is permitted, though, to acquire newly issued Treasury debt in a rollover in which maturing Treasury securities are exchanged for new ones.
16. Indeed, the Fed transfers excess earnings to the Treasury in amounts that in some recent years reached $100 billion.
17. Other functions of the Fed are subject to GAO audit. In defending the exemption from GAO audit of its monetary policy function, the Fed has argued that subjecting the Fed to such audits could have an adverse impact on inflation expectations—which play a key role in the macroeconomic process and in influencing actual inflation.
18. See Ben S. Bernanke, "Central Bank Independence, Transparency, and Accountability," Board of Governors of the Federal Reserve System, May 25, 2011.
19. In the wake of the financial crisis and Great Recession, financial stability has been deemed to be of comparable importance to monetary policy—returning

to the status that it held at the time of the founding of the Fed. This will be discussed in more detail in Chapter 15. The recent period has punctuated the interdependence between the pursuit of monetary policy goals and financial stability.

20. The terms *supervision* and *regulation* are commonly used together. Regulation refers to the rules that are issued for commercial banks and other financial institutions. Supervision refers to the monitoring of regulated financial institutions to ensure that they are following the rules and that they are not taking excessive risks. Because of their special status and special protections, these institutions are subject to a moral hazard situation, encouraging more risk taking. Supervision is intended to counter this. More will be said on this topic in Chapters 15 and 17.

21. Balances held at the Fed can be used to transfer funds for customers who are making payments—that is, they can be actively used for the vast multitude of standard payments that are made each day in our diverse and complex economy, including settling transactions that are processed through automated clearinghouses. Thus, banks tend to find it advantageous to hold balances at the central bank in excess of their required reserves to facilitate ordinary business needs related to customer transaction activity. In addition, banks may want to hold a cushion of excess reserves to avoid penalties that are imposed if they should unexpectedly end up with a shortfall of actual reserve holdings in relation to their reserve requirements.

22. The statute authorizes the Board to also set reserve requirements on so-called nonpersonal time deposits and net eurodollar liabilities. These are essentially managed liabilities, discussed in Chapters 3 and 17. Since 1990, the Board has set the required reserve ratio on these at zero, as these reserve requirements were seen to be an unnecessary tax on financial intermediation that raised the cost to borrowers.

23. Net transaction deposits exclude balances that banks hold with other banks and checks that have been deposited into customer accounts and are in the process of being collected from other banks. These deductions are allowed to avoid double counting. Also, in practice, the 10 percent reserve ratio is applied to net transaction balances in excess of some threshold—around $75 million per bank. This amount is indexed to the change in transaction deposits and other liabilities subject to reserve requirements. On very small levels of deposits, around $12 million, there is no reserve requirement. On amounts in excess of this amount and up to roughly $75 million, the reserve requirement is 3 percent. Cash in bank vaults can be used to satisfy reserve requirements; thus to determine the amount of balances that a bank needs to hold in balances at the Fed, one subtracts from its calculated reserve requirement the amount of vault cash that it holds.

24. In recent years, the Fed has been able to pay interest on banks' holdings of excess reserves, thus reducing the opportunity cost. In effect, the opportunity cost is the margin of the interest rate that could be earned if these excess reserves were invested in another (higher yielding) short-term instrument over the rate paid on excess reserves.

25. The negative slope of the demand for reserves also reflects an indirect influence through reserve requirements. A rise in short-term interest rates will induce depositors to hold fewer transaction balances to take advantage of the higher yields on money market instruments. As they reduce their holdings of transaction deposits, bank-required reserves decline.

26. Another factor that results in day-to-day fluctuations in nonborrowed reserves is Federal Reserve float, resulting from the check-clearing process. When commercial banks and other depository institutions use the Fed to collect on checks placed in customer accounts, the Fed agrees to give them deferred credit on each check deposited. Credit typically is given in one or two days, depending on when it is estimated that the check can be presented to the bank on which it is drawn. Ordinarily, there is no effect on the supply of nonborrowed reserves because the bank depositing the check will be getting a credit to its Fed account on the same day that the bank on which the check is drawn is losing balances at the Fed. However, there are times—usually associated with adverse weather or a major power outage—when the credit will be given to the depositing bank before the check can be presented to the bank on which it is drawn. This leads to Federal Reserve float and a temporary increase in the supply of nonborrowed reserves. For various reasons, including the substitution of electronic payments for paper checks, Federal Reserve float has been declining in importance over time and ordinarily is not an important consideration in reserve management by the Fed.

27. Note the positive slope to the supply of (total) reserves when the federal funds rate is above the discount rate. This happens because commercial banks have historically been reluctant to go to the discount window for reserves. In part, this is because there is perceived to be a stigma associated with using the discount window, and, even though the Fed does not release the names of banks getting discount window credit, there is a concern that, if word got out, this would be perceived as a sign of weakness. Also, the Fed in the past has deemed getting credit from the discount window to be a privilege and has used administrative measures to limit usage of discount window credit. The Fed no longer is as restrictive in providing access to the discount window—in part because it sets the discount rate as a penalty rate—but banks still show a reluctance to utilize this source of reserves, preserving the upward slope to the supply schedule.

28. To keep things simple, the discount rate has been set high, so that the amount of borrowed reserves is nil and the quantity of total reserves equals the quantity of nonborrowed reserves.

29. We will see in the next chapter that transactions in foreign currencies are an important component of fixed exchange rate regimes. In essence, central banks conduct open market operations in foreign currencies to achieve their goals for the exchange rate.

30. The Fed from time to time has acquired GSE—Freddie Mac and Fannie Mae—debt and mortgage-backed securities. In the wake of the financial crisis and Great Recession, it acquired these securities to place differential downward pressure on mortgage interest rates to foster better conditions in the moribund housing sector.

31. When conducting open market operations, the Fed has an approved list of counterparties for which it is willing to deal. These are mostly very large commercial banks and some major foreign banks. These counterparties are called *primary dealers* and were discussed in Chapter 7. The Fed sets stringent requirements to qualify as a primary dealer, including solid capital positions and a commitment to be an active market maker in Treasury securities.

32. The payment of interest on required reserves will also affect the nonhorizontal portion of the demand for reserves. Most importantly, it causes the demand

for reserves to be less interest-sensitive—more vertically sloped. This is because banks are likely to pass along at least some of the change in the rate paid on required reserves to their depositors in the form of the remuneration that they pay on deposits. As a consequence, the opportunity cost on deposits varies less and the demand for transaction deposits will not move as much as interest rates change.

33. In practice, the federal funds rate does fall below the interest rate paid on excess reserves. The reason for this has to do with some nonbank financial institutions—notably GSEs—being able to raise and place funds in the federal funds market, but not being eligible for an account at the Fed that would earn the interest rate on excess reserves. When these institutions have funds that they want to place in the federal funds market, they may need to accept less than the rate on excess reserves because they are unable to let the funds earn the interest rate on excess reserves in an account at the Fed.

CHAPTER 13

Monetary Policy: The Basics

WHAT YOU WILL LEARN IN THIS CHAPTER

- What causes inflation.
- Why stable prices (or low inflation) has become a primary goal of monetary policy around the globe today.
- How the goals of the U.S. central bank tend to differ from those elsewhere.
- How measures of prices and inflation are calculated.
- How the degree of resource utilization is determined, notably in the labor market.
- How fast the economy can grow on a sustainable basis.
- How changes in unemployment are related to economic growth and the rate at which the economy must grow for unemployment to fall.
- How the central bank affects the position of the economy by influencing aggregate demand.
- What happens when the economy is operating at a subpar level.
- What happens when it is overheating.
- What is meant by an output gap.
- How inflation expectations fit into the picture.
- How a central bank goes about lowering inflation.
- How a central bank goes about boosting a subpar economy.

BACKGROUND

Chances are that the financial crisis and the damage it caused to the macroeconomy—the Great Recession—continue to affect you. It also created one of the most serious challenges to the Fed in its first century. Moreover, worries on the inflation front have shifted from being on the side of rising inflation—where they had been since the 1960s—to being on the side of disinflation in recent years. Were you aware that the United States and many other industrial nations faced double-digit inflation in the late 1970s, and the American public deemed this to be the most serious problem facing the country, even more serious than nuclear confrontation with the Soviet Union? Have you wondered about how the Fed can address these problems with the tools at its disposal—the tools discussed in Chapter 12? In this chapter, we will discuss the goals of monetary policy and how central banks set about trying to achieve them with the tools at their disposal. In particular, we will develop a model that illustrates key macroeconomic relationships that bear on the policy process. In the next chapter, we will address the specific challenges that monetary policymakers face in pursuing the goals of policy, especially those faced in recent years.

EFFECTS OF MONETARY POLICY ON OUTPUT AND PRICES

It is universally agreed by macroeconomists that, in the long run, central bank monetary policy affects the price level—or the rate of inflation—but can do little to boost output and employment.[1] The latter are determined by the amount of labor and capital in the economy, resource productivity, and the effectiveness of markets in allocating resources. Other public policies, such as those that improve the skills of the workforce or the flexibility of markets, will be able to enhance output and employment levels in the long run.

Also worthy of note is the nearly universal agreement that monetary policy, despite being unable to influence output and employment in the long run, can affect these variables in the short and intermediate runs. An expansionary monetary policy will boost aggregate demand and, in normal circumstances, will lead to higher levels of output and employment for a while, with little impact on prices. But those higher levels of output and employment will later be reversed and prices will rise. Conversely, a contractionary monetary policy will lower aggregate demand and lead to a drop in both output and employment, but later that effect will be reversed as prices start to ease.

The Goal of Price Stability

In view of these relationships, in a vast number of countries today, the central bank has been given responsibility for achieving a goal for prices: price stability or low inflation. That is, the charter of the central bank specifies price stability as the primary goal of monetary policy. In a setting of stable prices, it is believed that the microeconomic role of (relative) prices can work more effectively in allocating resources and that businesses and households will be more willing to save as well as invest in productive projects, fostering a higher level of overall output and well-being. In some cases, the charter specifies other macroeconomic goals, such as sustainable levels of employment or output, as subordinate goals of monetary policy. Essentially, this enables the central bank to pursue a policy that will stimulate the economy, so long as it does not jeopardize the goal of price stability. But it does not authorize the central bank to pursue such a stimulative policy if that would compromise the goal for prices.

The Dual Mandate in the United States

In contrast, the Federal Reserve in the United States is charged with so-called twin goals of maximum employment and price stability—sometimes referred to as the dual mandate. That is, the charter of the Federal Reserve System—the Federal Reserve Act—states that the Fed is to pursue the goals of both price stability *and* maximum employment. It also specifies moderate long-term interest rates as a primary goal, but most analysts and public officials believe that this is redundant and will take care of itself if the other two goals have been achieved. In practice, the goal of moderate interest rates has little direct impact on the decision making of the Fed.

For Fed policymakers, the twin goals of maximum employment and price stability can pose a dilemma when the economy is weak and price stability is threatened by unwanted inflation pressures. In these circumstances, focusing on one of these goals will work to the detriment of the other, at least in the near term.

Some have argued that when such a conflict between maximum employment and stable price goals occurs, the Fed should opt for achieving price stability. In this way, it is argued, the Fed will develop a reputation for keeping inflation under control and this will lead to behavior on the part of the public that will complement the Fed's efforts to reach price stability, and, at the same time, will help to stabilize employment. More on this in Chapter 14.

THE OPERATIONAL COUNTERPARTS TO MAXIMUM EMPLOYMENT AND PRICE STABILITY

To be useful as goals of monetary policy, there must be operational counterparts to maximum employment and price stability that can guide the Fed and at the same time help the public assess whether the Fed is meeting its statutory responsibility. In other words, there should be some way of calibrating maximum employment and price stability using statistical information available to the Fed and to the public.

Maximum Employment

In the first place, what is maximum employment? Is it achieved when 100 percent of the work force is employed, or some smaller fraction? In practice, 100 percent employment is not feasible in a dynamic economy like that of the United States. At any point in time, new products are supplanting existing ones and some firms are gaining market share at the expense of others because they offer more attractive or lower-priced products. This requires that resources move from the declining sectors to the expanding ones. During this process, some workers and other resource owners will be discharged and face unemployment. This is sometimes referred to as *frictional unemployment*. It is basically an unavoidable by-product of an ever-changing economy and is largely self-correcting. To put some flesh on these bones, nearly 50 million people enter new jobs each year in a labor force that is a little larger than 150 million. At the same time, the number of separations—quits, layoffs, discharges, and retirements—is nearly as large. These figures indicate that turnover in the labor market is huge, resulting in significant frictional unemployment.

Another type of unemployment—*structural unemployment*—is typically not as short-lived and frequently involves considerable hardship for those affected. Some unemployed workers have not developed the skill sets needed for an advanced economy such as ours, making them less employable. It takes them a long time to find employment because most employers with job openings are seeking a more advanced skill mix; but, once they gain employment, they often acquire valuable job experience that enhances their skills. Others out of work are disinclined to move to places where the new jobs have become available. Still others may be unwilling to take an available job because they deem the work or pay to be demeaning, which becomes more feasible when the employee is eligible for unemployment insurance benefits or other types of public assistance. The latter is sometimes referred to as replacement earnings; the higher the replacement earnings relative to what the individual can earn through employment, the less inclined this person will be to accept employment and more willing to remain unemployed.

The Great Recession is believed to have resulted in a shaking out from the labor force many workers whose skills had lagged and are no longer aligned with the requirements of employers. They have contributed to an unprecedented number of long-term unemployed workers. Moreover, for many of these workers, the absence of employment has resulted in an atrophy of job skills, which is compounding the problem of their employability. These types of unemployment fall into the structural unemployment category. This type of unemployment is not so self-correcting, but often requires public policies other than monetary policy to address the problem.[2]

We generally deem the level of employment corresponding to the sum of frictional and structural unemployment—that is, the total labor force less the sum of these levels of unemployment—to be achievable through monetary policy. However, there are no reliable direct measures of this level of employment or its counterpart for the unemployment rate. As a consequence, researchers have adopted various indirect methods for measuring them. Most such estimates suggest that maximum employment is achieved when roughly 94 to 95 percent of the labor force is employed, or when approximately 5 to 6 percent of the labor force is unemployed. This level of the unemployment rate is sometimes called the *nonaccelerating inflation rate of unemployment (NAIRU)* or the *natural rate of unemployment*.[3] In our discussions, we will regard the NAIRU to be around 5.5 percent.[4]

The actual unemployment rate can be above or below this level, but when the actual unemployment rate departs from the NAIRU the situation is not sustainable. We know from the theory and evidence involving macroeconomic relationships that when the actual unemployment rate exceeds the NAIRU, the inflation rate tends to decline. And when the actual unemployment rate is below the NAIRU, inflation tends to rise.

We have focused our discussion on employment and have not discussed output. In practice, there tends to be a one-to-one correspondence between the level of employment and output in the short run. More employment (less unemployment) will give rise to a higher level of aggregate output, and vice versa. Thus, corresponding to maximum employment or the NAIRU will be a maximum sustainable level of output. This is often referred to as *potential real GDP* or *potential output*. Thus, the goal of maximum employment can be expressed either in terms of the unemployment rate or the level of aggregate output.[5]

Price Stability

We now turn to the operational measure of price stability. When discussing prices in the macroeconomic context, we usually deal with indexes of prices that are constructed to represent the average price of things bought. The most commonly followed indexes of prices are those for the prices that consumers pay. There are also indexes for some other types of prices, notably the index for gross domestic product (GDP), which is related to the average price of a unit of GDP. It includes, in addition to consumption goods and services, investment, government, and net exports.

Consumer price indexes are based on expenditure patterns for what households actually buy. Price enumerators around the country collect prices of each item appearing in a typical basket of goods and services bought by households. These are combined with data on the share of the household budget spent on each of these items—the weight of that item in the budget. The price of each item is then multiplied by its weight and each of these calculations is summed. That sum, corresponding to the average price in this period, is then divided by the average price during a base period to get the index number for this period. The index number for the period in question gives the average level of prices in that period relative to the average price in the base period. An index number of 1.23, sometimes expressed as 123, indicates that prices are 23 percent, on the average, higher than in the base period. If the index were to increase to 1.27 in the next period, we would say that inflation had been 3.25 percent (0.04/1.23).[6]

Because food and energy prices can fluctuate a great deal, the Fed—and some other central banks—tends to focus on measures of consumer price inflation that exclude these volatile components, so-called measures of *core inflation*. For example, a big run-up in food prices, owing to a bad harvest, may distort the underlying pace of price increases, especially as the run-up in food prices likely will be reversed before long. Excluding these components can give a better reading on underlying inflation trends.

The Fed, like many other central banks, does not seek an unchanged level in the price index, but, for various reasons, finds a small rise in the price index to be acceptable.[7] The Fed in recent years has specified a 2 percent objective—or target—for consumer prices and deems this to be consistent with its statutory mandate for price stability.

AGGREGATE DEMAND AND AGGREGATE SUPPLY

Aggregate Supply

We are now in a position to develop a useful model of aggregate demand and aggregate supply. Let us begin with aggregate supply. We can think of total output produced—aggregate supply—as the product of the number of workers employed and the average productivity per worker (output per worker). This can be expressed as

$$y = L \cdot \Pi \tag{13-1}$$

where y is the level of real GDP (the total amount of goods and services produced in the economy), L is the amount of labor employed, and Π is the average productivity of workers. This can be transformed into growth rates as follows:

$$\dot{y} = \dot{L} + \dot{\Pi} \tag{13-2}$$

in which $\dot{y}$ is the percent change in real GDP, $\dot{L}$ is the percent change in labor input, and $\dot{\Pi}$ is the percent change in labor productivity.

Equations (13-1) and (13-2) tell us that output can grow to meet expanding demand through an increase in employment or through more output per worker. In practice, growth in potential output or aggregate supply—$\dot{y}$ in Equation (13-2)—is estimated to be a little less than 2.5 percent per year. Both growth in labor and growth in underlying productivity contribute to this growth in potential output. The growth in labor—$\dot{L}$ in equation (13-2)—is estimated to be about 0.5 percent or a bit higher per year and growth in underlying productivity—$\dot{\Pi}$ in Equation (13-2)—is estimated to be around 2 percent or a little less per year.[8]

In light of this discussion, one can see why so much attention has been given to productivity. Strong gains in productivity get translated into more rapid growth in output and income, which have far-reaching benefits.

Aggregate Demand

Let us now turn to aggregate demand. When deriving aggregate demand, we usually view it from the perspective of the principal components of GDP—consumption, investment, government spending, and net exports. Indeed, we follow the definition of GDP:

$$y = c + i + g + (x - m) \tag{13-3}$$

In this expression, c represents real consumption (nominal consumption outlays divided by an index of consumption prices), i represents real investment, g represents real government spending on final goods and services by all levels of government, and $(x - m)$ represents real net exports (exports, x, minus imports, m).

Aggregate consumption is driven by three principal factors: real income, wealth, and interest rates. Consumption tends to be proportional to income, implying that it grows at about the same rate as income. Consumption also varies directly with wealth. Commonly, wealth and income grow together, resulting in consumption growth at that same rate. In the event wealth increases relative to income, consumption will increase and saving (the portion of income not spent) will decrease. In other words, more wealth will enable people to get closer to their goals for retirement, college for their children, bequests, and so forth, and they will not need to save as much. A decline in wealth relative to income will conversely lead to a drop in consumption and a rise in saving. Finally, higher (real) interest rates will tend to reduce spending as the return on saving more increases as do the costs of borrowing to finance spending. Conversely, a decline in interest rates will tend to boost spending by lowering the returns from saving and by lowering borrowing costs (which will encourage more debt-financed spending). A change in interest rates will also affect the value of equities and many other assets. A decline in interest rates increases the present values of the cash flows from those assets and thereby raises wealth. Thus, monetary policy also affects household demands through wealth effects. A lower interest rate boosts wealth and the higher wealth boosts spending. Conversely, a rise in interest rates lowers consumption through wealth effects.

Thus, monetary policy affects consumption through changes in interest rates and borrowing costs—especially for big-ticket items financed with credit. Those changes in interest rates also affect wealth through the discounting (present value) process developed in Chapter 4. We can unambiguously conclude that a decline in interest rates will increase consumption through interest rate and wealth effects, and vice versa.

The second category of aggregate demand—investment—is a collection of various items. It includes business fixed investment, which takes the form of such things as plants, equipment, software, and other intellectual property. Businesses undertake these investments to enhance their profits. So long as the rate of return on an investment project exceeds its financing cost (basically, the interest rate that must be paid on a loan or on bonds issued to finance the project), the business can add to long-term profits by making the investment. As a consequence, a decline in interest rates will render some investments profitable that previously were not. Conversely, a rise in interest rates will render some investment projects unprofitable that previously were worthwhile, and the firm will cut back on investment. A second type of investment takes the form of investment in inventories.[9] Businesses hold inventories to make more sales, and thus profits. Acting to limit inventory holdings are financing costs. Higher interest rates raise financing costs and encourage businesses to manage with fewer inventories. As a result, inventory investment declines. Conversely, lower interest rates tend to raise inventory investment.[10]

Monetary policy might also affect both types of investment to the extent that it affects business perceptions of the outlook for the economy. Should it become clear to businesses that the monetary authorities are pursuing policies that will result in faster growth in output, they will see sales prospects as improving, which tends to increase the prospective profitability of investments. As a consequence, investment spending would rise.

The remaining category of investment is residential investment—that is, investment in housing. Most housing is owner occupied, as noted in Chapter 10, and thus housing investment decisions are made by individuals (consumption units). Mortgage interest rates have a major impact on this type of investment spending, with declines in mortgage rates making housing more affordable, which boosts residential construction outlays.

Thus, monetary policy affects each of these categories of investment through changes in interest rates, and also potentially through the outlook for the economy and sales.

The third broad category of aggregate demand—government spending—is not very responsive to monetary policy, especially spending by the federal government.

However, the final category, net exports, is potentially very sensitive, but mostly through exchange rate effects. We will see in Chapter 16 that interest rates are a major factor affecting exchange rates and that exchange rates play a key role in influencing the competitiveness of a country's exports relative to other parts of the world. Thus, a decline in interest rates will lower the exchange value of an economy's currency. This will add to its price competitiveness in global markets and raise the price of imports coming into its market. In turn, this will lead to stronger exports and weaker imports. The flip side of weaker imports will be more demand for domestically produced goods that compete with imports. In other words, lower interest rates will boost the demand for net exports through their effects on the exchange rate. Higher interest rates will have the reverse effect on the exchange rate, and export and import competitiveness.

Aggregate demand can also be affected by uncertainty. More uncertainty about the economic outlook—and perhaps, future public spending, tax, and regulatory policies—can adversely influence business and household spending, causing a downward shift in aggregate demand.

Monetary Policy and Aggregate Demand

Figure 13.1 illustrates how monetary policy affects aggregate demand by affecting the level of interest rates. In this diagram, the initial level of interest rates is i_1 and the corresponding aggregate level of goods and services demanded is y_1. If the monetary authority wanted to boost the amount of goods and services demanded to y_2, it would seek to lower the level of interest rates to i_2.[11] Note that the interest rate that affects spending decisions by businesses and households is the interest rate that they face in the marketplace. That interest rate can be expressed as

$$i = i_T + \rho \tag{13-4}$$

where i is the interest rate faced by private borrowers, i_T is the benchmark (Treasury, risk-free rate), and ρ is the risk premium that private borrowers pay over and above the benchmark yield. As we noted in Chapter 5, interest rates i and i_T are intermediate or longer-term rates while the central bank controls a very short-term rate (and may affect expected short-term rates through forward guidance). In the discussion that follows, we will see how actions taken by the monetary authority to affect aggregate demand alter the position of the economy relative to potential output.

In sum, a more expansive monetary policy will raise aggregate demand by boosting the demand for consumption, investment, and net exports. A more restrictive monetary policy will have the opposite effect on aggregate demand by raising interest rates faced by businesses and households.

A disruption to the financial system, as occurred during the financial crisis, can lead to a "credit crunch" in which credit becomes more difficult to get by businesses and households. This corresponds to an increase in the interest rate in Figure 13.1 caused by an increase in the risk premium term, ρ, in Equation (13-4).[12] Borrowing costs rise for businesses and households, even though the central bank

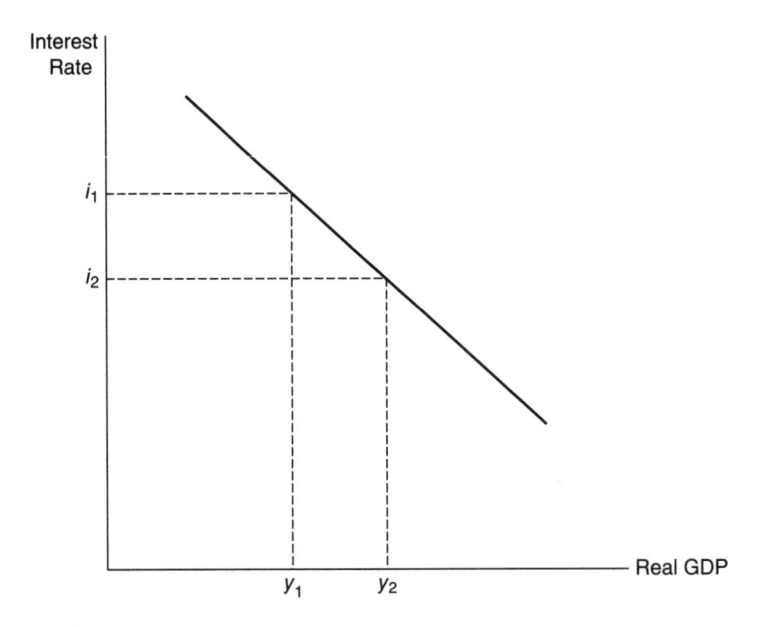

FIGURE 13.1 Aggregate Demand

Monetary Policy: The Basics

has not changed its policy rate. As a consequence, aggregate demand is reduced. This proved to be a major factor contributing to the large downward shift in aggregate demand during the Great Recession. It also limited the extent to which efforts by the Fed to lower benchmark interest rates were able to reverse the decline in demand; increases in the ρ term were tending to offset the drop in the benchmark interest rate term, i_T, brought about by Fed policy easing and flights to safety by private investors.

THE MODEL

We can now put these together in a diagram. Figure 13.2 presents what is an unconventional supply-and-demand relationship. It plots aggregate demand schedule, DD, and aggregate supply schedule, SS. Real output is presented on the vertical axis and time on the horizontal axis. The aggregate supply schedule plots potential output and thus it increases with the labor force and productivity. It is also true that along the aggregate supply schedule the unemployment rate equals the NAIRU. In the very short run, actual output will be set by the amount of aggregate demand, shown by the aggregate demand schedule, DD.[13] Aggregate demand could be the same as aggregate supply or it could be higher or lower.

Steady Inflation

The relationship between aggregate demand and aggregate supply has implications for prices, actually the inflation rate (the missing dimension in Figure 13.2). When actual GDP equals potential GDP, illustrated by A in the diagram, the inflation rate tends to be steady, be it high, low, or somewhere in between. The labor market counterpart to situation A is that the unemployment rate equals the NAIRU.

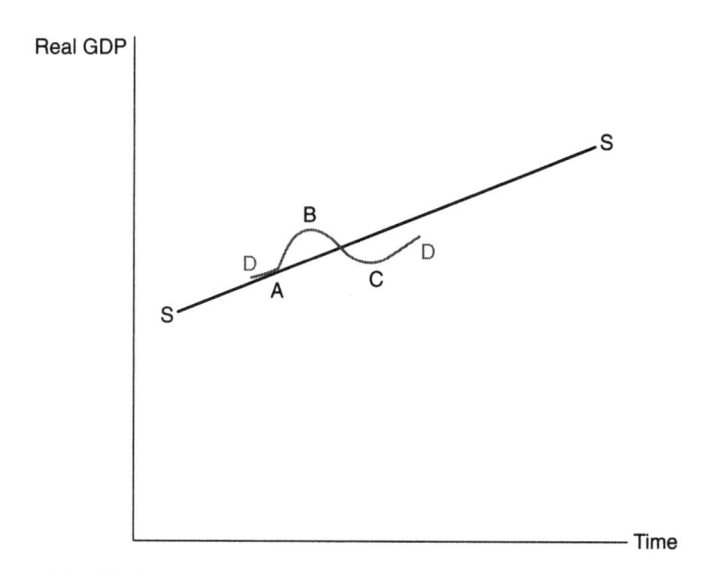

FIGURE 13.2   Aggregate Demand and Supply

Rising Inflation

In contrast, when aggregate demand rises above potential, as in B in Figure 13.2, the inflation rate rises (prices accelerate). The labor market counterpart to this situation is an unemployment rate that is below the NAIRU. The greater the extent to which aggregate demand exceeds aggregate supply, the larger the rise in inflation.

Falling Inflation

Conversely, when aggregate demand drops below potential, as in C, the inflation rate falls—there is *disinflation*. Once the inflation rate has dropped into negative territory, we say that there is *deflation*. That is, deflation occurs when the average level of prices is actually declining on a sustained basis. Clearly, the larger the shortfall of actual output from potential, the greater the disinflation. The labor market counterpart to this situation is an unemployment rate that is above the NAIRU and employment that is below maximum.

In the long run, macroeconomic principles tell us that situations B and C are unsustainable. The economic forces that result in the inflation rate rising or falling, respectively, will also tend to push the actual level of output toward the level of potential.[14] However, this could take some time—from a public policy perspective, an unacceptably long period of time. For this reason, the Fed's charter calls for it to, in effect, pursue policies that hasten the move of actual output to potential—or aggregate demand to aggregate supply.

The Important Role of Inflation Expectations

Thus far, we have discussed how an output gap affects inflation—a positive output gap results in rising inflation and a negative output gap results in disinflation. However, there is another important factor affecting inflation, and that is expectations of inflation. When businesses and workers expect more inflation, they act to protect themselves from losses of purchasing power by raising their prices more quickly and by seeking larger increases in wages (more appropriately, labor compensation). We noted in Chapter 4 that expectations of more inflation also boost (nominal) interest rates, sometimes called the Fisher effect.

The contribution of expected inflation is shown in reduced-form Equation (13-5):[15]

$$\dot{P} = \dot{P}^e + \gamma \left(\frac{y - y^*}{y^*} \right) \qquad (13\text{-}5)$$

In this equation, $\dot{P}$ is the rate of inflation, $\dot{P}^e$ is the expected rate of inflation, y is the actual level of output, y^* is the level of potential output, and γ is a positive coefficient representing the translation of the output gap into the rate of inflation. The coefficient on inflation expectations is, in effect, unity, implying that a change in inflation expectations passes through one-for-one to a change in the actual inflation rate.[16] This expression tells us that the inflation rate can go down either through a negative output gap or through a reduction in inflation expectations.

Actual and Potential Output in Practice

The model that we developed in Figure 13.2 is somewhat simplified from actual experience. The actual relationship between actual and potential output is presented in Figure 13.3. In this diagram, actual output (aggregate demand) is depicted by the more variable line and potential output (aggregate supply) by the continuous line. Note that the potential output line is curved upward. This occurs because output increases at an exponential rate, not at a linear rate as implied by Figure 13.2.[17] Periods designated by recessions—usually characterized by declining output and employment—are shaded. These are periods during which output drops below potential (unemployment rises above the NAIRU) for some time—a negative output gap. With actual output being below potential, inflation eases. Note that the period of the Great Recession and its aftermath has had the largest and most protracted negative output gap. We can now address monetary policy in situations in which the central bank is not achieving its mandate.

ADDRESSING INFLATION

We will first turn our attention to the situation of unwanted inflation—inflation above the central bank's target. This corresponds to B in Figure 13.2 where aggregate demand is above aggregate supply.[18] In this situation, unemployment will be below the NAIRU.

Absent being able to lower inflation expectations, the central bank will need to pursue a policy that restrains aggregate demand by raising interest rates through increases in its policy rate—a tightening of policy that raises benchmark interest rates, i_T. This tightening of policy has to be sufficient to bring aggregate demand

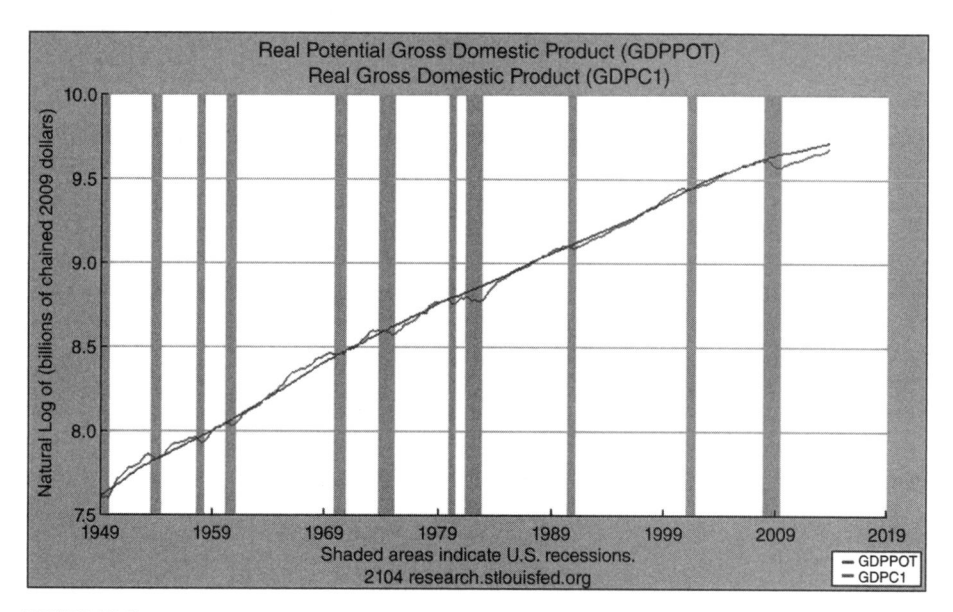

FIGURE 13.3 Real Actual and Potential Real GDP
Sources: Bureau of Economic Analysis and Congressional Budget Office.

below aggregate supply in order for the inflation rate to fall. This is illustrated in Figure 13.4. At point A, inflation is rising even further above the central bank's target. Not only does the acceleration in prices need to be arrested, but inflation needs to be brought down to the target pace. To achieve this, policy needs to be tightened enough for *growth* in aggregate demand to be brought below *growth* in aggregate supply or potential output. When this occurs, the aggregate demand line will move closer to the aggregate supply line and then drop below it as shown by the move along the broken line from A to B. Once the *level* of aggregate demand has dropped below the *level* of aggregate supply, such as at B, inflation will be falling and moving toward the central bank's target. At some point, the inflation rate will be getting sufficiently close to an acceptable pace and the central bank will need to focus on stimulating aggregate demand so that it rises to potential output, point C in Figure 13.4.[19] This will require that the policy rate be lowered sufficiently so that growth in aggregate demand will exceed growth in potential output for a while, until the level of aggregate demand reaches the level of potential output. As that point is approached, policy will need to be tightened enough to slow growth in demand to the same pace as growth in aggregate supply. Once there—point C—maximum employment and price stability (or low inflation) will be achieved and should be sustained until the economy is blown off course. More on that in the next chapter.

Alternatively, the central bank could lower inflation if it could convince the public that inflation was going to be lower in the future, and the public reduced its inflation expectations, $\dot{P}^e$ in Equation (13-5). Doing so eliminates the need for a negative output gap to lower inflation. If inflation expectations could be lowered sufficiently for inflation to drop to the target, all the central bank would need to do would be to tighten policy sufficiently for the economy to go from point A in Figure 13.4 to potential output and close the positive output gap. With an output gap of zero and inflation expectations in line with the target rate of inflation, actual inflation would settle at the target pace. There would be no need for output to fall below the level of

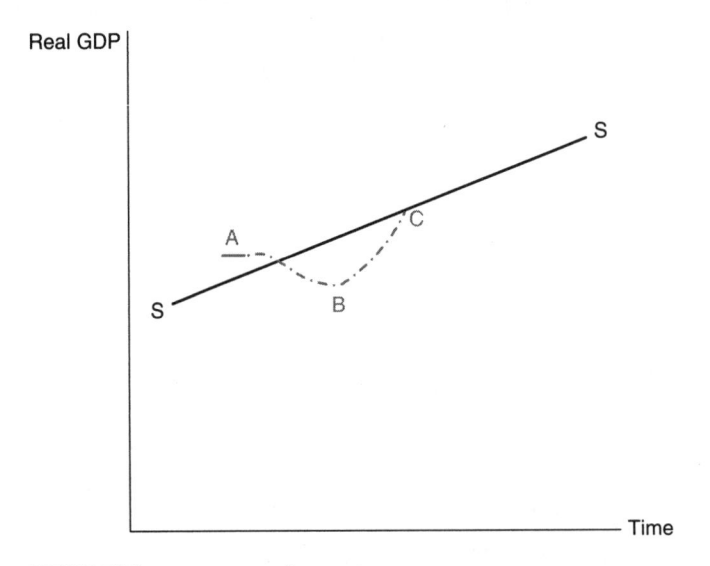

FIGURE 13.4 Bringing Inflation Down

potential (or the unemployment rate to rise above the NAIRU). The success of such a painless scenario depends critically on whether the central bank can articulate its commitment to achieving its inflation target and, perhaps more importantly, whether the public believes that it will. That is, whether the central bank's statements have credibility. This, too, will be discussed more fully in the next chapter.

Perhaps an example will help. In the 1970s, inflation became a serious problem in the United States and many other parts of the world. Inflation in the United States had risen throughout the 1970s and by the end of the decade had climbed solidly into double digits and seemed to be heading higher. The problem of inflation routinely topped the list of problems facing the nation according to various public opinion polls. In October of 1979, the Fed—under the leadership of its new Chairman, Paul Volcker—decided to tackle this problem aggressively.[20] It determined to tighten monetary policy sufficiently to bring inflation down to a low rate. It made public statements to this effect, but they did not make much of a dent in lowering inflation expectations. As a consequence, the economy moved from a point such as A in Figure 13.4 to a point such as C. The recession turned out to be the worst of the postwar period—until the Great Recession—as can be seen in Figure 13.3. The large negative output gap did the job of bringing inflation below 5 percent. However, if people had instead believed Fed statements and had acted accordingly in lowering their expectations of inflation, the same result could have been achieved at a much lower sacrifice of output and employment. It is noteworthy that the reduction in inflation and inflation expectations set the stage for a couple decades of prosperity and low inflation, sometimes referred to as the Great Moderation.

ADDRESSING A SHORTFALL IN OUTPUT

We next examine the policy response to a shortfall in output and employment. This corresponds to situation C in Figure 13.2. The unemployment rate will be above the NAIRU. In this circumstance, inflation will be under downward pressure, and efforts to stimulate the economy should not pose inflation concerns as long as actual output stays below potential.

In this situation, the central bank will need to lower its policy rate—ease monetary policy—sufficiently to get *growth* in aggregate demand to exceed *growth* in aggregate supply. This is illustrated in Figure 13.5. At point A, the level of output is below potential. Once the policy action takes hold and aggregate demand grows more rapidly than supply, the *level* of aggregate demand will draw closer to the *level* of aggregate supply. As this occurs, the central bank will need to begin raising the policy rate to restrain growth in aggregate demand. Indeed, it will want to raise the policy rate sufficiently to bring *growth* of aggregate demand into alignment with *growth* in aggregate supply at point B in Figure 13.5.[21]

Throughout the postwar period, the Fed had enough scope to lower its policy interest rate sufficiently to put the economy on an upward trajectory, as in Figure 13.5, and close the negative output gap over a year or two, as shown in Figure 13.3. However, as we will see in the next chapter, the situation that developed during the Great Recession resulted in a very large output gap that required a larger drop in the policy interest rate than could be achieved, given that the Fed had lowered that rate to its zero lower-bound limit.

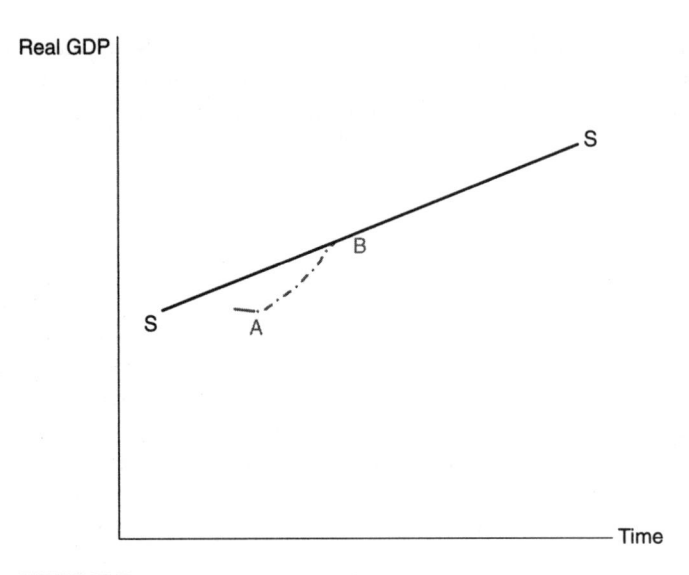

FIGURE 13.5 Restoring Full Employment

OKUN'S LAW

There is a relationship between growth in output and the change in the unemployment rate—referred to as Okun's Law, after its author, Arthur Okun.[22] It can be expressed algebraically as

$$\dot{y} - \dot{y}^* = -\Delta u \qquad (13\text{-}4)$$

In this expression, $\dot{y}$ represents the actual growth in real GDP, $\dot{y}^*$ represents the growth in potential output, and Δu represents the change in the unemployment rate. This expression states that if actual output grows at the same rate as potential, the unemployment rate will be unchanged (at a level at, above, or below NAIRU). If actual output grows faster than potential, the unemployment rate will decline. And if actual output grows slower than potential, unemployment will rise. For example if growth in potential is 2.5 percent and real GDP grows 3.5 percent over the next year, the unemployment rate will fall by 0.5 percent—$1 = -1/2 \cdot \Delta u$ or $\Delta u = -1/2$.

SUMMARY

1. In the long run, the principal effect of monetary policy is on prices. In the short and intermediate run, though, monetary policy can affect output and employment.
2. The charters of most central banks today specify price stability as the principal goal of monetary policy, recognizing that monetary policy can do little to affect output and employment in the long run. However, the Fed's charter specifies a dual mandate of price stability *and* maximum employment. In most circumstances, these two goals are not in conflict.

3. In practice, the Fed translates its mandate into operational objectives of a small increase—about 2 percent per year—in a core measure of prices and actual output equaling potential output (corresponding to an unemployment rate of around 5.5 percent, the so-called NAIRU).
4. Aggregate supply—potential output—grows over time at a pace determined by the rate of growth of labor input and the growth in labor productivity—in practice, nearly 2.5 percent per year.
5. Monetary policy affects aggregate demand, primarily by affecting interest rates (borrowing costs) faced by businesses and households. Higher interest rates reduce aggregate demand and lower interest rates raise aggregate demand. A disruption to the financial system—credit crunch—has much the same effect as tighter monetary policy by raising borrowing costs (and making it more difficult to qualify for a loan and reducing the amount that can be borrowed, if one can qualify).
6. When the *level* of aggregate demand matches potential output, inflation is stable. When the *level* of aggregate demand exceeds potential, inflation increases. And when the *level* of aggregate demand falls below potential, inflation declines (disinflation occurs).
7. When inflation is running above the central bank's objective, the *level* of output generally must be brought below potential through higher interest rates. This implies that *growth* in aggregate demand must, for a while, drop below *growth* in potential output.
8. Also affecting inflation are inflation expectations. Higher inflation expectations act to boost actual inflation, and, conversely, lower inflation expectations act to lower inflation. Thus, the central bank could achieve a desired reduction in the inflation rate by convincing the public that inflation will be lower. In these circumstances, a loss of output and employment can be avoided.
9. When the level of output drops below potential and slack develops in resource markets (unemployment rises above NAIRU), interest rates must be lowered by the central bank to boost growth in aggregate demand to exceed growth in potential output.
10. Okun's Law calibrates the relationship between the difference between growth in actual and potential output and the change in the unemployment rate. When growth in actual output exceeds growth in potential, the unemployment rate declines by half that margin.

QUESTIONS

1. In practice, which interest rates are most important for spending decisions? What is the connection between these rates and Treasury benchmark interest rates? How does the Fed affect benchmark interest rates? How do these rates vary in relation to Treasury benchmark rates over the business cycle?
2. Under what circumstances might the Fed's maximum employment goal conflict with its price stability goal?
3. How does monetary policy affect aggregate demand through wealth effects?
4. How would a credit crunch affect the relationship between the Fed's policy rate and the interest rate and terms faced by business and household borrowers?

How would this affect aggregate demand? What would the Fed need to do to avoid this from affecting the economy and employment?
5. Is there a role for communication policy to enhance the effectiveness of Fed policy? Does it make any difference whether people believe Fed public statements (whether the Fed is credible)?
6. If the Fed seeks to stimulate growth in aggregate demand, what should it do with its policy rate? Communications?
7. Output is currently below potential. What are the implications for inflation? How should the Fed set its policy rate to achieve its twin goals? What will happen to the growth in aggregate demand as a result? Should it then be growing faster or slower than potential output (aggregate supply)? At what point will the Fed want to readjust its policy stance to avoid an inflation problem? At this point, what should it seek for the relationship between aggregate demand and aggregate supply? What will happen to inflation when this is achieved? What will be the unemployment rate?
8. If the unemployment rate is currently around 9.5 percent, how many years of growth in real GDP of 4.5 percent per year would be required to restore the unemployment rate to the natural rate (NAIRU) and actual output to potential? (Assume that growth in potential output is 2.5 percent per year and the NAIRU is 5.5 percent.)
9. If actual output currently is equal to potential output and inflation is not a concern, should aggregate demand be stable or growing over the next couple years? What would be the implications of holding aggregate demand steady at that level for the next few years? Would the Fed continue to achieve its goals?
10. If the unemployment rate were to be stable over the next few years, what would you infer has happened to growth in real GDP?
11. What is meant by disinflation? If the United States were experiencing disinflation, what would you conclude about the relationship between actual output (aggregate demand) and potential output (aggregate supply)? The unemployment rate?
12. At the present time, is inflation or disinflation more of a concern for the United States? Why? What is the outlook for inflation? Why?
13. If inflation expectations were to increase, what would be the implications for actual inflation? How would this affect the twin goals? What would be required to return inflation to its previous rate?

NOTES

1. In practice, central banks can permanently *reduce* output and employment by following disruptive monetary policies that, for example, result in high and volatile inflation.
2. Policies that can ameliorate structural unemployment are training programs, including those offered by community colleges and trade schools, and relocation assistance to enable unemployed workers to get to the places where there are jobs.
3. There has been an unusual amount of uncertainty about the estimate of the NAIRU in recent years, owing to the extent of the mismatch of job skills that became evident in the wake of the Great Recession.

4. The NAIRU can vary over time in association with demographic or structural factors. Younger workers have less experience and tend to have higher unemployment rates. Thus, when young people comprise a large share of the labor force, the NAIRU tends to be high. Currently, the labor force has a disproportionate share of older and more experienced workers, which is tending to pull down the NAIRU.
5. Complicating the relationship between the unemployment rate and the level of output are variations in the labor force participation rate. The unemployment rate is calculated as the number of adults surveyed who regard themselves as in the labor force less those actually employed (divided by those in the labor force). However, when the economy is weak and some adults see their prospects for employment to be dim, they classify themselves as not in the labor force. When this happens, the measured unemployment rate is reduced compared to what it would be if these people classified themselves as being in the labor force and seeking work. In other words, the labor force participation rate—the number of people classified as being in the labor force divided by the adult population—drops, and the relation between the measured unemployment rate and the level of output is distorted (unemployment is low in relation to output). When the economy strengthens, these people see better employment opportunities and regard themselves as being in the labor force. The associated increase in the participation rate will give rise to a higher unemployment rate. The distortion caused by lower labor force participation has been exaggerated in the Great Recession and its aftermath.
6. The rate of inflation is usually presented as an annual rate. When computing the inflation rate from the same period—month or quarter—a year earlier, the result will be an annual rate. However, if one calculates the rate from an adjacent period—quarter or month—one needs to annualize the change by multiplying the percent change by 4 (if quarterly) or 12 (if monthly). High-frequency changes in prices—such as quarterly or monthly—contain a substantial amount of "noise" and may not be reflective of underlying inflation. As a result, many analysts focus on year-over-year measures.
7. One reason the Fed and other central banks have been willing to tolerate a small increase in the measured level of prices is that these indexes are known to have an upward bias, which could be as much as 1 percentage point per year. Another reason has to do with problems that are encountered when the inflation is very low. In these circumstances, the central bank will need to set a low policy rate to avoid having a real interest rate that is too high and would lead to disinflation and ultimately deflation. It could fall behind the curve in its effort to prevent deflation if it lowers the policy rate at a slower pace than inflation is dropping and thereby allows the real interest rate to increase. By falling behind, it might be unable to prevent deflation once it hits the lower bound on its policy rate, which is zero. Japan faced this problem during the 1990s and the United States has faced something similar in its efforts to restore the economy to full employment in the wake of the Great Recession.
8. The growth in labor has slowed from a 1 percent rate or so not so long ago. This owes to a leveling off of labor force participation on the part of women—after decades of steady increases—and withdrawals from the labor force of a growing volume of mature adult males, many to retirement. Productivity growth,

in contrast, has been relatively strong since the 1990s, reflecting advances in information technology, the life sciences, and managerial efficiencies. Note that it is growth in underlying productivity that contributes to growth in potential output, not necessarily growth in actual productivity. Over shorter periods, the latter also reflects aggregate demand. Weakness in aggregate demand will result in slow growth in actual (measured) productivity because actual production will be constrained by the weakness in demand and will fall short of what could be produced with available resources and existing technology.

9. Note that it is the *change* in the level of inventories, not the level itself, that enters into real GDP.
10. The change in inventories represents the difference between demand and production in any period. When demand exceeds production, firms will draw down inventories to satisfy demand. Conversely, when demand falls short of production, firms will find themselves accumulating inventories. Generally, demand and production track each other fairly closely over time and we will use the terms *demand* and *production* interchangeably.
11. We will see in the next chapter that the ability of the monetary authority to exert control over aggregate demand is complicated by several factors. One of these is the imprecise relationship between the interest rate it controls, a very short-term rate (the policy rate that, in the United States, is the federal funds rate), and the interest rates on which households and businesses base their spending decisions, intermediate- and long-term interest rates. Moreover, those interest rates embody risk premiums that vary over time and in somewhat unpredictable ways.
12. Actually, a credit crunch affects not only borrowing costs, but also whether a business or household can get credit, and, if so, how much it can get. In other words, it raises the bar for being able to get a loan, as well as the amount of credit that a borrower getting over the bar can get and the spread of the interest rate that the borrower must pay over the benchmark interest rate. A tightening along any one of these dimensions of the credit process can be thought of as raising the interest rate in Figure 13.1. Of course, if credit were to tighten along all three dimensions, this would be illustrated by an even larger increase in the interest rate in Figure 13.1. An increase in the ρ term could occur because commercial banks and other lenders have lost capital (net worth) and must cut back on their assets, including loans, to realign their assets with their reduced capital. This is discussed more fully in Chapter 15 dealing with financial crises.
13. This model, while simple in construct, is based on widely accepted principles of macroeconomics. In particular, those principles indicate that the actual level of real output will be determined by aggregate demand in the short run. Moreover, they indicate that when output departs from potential (unemployment from the NAIRU), the inflation rate will change—sometimes called the short-run Phillips curve.
14. In terms of underlying aggregate demand and supply schedules, the tendency for output to gravitate toward potential in the long run is the same proposition as the aggregate supply schedule, drawn in typical price and output space, shifting from a horizontal position in the short run to a vertical position in the long run (at potential output).

15. A reduced-form equation distills a key relationship between a few variables based on a more complex set of macroeconomic relationships involving many more variables.
16. The coefficient γ has been estimated to be on the order of 0.3 when inflation and the output gap are expressed as percentages. Thus, a 1 percent negative output would lead to a reduction in inflation of 0.3 percentage points.
17. The linear diagram of Figure 13-1 is a little simpler to work with and, for expositional purposes, adequately captures the important concepts being developed.
18. Inflation above the Fed's target could also occur when actual output is at potential. In this case, inflation is stable, but too high. In the situation illustrated by Figure 13.4, the inflation rate is rising. Both cases will require that policy be designed to bring actual output below potential for a while during which inflation is falling and approaching the target.
19. Because of lags involved between changes in the policy rate and their effect on aggregate demand—which tend to average around six months—the central bank needs to be lowering its policy rate before point B is reached to avoid overshooting on the downside. Similarly, it will need to begin reversing this policy rate decline before point C is reached to avoid overshooting on the upside. Policy lags will be discussed in Chapter 14.
20. See John B. Taylor, "The International Implications of October 1979: Toward a Long Boom on a Global Scale," *Federal Reserve Bank of St. Louis Review* 87, no. 2, part 2 (March/April 2005): 267–275.
21. Again, the central bank will need to initiate the increase in the policy rate before point B is reached, given policy lags.
22. Arthur Okun, "Potential GNP: Its Measurement and Significance," American Statistical Association, *Proceedings of the Business and Economic Statistics Section* (1962): 98–104.

CHAPTER 14

Monetary Policy: Challenges Faced by Policymakers

WHAT YOU WILL LEARN IN THIS CHAPTER

- The kinds of shocks to aggregate demand and aggregate supply that push the economy off course and require central bank action.
- The critical role played by expectations when inflation departs from the central bank's objectives.
- The time lags involved between the time the economy or inflation move off course and actions taken by the central bank begin to correct the situation.
- How these lags require the central bank to be forward looking in setting its policy.
- The potential benefits from having the central bank follow a well-articulated monetary policy rule instead of discretion.
- How central banks have used forward guidance to increase the effectiveness of their actions.
- How central bank credibility is critical to its effectiveness in stabilizing inflation and output and employment, and how central bank independence buttresses credibility.
- Whether there would be gains to be achieved if the United States were to follow the lead of other countries and have a single goal of inflation instead of its current dual mandate.
- How the Fed has utilized conventional and unconventional monetary policy tools to counter the Great Recession.

BACKGROUND

Perhaps you thought from the discussion of the previous chapter that central banking isn't so difficult after all. You need to figure out where the economy is in relation to potential output and engineer policy settings that place aggregate demand on a trajectory to reach potential output, and, once there, you choose policy settings that keep the economy expanding at the rate of growth of potential output. Pretty straightforward, isn't it? So why in practice do we so seldom achieve even one of the twin goals of monetary policy, let alone both? What are the gremlins that keep us from achieving the twin goals?

Perhaps you have noticed that Fed policymakers talk a lot. What are they trying to accomplish by their public statements? How might they be trying to affect our behavior? On another matter, could the central bank achieve better results if it stuck with a well-articulated rule for conducting policy instead of relying on policymaker discretion (some would say whim)? Further, is there something to be said for following the practices of other parts of the world by specifying a single goal of monetary policy—stable prices—rather than complicate the process with the dual mandate? Finally, how was the economy pushed so far off course during the Great Recession, and why has the Fed faced prolonged difficulties in getting the economy back on track? In this regard, what has been the purpose for the Fed buying unprecedented amounts of assets in the open market?

This chapter addresses these issues using the framework that we developed in Chapter 13.

OTHER FORCES AFFECTING OUTPUT AND INFLATION

In practice, forces other than monetary policy affect output and inflation. Often, we refer to these as *shocks* or unexpected forces that affect the trajectory of aggregate demand and push it above or below aggregate supply. Shocks also occur to aggregate supply.

Aggregate demand shocks are illustrated in Figure 14.1. The economy has been operating at potential, point A in Figure 14.1, and inflation has been low and acceptable.

A positive aggregate demand shock is illustrated by the move to point B. Households or businesses may decide to spend more on consumption or investment than normal relationships would suggest. For example, businesses may be driven by "animal spirits" to spend more, to use an expression coined by John Maynard Keynes.[1]

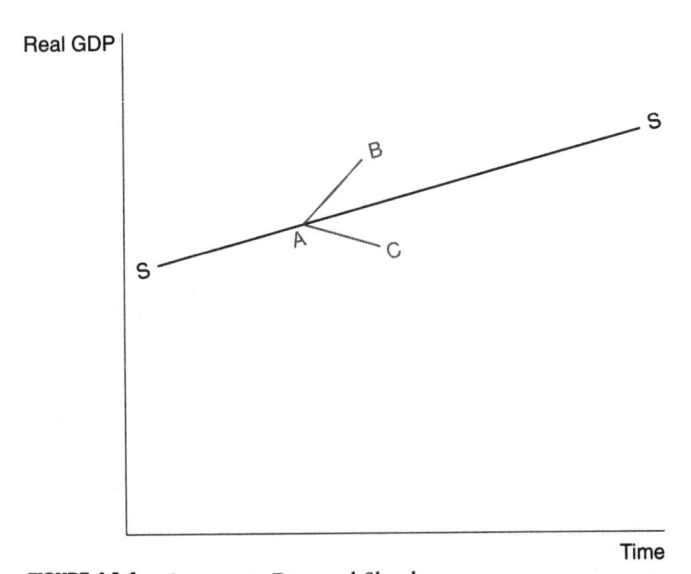

FIGURE 14.1 Aggregate Demand Shocks

In any event, the central bank will begin to realize that the economy has been blown off course and unwanted inflationary pressures are building. If it does not see this positive demand shock as reversing itself soon, it will need to subdue this inflation threat by tightening monetary policy through an increase (or increases) in the policy rate. The way in which policy will restore price stability—or low inflation—is the same as described in the context of Figure 13.4.

A negative demand shock could occur for the opposite reasons as a positive shock. For example, it could result from a credit crunch or a major sell-off in the stock market causing a big loss of wealth. This is illustrated in the move from A to C in Figure 14.1. With inflation not a concern, if the central bank does not see this shock as being one-off, it will need to attempt to counter the loss of output and employment by easing monetary policy and stimulating growth in aggregate demand through a reduction (or reductions) in its policy interest rate. The prescription for monetary policy is the same as that described in the context of Figure 13.5.

Similarly, there are shocks that affect the aggregate supply schedule, enabling more or less output to be produced with existing resources. A negative aggregate supply shock is illustrated by line segment B in Figure 14.2. In this situation, demand is unaffected and keeps expanding in line with the previous expansion in potential output, while supply dips lower. This could be caused by a surge in the price of oil or some other commodity that is imported in substantial amounts. In essence, the higher price for this commodity means that less can be purchased from abroad and thus less is available as an input for the production of goods and services domestically—pulling aggregate supply downward, at least temporarily. The result is a gap between aggregate demand and aggregate supply that could be inflationary.[2]

Much depends on whether the shock is one-off or persisting. If it is thought be temporary, then the issue for the central bank will be whether the rise in inflation will result in the public expecting more inflation or whether the public will realize that the inflationary pressures will ebb and they expect inflation to return to its

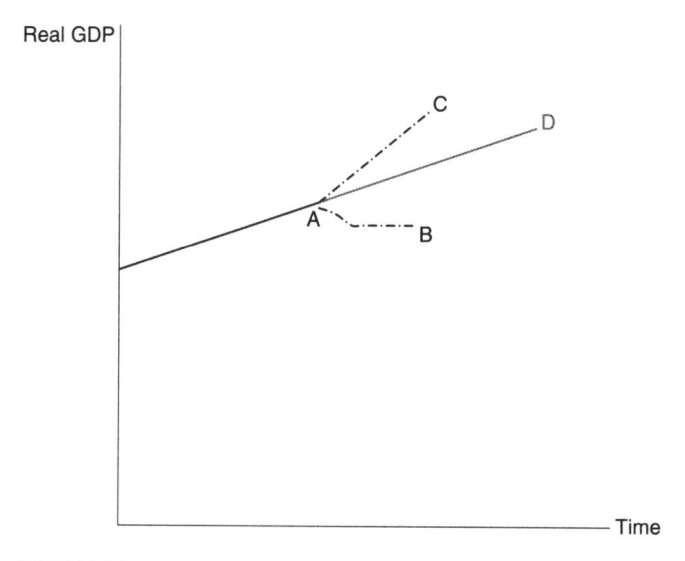

FIGURE 14.2 Aggregate Supply Shocks

preshock pace. In the case of the former, to avoid inflation's staying higher as a result of higher inflation expectations, the central bank would need to lower aggregate demand through a tighter monetary policy that brings aggregate demand below aggregate supply until inflation and inflation expectations return to their former rate. If it is thought to be a more lasting shock, then aggregate demand would need to be brought down to the new aggregate supply (line segment A) or below, if inflation expectations rise, to prevent inflation from staying higher. The outcome will be lower output and employment, and, at least temporarily, more inflation.[3]

Supply shocks can be positive as well as negative. For example, growth in productivity could strengthen. This is illustrated by the line segment C. In this case, growth in potential output has increased on a sustained basis, as indicated by the steeper slope of the aggregate supply schedule. In this example, a gap develops between potential output and aggregate demand.[4] The slack that emerges in product and labor markets puts downward pressure on inflation, unless the central bank boosts aggregate demand and brings it up to the new level of aggregate supply. Notice in this example that aggregate demand will need to be growing at a faster rate than before, or slack will be developing, because aggregate supply is now growing more rapidly.

LAGS AND OTHER COMPLICATIONS

Information about the performance of output and inflation is only available with a time lag. Thus, the central bank will typically be getting readings on where the economy has been some time ago and not where it is at the moment.[5] As a consequence, the central bank can never be sure whether the economy and inflation are on the intended path or are drifting off course.[6]

In addition, there are lags between actions taken by the central bank and their effects on the economy and prices.[7] Changes in the policy rate are generally thought to have their primary impact on output and employment about six months later, although these lags can vary in unpredictable ways. The lag between a change in the policy rate and prices (or inflation) is commonly believed to be longer, on the order of two years.

Need to Be Forward Looking

For these reasons, the central bank needs to be forward looking, trying to anticipate where the economy will be in a couple of quarters and where inflation will be after that. Actions taken today will not have much impact before then. Moreover, these lags require that the central bank be fairly good at forecasting the path of the economy and prices to be able to determine if policy actions are required now to achieve its goals later on and to keep departures from those goals to a minimum.

Beyond these lags, there is uncertainty about what the effect on the economy and prices will be from any change in the policy rate. At times, a given change in the policy rate will have a greater impact on output or prices than at other times. Thus, the central bank will be uncertain about how much the policy rate will need to be changed, even when it has confidence about its assessment of the economy and the outlook for the economy.

Importance of the Expected Path of Short-Term Rates

Some of this uncertainty stems from slippage in the relationship between changes in the policy rate, which the central bank can control with considerable precision, and changes in those intermediate- and longer-term interest rates that influence spending decisions. To appreciate this, we will go back to the term structure of interest rates model that was developed in Chapter 4.

Figure 14.3 presents the two-paneled diagram that was developed in Chapter 4. It illustrates the crucial relationship between the path of expected short-term interest rates that will be set by the central bank over time and the yield curve. The current level and expected path of short-term rates is illustrated by schedule AA in the lower panel. To keep things simple, market participants expect that short-term rates will be steady at i_0. Corresponding to this set of expectations is a yield curve, shown in the upper panel by schedule AA. Note that the yield curve slopes upward, even though the expected path of short-term rates is flat, because of term premiums that reflect increases in interest rate (price) risk as maturity increases.

Next, suppose that the economy has weakened unexpectedly, and the Fed responds by cutting the policy rate to i_1. This will cause longer-term rates to decline. But the extent of the decline will depend on how market participants revise their outlook for the path of short-term interest rates. Two possibilities are shown in Figure 14.3. In the first, illustrated by line segment B in the lower panel,

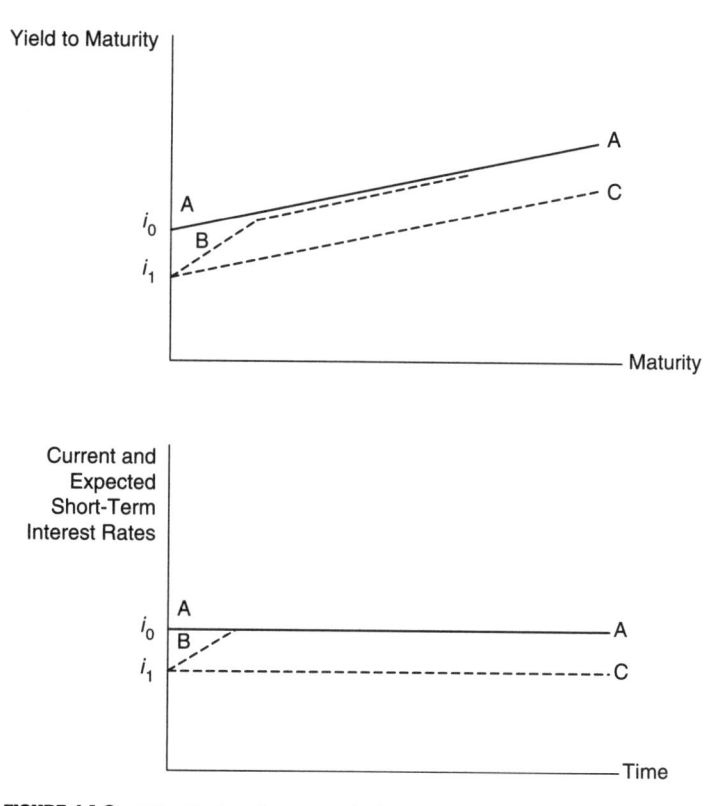

FIGURE 14.3 The Path of Expected Short-Term Rates and the Yield Curve

market participants expect the drop in short-term rates to be only brief, and the policy rate to return fairly promptly to its initial level, i_0, and path. In these circumstances, the impact on the yield curve, especially beyond the near term, is minimal. This is illustrated by line segment B in the upper panel. Those types of spending that are affected by intermediate- and long-term interest rates—household and business spending—will be only minimally boosted by this policy action.

In contrast, should market participants come to expect that the new lower policy rate, i_1, will persist throughout the years ahead, the expected path of the short-term interest rate will remain uniformly below the old one. This is illustrated by line segment C in the lower panel. As a consequence, the entire yield will drop by the same amount, illustrated by line segment C in the upper panel. Because intermediate- and long-term interest rates will fall by much more than in the first case, spending will be boosted considerably.

These examples illustrate the critical role that expectations of market participants play in the impact of changes in the policy rate by the central bank. The more the change in the policy rate affects the expected future path of the policy rate, the greater the impact of a given change in the policy rate on aggregate demand.

Forward Guidance

For this reason, the central bank will be concerned about expectations of the future path of short-term interest rates. Suppose the central bank foresees much weaker aggregate demand going forward. In this case, the central bank will want market participants to be convinced that the policy rate will be lower for the foreseeable future. This will result in a large reduction in intermediate and long-term interest rates—along the lines of line segment C in Figure 14.3—and a large boost to aggregate demand. To ensure that this occurs, the central bank may wish to convey to the public that it envisions that conditions will require a low policy rate for some considerable time. At other times, the central bank will foresee only a small shortfall in aggregate demand and will seek only a small change in intermediate- and long-term interest rates—along the lines of line segment B in Figure 14.3—to avoid overstimulating aggregate demand.

Just the reverse will hold when the economy is overheating and the central bank seeks to relieve inflationary pressures. The more aggregate demand is seen to exceed aggregate supply, the more the central bank will want market participants to extrapolate a higher policy rate into the future. In this way, the impact of the policy action will be greater on intermediate- and longer-term interest rates, and the slowing in growth of aggregate demand will be more pronounced and consistent with reachieving price stability. A statement by the central bank conveying its expectations that short-term rates will remain high for some time will help to shape expectations by the public that the path of short-term interest rates will stay elevated, and this will help to ensure that the response of intermediate- and long-term interest rates will be in keeping with the central bank's policy objectives.

This type of public communication has come to be known as *forward guidance*. Increasingly, central banks have come to regard forward guidance as an additional instrument of monetary policy.

POLICY RULES

There are advocates of policy rules to guide or to discipline monetary policymakers, arguing that adherence to the right policy rule will result in better performance of output and prices.

Money Stock Rule

In the past, there have been advocates of establishing a rule for growth in the money stock—targeting the money stock. It was maintained that if the central bank established a money stock target, based importantly on achieving price stability, then this would be effective in achieving price stability. But it would also be effective in stabilizing the economy if shocks to aggregate demand were to push the economy off course. Basically, it was argued that the central bank should set a target for money growth that was broadly in line with the growth in potential output. This target, it was maintained, would ensure that aggregate demand was growing near the pace of growth in potential output. The result would be a reasonably stable price level. In the event that a negative demand shock were to threaten to push the economy below potential, money demand would weaken with the softening economy and steady growth in the money stock would result in an excess supply of money balances which would lead to a decline in interest rates. Lower interest rates would boost aggregate demand and help the economy return toward potential.

For money stock targeting to work, the demand for money must be reasonably stable, predictable, and not highly sensitive to movements in interest rates. As noted in Chapter 3, the experience in the United States and other developed economies over recent decades has been one of very unstable and unpredictable money demand. This means that money stock targeting will be counterproductive in stabilizing output and achieving price stability. In other words, in these circumstances, disturbances to money demand will get translated into disturbances to aggregate demand, output, and employment, pushing the economy away from the objective instead of toward it. Moreover, because the money stock no longer tracks movements in economic activity—gross domestic product (GDP)—very closely, it is not of much value as an indicator of the economy.[8] As a result, most countries have abandoned the use of measures of the money stock as either a target or an indicator of monetary policy. The evolution of the financial system is believed to have loosened the relationship between the money stock and output, rendering the money stock of minimal value for monetary policy purposes.

Taylor Rule

In recognition of the shortcomings of a money stock rule, some have advocated setting the policy interest rate based on the twin goals of policy—maximum employment and stable prices—more directly. The most popular such rule is the Taylor rule, developed by noted Stanford economist John Taylor.[9] Specifically, the standard Taylor rule is specified as

$$i_{ff} = 2 + \dot{P} + 1/2(\dot{P} - 2) + 1/2\left(\frac{y - y^*}{y^*}\right) \tag{14-1}$$

In this expression, i_{ff} is the setting of the policy (federal funds) rate, $\dot{P}$ is the rate of inflation, y is the *level* of real GDP, and y^* is the *level* of potential real GDP. This version of the rule treats price stability as a 2 percent annual increase in the price level. If the economy were at potential output $\left(\frac{y-y^*}{y^*}=0\right)$ and if prices were rising at a 2 percent rate, the setting of the federal funds rate would be 4 percent—that is, $i_{ff} = 2 + 2 + 0 + 0 = 4$ percent. If, instead, prices were rising at a 3 percent rate, the policy rate would be set at $i_{ff} = 2 + 3 + ½(3 − 2) = 5.5$ percent. Note that the inflation rate rose to 1 percentage point above target, but the policy rate rose 1.5 percentage points. This means that following the Taylor rule would result in the real interest rate rising by 0.5 percentage points to slow down aggregate demand to bring inflation down.[10] Should, instead, a negative aggregate demand shock cause output to fall 2 percentage points below potential output, the Taylor rule would call for $i_{ff} = 2 + 2 + ½(−2) = 3$. The policy interest rate (and the real interest rate) would be lowered 1 percentage point to counter the weakness in the economy.

The chart in Figure 14.4 illustrates the actual federal funds rate with the solid line and the federal funds rate path suggested by the Taylor rule with the dashed line. The chart illustrates that the actual rate set by the Fed varied with the contours suggested by the Taylor rule over much of the 2000s. However, it was routinely

The Target Rate and the Taylor Rule Prescriptions using Real-Time Inflation Forecasts

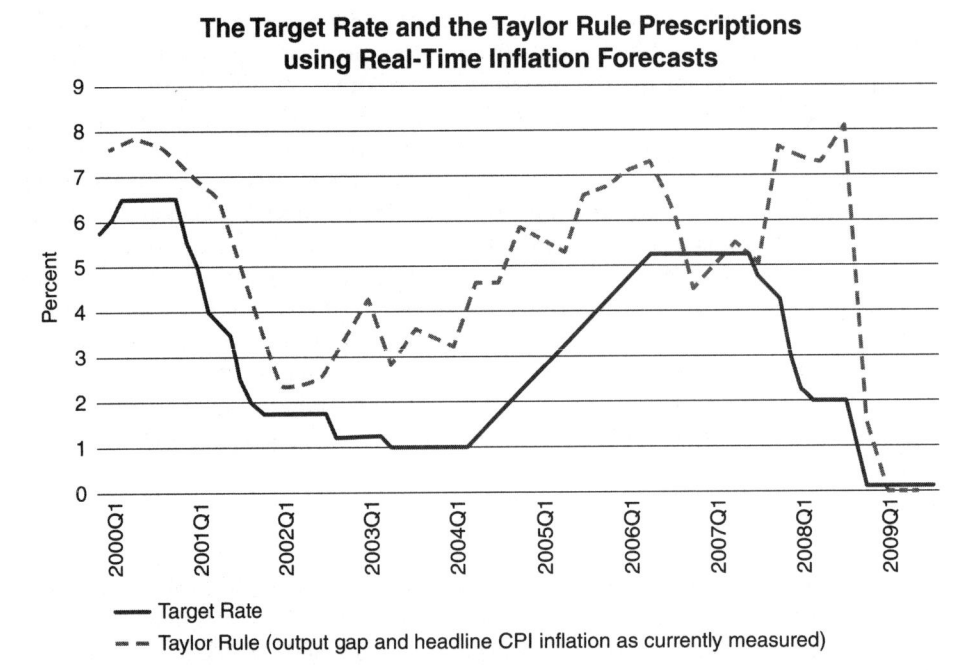

— Target Rate
- - Taylor Rule (output gap and headline CPI inflation as currently measured)

FIGURE 14.4 Actual Target Federal Funds Rate (solid line) and Two Versions of Taylor Rule Prescriptions (broken and dotted lines)
Source: Federal Reserve Board, Bureau of Labor Statistics, Bureau of Economic Analysis, and Federal Reserve staff calculations.

below that level over much of that period. Professor Taylor has argued that this shortfall in setting the federal funds rate contributed to the bubble in housing prices during this period and the major losses in mortgage-related financial assets once the bubble began to burst.[11]

Well-designed policy rules, it is argued, can help to anchor inflation expectations. If the public understands the rules and has confidence that their pursuit will result in the inflation goals being met, then they can help to bring the behavior of private economic agents in harmony with those goals.

EXPECTATIONS AND CENTRAL BANK CREDIBILITY

The discussion in this chapter and the previous one highlights the importance of expectations on the part of economic agents in a market economy. In particular, we have seen how inflation expectations play a key role in the macroeconomic process and in the effectiveness of monetary policy. We saw how higher inflation expectations lead to higher inflation and a loss of output if the inflation is to be reversed. We also saw how a shock causing higher inflation need not require a loss of output and employment if it does not adversely affect inflation expectations. If the public is convinced that the central bank will take the necessary action to curb the higher inflation—that is, inflation expectations are well anchored—the rise in inflation can be unwound fairly easily without much loss of output and employment. However, the more stubborn those inflation expectations are—because the public is skeptical of the central bank's commitment to bring inflation back under control—the more persistent the problem will be.

Furthermore, we saw in the previous section that expectations of market participants regarding the path of the policy rate are key to intermediate- and long-term interest rates. If the central bank, for example, foresees that aggregate demand will be running well above aggregate supply for some time, imparting serious inflationary pressures, it will want market participants to believe that the policy rate will be higher for some time to have the biggest impact on curbing aggregate demand through a bigger increase in intermediate- and long-term interest rates. As we noted, it may need to help that process by communicating to the public that it foresees the policy rate being high for an appreciable time.

To get the right outcome for both inflation expectations and intermediate- and longer-term interest rates, the central bank will want to shape those expectations. This will require clear communications with the public and belief by the public in the statements of the central bank—credibility. Thus, if inflationary pressures are developing, the central bank will want the public to believe that it will take necessary actions to keep inflation under control. If credible, this should keep inflation expectations anchored and thereby limit adverse results for both prices and output. In other words, credibility of the central bank's commitment to price stability will limit the inflationary consequences of an adverse shock to aggregate supply as an actual upturn in inflation will not be translated into an increase in inflation expectations, with implications for output losses and more inflation. Similarly, overheating caused by aggregate demand climbing above aggregate supply will need to be countered by higher benchmark interest rates. Here again, if market participants believe that the path of the policy rate is going to be higher for some time—perhaps because of explicit forward guidance by the central bank—the impact on those key interest rates and aggregate demand will be greater. Conversely, lack of central bank credibility can make the central bank's task much more difficult, with adverse consequences for output and inflation.

For these reasons, central banks today seek to be convincing in their commitment to the goals of monetary policy, especially price stability, and they need to demonstrate their competence in being able to achieve those goals. Credibility has come to be seen as a separate instrument of monetary policy. It is key to getting the public to take actions that are in harmony with its policies. Central bank independence, which we discussed in Chapter 12, is an important contributor to central bank credibility. If the central bank does not have sufficient autonomy to pursue the goals of monetary policy, the public could well be skeptical of whether those goals will be achieved—especially price stability. The public might see the central bank's efforts to achieve price stability, for example, being compromised by pressure from the government or a powerful special interest group to back off an anti-inflationary policy because of its temporary adverse consequences for output and employment. This would result in inflation expectations drifting away from the target.

On a related issue, because markets are very forward looking, they respond to every bit of news bearing on the outlook for the economy. In other words, they will anticipate policy actions before they occur and build these into a revised path for short-term interest rates. This, in turn, will affect intermediate- and longer-term interest rates before any policy action is actually taken. As a consequence, aggregate demand will be affected sooner. For example, should news related to consumption spending show that unexpected weakness is developing in aggregate demand with adverse consequences for output and employment, market participants will begin to anticipate a lower path for the policy rate. That lower path will lead to declines in benchmark interest rates. This will start the process of stimulating spending by businesses and households prior to any actual lowering of the policy rate by the central bank. So long as market participants correctly assess the implications of the news for the economy and monetary policy, their actions will help to stabilize the economy faster than if they only responded after the central bank's policy action.

INFLATION TARGETING

Some countries have adopted formal targets for inflation. These are usually announced on an annual basis, typically with the government concurring on the target announced by the central bank. Among the notable examples are the United Kingdom, Canada, and New Zealand (the first to introduce an inflation-targeting regime).

Advocates of inflation targeting maintain that commitment by both the central bank and the government to a specific inflation target will have a salutary effect in anchoring inflation expectations around that target, and will convince the public to take actions in harmony with that target. With anchored inflation expectations, departures of inflation from target will not cause the revisions to inflation expectations that require the central bank to take actions affecting output and employment that in time stabilizes inflation and returns inflation expectations to align with the central bank's target. We saw in the earlier parts of this chapter that shocks to aggregate demand and supply will have more substantial consequences for departures of output and employment from policy objectives when inflation expectations are adversely affected. In other words, the absence of anchored inflation expectations results in more variability of output and inflation when there are shocks as the central bank acts to avoid inflation from sustained departures from the goal.[12]

Studies of the experience of the economies with inflation targets suggest that inflation expectations have been reasonably well anchored under inflation targeting, and macroeconomic performance has been favorable overall.

It has been argued that the United States should follow the examples of these other countries and adopt an inflation target. However, critics maintain that an inflation target would give precedence to the goal of price stability over maximum employment. It is argued by critics that if the Fed were faced with a combination of inflation pressures and weakening output and employment, it would need to address the inflation risk at the expense of output and employment. Advocates of inflation targeting, however, maintain that credible inflation targeting would more firmly anchor inflation expectations and would not require aggressive monetary policy actions to counter higher inflation and inflation expectations. This would then give the Fed the flexibility to pursue emerging weakness in employment without needing to be concerned about igniting worries about inflation. Thus, they argue that inflation targeting would better enable the Fed to achieve both of its twin goals.

The experience of the United States over the past decade or so, however, has demonstrated that inflation expectations have remained fairly stable in the face of a variety of shocks that caused actual inflation to rise above the Fed's objective—and at other times to fall below. Among these were supply shocks causing large increases in energy and other commodity prices. In these circumstances, the Fed has had flexibility to pursue policies that supported output and employment growth without having to be overly concerned about inflaming inflation expectations. This has happened at a time when the Fed has pursued its dual mandate, even before it specified the numerical target of 2 percent for inflation in 2012. Prior to the specific numerical target, the Fed stated that it was seeking low inflation and it took actions suggesting that its inflation objective was on the order of 1.5 to 2 percent per year. This experience has led many to believe that inflation expectations have been sufficiently well-anchored under the dual mandate and to question whether the dual mandate needs to be replaced with a sole target of inflation.

THE ZERO-BOUND CONSTRAINT AND THE SLOW RECOVERY FROM THE GREAT RECESSION

The financial crisis and the associated credit crunch and large loss of wealth caused a major negative shock to aggregate demand, pushing the economy far off course. Recall from the previous chapter that a loss of wealth causes a downward shift in aggregate demand. Utilizing the framework developed in Figure 13.1, this is illustrated in Figure 14.5 by the shift in aggregate demand schedule from DD to D'D'. This caused the amount demanded to shift from A (output y_0) to B (y_1) at interest rate i_0. At the same time, the credit crunch was causing the premium that borrowers had to pay over benchmark interest rates (the ρ term in Equation 13-4) to

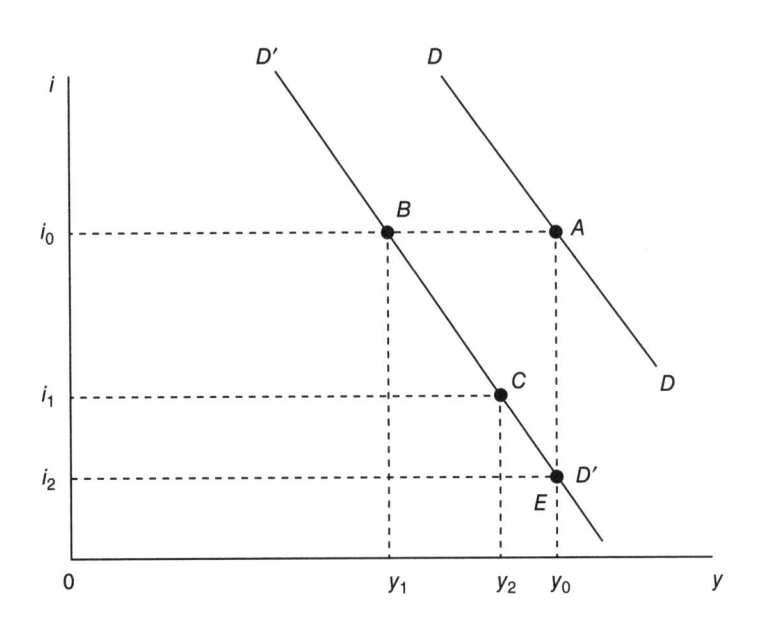

FIGURE 14.5 The Great Recession

rise, which, absent declines in benchmark yields, raised the borrowing cost faced by businesses and households and further curbed aggregate demand. The Fed responded by aggressively lowering the policy rate to zero (actually zero to 25 basis points). Its actions helped to bring down benchmark interest rates but proved inadequate for turning the economy around quickly and increasing the amount of aggregate demand sufficiently to return actual output to potential output. This is shown by the reduction in the interest rate faced by private borrowers from i_0 to i_1. Output was able to increase from y_1 to y_2 (from point B to point C). But there was still a shortfall because borrowing rates faced by private borrowers needed to fall by more, to i_2, to boost the amount demanded to E in the diagram, which corresponds to potential output. The zero-bound constraint meant that the Fed could not use its traditional policy tool anymore to stimulate the economy. In other words, to lower the benchmark rate to i_2, the federal funds rate would need to move into negative territory—which cannot happen—or the Fed would need to take other measures to place downward pressure on benchmark rates.

To get more leverage on borrowing costs once the zero-bound constraint was reached, the Fed refined its communications policy to sharpen forward guidance on the path of the federal funds rate. This included statements such as the Federal Open Market Committee (FOMC) expected its policy to remain very low for an "extended period" and later to link its setting of the federal funds rate to economic performance (the unemployment rate dropping to 6.5 percent or lower was specified for a time). As the unemployment rate was approaching this quantitative specification and the economy was not as robust as contemplated, the Fed substituted qualitative factors that would influence the decision to raise the federal funds rate for this quantitative statement.

Meanwhile, the Fed embarked on large-scale (long-term) asset purchase programs, known as LSAPs, in an effort to lower longer-term interest rates by tamping down term premiums in those rates. It came to be dubbed *quantitative easing* (QE). Beyond this, at one point, the Fed attempted to put even more downward pressure on term premiums embedded in long-term rates by reallocating its portfolio by selling short-term Treasury securities and using the proceeds to buy more long-term Treasuries. This was popularly known as "Operation Twist." While these nontraditional policy tools no doubt contributed to lower benchmark interest rates—especially the Fed's forward guidance—they have proven to be controversial, notably the asset purchases that ballooned the Fed's balance sheet. They also proved to be insufficient in getting the economy to return to potential output as quickly as the Fed wanted.

SUMMARY

1. In practice, shocks to aggregate demand and aggregate supply are frequently pushing the economy off course, requiring adjustments in the stance of monetary policy. These shocks affect the relationship between aggregate demand and aggregate supply and thus the actual rate of inflation and possibly inflation expectations.
2. Inflation expectations play an important role in the relationship between output and inflation. Higher inflation expectations tend to raise actual inflation. In these circumstances, departures of inflation from target would be met by tighter monetary policy and a loss of output and employment. For these reasons, policymakers pay close attention to inflation expectations and seek to anchor them at low levels consistent with their price stability goals.
3. There are various time lags involved between the time the economy starts to go off track and actions taken by monetary policymakers start to return the economy to potential output. The information about the position of the economy becomes available only after some time and it may take additional time before the policymakers take action to counter the departure. It then takes significant additional time before the change in the policy settings affects the economy.
4. Moreover, policymakers have uncertainties about their assessment of the economy and about how their policy actions will affect the economy and inflation, further complicating the task of policymakers.
5. Forward-looking markets can help reduce the lags when information becomes publicly available that suggests the economy has moved off track. Market participants will anticipate policy action by the central bank, which will affect prices of financial assets even before the central bank acts.
6. Because central banks do not control benchmark interest rates directly and must work through the term structure of interest rates, they have increasingly made public statements—forward guidance—about their expectations for the future path of the policy rate. In this way, they seek to shape expectations of market participants of the future path of short-term interest rates in ways that better achieve their desired change in benchmark interest rates—and thereby interest rates faced by businesses and households as they make their spending decisions.
7. Policy rules have been suggested to guide central banks. Setting a target for money stock growth has been one such policy rule. However, instability in the money demand relationship has rendered such rules impractical for achieving the ultimate goals of monetary policy. Alternatively, the Taylor rule—which focuses on setting the policy rate based on departures in inflation from price stability and

departures of output from potential—has been offered as a better way to achieve the final goals of policy.

8. Central bank credibility is important for central bank effectiveness in achieving its monetary policy goals. In particular, it is important whether the public's expectations of inflation and the path of short-term interest rates is in harmony with statements by the central bank and its stated goals.
9. Inflation targeting is practiced in a number of countries, but the United States has a dual mandate. Some have advocated inflation targeting for the United States on grounds that a single such mandate would better anchor inflation expectations.
10. The zero-bound constraint on the federal funds rate proved to be a serious obstacle for the Fed to return the economy to potential (lower the unemployment rate to the nonaccelerating inflation rate of unemployment [NAIRU]) during the Great Recession and its aftermath. Accordingly, the Fed sought to use unconventional means to put downward pressure on borrowing costs—notably forward guidance and large-scale asset purchases.

QUESTIONS

1. Does a positive aggregate demand shock have the same effect on output and inflation as a positive supply shock? How do inflation expectations come into play?
2. How do the consequences of a one-off shock differ from a more persistent shock? How do inflation expectations come into play?
3. What is meant by "anchored" inflation expectations? Do these aid a central bank in stabilizing output and inflation? If so, how?
4. How do forward-looking financial markets shorten the time between departures of the economy from the intended path and the effects of policy actions in returning it to that path?
5. How does credibility affect the ability of a central bank to stabilize output and inflation? Its ability to affect benchmark interest rates?
6. How might central bank independence affect its credibility? What other factors will affect its credibility?
7. How do lags in the effects of policy action on output and inflation bolster the case for central bank independence?
8. Under what circumstances would a money stock target be effective in stabilizing inflation? Output?
9. What is meant by a Taylor rule? What would the Taylor rule call for in the setting of the policy interest rate if inflation were 3 percent, the target for inflation were 1 percent, and there were a positive output gap of 1 percent? What would be the setting if inflation were 1 percent and there were no output gap (positive or negative)?
10. How might an announced single goal of an inflation target help to achieve that objective? What would be the consequences for output and unemployment? In practice, how would you characterize experience in the United States under the dual mandate?
11. Go to the Board's website and read the most recent statement issued by the FOMC. Identify the sentences that are intended to influence expectations held by the public.

12. What is meant by the zero-bound constraint? How has it affected the ability of the Fed to achieve its goals? How has the credit crunch affected the ability of the Fed to achieve its goals?

NOTES

1. John Maynard Keynes, *The General Theory of Employment, Interest and Money* (London: Macmillan, 1936), 161–162.
2. Actually, the increase in the commodity price, say oil, will reduce purchasing power of economic agents and depress aggregate demand as it is passed along to the price of final goods—gasoline and other fuels. The drop in demand will usually fall short of the drop in aggregate supply and there will be a remaining gap that is inflationary. Also, the higher prices of goods directly affected by higher oil prices will tend to push up headline prices on a one-off basis, even if the central bank attempts to close the gap—that is, if it acts to contain core inflation.
3. This framework can help to explain the process by which a change in expected inflation affects actual inflation, as captured in Equation (13-5) in the previous chapter. That equation states that higher expected inflation will pass through to higher actual inflation. This is akin to a negative supply shock, as in Figure 14.2. In effect, if expected inflation increases, producers will want to produce less and workers will want to work less at the previous inflation rate (they will produce the same and work the same hours if inflation rises in line with their expectations of inflation). As a result, a positive output gap develops, which results in more actual inflation.
4. In practice, the greater output made available by more productivity will boost profits, leading to more stock market wealth, and also higher real wages. Increases in both will also boost aggregate demand. Thus, the gap between aggregate demand and aggregate supply will be smaller. The disinflationary effects will be greater if businesses compete their higher profits away through lower prices, which appears to have happened when productivity growth jumped in the mid-1990s. Many attributed this to global competitive price pressures.
5. The Federal Reserve and other central banks supplement lagging statistical data with anecdotal information that can be gathered more quickly. Reserve Banks survey key players in their districts with some frequency for this purpose. However, anecdotal information needs to be used carefully, because it is typically less comprehensive and less reliable than regular statistical releases.
6. The time lag between when a development pushes the economy off course and the recognition of this development and policy action by the central bank is sometimes called an *inside lag*.
7. The lag between the action by the central bank and its effect on the economy sometimes is called an *outside lag*. In practice, the effect of a policy action is not all felt at one time, but is distributed over a period of time.
8. An economic variable, such as the money stock, can be used as an *indicator* without being used as a *target*. Using the money stock as an indicator would involve using movements in the money stock as a gauge of movements in the economy. For example, a pickup in growth of the money stock might be indicating a pickup in the rate of growth of output. Measures of the money stock

are typically statistically reliable, are available on a timely basis, and potentially could be used as an indicator of the economy—along with other timely information—so long as variations in the money stock reflect variations in the economy. In these circumstances, the monetary policy action would be based on assessments of the trajectory of output, which in turn would be informed by movements in the money stock. Using the money stock as a target, by contrast, would involve using the instruments of monetary policy, such as open market operations, to achieve a target for the money stock as an intermediate means of achieving an objective for output (GDP).

9. John B. Taylor, "Discretion versus Policy Rules in Practice," *Carnegie-Rochester Conference Series on Public Policy* 39 (December 1993): 195–214.
10. A policy rule that results in an increase in real interest rates when inflation is rising above the target rate (or decreases when inflation falls below the target rate) is called the Taylor Principle. Such a movement in real interest rates is needed to bring inflation back to the target rate.
11. John B. Taylor, *Getting Off Track: How Government Actions and Interventions Caused, Prolonged, and Worsened the Financial Crisis* (Stanford: Hoover Institution, 2009).
12. Some have argued for a price level target instead of an inflation target. Instead of, say, a 2 percent annual target for inflation, it is argued that the central bank should develop a path for the level of prices that rises 2 percent per year. With an inflation target, a miss in the inflation target in a year—say, inflation turned out to be 1 percent—would ordinarily not be made up in the future, but the central bank would continue to pursue 2 percent inflation each subsequent year. However, a miss under a price-level target would need to be made up, and thus inflation for a period of time would need to run above 2 percent. Whether a price-level target would be more effective in stabilizing inflation expectations would depend on whether the public understood its working and the public believed that a makeup of a shortfall was not going to lead to an ongoing pickup in inflation.

CHAPTER 15

Financial Crises

WHAT YOU WILL LEARN IN THIS CHAPTER

- How financial crises have been an important part of our history.
- Why some bursts of asset bubbles have major consequences for the functioning of the financial system and the economy and others do not.
- How recessions caused by financial crises tend to be more severe and recoveries from those downturns less robust.
- How large losses of asset values at commercial banks and other financial institutions and maturity mismatches between assets and liabilities are at the heart of financial crises.
- How recent financial crises and classic banking panics have many similarities.
- How the recent financial crisis compares with that of the Great Depression.
- The meaning of the *shadow banking system*.
- The meaning of *systemic risk* and its implications for public policy.
- How public policy toward large, systemically important financial institutions has changed in response to the recent financial crisis, including as prescribed by Dodd-Frank legislation.

BACKGROUND

The recent financial crisis has touched nearly everyone on this planet—leaving deep scars on many. A consequence of the financial crisis was the Great Recession, the worst in the postwar period. Moreover, the recovery from this recession has been tepid, as has been typical of previous recoveries from financial crises.[1] Some have laid the blame for this debacle on government policies, while others have pointed the finger at reckless, unbridled commercial banks and other private financial institutions. Meanwhile, governments around the globe have responded by expanding the scope of regulation of the financial system, focusing on large, systemically important institutions that pose risks to the entire financial sector and to their economies.

Financial crises have played an important role in U.S. financial history. The most severe have been associated with a vicious dynamic: a tailspin in the financial system interacts negatively with the economy, bringing both lower. At times, there has been outright panic and the financial system has frozen up, causing output and employment to plunge. In their aftermath, the most severe have led to major changes to our financial system—some drastic.

To develop some appreciation for the central role played by financial institutions—primarily commercial banks—in financial crises, we can compare two recent bubble episodes. In the late 1990s, a bubble developed in the stock market, especially in tech stocks. Prices reached a peak in March 2000, and then began a two-and-a-half-year slump, falling by nearly half over that period. The second bubble was the residential real estate bubble that followed. Real estate prices climbed rapidly until mid-2006 and then began to drop steadily. The cumulative drop over the next few years was about a third. The size of both markets was comparable at their respective peaks, about $20 trillion for the stock market and $25 trillion for the residential real estate market. These figures indicate that the dollar loss was a little greater for the stock market decline.

However, the damage to the broader financial system and to the economy was much greater in the bursting of the housing bubble. A number of our major commercial and investment banks nearly failed (and one major investment bank failed), as did a major insurance conglomerate. The drop in output and rise in unemployment was considerably greater for the financial crisis brought on by the bursting of the real estate bubble, despite a much more aggressive monetary policy response. In contrast, no major financial institutions came close to failing after the bursting of the stock market bubble. The difference between the two episodes is that the drop in asset values from the bursting of the stock price bubble went directly into investor portfolios, while the losses arising from the bursting of the real estate bubble wiped out massive amounts of capital of major financial institutions. Because the capacity of commercial banks and other financial institutions to provide financing for business and household spending is directly related to their capital positions, this meant that these institutions had to cut back substantially.[2] The result was a credit crunch that caused cutbacks in spending and a contraction in output and earnings, which caused credit losses at financial institutions and further losses of capital. The vicious downward spiral that ensued has been referred to as an *adverse feedback loop*.

In view of this painful episode, the Fed has elevated stability of the financial system to a priority status comparable to that of monetary policy, noting the interconnection between a stable financial system and a well-performing economy. When the financial system faces severe stress, it spills over to the macroeconomy. And when the macroeconomy is seriously underperforming, losses mount among financial institutions and financial stability is threatened.

We will now look more closely at the dynamics of a shock affecting the stability of financial institutions, most notably the commercial banking system.

CLASSIC BANKING PANICS

In earlier times, financial crises involved the banking system. In these times, the bulk of financial activity took place through commercial banks and there was no government safety net, such as deposit insurance, that covered commercial banks and gave their depositors comfort about the safety of their bank balances. Also, as we noted in Chapter 3, commercial banks have traditionally received short-maturity deposits (much of which can be redeemed on demand) and have used the bulk of the proceeds from these deposits to acquire longer duration—and usually illiquid—assets. The remainder would be used to acquire liquid assets to serve as a buffer to meet withdrawals.[3] As a consequence, commercial banks have always had a vulnerability to large-scale deposit withdrawals—those exceeding their buffer of liquidity. This is a consequence of the maturity transformation process discussed in Chapter 3.

At times, a major bank or several banks found themselves with insufficient liquid assets to meet customer requests for withdrawal. More often, this was triggered by a drop in asset prices—be they bonds, real estate, or other assets—that called into question whether banks' assets had lost so much value to render some banks insolvent. Once it was suspected that some banks might be insolvent or have insufficient cash to meet withdrawals, those under suspicion lost funds, as nervous customers withdrew balances. These losses of funds were from retail deposit customers and from other banks that had been a steady source of funds through the interbank market. So often, anxious depositors of the banks under suspicion queued up in lines that extended outside banking offices as depositors sought to get what they could. This placed even greater strain on those banks' holdings of cash assets.

To attempt to meet these withdrawals, banks under stress tried to sell marketable assets. Meanwhile, skittish customers of other banks became concerned about the safety of their deposits and withdrew their funds, prompting those banks to sell assets. This strained the capacity of affected asset markets to absorb these sales, causing asset liquidity to diminish and asset values to sink. In essence, a cloud of uncertainty about the health of commercial banks broadly developed in light of an absence of real-time information about the liquidity and solvency of individual institutions allowing the public to discriminate between the still-healthy and unhealthy institutions.

The spreading difficulties facing the entire banking system (holding only a fraction of deposits in cash), in turn, triggered even more widespread depositor panics. Depositors everywhere, fearful that their bank did not have enough cash on hand to meet escalating withdrawal requests, sought to line up ahead of other depositors. As banks tried to meet those mounting withdrawals, they needed to engage in greater efforts to dump assets for cash to pay depositors. Increasingly, banks, having blown through their liquid assets, needed to sell less liquid assets under fire sale conditions. This caused heavy losses across asset categories, especially the illiquid ones requiring large price discounts to bring in buyers.

Losses on assets pass through to the bank's net worth. We know that $A = L + NW$ or $NW = A - L$. Thus, the drop in the value of assets, A, feeds through to the institution's net worth or capital, dollar for dollar. A large drop in A will raise concerns, especially about those institutions thought to be holding large concentrations of such assets.

Meanwhile, potential buyers of bank assets became more uncertain about fundamental asset values, and pulled back from taking them off the hands of desperate banks. In effect, the markets for many of the assets held by banks seized up. Not only did the drop in asset prices threaten the banks' solvency, but the growing inability to find buyers meant that banks were unable to get the cash they needed to redeem deposits and relieve some of the pressures on the system. In these circumstances, many banks had no alternative to suspending deposit conversions or closing their doors, sometimes permanently.

Moreover, as banks lost liquidity and watched their net worth slip away, they were unable to satisfy loan demand. Shrinking net worth meant that banks had to cut back on assets, including loan portfolios.[4] All loan customers found credit less available and more costly, but riskier customers were hit the hardest. In essence, credit supplied to the economy was curtailed sharply—a "credit crunch" developed. This forced a cutback in spending by businesses and households. The result was a marked weakening in the economy and deterioration in profits and earnings of households. This deterioration reduced the ability of borrowers to service their debts, creating credit losses and further reducing losses of net worth at banks and further compounding the crisis.

These conditions were usually accompanied by unsettled conditions elsewhere in the financial system. In particular, there frequently were heavy sell-offs in the stock market, as profits fell and risk in the economy was repriced upward. Using the equity pricing framework developed in Chapter 10, risk premiums embedded in share prices (the equity premium) soared, causing share prices to plunge. This further unnerved bank depositors and further led to cutbacks in spending by households and businesses. Today, we refer to this vicious downward spiral of tightening financial markets and a weakening economy feeding on each other as an adverse feedback loop.

Panics along the lines described above occurred with some frequency in the latter part of the nineteenth and the early part of the twentieth centuries—1873, 1884, 1890, 1893, and 1907. The serious damage caused by these panics contributed to a political consensus for creating a central bank in the United States, along the lines of those in other major countries, described in Chapter 12. It was clear to observers that these other countries did not have severe banking panics like the United States because their central banks provided funds to struggling banks to replace withdrawals. This was achieved through their discount windows by extending collateralized loans to affected banks or by discounting assets submitted by them. The result of this new consensus was the creation of the Federal Reserve in 1913.

THE NIGHTMARE OF THE GREAT DEPRESSION

Over the first decade and a half of the Federal Reserve, the financial system and economy performed reasonably well. But in the early 1930s, a series of severe banking panics, the worst in U.S history, occurred. These, combined with other forces, propelled the nation into the worst economic downturn in its history—an event that left an indelible imprint on the minds of those who survived and led to sweeping change in our governmental institutions. It is ironic that this was exactly what the Fed was created to prevent.

Gold Standard Restraints

Basically, the Fed did not respond in a coherent manner to the developing crises in the banking system. Moreover, its tasks were complicated by the nation's participation in a global gold (exchange) standard, which limited the Fed's ability to use monetary policy to address emerging weakness in the economy. Indeed, at one point, in an effort to defend the dollar price of gold in the face of large gold outflows, the Fed actually tightened monetary policy by raising the discount rate to stem gold outflows as the economy was sinking. The conflict between the workings of a fixed exchange rate regime—of which the gold standard is a form—and monetary policy aimed at stabilization of output and prices will be discussed in the next chapter.

The Stock Market Crash

The most widely cited precipitating event for the catastrophe of the 1930s was the stock market crash of October 1929. Prior to this event, stock and real estate prices had registered large gains, reaching levels that were unsustainable. The Fed had expressed concern about overextended stock prices and addressed this concern by raising its discount rate in several steps over 1928 and 1929 in an attempt to deflate share prices—which no doubt helped trigger the eventual large-scale sell-off. The resulting loss of wealth and deterioration of financing conditions for businesses led to weakness in aggregate demand.

Bank Runs

The first of a series of banking crises began a year later, in October 1930. An already bad situation was compounded by the failure of a large New York bank having the name Bank of the United States, which many had mistakenly believed conveyed an official connection with the U.S. government. Not many months later, a major Austrian bank failed, leading to banking panics in Europe and exacerbating worries about commercial banks in the United States. With the Fed ineffective as a lender of last resort, banks under stress found themselves needing to dump assets to get cash to meet depositor withdrawals. As they dumped assets, banks suffered losses to their net worth positions, which further curbed their ability to satisfy loan demand. As a result, financing became less available (and more costly) to businesses and households—a credit crunch. This added to weakness in aggregate demand and contributed to the downturn in the economy. An adverse feedback loop had taken hold.

Compounding global weakness was the working of the gold system that had been adopted in the 1920s—a gold exchange standard. The gold exchange standard, when it worked in line with intentions, allowed countries to hold selected currencies, such as the British pound and U.S. dollar, to back their currencies instead of using gold. This, in effect, allowed the global gold stock to be leveraged and support larger global demand. However, when the global economic and financial system came under stress, some countries holding these selected currencies instead of gold to back their own became concerned about the safety of these holdings and sought to exchange them for gold. This had many similarities to the bank runs that were occurring within these countries' borders. In effect, these actions reduced the base for the global money stock and aggregate demand, in much the same way that a contraction in the stock of gold would, and compounded the downturn in global aggregate demand.

The worst of the banking crises occurred in early 1933. It was so severe that the incoming president—Franklin D. Roosevelt—in March ordered commercial banks to be closed (a so-called bank holiday) temporarily to allow time to sort through problems and calm frayed nerves. At the same time, the United States left the gold standard. This relieved pressures coming from the gold standard and, in effect, allowed the dollar to depreciate, enhancing the competitiveness of U.S. exports and import-competing industries.[5] The lower exchange value of the dollar gave the economy a much-needed boost.

The bank holiday and suspension of gold payments were important steps that helped stabilize the financial system and the economy. In addition, the federal government introduced deposit insurance and created a new agency to administer the program—the Federal Deposit Insurance Corporation (FDIC). This assuaged many retail depositors concerned about the safety of their deposits and reduced their inclination to run on their bank whenever rumors surfaced that the bank might be in trouble. The federal government also developed programs to use public funds to place capital in banks, replacing some of the capital lost through declines in asset prices and loan losses. The resulting improvement in their net worth positions fostered the ability of recipient banks to resume their role as lenders.

Massive Damage

When all was said and done, the devastation proved to be immense. Real gross domestic product (GDP) fell about 25 percent over the five years from 1929 to 1934, and the unemployment rate soared to 25 percent. The level of prices also fell about 25 percent. Meanwhile, roughly half of all commercial banks closed their doors, either through liquidation or through being acquired by another bank. Moreover, poor policy decisions hindered natural regenerative efforts of the economy to recover over the second half of the 1930s and prolonged the misery. One notable policy blunder occurred when the Fed misread heightened caution by commercial banks that took the form of demands for massive holdings of excess reserves and other highly safe and liquid assets. Instead, the Fed viewed this as an unwanted build-up of liquidity that risked a surge in lending and spending and thereby posed an inflation threat. It responded by doubling reserve requirements over 1936 and 1937 to mop up the perceived excess liquidity. Instead, this action jolted the financial system and restrained the struggling economy as commercial banks sought to restore their liquidity cushions, leading them to cut back on lending.

Because of its weak governance structure and problems of accountability, the Federal Reserve System went through a major overhaul in 1935—as noted in Chapter 12—that centralized responsibility in the Board. Also, as noted earlier, Congress created a new agency, the FDIC, to insure bank deposits and quell fears of depositors in times of stress.

BROADER FINANCIAL CRISES

Recent decades have seen some major financial crises that have been broader in scope than the banking crises that characterized the period up to and including the Great Depression. Among the most notable were the stock market crash of 1987; the commercial real estate bubble of the late 1980s; the sharp reaction to the events of September 11, 2001; and the granddaddy of them all, the recent financial crisis that started in 2007. These affected a wider array of markets and financial institutions, but had many similarities to the classical banking crises described above.

Big Drop in Asset Values

These broader financial crises have typically stemmed from a precipitous decline in the price of a class of financial assets, such as mortgage securities, or physical assets, such as commercial or residential real estate. Typically, concerns developed in these markets that the prices had gotten overextended, well beyond levels based on economic fundamentals. Some were regarded as an asset price bubble. With an asset bubble process, as discussed in Chapter 6, a dynamic develops whereby the run-up in prices prompts investors to extrapolate expectations of further price increases. They then seek to get extraordinary expected returns by purchasing more of this asset—often with credit, which enables a leveraging of gains. At some point, this process comes to an end, and the price of the asset turns down.[6] A vicious downward dynamic can then unfold, taking financial institutions down in their wake.

The drop in prices can overshoot on the downside, further hurting financial institutions with exposure to such assets. Typically, some market participants look for profit opportunities when asset prices fall beyond levels that reflect market fundamentals and they step in and start buying. This cushions the drop in prices as these participants try to take advantage of buy opportunities. However, when prices fall sharply, many of these participants begin to question their understanding of what determines fundamental asset values and back off from taking such price-stabilizing actions. Indeed, panic may grip them as they lose their bearings, and they may switch from being buyers to being sellers—fearing that prices remain overvalued. This exacerbates market distress.

Financial institutions holding such assets, notably commercial and investment banks, will experience a reduction in their capital or net worth position. At the same time, with asset maturities longer than funding sources, they are vulnerable to losses of funding.

Runs on Suspected Institutions

Those customers or counterparties with exposures to suspected institutions—such as depositors and other short-term creditors or lenders of securities—would become more concerned about the potential losses that they may sustain as default no longer seems to be a remote possibility. Because the actual holdings of troubled assets is typically unknown by counterparties on a real-time basis, a large number of financial institutions come under suspicion. The heightened uncertainty leads to a pullback in financing provided to these institutions—those that actually had taken big losses and others that had come under suspicion. This can take the form of pulling out funds by not rolling over a short-term credit or calling back securities that had been lent. Because all these institutions had a maturity mismatch, they will need to pay out cash before the corresponding assets mature. As the institutions exhaust their cash to pay down such funding, they must turn to selling assets. First to be sold will be assets with prices least affected by the market turmoil, but at some point they will be down to troubled assets.

Fire Sales

As these institutions dump more troubled assets, the prices of these assets come under even greater downward pressure, which adds to concerns about the institutions' solvency. Their inability to secure replacement funding adds to pressures to sell assets at fire sale prices and they lose even more net worth. In such circumstances, these institutions are unable to perform their normal role of providing financing to the economy. Moreover, risk premiums faced by financial institutions—those with the largest asset losses and also others—climb, as investor concerns spread to all financial institutions and as investor tolerance for risk diminishes (they become more risk averse). These reactions result in further pull-backs of lending and other financing and losses in asset prices, such as stocks. The result is additional economic weakness, which feeds back on the condition of financial institutions—an adverse feedback loop. Absent effective action by the monetary authorities to stem the weakness in the economy and to address the liquidity shortfall in the financial system, an outcome resembling the Great Depression could occur.

By way of summary:

- A sharp drop in asset prices occurs.
- This raises questions about losses that may have been sustained by key financial institutions.
- Uncertainty about the health of these institutions causes a drying up of their funding sources, which compounds the problem because the assets funded have longer maturities—maturity mismatches magnify stresses.
- Loss of funding and widening uncertainty premiums cause financial institutions to cut back on lending or otherwise financing the economy.
- This—along with a more general decline in prices of risky assets—leads to a credit crunch and contributes to weakness in the economy, which in turn inflicts more losses on financial institutions.
- A vicious downward spiral—adverse feedback loop—is under way.

As noted in the introduction, the damage depends to a critical extent on the degree to which financial institutions are exposed to the drop in asset prices. The plunge in stock prices after the tech-related bubble in stock prices in the late 1990s led to losses of nearly half their peak values. However, these losses were largely passed to wealth holders directly, and did not pass through to the net worth of major financial institutions. This loss of wealth inflicted a lot of pain on those affected, but no major financial institution got into trouble. Moreover, the recession that accompanied this loss of wealth was one of the milder on record.

THE FINANCIAL CRISIS

Echoing the late 1920s and 1930s, the crisis that began after mid-2007 was linked to overvaluation of an asset class—this time, residential real estate. It was associated with excesses in the market for mortgage credit, especially adjustable-rate, subprime mortgages (discussed in Chapters 9 and 10). The unwinding of the bubble caused massive damage to the financial system in the United States and elsewhere, and led to the most severe recession of the postwar period. Although the market for subprime mortgages has been singled out as the cause, many other parts of the financial system also contributed. Excessively easy conditions characterized other credit markets and encouraged leveraging, resulting in vulnerable financial positions for a wide variety of borrowers.

Background Factors

Several forces were at work that contributed to the crisis. First, benchmark interest rates had been unusually low earlier in the decade. This prompted many investors to seek lost yield by acquiring exotic new assets, such as those involving subprime mortgages having more risk. They were said to be "reaching for yield." Second, there had been a belief that residential real estate prices would not decline on a national level, although they could decline in some local markets. This view was based on evidence from the postwar period in the United States in which real estate prices did not decline in a sustained manner on the national level, although local residential markets did from time to time experience declines. Thus, it was thought that investments backed by a diversified pool of residential real estate would not cause serious losses to investors, even if the loans supporting them were to default. In the event of default, the real estate collateral could be sold at prices no lower than the purchase price on which the mortgages were made. In other words, there was the belief that there was little or no downside risk associated with holding mortgage assets, yet they provided their owner an attractive yield. Third, a long period of fairly stable economic growth and low inflation had lulled investors into a false sense that there was low underlying risk in the economy. The period following the early 1980s has come to be known as the Great Moderation, characterized by historically low economic volatility and correspondingly limited investment losses. This engendered a belief among investors that such conditions would persist indefinitely and a sense of complacency on their part about the risk of investments involving real estate and leverage. Fourth, this had been a period of financial engineering involving, among other things, securitized financial assets—complex financial products produced from ordinary loans, often subprime mortgages, and other leveraged and risky components (discussed more fully in Chapter 9). These products reassigned claims to the underlying cash flows in very complicated ways and created the impression that they had achieved overall considerable risk reduction in the process—including through diversification. Moreover, statistical measurements of the risk properties of the new securitized products had been based on a relatively short historical period that had been characterized by unusually good economic and financial performance; in other words, these statistical measures of risk were biased downward.

Proliferation of Nonstandard Mortgages

As noted in Chapter 10, subprime mortgages are those made to persons falling well short of the standards for a conforming (prime) mortgage. The market for subprime mortgages had been characterized by cautious evolution until around 2003. At that time, it changed dramatically as many mortgage companies and lenders saw the relatively favorable performance of subprime loans and their higher yields as reason for becoming very aggressive—and lax—in expanding the availability of mortgage credit to a broader set of borrowers. At the same time, mortgage credit became increasingly available to other nonstandard (or nonconforming) borrowers, too—those eligible for so-called Alt-A mortgages (somewhere between prime and subprime status) and those seeking jumbos (mortgages exceeding the conforming size limit). The expanding availability of mortgage credit and the generally low level of interest rates both contributed to a pickup in home demand, and thus home prices.

Originators of these nonstandard loans were selling them to pools, following the originate-to-sell model. Participations in these pools were then sold to investors directly or the pools were restructured into complex mortgage securities—the structured investment products described in Chapter 9. Institutional investors were quite willing to gobble these up to get the seemingly attractive higher yield—turning a blind eye to their underlying risk—and were clamoring for more. This persistently strong demand got translated in looser underwriting criteria for nonstandard mortgages and led to very attractive pricing for nonstandard adjustable-rate mortgages.

The rapid run-up in home prices was encouraging many to extrapolate further gains, and speculative purchases of residential properties jumped, adding to upward pressure on home prices. A building boom and price bubble were in full swing.

Meanwhile, other financial organizations became involved. Credit rating agencies were asked to rate many of these complicated products and generally gave them high marks. Also, some insurers got involved, insuring these new structured, securitized products against credit losses for investors (notably through credit default swaps [CDSs]) at underpriced premiums. Actions by both credit agencies and insurers added to the appeal of these complex financial products to investors and to the already strong demand for them.

Growing Exposures of Key Financial Institutions

Key financial institutions became exposed to this situation in various ways. To some extent, they originated and held various nonstandard, mortgage-related products. Many also were involved in developing, underwriting, and distributing these products; in the course of doing so, they unavoidably held positions in these assets and had to finance those positions. They sought other ways, too, to profit from these products by creating special off-balance-sheet vehicles (structured investment vehicles [SIVs]) that would take these assets off the balance sheet of the financial institution and place them in a specially created legal entity, as described in Chapter 9; this entity would then be able to buy the assets using the proceeds from short-term borrowings, such as commercial paper, collateralized by the assets. As we saw in Chapter 7, such commercial paper is referred to as asset-backed commercial paper (ABCP). Creators of these vehicles were thus making a play on both credit risk and the yield curve, as they expected to profit from the spread between the returns on the risky assets and financing costs. These were enlarged by inexpensive sources of finance because short-term yields tend to average below longer-term yields. Although these SIVs were constructed in such a way that the bank or other major financial institution was not legally liable in the event of default, that institution's reputation was on the line if it did not step in to prevent investor losses.

Moreover, the numerous ways in which key financial institutions were connected to each other led to a vulnerability of the entire financial system to the fortunes of any single key player—so-called *systemic risk*. Should one player be unable to discharge its obligations—that is, should it default—its multiple complicated exposures to others would pose threats to those counterparties, as they would be unable to collect from the defaulting party. This could bring the entire financial system down. Moreover, the time required to unwind transactions involving that one player could freeze the financial system for days, compounding the sense of panic in financial markets. In other words, the externalities associated with the problems of one major financial player—commercial bank, investment bank, or even insurance company—could jeopardize the entire financial system and spill over to the economy.

The Unraveling

By mid-2007, the situation shifted dramatically. Declines in real estate prices were threatening to become more pervasive and to intensify. Moreover, attention turned to deteriorating prospects for the performance of a large share of the nonstandard mortgage products. As a consequence, the market for nonstandard mortgage products worsened dramatically, and buyers of these products vanished. Attention turned to those financial institutions that might have developed large direct and indirect exposures to this market. Uncertainty about the underlying condition of major financial institutions gripped the system, with an inability to pinpoint which might be on the edge, and with it came a widespread, substantial pull-back in the funding provided to these institutions. As noted, these institutions were financing positions in longer-term assets with short-term borrowing, which required regular rollover of borrowings. As it became more difficult to roll over this financing, they were pressured to sell troubled assets. As asset prices dropped, they were forced to realize losses, and asset losses flowed through to losses in their net worth. Among the casualties was the interbank market as lenders of funds in this market became concerned about the health of their counterparties and cut back on their lending; maturities of such loans shortened and costs rose appreciably.

Not only were major U.S. financial institutions coming under severe stress, but similar difficulties developed in other parts of the world. In some cases, these difficulties resulted from exposures that non-U.S. institutions faced in the United States, and in others they arose from a similar buildup of exposures to inflated real estate values in their own markets.

An ongoing deterioration, along the above lines, persisted through the end of 2007 and over most of 2008. In the process, a major investment bank, Bear Stearns, was absorbed and Lehman Brothers failed, triggering the global financial tsunami. Some major commercial banks and savings institutions—specifically, Wachovia, National City, Indy Mac, and Washington Mutual—needed to be rescued by other institutions.

Shadow Banking Stress

Beyond the disappearance of these investment banks and depository institutions, serious problems developed elsewhere in the financial system. These other parts of the financial system have come to be known as the *shadow banking system*. The shadow banking system was performing some of the intermediation functions of commercial banks, but outside the purview of standard depository institution regulation. Notably, money market mutual funds faced huge customer withdrawals as one prominent fund experienced big credit losses from its holdings of commercial paper issued by Lehman. It had to "break the buck" as the value of its shares dropped below $1 per share (discussed in Chapter 18). This prompted worries by customers of other money funds, leading to a stampede from these funds. This, in turn, resulted in a collapse in the demand for commercial paper from this largest institutional holder of commercial paper. In addition, the SIVs mentioned earlier came under strain. Holders of commercial paper issued by SIVs and backed by exotic assets got nervous and were unwilling to roll over their ABCP. This left the SIV sponsors—large commercial and investment banks—with the dilemma of replacing the lost funding using their own dwindling resources or selling the longer-term assets at a loss and not getting enough proceeds to avoid defaulting on the SIVs' commercial paper. This threatened to undermine the sponsor's own reputation.[7] Furthermore, AIG, a major insurance company that had been prominent in underwriting insurance on new and complex financial instruments, nearly failed.

Major Credit Crunch

Meanwhile, the ongoing loss of net worth at financial institutions around the world and sharply higher risk premiums embedded in funding costs acted to curtail the availability of financing to households and businesses. That is, a serious "credit crunch" intensified. This acted to hold down spending, weakening the U.S. economy and economies around the world, which led to a further deterioration in the ability of borrowers to service their debts. An adverse feedback loop had developed and was worsening.

Policy Responses

The deteriorating situation brought forth unprecedented policy actions. The Fed introduced a series of programs to replace lost funding at major financial institutions, thereby reducing the need for these institutions to sell assets. This helped to relieve pressure on interbank funding markets. The Fed also initiated programs to purchase assets to revive certain key markets, such as commercial paper, securitized consumer loans, and mortgage securities.

Meanwhile, Congress passed a massive rescue package—the Troubled Asset Relief Program (TARP)—giving the Treasury considerable flexibility to deploy public monies to shore up the financial system. In part, the sheer size of the package was intended to convince market participants that public policy would be able to restore stability to the financial system and thereby reduce uncertainty about the outlook for the financial system and the economy; it was hoped that this would bolster asset prices by reducing risk premiums.[8] In practice, a good portion of these funds were used to make capital injections into major financial institutions by acquiring preferred stock along with warrants to purchase stock in those institutions, as discussed in Chapter 11. The choice of preferred stock placed the taxpayer ahead of common stock shareholders as claimants on the assets and cash flows of these institutions, and the warrants provided taxpayers an opportunity to share in the upside gains should the fortunes of these institutions turn positive.

The highly proactive approach taken by the Fed and Treasury was, in time, able to have the intended effect of turning around the financial system. It prevented much of the devastation experienced during the 1930s. In the end, these efforts, while exposing taxpayers to downside losses, did not have net losses. Also contributing to this turnaround was the highly aggressive monetary policy of the Fed that resulted in a lowering of its policy interest rate to zero.

Dodd-Frank

The shortcomings of the regulatory system in containing systemic risk were addressed in landmark legislation enacted in 2010—the Wall Street Reform and Consumer Protection Act (Dodd-Frank). This far-reaching legislation, among other things, establishes a framework for subjecting institutions deemed to pose risk to the stability of the financial system—systemically important financial institutions (SIFIs)—under federal regulation. In particular, the bill created a Financial Stability Oversight Council (FSOC) comprising the heads of the federal financial regulatory agencies—including the Fed, Securities and Exchange Commission (SEC), Office of the Comptroller of the Currency (OCC), and FDIC—and chaired by the Secretary of the Treasury. The FSOC can determine that a financial institution poses risk to the system and place it under Fed regulation. This provides a means for addressing worrisome risk that can build up in the shadow banking system.

The bill puts special emphasis on capital levels of larger regulated institutions as a means of reducing risks to individual institutions and to the system (discussed more fully in Chapter 17). Higher capital provides more of a buffer for losses from an institution's assets to be absorbed by capital before that loss poses a threat to holders of its liabilities. Systemically important institutions are to have higher capital requirements than others because their very nature implies that any difficulties that they get into will have adverse consequences for others—they pose serious externalities. In addition, the bill requires that standards be established to ensure that systemically important institutions have adequate holdings of liquid assets to be able to meet a sustained roll-off of liabilities (a run); this provision addresses the maturity mismatch between assets and liabilities that is common among major financial institutions. Further, the legislation has a provision that requires large systemically important institutions to have a so-called living will, which would serve as a guide to regulators in the event the institution were on the brink of failure and needed to be unwound.

Beyond these provisions of the bill, the Fed has introduced regular (annual) stress tests for very large systemically important institutions. These institutions are to assess the impact of a scenario of very adverse financial and economic assumptions on their net worth. Based on the results of the stress test, they would need to bolster their capital in the event that they did not have enough capital to absorb the losses posed by the scenario.

At the same time, a global effort among regulators from various jurisdictions, so-called Basel III, has been intended to coordinate and strengthen global capital and liquidity standards and to foster better risk management by important global banks. This was intended to reduce the prospects for another financial crisis that would threaten a meltdown of the global financial system.

COMMON THREADS

There are some common threads in the kinds of financial crises described above. First, they result from risk exposures of financial institutions, principally commercial banks, that threaten their ability to repay their obligations on schedule and even their solvency. When such exposures and losses occur outside financial institutions, such as when the tech bubble burst in 2000, the consequences for the financial system and the economy are much less severe. Second, they involve financial institutions holding assets with longer maturities than the deposits or other funding that they rely on to finance these assets. In other words, they have short funded their assets and are in a position of needing to roll over the financing of these assets. This makes them vulnerable to a reluctance of depositors or other creditors to roll over this funding. Third, problems develop when there is a sharp drop in asset prices and uncertainty becomes pronounced about the health of the financial institutions that might be exposed to losses. Lenders (and depositors) pull back from these institutions and risk premiums rise. Problems in rolling over funding places pressure on these institutions to unload assets, adding to selling pressures in troubled asset markets. Meanwhile, problems in replacing funding and declines in asset values feed through to the net worth of these institutions and result in a cutback in the supply of credit to businesses and households. This can lead to a full-blown credit crunch, which results in severe headwinds on the economy. At this point, an adverse feedback loop develops, requiring bold initiatives by the central bank and government to contain the crisis.

SUMMARY

1. Financial crises have left deep imprints on our financial system and economy and have led to major changes in the role of government in regulating the financial system.
2. A large decline in asset values can lead to a financial crisis if it threatens to affect the net worth of major financial institutions. This can result in a cut back of regular funding, leading to the need to sell assets—at a loss—to raise cash to pay back creditors. Net worth of these institutions is thereby impaired, and they need to cut back on lending to their customers—causing a credit crunch.
3. Uncertainty premiums embedded in risky assets also increase, leading to more generalized declines in wealth.
4. Tighter credit and losses of wealth lead to a cutback in spending by businesses and households, which adds to weakness in the economy and credit losses at financial institutions. The vicious downward spiral is referred to as an adverse feedback loop.
5. Financial crises have come to involve a broader set of financial institutions than just commercial banks—though the process remains much the same.
6. The recent financial crisis centered on the residential real estate market and the various mortgage instruments that were used to finance the real estate bubble. However, a number of other factors were at work as well, contributing to various financial excesses. The financial collapse could have rivaled the Great Depression had it not been for aggressive policy measures, informed by the experience of the 1930s.
7. The recent financial crisis also highlighted the interconnectedness of major financial institutions that gives rise to systemic risk.
8. The recent financial crisis also illustrated that a shadow banking system outside standard regulation can pose systemic risk.

9. As a result, new financial legislation was enacted that was intended to prevent such systemic events. It applies to all financial institutions, not only commercial banks, deemed to pose a systemic threat.
10. Public policy around the globe has placed more emphasis on requiring sufficiently large capital positions, and, to a lesser extent, adequate amounts of liquidity.

QUESTIONS

1. What is meant by a financial crisis? What is the role of financial institutions?
2. Could a large decline in asset prices occur without prompting a financial crisis? Any examples?
3. Why do major financial institutions face the need to sell assets during a crisis? Why are these sales frequently characterized as fire sales? During such times, why do markets for risky assets function poorly? Why are investors who normally look for bargains reluctant to step in to cushion the drop in asset prices?
4. How did the financial crisis of the 1930s contribute to the Great Depression? How did policymakers deal with this situation?
5. What is an adverse feedback loop? How does this work to worsen the financial system and the economy?
6. When net worth of financial institutions drops because asset prices fall, how does leverage of these institutions compound the need to cut back on lending? How is a credit crunch involved?
7. During a financial crisis, what do you suppose happens to the price of Treasury securities? Why?
8. What is meant by systemic risk? How does this relate to externalities as a microeconomic principle?
9. How did financial institutions other than commercial banks contribute to the financial crisis of 2008? What is meant by the shadow banking system?
10. What approach has the Dodd-Frank bill of 2010 taken to prevent financial crises from developing? Explain.
11. Why has so much attention focused on capital regulation in recent years? Liquidity regulation?

NOTES

1. See Carmen M. Reinhart and Kenneth S. Rogoff, "The Aftermath of Financial Crises," NBER Working Paper No. 14656, January 2009.
2. In principle, these large financial institutions could have raised additional net worth by selling stock and thereby avoiding cutbacks in lending and other financing of business and household spending. In practice, however, this was not a viable option at the time because the stock market was plunging as investors pulled back on risk. With equity prices so low, stock offerings would not bring in much capital.
3. For expected withdrawals, the bank can acquire assets that mature at the time of the withdrawal and thereby have funds to meet the redemption.

4. To illustrate, a bank that was leveraged 10-to-1 would have to shrink its assets by $10 for every dollar loss of net worth. Thus, if it incurred a capital loss and decline in net worth of $1, it would need to reduce its other assets—including loans—by $9.
5. A year later, in 1934, the United States returned to the gold standard, but at a much higher price per ounce of gold—$35 instead of $20.67. This was a 40 percent devaluation of the dollar.
6. Some view asset bubbles as inconsistent with principles of efficient markets, as discussed in Chapter 6. However, there is a strain of thinking that says a bubble can involve rational decision making by investors. With a rational bubble, investors believe that prices have exceeded levels justified by fundamentals, but also believe that there remains upward momentum and that prices will rise further. By adding to their holdings of these assets, they see themselves able to earn extraordinary returns until prices turn down. They also believe that they will be able to identify that point at which prices begin turning down and will be able to exit more promptly than other investors. This strategy relies heavily on markets remaining liquid, especially after prices begin their descent. History shows many examples when asset liquidity dried up, leaving those practicing such strategies holding the bag.
7. The so-called tri-party RP market also experienced serious strains. Dealers in Treasury securities had relied on short-term RPs to finance their positions in longer-term securities, relying on a couple large clearing banks to ensure that any short-term funding needs were met. Some RP investors became reluctant to continue funding these dealers, putting stress on the clearing banks that were providing backstop support.
8. See Henry M. Paulson, Jr., *On the Brink: Inside the Race to Stop the Collapse of the Global Financial System* (New York: Business Plus, 2010).

CHAPTER 16

The Foreign Exchange Market and Exchange Rate Regimes

WHAT YOU WILL LEARN IN THIS CHAPTER

- What the distinction is between spot and forward exchange rates and the role of currency swaps.
- How foreign exchange is traded around the globe.
- How spot and forward exchange rates are linked through interest rate differentials.
- How the law of one price and purchasing power parity result in prices being the same across borders, allowing for the exchange rate, in the long run.
- What is meant by the real exchange rate and its importance.
- How a floating exchange regime works and how it frees up monetary policy to pursue inflation and output goals.
- How a fixed exchange regime works and how it constrains monetary policy.
- What is meant by dollarization, currency boards, and adjustable pegs.

BACKGROUND

Chances are you have traveled abroad. In doing so, you had to convert your home currency (dollars, if you are an American) for the local currency of the country you were visiting. You may have done this at an airport, at a currency exchange shop in the heart of a big city, or you may have gone to an automated teller machine (ATM). Is that how all foreign exchange transactions get done in this increasingly globalized world? Certainly, big commercial and financial transactions must be done differently. You may have heard politicians say that a strong dollar is good for America. Is this always true, or might a weaker dollar be of some benefit? The value of the U.S. dollar fluctuates a good bit, but the Chinese currency—the yuan—is very stable. Why? Is one better than the other?

Foreign exchange rates play an important role in a wide variety of economic decisions. Moreover, exchange rates have become increasingly important as the globalization process continues at a brisk pace—imports and exports have been growing at a much faster pace than global output.[1] The preponderance of these international trade transactions involves the conversion of one currency into another in the foreign exchange market. In addition, there are a vast and rapidly growing number of cross-border investments that also require the conversion of one currency into another. The rapid rise in such cross-border financial transactions owes importantly to the application of the portfolio diversification principles that we discussed in Chapter 6. Adding to foreign exchange trading volume has been the growing availability of financial derivatives that help investors lock in returns from cross-border transactions, some of which will be discussed shortly. In view of these considerations, it should not be surprising that the *daily* volume of foreign exchange transactions exceeds $5 trillion.[2]

When dealing with the market for foreign exchange, there are a few things worth noting up front. For purposes of analysis, we typically measure the exchange rate as the number of units of foreign currency one can get for a unit of domestic currency. This can be expressed as follows: the exchange rate, e, is shown as $e = f/d$, where f denotes units of foreign currency and d units of domestic currency. When this measure increases—that is, a unit of domestic currency can be exchanged for more foreign currency—we say that the currency has *appreciated*. In contrast, when it decreases—a unit of domestic currency buys fewer units of foreign currency—we say that the currency has *depreciated*. An appreciation of the country's currency causes its exports to be more expensive to buyers abroad; they need more of their currency to get a unit of domestic currency to buy the export. Similarly, it causes imports to be cheaper, because fewer units of domestic currency are needed to get the foreign currency to buy the import. Conversely, a depreciation of the currency causes exports to be cheaper to buyers abroad and imports to be more expensive to folks at home. A depreciation of the country's currency will stimulate foreign demand for domestically produced output and increase exports. It will also induce domestic buyers to substitute away from imports and toward domestically produced goods. An appreciation will have the opposite effect—curbing exports and boosting imports. Note that the value of a currency is a relative matter. If the domestic currency has appreciated, the foreign currency has depreciated.

It is also worth noting that some of the common ways that exchange rates are reported can give the wrong impression of whether the U.S. dollar has appreciated or depreciated. This is especially true of the standard way in which the value of the dollar is expressed in terms of the euro (€) and the British pound (£). Both are commonly quoted in terms of dollars per euro and dollars per pound, such as $1.40 = €1 or $1.60 = £1. For the latter, a market participant might say, "The dollar is trading at one-sixty against the pound." Thus, if this measure were to rise to $1.65 = £1, the value of the pound would have risen, but the value of the dollar would have fallen. We can now see that these standard ways of quoting the values of the euro and pound are for those living in places that use the euro and the pound and not for those using the dollar; the reciprocals of these—that is, dividing one by them—gives the value of the dollar. In contrast, the dollar-yen (¥) exchange rate is commonly expressed in terms of yen per dollar, such as ¥95 = $1. If the exchange rate rose to ¥100 = $1, the dollar would have appreciated and the yen depreciated.

FEATURES OF THE MARKET

The bulk of transactions in the foreign exchange market are wholesale transactions. That is, they are very large in size and are made for commercial or financial transactions. Transactions involving bank notes—currency—are trivial in comparison, although they are the ones with which we are most familiar.

The market for foreign exchange is an over-the-counter market in which global commercial banks are the principal market makers, posting bid and ask prices for a considerable variety of currencies. The hub of the market is London, where European trading is concentrated. In the Western hemisphere, New York dominates trading, but, overall, is dwarfed by London. Trading in Asia is distributed among Tokyo, Hong Kong, Singapore, and Sydney. The preponderance of transactions involves U.S. dollars—primarily against euros, British pounds, and Japanese yen.

Foreign exchange transactions mainly take the form of either *spot transactions* or *foreign exchange swaps*—which includes both a spot and a *forward* transaction.[3] With a spot transaction, currencies are exchanged for immediate delivery. That is, the currencies are exchanged at the time the transaction is negotiated (actually, by convention, two days later in the wholesale market). Moreover, they involve the exchange of bank deposit balances, not physical cash. For example, the exchange of British pounds for Japanese yen typically involves the seller of pounds paying from an account with a commercial bank denominated in pounds and, in return, receiving yen in a yen-denominated account.

In contrast, a forward transaction is one that is negotiated now for delivery at some later date. A foreign exchange swap is one for which a spot transaction occurs up front, but this transaction is reversed at some agreed-upon future date. That later leg of the transaction is a forward transaction. For example, someone with Euros may want to exchange them for Canadian dollars now, and anticipates wanting to swap those Canadian dollars back into euros in 30 days. If the Canadian dollar drops in value over this period in terms of the euro, our individual would end up with a loss, and as a result, may want to lock in the exchange rate at which euros are exchanged for Canadian dollars in 30 days. This person could enter into a 30-day Canadian dollar-euro swap in which he or she would surrender euros today (actually, in two days) and get Canadian dollars in return. In 30 days, the two parties would reverse this transaction, and our person would surrender Canadian dollars and receive back euros.

Parties wanting to invest in a financial asset in another market that uses a different currency commonly use foreign exchange swaps to lock in exchange rates and thereby returns. Our individual with the Euros may want to acquire a 30-day money market instrument in Canada and lock in the returns on that investment through a foreign exchange swap.

In addition to foreign exchange swaps, outright forward transactions are conducted in substantial volume in the foreign exchange market. A standard foreign exchange forward is one in which a customer negotiates to buy or sell foreign currency for delivery at some date in the future. For example, a U.S. manufacturer of machine tools may have negotiated the purchase of a key component input from a firm in Japan for ¥800 million for delivery in 60 days. The manufacturer may be concerned that the U.S. dollar will weaken over the next two months—buying those yen will be a lot more expensive—and wants to fix the price of the yen today. This can be done through an outright forward contract. In 60 days, the manufacturer will surrender dollars from its dollar deposit account (roughly $9 million) and will receive—or can direct the payment to the parts seller—the ¥800 million needed to complete the transaction at the previously negotiated terms.

Businesses requiring foreign exchange usually turn to their commercial banks for the currency—whether it is a spot, swap, or outright forward transaction.

Forward transactions—both swaps and outright forwards—can be customized to the requirements of the business customer of the bank, the amounts, and the dates of delivery.

In the course of conducting such transactions with customers, an individual bank will likely develop risk exposures to different currencies on its book that vary from day to day. For example, the bank may find itself in a situation in which it has agreed to sell more euros for dollars for delivery in 14 days to one group of customers than it has agreed to buy from another group of other customers. After netting these positions, the bank is committed to come up with more euros in 14 days—it is said to be in a net short position in euros (and long in dollars). If the value of the euro rises between now and then, the bank will face a loss on this position unless it hedges its position. A hedge could be achieved by entering into a forward transaction with another bank—one that is a market maker—in which it would buy euros for 14-day delivery in an amount that fully covered its net short position.

Alternatively, the bank could purchase a futures contract that would deliver euros for dollars in as close to 14 days as possible. Futures contracts are forward agreements that are standardized in terms of size and delivery dates. They are typically traded on organized exchanges. They lend themselves to covering net positions by market makers. Alternatively, the bank could acquire an options contract in euros—a put or a call. A put would give the bank the right to sell euros and a call the right to buy euros at a predetermined price—the so-called strike price. In the preceding example, the bank would want to acquire a call option, which would enable the bank to buy euros at the strike price if the value of the euro increases appreciably.

THE RELATION BETWEEN SPOT AND FORWARD EXCHANGE RATES

We noted that a foreign exchange swap involves a combination of a spot exchange of currencies that is followed by an offsetting forward transaction at a specified later date. Going back to our example of the person wanting to swap Canadian dollars for euros, interest rate differentials will govern the terms of the forward leg of this transaction. For example, if the 30-day yield were 2 percent in Germany and 3 percent in Canada, arbitrage would ensure that the implicit forward rate on the unwinding of the transaction in 30 days would result in a weaker Canadian dollar (and favor the euro). To illustrate, if the spot exchange rate is C$1.40 per euro (note that this treats the euro as the domestic currency), then one euro invested at 3 percent will provide the investor with C$1.40 × 0.03 or 4.2 Canadian cents on an annual basis. Over the 30 days, this will be approximately 4.2/12—that is, a twelfth of the annual interest—or 0.35 Canadian cents interest. That same euro invested in Germany will provide the investor with the equivalent to C$1.40 × 0.02 or 2.8 Canadian cents on an annual basis, if the exchange rate stayed at C$1.40. Over 30 days, this would be approximately 2.8/12 or nearly 0.25 Canadian cents, well below the interest that can be earned in Canada. Arbitrage—taking the form of investors wanting to convert euros to Canadian dollars for 30 days and to reverse this transaction in 30 days—will result in investors wanting to sell Canadian dollars in 30 days for euros, which will drive down the forward value of the Canadian dollar to below the spot rate.

How much below the spot rate will be the forward rate? The following formula provides the answer:

$$F = S\left(\frac{1+i_A}{1+i_B}\right)^t \qquad (16\text{-}1)$$

In this expression, F represents the forward rate, S the spot rate, i_A the interest rate in the country having the currency that is being bought spot for investment (Canada, in our example), i_B the interest rate in the country having the currency that is being sold spot for the investment (Germany), and t represents the length of time (measured in years). In our numerical example, S is C\$1.40, i_A is 0.03, i_B is 0.02, and t is approximately 1/12 (approximately one-twelfth of a year). Or

$$F = 1.40\left(\frac{1.03}{1.02}\right)^{1/12} = 1.401$$

Note that the higher the interest rate in the other country (Canada), i_A, or the lower the interest rate in the home country (Germany), i_B, the larger the premium of forward over spot. This relationship between spot and forward exchange rates and interest rate differentials is sometimes called *covered interest arbitrage*.

The preceding discussion relates to currencies that can vary against each other over time. We call this a floating exchange rate regime and will discuss this regime in more detail later in the chapter. If, instead, the exchange rate is fixed between two currencies, the forward exchange rate must equal the spot rate, and thus Equation (16-1) implies that interest rates must be the same in the two countries. We will also discuss fixed exchange rate regimes later in this chapter.

LONG-RUN EXCHANGE RATE RELATIONSHIPS

In the long run, exchange rate relationships are thought to be determined by forces expressed by the *Law of One Price*. The law of one price says that the price of an item traded in two markets using different currencies will be the same in those two markets, allowing for exchange rates. It presumes that there are no barriers to competition in the two markets—including restrictions on imports and exports—and that transportation costs are not very important.

An illustration may help. Suppose that the price of a Canon PowerShot ELPH digital camera is \$125 in the United States and ¥13,500 in Japan. If the exchange rate is ¥90 = \$1, then this camera will be cheaper in the United States than in Japan (where it is \$150 equivalent). The law of one price says that this price differential cannot persist. Arbitrage will tend to equalize the price of the item in both markets. Traders will seek profit from this situation by purchasing Canons in the United States and selling them in Japan. This process will continue so long as there is any material price differential in the two markets.

How prices become equalized in the two markets depends importantly on the exchange rate regime that prevails between the United States and Japan. If it is a *fixed exchange rate regime*, equilibrium will be achieved by the camera prices adjusting in the two markets. In the preceding example, if the authorities in the United States or Japan are committed to an exchange rate of 90 yen per dollar, the price of Canons will rise in the United States and will fall in Japan. The process will end when the price of the camera is the same in both markets, allowing for an exchange rate of ¥90 = $1. This might occur when the price in the United States rises to $137.50 and the price in Japan falls to ¥12,375 (equivalent to $137.50 at this exchange rate).

In contrast, if there is a *floating exchange rate regime,* the yen-dollar exchange rate will be allowed to move with market supply and demand. In this case, actions by arbitrageurs will bring about a new equilibrium, either through a movement in the exchange rate or a combination of a movement in the exchange rate and change in the price of the good (or goods). Actions by arbitrageurs will put upward pressure on the exchange value of the dollar as they purchase dollars to buy the cameras in the United States. By the same measure, the yen will weaken as the cameras are sold for yen in Japan. If the exchange rate appreciated to ¥108 = $1, the law of one price would be achieved (the price in Japan would be ¥13,500/108 or $125 equivalent). More likely, the new equilibrium will be achieved by a combination of exchange rate and price movements. That is, both the dollar may appreciate against the yen and the price of Canons may rise in the United States and fall in Japan. For example, the dollar may strengthen to ¥100 and the price of the camera may rise to $130 in the United States and fall to ¥13,000 in Japan (¥13,000/100 = $130 equivalent).

An extension of the law of one price to a broader array of goods is referred to as *purchasing power parity (PPP).* In essence, PPP says that the average price of a basket of goods—common to both economies—will be the same in both economies, allowing for the exchange rate. This relationship can be expressed algebraically as

$$P_A = e \cdot P_B \qquad (16\text{-}2)$$

In this expression, P_A represents the average price of the basket in country A, P_B is the average price of the basket in country B, and e is the exchange rate calibrated as the number of units of currency A per unit of currency B (the expression for the exchange rate for country B). Commonly, this expression relates price indexes for each of the countries. That is, P_A is the price index for country A and P_B is the price index for country B.

Arbitrage helps to ensure that PPP is achieved over longer periods. Thus, movements in the exchange rate, where floating exchange rates prevail, will reflect changes in the price level of one country in relation to that of the other country. The country with the price level rising more rapidly will have its currency depreciate relative to the country with more stable prices. Turning to Equation (16-2), if the price level in country B rises 10 percent and that in country A is unchanged, then the exchange rate of country B will need to decline 10 percent (the term on the left of (16-2) is unchanged which tells us that the product of the terms on the right must be unchanged—the percent increase in P_B must be matched by the percent decrease in e). That is, if the price of an item in country B has risen 10 percent, for this item to have the same price as in country A the exchange rate would need to fall 10 percent. The drop in the exchange rate by 10 percent allows buyers in country A to get 10 percent more of currency B, which covers the higher price of the item in country B.

In contrast, when the exchange rate is fixed, price levels in countries A and B will need to adjust to satisfy PPP. That is, if e in (16-2) is fixed, then P_A and P_B must be in alignment.

THE REAL EXCHANGE RATE

The concept of the real exchange *rate* is used routinely in economic analysis. It is the real exchange—as opposed to the *nominal exchange rate*—that drives important production and spending decisions. Nominal exchange rates are those that are quoted routinely, such as the rates we were using previously in this chapter. The real exchange rate adjusts for differential movements in the price level between one country and the other. The relationship between the nominal and real exchange rate can be expressed as follows:

$$\varepsilon = e \times \frac{P_d}{P_f} \qquad (16\text{-}3)$$

In this expression, ε represents the real exchange rate, e the (nominal) exchange rate, P_d the domestic price level, and P_f the price level in the foreign country.

Equation (16-3) states that the real exchange rate, ε, could increase by 10 percent either because the nominal exchange rate, e, has increased by 10 percent or because domestic prices have increased relative to foreign prices by 10 percent. From the perspective of economic decision making, it should not make a difference whether it was achieved by an increase in the nominal exchange rate or a rise in domestic prices.

An example will help. Let us look at the decision to buy an export of the United States—a CD of an American vocal group—by someone who lives in Europe. Suppose that the CD is originally priced at $15 and the exchange rate is $1.50 = €1. For the person living in Europe, the price of this U.S. export in euros is €10. Now, suppose that the price of goods in the United States increases 10 percent. This leads to the price of the CD increasing to $16.50. The price to someone in Europe would also increase 10 percent to €11 (16.50/1.50) if the nominal exchange rate remains unchanged at $1.50 = €1. Likewise, if the dollar appreciates 10 percent (the number of euros per dollar falls 10 percent) to $1.35 = €1, the price of the CD to someone in Europe will also be 10 percent higher.[4] A worthwhile exercise to test your understanding is to verify that the 10 percent appreciation in the real exchange value of the dollar against the euro will have the same impact on the price in the United States of an imported item from Europe whether it occurs because the nominal exchange value of the dollar has appreciated 10 percent or the price of this foreign good has fallen 10 percent (recall that the price of foreign goods appears in the denominator of Equation (16-3)).

EXCHANGE RATE DETERMINATION IN THE SHORTER RUN

We now turn to the determination of the exchange rate over shorter periods. To do so, we will develop a model of supply and demand for the currency in the foreign exchange market. This will help us better understand why exchange rate regimes are so important, and why countries that choose to pursue a fixed exchange rate largely give up their ability to use monetary policy for other purposes, such as the pursuit of price stability or maximum employment.

Demand Schedule

To illustrate the forces that affect exchange rates, let us begin by examining the determination of the exchange value of the British pound in terms of the U.S. dollar. We will be viewing this from the perspective of those living in the British Isles, for whom the pound is their regular currency. The demand for pounds is illustrated in Figure 16.1. On the vertical axis is the value of the pound expressed in dollars ($/£). On the horizontal axis is the quantity of pounds demanded by people residing outside Britain. It is downward sloped, like all good demand curves. This is because, as the value of the pound falls, the price of British goods (and travel in the United Kingdom) declines and people abroad want more.[5] As shown, when the value of the pound falls from $1.60 to $1.40, the demand for pounds increases from $£_1$ to $£_2$. Conversely, as the value of the pound increases, the amount of pounds demanded falls.

Another important factor affecting the demand for a currency is interest rates. Suppose that interest rates in the United Kingdom rise. This will make investments in British money market instruments more attractive. As a consequence, the demand for British pounds will increase as investors outside the country seek pounds to be able to purchase these more attractive instruments. The demand schedule will shift out from DD to D'D',

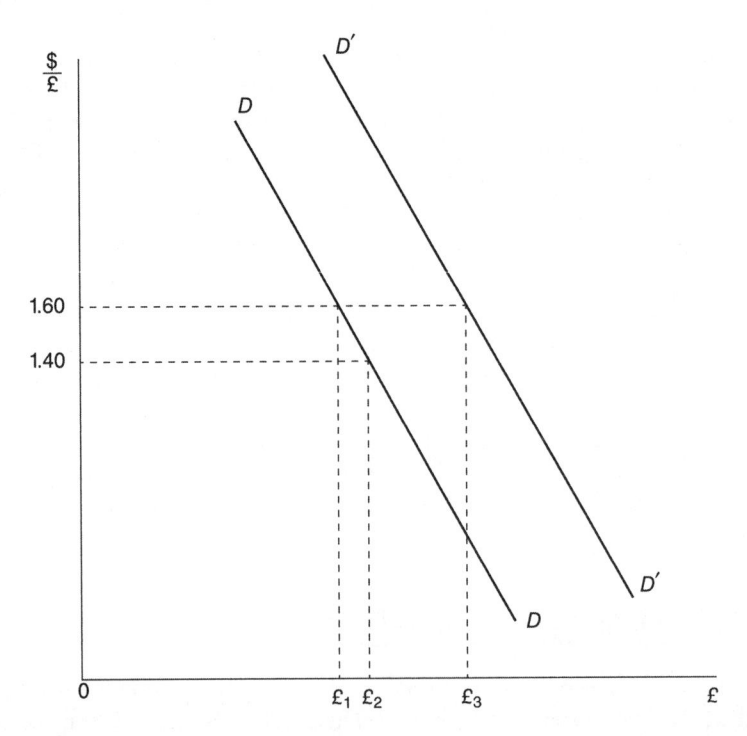

FIGURE 16.1 Demand for a Currency in the Foreign Exchange Market

The Foreign Exchange Market and Exchange Rate Regimes 271

and the quantity of pounds demanded at an exchange rate of $1.60 would increase from £$_1$ to £$_3$. It should be noted that a decline in interest rates abroad will have the same impact on the demand for pounds. For example, if interest rates declined in the United States, the demand for pounds would shift to the right as in Figure 16.1.

Supply Schedule

Let us now turn to the supply of British pounds in the foreign exchange market. People living in the United Kingdom who want to exchange local currency for foreign currency supply these pounds. The situation is shown in Figure 16.2. The supply schedule has a positive slope for reasons analogous to the reasons for the negative slope of the demand schedule. If the value of the pound increases, say from $1.40 to $1.60, foreign goods will become cheaper for those residing in Britain and they will want more.[6] The supply of pounds will increase from £$_1$ to £$_2$.

Of course, if the pound drops in value, foreign goods will become more expensive to those living in Britain and the amount demanded will decline, leading to a drop in the amount of pounds supplied.

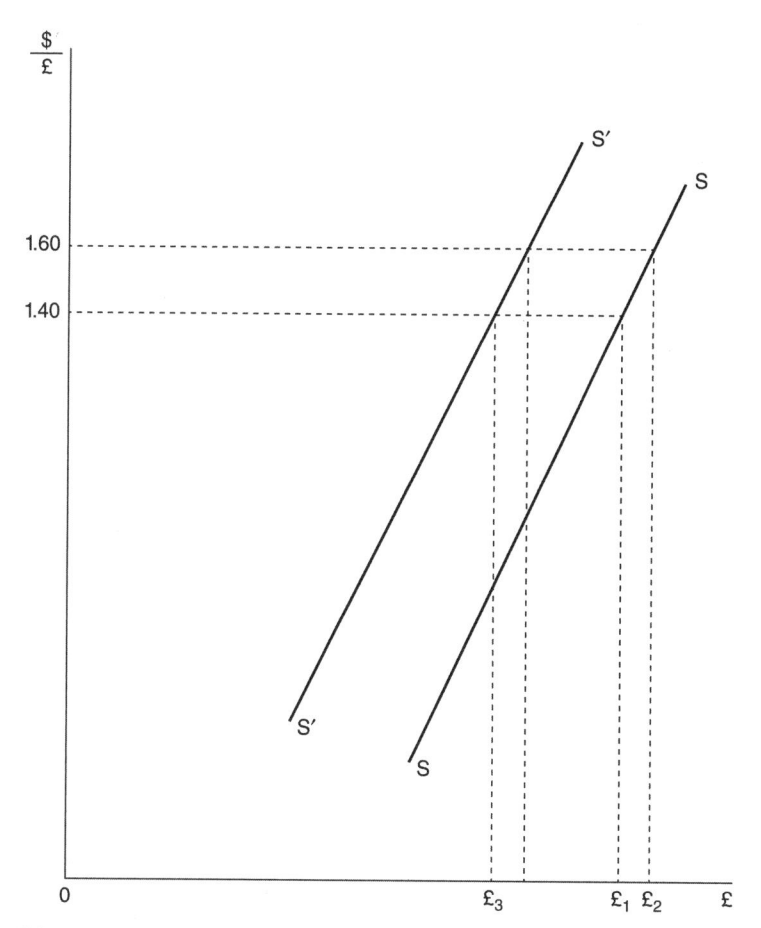

FIGURE 16.2 Supply of a Currency in the Foreign Exchange Market

A change in interest rates will also affect the supply of currency on the foreign exchange market. For example, if interest rates in the United Kingdom increased, the amount of currency supplied would decrease. This is shown by the shift to the left of the supply schedule in Figure 16.2 from SS to S'S'. British investors who have been investing outside the country will now find investments at home to be more attractive and will reduce the amount of pounds that they want to sell (to make investments abroad). At an exchange rate of $1.40 = £1, the quantity of pounds supplied would be £$_3$. Having a similar impact on supply would be a decline in interest rates abroad.

Equilibrium

As in other markets, equilibrium in the foreign exchange market occurs when the price—exchange rate—is such that the quantity supplied equals the quantity demanded. This is illustrated in Figure 16.3. The demand schedule, DD, intersects the supply schedule, SS, at the price of $1.50 per pound. The equilibrium quantity of pounds is £$_0$. If central banks have a policy of allowing the market to set the

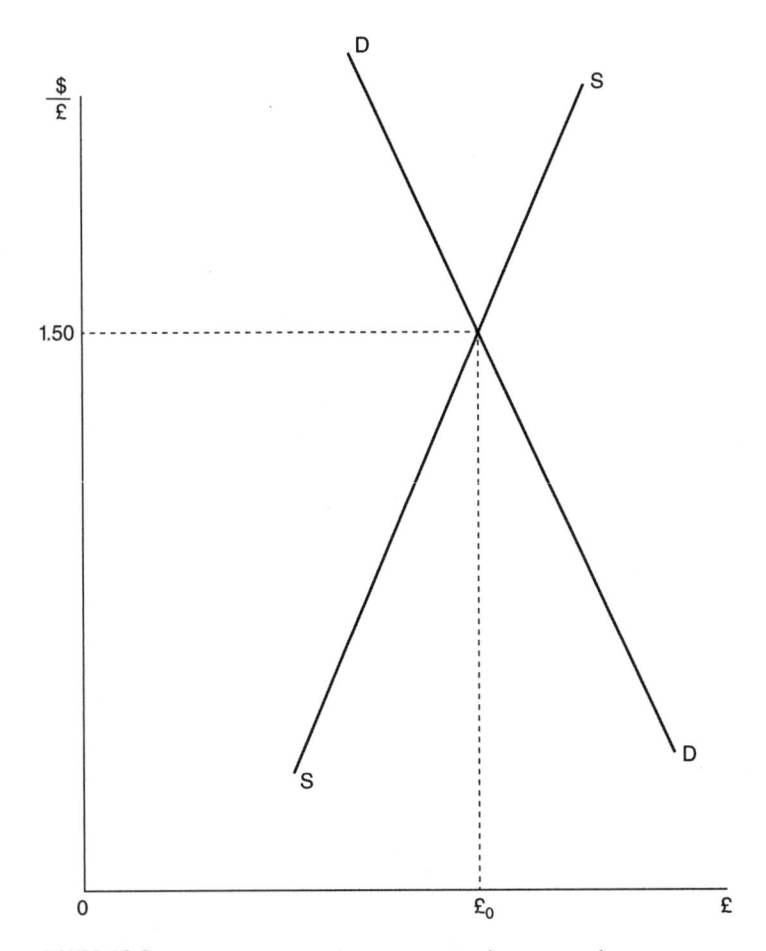

FIGURE 16.3 Equilibrium in the Foreign Exchange Market

exchange rate, this will be the exchange rate that will prevail. This is not to say that central banks have no effect on the exchange rate in a floating exchange rate regime, as we will see. But when they do, it is incidental to pursuing other objectives. In contrast, in cases in which the central bank seeks to fix the exchange rate, when the exchange rate that they attempt to set differs from the equilibrium rate, they must undertake monetary operations—which will have important consequences for financial markets and the economy, as we will also see.

FLOATING EXCHANGE RATE REGIME

In the purest form of a floating exchange rate regime, the central bank treats the exchange rate with "benign neglect." That is, the central bank lets market forces set the exchange rate and does not attempt to influence the value of its currency by stepping into the foreign exchange market to buy or sell its currency. Instead, it pursues other goals with the instruments of monetary policy, and, in so doing, takes the value of the exchange rate into account in those pursuits.

However, some central banks with floating exchange rate regimes will from time to time enter the foreign exchange market to influence the value of their currency. Often, this is done to signal to market participants that the central bank has a different view on where its currency should be trading. The central bank may be of the view that its currency is oversold—that is, it is undervalued in terms of what it believes to be the exchange rate that is consistent with market fundamentals. Buying its currency in a high-profile market transaction is a way to register this signal. At other times, the central bank may be of the view that the market value of its currency is too high—and is holding down its economy—and uses currency market intervention to transmit this view. Central banks that frequently enter the market for their currency are said to engage in a *managed float*—sometimes called a "dirty float."

A variety of factors will cause the demand for and supply of a currency to change, and thus for the exchange rate to fluctuate. Very prominent among these are interest rates—at home and abroad. We illustrate the impact of a decline in interest rates in Figure 16.4, again using the British pound. In this diagram, DD and SS represent the initial demand and supply schedules, implying an exchange value of the pound of $1.60. Next, suppose that interest rates in the United Kingdom decline, leading to both a shifting rightward of the supply curve to S'S' and a shifting leftward of the demand curve to D'D'. As a consequence, the value of the pound drops—depreciates—to $1.40. The quantity of pounds in this diagram does not change—it remains at $£_0$. It could, however, increase or decrease, depending on whether supply or demand changes most. Similarly, an increase in interest rates outside the United Kingdom would result in the pound depreciating in the foreign exchange market in the same way as shown in Figure 16.4.

Conversely, an increase in interest rates in the United Kingdom will cause the supply schedule to move leftward and the demand schedule to move rightward, leading to an unambiguous increase—appreciation—in the exchange value of the pound. Similarly, a drop in interest rates in the United States would have the same impact on the value of the pound as an increase in British interest rates.

An important feature of floating exchange rates is that the exchange rate will weaken when the economy weakens and will strengthen when the economy overheats.

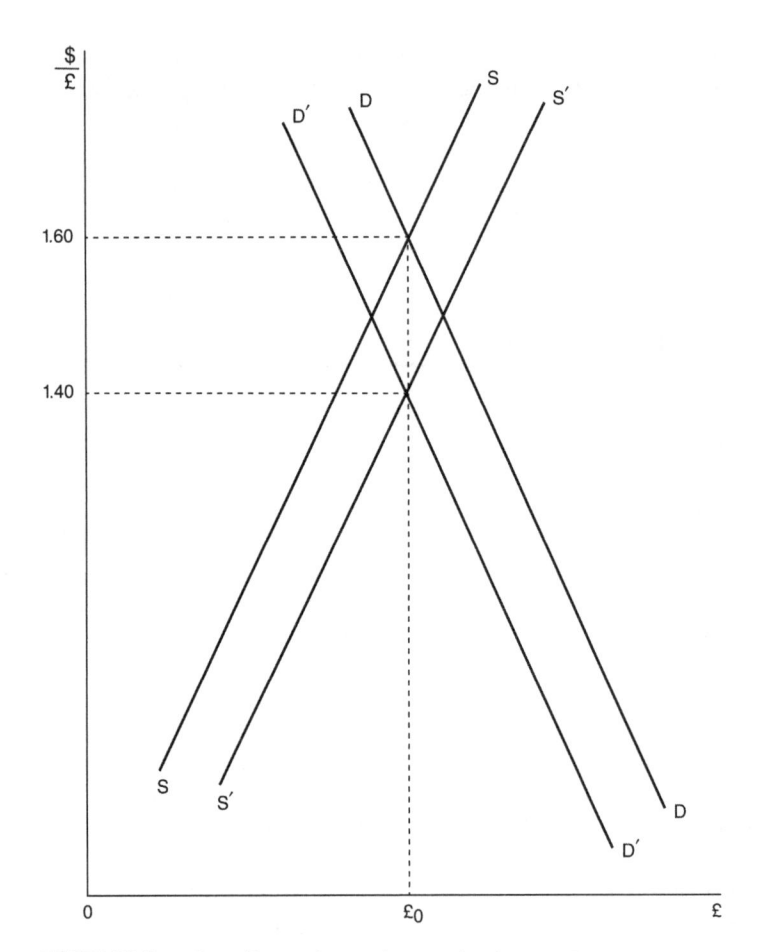

FIGURE 16.4 The Effects of a Decline in the Interest Rates

We have seen in previous chapters that interest rates decline when the economy is weak, in part because the central bank will be using monetary policy to counter the economic weakness by lowering its policy interest rate. As we can see from Figure 16.4, this leads to a decline in the demand for the currency and an increase in supply—both acting to push down the exchange rate. The drop in the exchange rate acts to make exports more competitive and imports more expensive. The resulting higher demand for domestically produced goods will serve to counter some of the weakness in the economy. In other words, the drop in the exchange rate can be thought of as an automatic stabilizer, helping to attenuate movements in the economy.

Conversely, when the economy is very strong and threatening to boost inflation, an increase in interest rates will lead to a rise in the value of the currency on the foreign exchange market. This will act to make exports less competitive and imports more attractive, easing inflationary pressures by reducing resources devoted to export production and diverting demand away from domestically produced goods to imports.

Thus, exchange rate movements complement monetary policy actions in economies with a floating exchange rate. An easing of monetary policy will weaken the exchange rate, as well as lower interest rates. As a consequence, net exports will increase, in addition to domestic spending. Conversely, a tighter monetary policy will lead to an appreciation of the exchange rate, as well as higher interest rates. Net exports will be curbed as will domestic spending, and both will help to cool an overheating economy.

This enhanced effectiveness of monetary policy and the automatic stabilizing feature, along with the ability of the monetary authorities to pursue objectives other than exchange rate stability, has led most advanced economies to adopt floating exchange rate regimes. It also has contributed to monetary policy becoming the principal macroeconomic stabilization policy. The manner in which fixed exchange rates constrain monetary policy will be demonstrated in the next section.

FIXED EXCHANGE RATE REGIME

For much of our history, the United States has been on a fixed exchange rate regime—mostly a gold standard of one form or another. The rules of a fixed exchange rate system require that the tools of monetary policy be directed toward keeping the exchange rate fixed, even when doing so might undermine other goals—such as price stability or maximum employment. Let us see why.

An Undervalued Exchange Rate

When the target value of the exchange rate is below the rate that would clear the market, we refer to this as an undervalued exchange rate. China has pegged its currency to the U.S. dollar and has had a conscious policy of undervaluing its currency—the yuan—for many years, in order to favor its export sector.

We illustrate this situation in Figure 16.5. The demand schedule, DD, represents the demand for Chinese yuan by businesses and people outside China. The supply schedule, SS, represents the supply of yuan by businesses and people in China. They intersect at exchange rate P_e. However, the Chinese authorities have a policy of seeking an exchange rate of P_1, below P_e. By seeking an exchange rate below the equilibrium level, the demand for yuan at P_1, $yuan^D$, will exceed the supply, $yuan^S$. To succeed in hitting their target for the exchange rate, the Chinese authorities will need to satisfy all the demand at that price, just like any other scheme to fix a price below its equilibrium value. This means that the Chinese central bank—the People's Bank of China (PBOC)—will need to create more yuan and sell them for dollars to avoid an appreciation in their exchange rate. They will need to intervene in the market for their currency. Indeed, they will need to sell $yuan^D - yuan^S$ for dollars. This is, in effect, an open market purchase of an asset—dollars—that leads to more reserves in the banking system.

It is noteworthy that the sale of yuan for dollars provides the Chinese authorities with dollars. Rather than hold them in a checking account at little or no interest, they wish to get a better yield on their accumulation of dollars by investing the proceeds. Given their preference for liquidity and safety, the proceeds get invested largely in U.S. Treasury securities. The persistent undervaluation of the yuan—for reasons explained shortly—has led to a considerable accumulation of Treasury securities by the Chinese authorities.

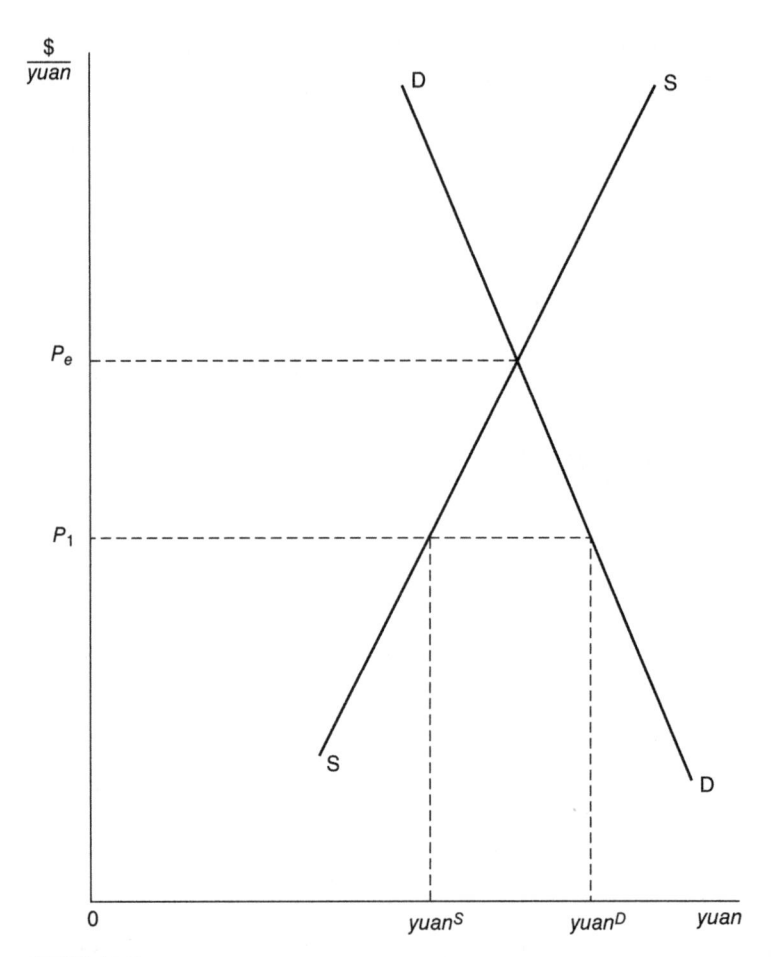

FIGURE 16.5 An Undervalued Currency

The Dynamics of an Undervalued Currency

Things do not stop here. The monetary operations performed by the PBOC—the creation of more reserves in the banking system—leads to (temporarily) lower interest rates, faster growth in money, and inflationary pressures. Lower interest rates will make investments in Chinese financial assets less attractive, and higher prices of Chinese goods will reduce the appeal of Chinese goods to foreign buyers and increase the appeal of foreign goods to businesses and people in China.

As a consequence, the demand schedule for yuan will shift left and the supply schedule will shift to the right, as shown by D'D' and S'S' in Figure 16.6. This will reduce the excess demand for yuan and the extent of the PBOC's intervention in the foreign exchange market—dropping to $yuan^{D'} - yuan^{S'}$. Though smaller, the further addition of reserves to the banking system will continue the process of boosting prices in China. As a result, the demand for yuan will continue to shift left and the supply will continue to shift to the right until they intersect at P_1. This is shown by demand schedule D"D" and supply schedule S"S".

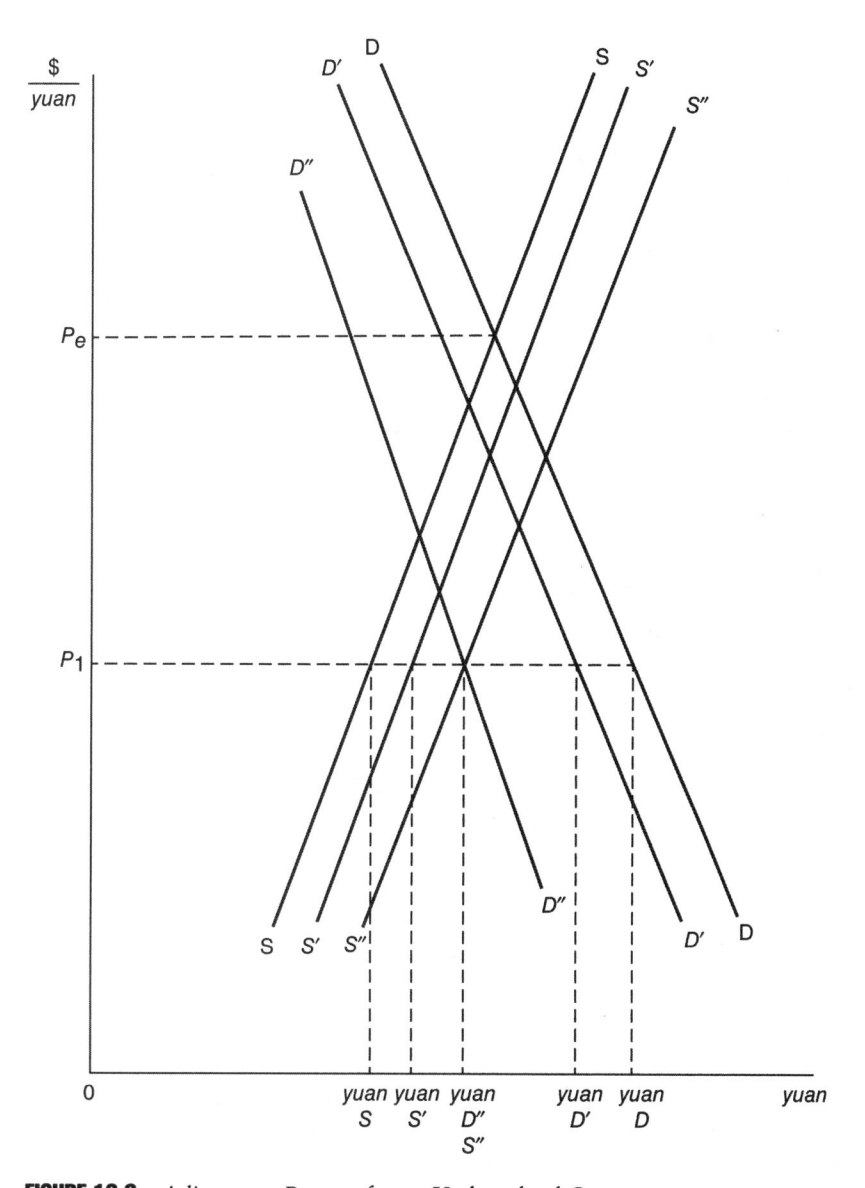

FIGURE 16.6 Adjustment Process for an Undervalued Currency

Thus, a fixed exchange rate system is self-equilibrating. Eventually, equilibrium will be achieved at the targeted exchange rate, but at the expense of higher prices in China. Indeed, the real exchange rate will rise to establish equilibrium, but through higher prices in China rather than a higher nominal exchange rate for the yuan. That is, the real exchange rate will need to be the same at equilibrium, whether this occurs from nominal appreciation or from higher domestic prices—so long as the Chinese authorities allow the process work to its completion. Among the implications is the Chinese must sacrifice the goal of price stability to achieve the exchange rate goal.

In practice, there is another solution for a country with an undervalued currency—*sterilized intervention*. Sterilized intervention involves the central bank neutralizing its foreign exchange operations through other measures. More specifically, if the Chinese do not want the inflation that is a by-product of an undervalued currency, they can seek to withdraw the reserves that are created through purchases of foreign exchange by selling another asset. For example, they can sell Chinese government securities from their portfolio—conduct a standard open market sale. Alternatively, they can have a comparable effect by raising reserve requirements on bank deposits; that is, by fostering an increase in the demand for reserves they will have the same impact on the reserves market and short-term interest rates as a comparable reduction in supply. These sterilization measures can be undertaken as long as the central bank has other assets to sell or as long as it is feasible to raise reserve requirements.[7] Sterilization, though, results in a persistent excess demand for yuan and the need for persistent intervention by the Chinese authorities. This implies that the Chinese authorities will be perpetually accumulating dollars and thus U.S Treasury securities.

An Overvalued Currency

A country with a fixed exchange rate regime may face a situation in which its currency is overvalued—its exchange rate target is above the market-clearing price of its currency. In this case, the supply of the country's currency will exceed demand at the target exchange rate, and the process that follows will be the reverse of that associated with an undervalued currency. The central bank will need to sell foreign exchange, as long as it has an inventory.

We illustrate in Figure 16.7. In this diagram, we look at the market for British pounds in terms of the German Deutsche mark (DM). The DM had been the currency used by Germany prior to its adoption of the euro. Countries that were committed to adopting the euro—which included Britain for a time—were required to peg the exchange value of their currency in terms of the DM. For the United Kingdom, the exchange rate was approximately DM2.9 = £1 (P_1 in the chart). In 1992, circumstances resulted in Britain having a considerably overvalued currency. The supply of pounds at that exchange rate is illustrated by £^{S} and the demand for pounds by £^{D}.

To maintain the exchange rate at the target level, the Bank of England had to absorb this excess supply by selling an asset—DM. This was an open market transaction that withdrew £^{S} − £^{D} reserves from the banking system. Such actions led to a rise in interest rates and restricted aggregate demand and money growth in the United Kingdom. It created a negative output gap that placed downward pressure on prices in Britain. Through its commitment to the exchange rate, the Bank of England was foregoing its ability to counter the emerging rise in unemployment. In time, prices in the United Kingdom would have fallen in relation to those elsewhere in Europe and equilibrium would have emerged as the demand for pounds shifted out and the supply shifted in.[8] However, there would be an unwanted loss of output and employment in the meantime. The British authorities faced a dilemma between their commitment to join the euro, requiring them to keep the exchange rate at DM2.9 = £1, and their desire to keep employment levels high. They chose to drop their commitment to the euro and instead to let the pound depreciate in order to free up

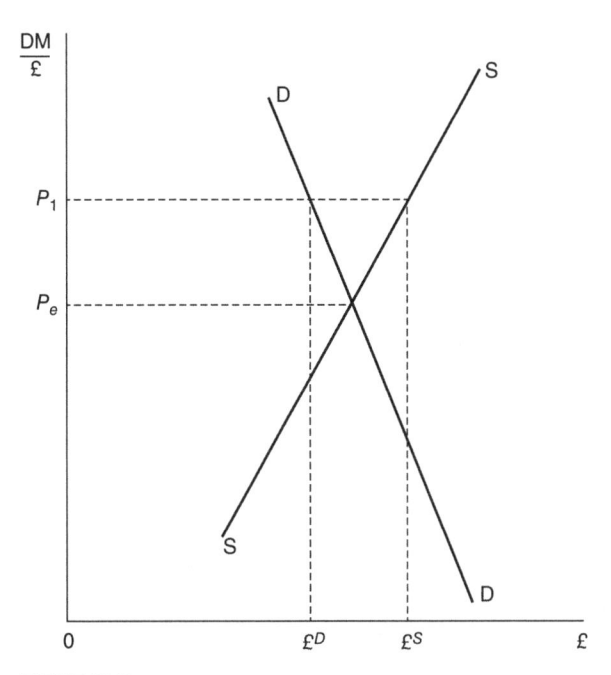

FIGURE 16.7 An Overvalued Currency

monetary policy to address the weakening economy. This illustrates the point made previously that a fixed exchange rate regime requires that monetary policy must be directed to the exchange rate and not to other objectives, if the process is allowed to work to a new equilibrium.

Instead, if the authorities having an overvalued currency are unwilling to relinquish monetary policy solely to achieve the target exchange rate, they may be tempted to engage in *exchange controls*. With exchange controls, the central bank deals with the excess supply of its currency—excess demand for the foreign currency—by rationing foreign exchange. In other words, the excess supply of local currency in Figure 16.7 (pounds in that diagram) can be thought of as an excess demand for the other currency (DM in the diagram). A wide variety of rationing methods have been used over time—and often invite corruption by those involved in administering the rationing. Like the methods associated with sterilized intervention, discussed above, exchange controls lead to inefficiencies in the performance of the economic system. Among those inefficiencies is lower investment in the country by those who can choose to invest elsewhere. The reason is that exchange controls pose risks to those investors (portfolio and direct investors) in the form of not being able to repatriate their investment earnings—convert them from local currency into foreign exchange. Exchange controls also lead to a black market in foreign exchange. Many who are not awarded foreign exchange at the official pegged rate will be willing to buy that currency at a higher price in the black market. Thus, a dual exchange rate will emerge—the official rate for those fortunate enough to get an allocation, and the black market or "street" rate for the rest.

Variations on Fixed Exchange Rate Regimes

There are various forms of exchange rate regimes that involve a fixed exchange rate. A *currency board* is an extreme version of a fixed exchange rate regime. Instead of a central bank, a country with such a system establishes a currency board to exchange the country's local currency for the currency to which it is pegged—the so-called anchor currency. The local currency is fully backed by reserves held in the anchor currency—typically, holdings of money market assets denominated in this currency. That is, the amount of local currency issued cannot exceed the value of the anchor currency held as reserves by the currency board. The currency board passively issues local currency in exchange for the anchor currency and does not engage in monetary policy, meaning that it cannot pursue goals other than the exchange rate peg.

This system has similarities to using the anchor currency as the national currency—referred to as *dollarization* (even when the anchor currency is not the dollar). In other words, another currency is adopted as the domestic currency. Notable among countries that have dollarized are Ecuador, Panama, and El Salvador. Many other counties have been partially dollarized. Even though they still have their own national currency, the dollar (or some other foreign currency) is widely used for domestic transactions and for storing wealth. Usually, these countries have had high inflation rates (and thus erosion of the purchasing power of the local currency) and monetary turbulence. People in these countries hold dollars or other currencies because they are more stable in value.

The advantage of a currency board over dollarization is that a currency board enables the country to earn some income from money issuance—called *seignorage*. As noted, it does so by investing the reserves in the anchor currency in interest-earning assets; under dollarization, the issuer of the anchor currency receives the seignorage—the Federal Reserve, if the adopted currency is the U.S. dollar (actually the Treasury, because excess earnings of the Fed are remitted to the Treasury). Having currency boards are Hong Kong, Lithuania, and Bulgaria.

At the other extreme, some countries have an *adjustable peg*. That is, they fix their exchange rate in terms of another currency, but adjust that peg from time to time. For example, the central bank may have as a basic objective an inflation target and may use foreign exchange transactions to implement its policy directed toward hitting that target. If it perceives that inflation is running above the target, it will raise the value of its currency—appreciate its nominal exchange rate. By appreciating the nominal exchange rate of its currency, its price level will tend to fall in relation to that of other currencies, if the real exchange rate is unchanged. This is consistent with Equation (16-3). By raising the nominal exchange rate, domestic prices will fall in relation to foreign prices (or domestic inflation will fall in relation to foreign inflation). Conversely, if inflation is running below target, it can depreciate its nominal exchange rate. Among countries that have used an adjustable peg to pursue a price stability goal has been Iraq.

SUMMARY

1. Exchange rates are the prices at which currencies are converted into each other. The foreign exchange market has grown rapidly, owing to globalization.

2. The foreign exchange market is primarily a wholesale, over-the-counter market. Large global banks are the principal market makers. The market performs spot and forward transactions, including currency swaps and outright forwards. Forwards are customized by commercial banks to the requirements of their customers. Currency swaps—which contain a spot leg and a forward leg—have also become very large. Of lesser size are currency futures and options.
3. There is a distinct relationship between the forward exchange rate and the spot rate, which is based on interest rate differentials between the two countries. A higher interest rate in the foreign country than in the home country will cause the forward rate for the home country's currency to be above the spot rate, as the home country's currency appreciation compensates for its lower interest rates.
4. In the long run, PPP tends to determine exchange rates when exchange rates are flexible. If currencies are fixed, it affects price levels in the two countries. PPP is a broader version of the law of one price.
5. The real exchange rate is the nominal exchange rate adjusted for differential movements in price levels. Important economic decisions tend to be made on the basis of the real exchange rate more so than the nominal rate. Appreciation of the real exchange rate can be achieved either through appreciation of the nominal rate or by larger increases in domestic prices relative to those abroad.
6. The demand for and supply of a country's currency determine its equilibrium exchange rate. The actual exchange rate depends on its currency policy.
7. Under a floating exchange rate policy, the country allows the market to set the exchange rate—the actual exchange rate is the equilibrium rate or the rate determined by economic fundamentals as reflected in currency demand and supply. A floating exchange rate allows the country's central bank to pursue other objectives, such as stable prices and maximum employment. Also, movements in the exchange rate serve as an automatic stabilizer.
8. Under a fixed exchange rate regime, the target for the exchange rate can differ from its equilibrium value. When it does, then the central bank must take monetary actions—intervene in the foreign exchange market—to achieve the exchange rate target. These actions involve open market operations that affect the supply of bank reserves.
9. With an undervalued currency, the central bank will engage in expansionary open market operations that will, in time, lead to a new equilibrium at the target exchange rate. This takes place through more rapid increases in its price level—which cause the real exchange rate to appreciate.
10. With an overvalued currency, the central bank will need to undertake contractionary open market operations that will, also in time, lead to a new equilibrium at the target exchange rate. This is achieved through downward pressures on the price level—brought about by a weaker economy. In this case, the real exchange rate will depreciate through price level movements (smaller increases in this country than increases abroad) instead of a decline in the nominal exchange rate.
11. Countries that want to have a fixed exchange rate and short circuit the adjustment mechanism when the target exchange rate differs from the equilibrium rate will engage in sterilization when their currency is undervalued. This will take the form of the central bank reversing the open market purchase of the other currency by selling another asset or its equivalent. Countries with an overvalued currency are tempted to use exchange controls to deal with the excess supply

of their currency (excess demand for the foreign currency) in order to avoid the economic weakness that results when their central bank instead sells foreign exchange and reduces bank reserves.
12. Currency boards are an extreme version of fixed exchange rates. They have similarities to dollarization. At the other extreme are adjustable pegs, which can be used to achieve another objective—such as an inflation target.

QUESTIONS

1. Why has the foreign exchange market grown so rapidly over recent decades? Do you expect it to continue to grow rapidly?
2. Describe the basic structure of the foreign exchange market. Who are the major players?
3. What is the difference between a spot and a forward exchange transaction? In what category does a foreign exchange swap appear?
4. If the 90-day short-term interest rate is 5 percent (annual rate) in the United Kingdom and 2 percent in Japan, what will be the 90-day forward exchange rate of the pound? Suppose that the current spot rate is ¥128 = £1.
5. What is the real exchange rate? Explain why economic decisions will be based more on movements in the real exchange rate than the nominal rate.
6. Suppose that the real exchange value of the dollar in terms of the euro appreciates 10 percent. As a result, will the choice to a U.S. consumer be any different if this takes place through a nominal appreciation of 10 percent or a 10 percent decline in the price of a good denominated in euros? Suppose that the initial exchange rate is $1.50 = €1 and the initial price of the European good is €100.
7. What is the law of one price? How does it relate to purchasing power parity? How is the law of one price achieved under fixed exchange rates? Floating exchange rates?
8. What must a country with a fixed exchange rate do to hit its target for the exchange rate if its currency is undervalued? Overvalued? Is the country also able to pursue other goals with monetary policy, such as maximum employment and stable prices?
9. How will a reduction in interest rates in the United States affect the exchange value of the dollar? An increase? How would an increase in interest rates outside the United States affect the exchange value of the dollar?
10. Suppose the U.S. economy slips into recession and interest rates fall while other major economies hold up fairly well and their interest rates do not change. Will the movement in the exchange rate help to offset some of this weakness or compound the weakness? How would the situation differ if other economies weakened along with the U.S. economy?
11. China is experiencing inflationary pressures. How is this related to its exchange rate policy? Is its currency—the yuan—undervalued or overvalued? Why has China raised its reserve requirements on deposits over recent years?
12. What is meant by currency sterilization? Has China been engaging in sterilization? If so, how have they done this?

13. How do exchange controls aid a country with an overvalued currency that does not want to impose a contractionary monetary policy?
14. Compare a currency board with dollarization. Why might a country favor a currency board over dollarization?
15. If a country has an adjustable peg exchange rate regime and wants to slow its inflation rate, how will it want to adjust its exchange rate? Explain how this works using Equation (16-3).

NOTES

1. As a result, the value of cross-border trade in goods and services has expanded from around 40 percent of global GDP to roughly two-thirds in only three decades.
2. See Bank for International Settlements, *Triennial Central Bank Survey: Report on Global Foreign Exchange Market Activity in April 2013*, Monetary and Economics Department, December 2013.
3. According to the 2013 BIS survey cited in note 2 above, about 40 percent of transactions are spot transactions, 40 percent are swaps, 15 percent are forwards, and 5 percent are options.
4. Note that if you divide $15 by $1.35 per euro, the price will be a little higher than €11—it will be €11.11. The reason is that 10 percent is a fairly large change and the relationship is more precise for smaller—less discrete—changes.
5. It is presumed that the demand for traded goods is price elastic. That is, a decline in the price of British goods in the United States of 1 percent will induce an increase in the demand for such goods of more than 1 percent. This gives rise to the negative slope to the demand schedule for British pounds by people living in the United States.
6. It is presumed that the demand for foreign goods by British residents is price elastic for the same reason that it is presumed that the demand for British goods outside the United Kingdom is price elastic.
7. Raising reserve requirements is, in effect, raising the implicit tax on intermediation through commercial banks, which results in economic inefficiencies in the allocation of credit resources. Other measures that the authorities can pursue to limit the inflationary effects of the undervalued currency are to set limits on bank lending or to curtail household or business spending through other controls.
8. Note that prices in the United Kingdom can still be rising. However, they must be rising less rapidly than on the continent for the ratio of the price of goods and services in the United Kingdom to fall in relation to those on the continent.

CHAPTER 17

Depository Institutions

WHAT YOU WILL LEARN IN THIS CHAPTER

- How the size of commercial banks compares with savings institutions and credit unions and how they differ in the services that they provide.
- Why there are so many commercial banks in the United States and just a few large banks in other countries.
- Why cost considerations do not seem to greatly favor large institutions over smaller ones.
- Why interbank connections are important for the U.S. banking system.
- What is meant by relationship banking and bundling of services.
- How deposit insurance affects our depository system today.
- How the safety net provided to commercial banks and other depository institutions creates moral hazard incentives.
- How regulation and supervision seeks to counter moral hazard.
- Why so much emphasis by regulators around the world has been given to capital standards for depository institutions.

BACKGROUND

As you drive through some communities, there seem to be offices of depository institutions on virtually every corner. Some are branches of large, global banks; others are local institutions with the name "bank" in their title; and still others are credit unions. Are they all doing the same thing? Is their customer base the same? Do they compete with each other? Why do small banks seem to have no difficulty coexisting with mega-banks?

Further, have you wondered whether there is any longer a need for such bricks and mortar, or whether the services of depository institutions can be conducted over the Internet? Beyond this, why are banks and other depository institutions so heavily regulated in relation to other businesses.

Historically, commercial banks have been the largest and most important financial institutions. This has been true in the United States as well as in other parts of the world. Commercial banks have provided various services to businesses, governments, and less so, until recently, to households. Among these services are handling payments, supplying financing, and providing liquidity.

In the United States and some other parts of the world, other depository institutions have developed, mainly to serve middle- and lower-income households as repositories of their savings and as sources of credit. In the United States, these take the form of savings institutions and credit unions. Commercial banks are still the largest financial sector in the United States, but the industry has given ground to financial institutions other than depository institutions (to be discussed in the next three chapters) and to securities markets (discussed in Chapters 7 through 11).

We can get some idea of the relative importance of commercial banks by examining their size, measured by assets (as of end June 2013):

Institution	Assets (billions of dollars)
Commercial banks	13,350
Savings institutions	1,056
Credit unions	1,060
Total credit market assets	57,563

Sources: Federal Reserve Board, Federal Deposit Insurance Corporation, and National Credit Union Administration.

Commercial banks are clearly the largest of the depository institutions, being more than 10 times the size of savings institutions or of credit unions. Nonetheless, they hold less than a fourth of all credit market assets; the other credit market assets are either securities held directly in portfolios by investors or by all financial institutions (including the Fed).

Over time, commercial banks and other depository institutions have broadened the array of services that they provide to the public. Meanwhile, other financial institutions have emerged and have grown in importance as providers of financing and as holders of the public's assets. Nonetheless, commercial banks remain at the core of the financial system in the United States and elsewhere.

Because of their very special position in the financial system, commercial banks and other depository institutions are among the most regulated and supervised businesses, whether they are located in the United States or other parts of the world. Indeed, the degree of regulation has expanded over recent years, especially in the wake of the financial crisis.

In this chapter, we will look more closely at these institutions—their organization and size, the services they offer, and the way they are regulated.

ORGANIZATION OF COMMERCIAL BANKS AND OTHER DEPOSITORY INSTITUTIONS

As noted in Chapter 12, commercial banks can get their charter from the state in which they are organized or from the federal government (Office of the Comptroller of the Currency [OCC]). The same is true of other depository institutions—savings institutions and credit unions. Regardless of the source of their charter, the deposits that they offer to the public have federal insurance, and through the provision of federal insurance, federal regulators are able to standardize much of the regulation and supervision of these institutions.

Commercial Banks

In the United States, there are roughly 6,000 separately chartered commercial banks, which is down appreciably from the high-water mark of 15,000 in the early 1980s. Most of these are chartered by states. Moreover, these banks provide services to their customers through more than 80,000 branches, a number that has grown steadily over time. Whether the number of banking offices will continue to grow remains to be seen, as electronic delivery systems—notably, Internet and mobile banking—are providing convenient alternatives to bank customers. These systems do not require costly "bricks and mortar" and are changing the concept of banking markets.

Despite the decline in the number of separately chartered commercial banks over recent decades, the United States has a lot more commercial banks than exist in other parts of the world. This owes importantly to the federal nature of our banking system and concerns early in our history about concentration of financial power. The states were jealous of their authority to control commercial banking within their borders and were reluctant to allow commercial banks chartered in other states to conduct a banking business within their jurisdiction. Moreover, many states were so-called unit banking states and did not allow banks to branch within their state or placed tight limits on branching. This meant that each banking office had to be separately chartered and led to a proliferation of the number of commercial banks.

Role of the Interbank Market The interbank market provides a means by which the banking system comprised of many separate banks becomes connected in important and efficient ways. The interbank market enables banks that gather more core deposits than they want to lend to lay off the excess to other banks that want to lend more than their core deposits will allow. Smaller banks tend to have a solid core deposit base that provides them with more deposits than they find it worthwhile to lend. In contrast, large banks typically face a shortfall of core deposits in relation to the loans that they deem to be worthwhile to make. The interbank market—notably, the federal funds market described in Chapter 12—enables these imbalances to be ameliorated. Often, such smaller banks will lend their excess funds to their correspondent bank, discussed below.

The interbank market also provides banks facing shocks to their balance sheets a means for dealing with them. A bank that experiences an unexpected outflow of funds on a particular day can use the interbank market to cover its shortfall by getting finds from another bank—likely one that experienced a positive shock that day, getting an unexpected inflow. These types of shocks can be addressed by using the services of a federal funds broker, which specializes in arranging trades among banks, or through a correspondent banking relationship.

Further, the interbank market helps to ensure that all banks are facing the policy interest rate being set by the central bank and are taking this into account in making business decisions. Banks facing strong loan demand will be able to access additional funds through the interbank market at an interest rate linked to the level of the central bank's policy rate and keep making loans until additional loans are no longer profitable. Similarly, banks facing weak loan demand can make more profits by placing some of their funds in the interbank market rather than lending them out. In this way, the central bank monetary policy is influencing credit decisions more uniformly. In the process, credit is being allocated within the banking system more efficiently.

Role of Branches Outside the United States, most other countries did not have such restrictions and instead have experienced the development of a few large commercial banks with numerous branches. A branch is a component of the bank itself rather than an affiliate of the bank. With a branch system, the need for an interbank system is reduced—but not eliminated. Offices (branches) that routinely gather more core deposits than they lend can be used to transfer funds to other branches that routinely have insufficient core deposits to meet their lending. Also, a positive shock at one branch can be used to meet a negative shock at another. This reliance on branches likely reflects certain economies of scale in the provision of banking services—that is, when per unit (average) costs of these services decline as the volume of services provided expands.

Economies of Scale Today, economists disagree about the presence of *economies of scale* in banking—that is, the extent to which per-unit costs decline as the size of the institution increases. Much evidence, based on historical experience, tends to indicate that the per-unit cost of banking services does not change much—decrease or increase—as the size of the bank increases. This would suggest that there is no fundamental economic reason why the banking system would be dominated by large- or small-sized commercial banks. In these circumstances, small banks should be competitive with very large banks. Yet, in the United States, we have seen the share of banking system assets held by very large banks grow over time, which might suggest the presence of economies of scale in banking that enable larger banks to provide better or lower-cost services to the public.

The statistical evidence noted on economies of scale, based on long periods of time, may not fully capture the effects of new information technology. Modern software systems for commercial banks, so-called core banking software, enable bank management to have real-time information on transaction activity throughout the entire bank, regardless of the number of offices or portals in the organization and their locations. Such systems have large up-front costs and facilitate management of very large and complex banking businesses. This tends to favor larger institutions and can offset some of the diseconomies of scale that previously were a serious impediment to large size. Moreover, regulatory compliance has become a bigger component of commercial banking today. Compliance tends to have huge start-up costs and low marginal costs, which gives rise to economies of scale and favors larger commercial banks.

Over time, commercial banks in the United States have developed in ways that have enabled them to exploit some of the benefits of size within the legal constraints that prevailed until fairly recently. One such method has been the use of the bank holding company structure. *Multibank holding companies*—as their name suggests—are a collection of separately chartered commercial banks under the umbrella of a single holding company. That is, these banks have a common owner—the holding company. The banking organization's investors acquire shares (ownership) in the holding company and the holding company, in turn, acquires shares in the individual banks. Through the holding company, these organizations have been able to utilize common business plans, purchase inputs for the entire system, and jointly exploit processes that are characterized by economies of scale. Because of the benefits of such a structure, more than four-fifths of commercial banks today are part of a multibank holding company, with the remainder as stand-alone commercial banks.

Economies of Scope The holding company structure has also enabled banking organizations to engage in activities that are not standard banking activities, but are closely related or incidental to banking. These are activities that are characterized by *economies of scope*. Economies of scope refers to complementarities—synergies—in the provision of different services. When there are economies of scope, complementarities in the provision of separate services lower production costs or raise the appeal of the bank to customers by offering a variety of (complementary) services. In other words, the bank becomes a one-stop provider of a variety of financial services.

The coexistence of banks of different sizes suggests that smaller (and medium-sized) banks have economic reasons why they can hold their own, even in the face advantages favoring large banks. Important to banking have been relationships with customers along various complementary product lines—so-called relationship banking. The bank commonly provides its business customers a transaction account, a line of credit, payroll processing, credit cards for business expenses of employees, and so forth—a form of bundling of services. Through such a multifaceted relationship, the bank can get better information on the customer about its business prospects, reducing the asymmetric information problem. This improves its ability to make credit judgments. Relationship banking helps banks of all sizes to improve the attractiveness of the products that they offer to their business—and household—customers. It is thought that the management of smaller banks can be in an even better position to assess the prospects of business customers in their markets because, by living among such customers, they can accumulate more relevant information on the prospects for these businesses and their ability to repay loans. This is likely why smaller banks tend to be very competitive in offering products to smaller businesses.

For some of these services, law or regulation may prohibit the bank from offering the service. However, the service may be permissible if it is performed in another subsidiary of the holding company—an affiliate. The bank can then refer its customers to the holding company affiliate or even handle arrangements for the customer to acquire the service from the affiliate. For example, the holding company may have a subsidiary that performs data processing and this service can be offered to customers of the holding company's component banks. Also, securities underwriting has been an activity that frequently has been performed by a subsidiary of the holding company and offered to bank customers wanting more financing options than standard loans from the bank.

Securities underwriting by commercial banks was prohibited by the Glass-Steagall Act of 1933.[1] The intention was to limit the risk profile of banks, as securities underwriting (and trading) was perceived to be excessively risky. This was a time of massive bank failures and securities underwriting was thought to be a contributing factor. There were also thought to be conflicts of interest for a bank involved in both lines of activity because the information gathered about a business from a bank lending relationship may provide an advantage in managing or investing in the securities of the business. The provisions of Glass-Steagall were relaxed over time by federal bank regulators, and, in 1999, the Gramm-Leach-Bliley Act largely removed the remaining restrictions. As a result, commercial banks and securities firms were formally permitted to affiliate with each other (and with insurance companies). The landmark Dodd-Frank act of 2010 restored a few restrictions on commercial bank securities activities, notably prohibiting proprietary trading in securities—that is, trading in securities other than those of the federal government for the account of the bank.

Removal of Restrictions on Branching Over the 1980s, many states removed restrictions on out-of-state banks acquiring banks within their borders and on establishing branch banks within their jurisdiction. This was followed by federal legislation in the 1994—the Riegle-Neal Act—that effectively eliminated remaining restrictions on interstate acquisitions of banks and permitted interstate branching. As a consequence, the U.S. banking landscape has changed in important ways. These developments have made it easier for banks to expand the scale of their activities geographically through the bank itself by adding branches rather than adding separately chartered banks via the holding company. As a result of these liberalization measures, there has been a considerable amount of consolidation in the banking sector over the past couple of decades. A substantial number of mergers and acquisitions took place in the United States, particularly involving very large banking organizations. Some of these took place during the financial crisis and took the form of seriously impaired institutions being absorbed by healthier ones. As a result, today the largest commercial banks in the United States have become national in scope and control a large share of commercial bank assets. For example, the top five commercial banking organizations hold nearly half of banking system assets, much of these through their branch banking networks.

As part of the globalization process, foreign-chartered commercial banking organizations have also become an important presence in the U.S. banking market. They typically do so either through establishing U.S. branches of the bank itself or through owning a commercial bank in the United States having a federal or state charter. Foreign banks hold about a sixth of banking assets in the United States, up considerably from a few decades ago. As might be expected, offices of foreign banks are concentrated in New York City, the hub of the U.S. financial system.

Universal Banks It is worth noting that many foreign banks in their home markets are *universal banks*. A universal bank is one that offers many products within the bank that are not standard banking products. Many of these are not permissible for U.S. commercial banks or must be performed in the United States by a nonbank subsidiary of a holding company. A long-standing debate has been taking place about whether the United States should allow universal banking. Much of the debate centers on whether the other activities allowed by universal banking pose too much risk for them to be included in the protected bank—a matter discussed later in this chapter—or whether they should be placed in a separate holding company of the banking organization with ring fences protecting the bank from the risk of its affiliate. As the global financial system has become more closely integrated, differences regarding the structure of commercial banks and other financial institutions have become more prominent, and the matter of how to level the competitive playing field has been looming larger.

Today, commercial banks offer business, government, nonprofit organizations, and household customers a wide range of financial services. They offer transaction, savings, and time deposits, along with other types of investments. Some of these are structured as retirement accounts. On the credit side, they make a wide variety of loans to these customers—both secured (as with motor vehicle loans and mortgages) and unsecured.

Some larger commercial banks also provide services—such as check clearing—to other commercial banks, saving institutions, and credit unions. These are referred to as *correspondent relationships* and typically involve services for which there are distinct economies of scale, which the larger correspondent bank can exploit and provide the smaller respondent with these services at lower cost than if the respondent undertook these activities by itself.

Savings Institutions

As noted in Chapter 2, savings institutions—sometimes called *thrift institutions*—have traditionally served households with limited resources and with limited opportunities for getting basic financial services. These institutions began in the nineteenth century to hold the savings of and make loans—primarily mortgage loans for the purchase of a home—to such retail customers. Initially, they were chartered to operate by states, which also regulated them. Later, they were chartered and regulated by agencies of the federal government, too. Originally, they took the form of mutual organizations; that is, their retail customers owned them. Today, most are organized as corporations, owned by shareholders.

The deposits that savings institutions offered were called savings deposits and the funds in savings accounts could be withdrawn by appearing in person at the institution. Indeed, these institutions took on the names of (mutual) savings banks and savings and loan associations. Over time, they offered a wider variety of accounts—notably fixed-maturity time deposits—and later transaction and retirement accounts. They also expanded the types of loans that they offered their customers to include personal and auto loans, and later credit card loans.

These institutions became very competitive in garnering retail deposits at a time when household wealth was growing rapidly after the Second World War.[2] As a consequence, they developed into the principal residential mortgage lender. As noted in Chapter 10, savings institutions bundled the origination, servicing, and typically the holding (and funding) of mortgages to maturity. The alternative to holding these mortgages to maturity for these institutions was to sell them to the government-sponsored enterprises (GSEs)—Fannie Mae and Freddie Mac—that returned cash to make more mortgages.

The thrift institution model was highly vulnerable to interest rate risk associated with the serious mismatch between the maturity of their deposit liabilities and the maturity of (mostly mortgage) assets. The mortgage loans that they made typically had fixed interest rates and very long original maturities—usually 30 years. Their deposits had much shorter maturities. Savings (and transaction) deposits could be withdrawn essentially on demand, and time deposits had fairly short maturities, ranging from a few months to a few years. When interest rates surged in the late 1970s and early 1980s, much of this industry became insolvent. Their interest costs rose sharply while the interest income they got from mortgages was fairly stable. Viewed differently, the higher level of interest rates caused a much sharper drop in the present value of their assets than in their liabilities, resulting in negative net worth for many. Mitigating these losses to a small extent was a growing share of adjustable-rate mortgages (ARMs) that thrifts had put on their books. The interest earnings on these loans moved more closely with the interest expense on their deposits.

Later in the 1980s, savings institutions were given new powers by legislation—primarily to make commercial real estate loans for which they had little experience and expertise. Many of those that had not failed earlier in the decade ended up insolvent because of the bad commercial real estate loans that they made. As a result, a good portion of the savings institution sector either failed or was acquired by commercial banks wanting to expand their retail deposit base.

The number of savings institutions has fallen from nearly 4,000 in the 1980 to a little more than 1,000 today. The remaining savings institutions—many of which have taken on the title "bank"—are largely owned by holding companies established to hold savings institutions.

Today, savings institutions have many of the same powers as commercial banks—including being able to offer transaction deposits and the authority to make certain business loans. Nonetheless, their client base continues to be concentrated among retail (household) customers.

A number of savings institutions and commercial banks—and, to a lesser extent, credit unions—fall into the category of *community banks*. Community banks typically are smaller institutions that are locally owned and operated and focus on providing financial services to businesses and households in their local area. Notably, community banks account for a large share of loans made to small businesses.

Credit Unions

In the United States, credit unions are an outgrowth of the cooperative movement. With a cooperative, customers are members of the organization and jointly own the organization, as with a mutual organization. The law establishing credit unions requires that members of the credit union have some type of affinity connection—a so-called field of membership.[3] Typically, this affinity involves a common employer, including the military. Over time, this restriction has been modified to broaden eligibility for membership. For example, residents of the same community can now form a field of membership, and some credit unions will serve more than one employer. Credit unions gather funds from their members in the form of deposits (actually called shares) and use these funds to make loans to members.

There are roughly 7,000 separately chartered credit unions in the United States, most of which are very small. Some of the larger credit unions have branches. The aggregate number of credit unions is down a little over recent years, owing to mergers and failures. Consolidations take the form of mergers because acquisitions are very difficult with member-owned organizations; members of both organizations would have to concur that the combination would be beneficial to their interests, which tends to be a hard sell. Credit unions can be chartered by the federal government—the National Credit Union Administration (NCUA)—or by state chartering authorities.

Credit unions offer their members the same types of deposits as other depository institutions—transaction, savings, time deposits, and retirement accounts. On the asset side, they offer their members various types of loans. These include personal loans, credit card accounts, motor vehicle loans, and first and second mortgages (including home equity lines). Because of the interest rate risk associated with mortgages, credit unions tend to sell them in the secondary market, especially if have they have fixed rates. A small segment of the industry offers business loans if the owner of the business is a member.

ECONOMIC FUNCTIONS OF DEPOSITORY INSTITUTIONS

In Chapter 3, we discussed the special role of commercial banks. As we have noted in this chapter, savings institutions and credit unions have many similarities to commercial banks, and thus perform many of the same economic functions. Let us recap those economic functions.

Payment Services

Commercial banks and other depository institutions provide their customers with accounts that hold balances that can be used for making all kinds of payments. These accounts are accessible on demand, as they must allow payment orders from the customer to transfer balances when the order is submitted. In effect, these accounts should be regarded as having very short maturities. This service enables vast numbers of economically beneficial transactions to be completed each day throughout the economy. Traditionally, payment services involved the use of paper checks, but this is giving way to various electronic payments—including point of sale, the Internet, and mobile phones.

Liquidity Provision

Depository institutions also provide their customers with funds for unexpected needs on short notice. These take the form of loans, often under prenegotiated lines of credit. This is comparable to the provision of transaction balances for payment purposes in that it requires the institution to be able to provide good funds to the loan customer on little notice, which has the same effect as an unexpected withdrawal from a transaction account. That is, a customer needing funds immediately can draw down balances in a transaction account or the customer can tap a credit line. This function enables customers to meet unexpected contingencies that arise—shocks that have little or no advance warning.

Providing Credit When There Is Asymmetric Information

The presence of asymmetric information means that lenders will be reluctant to extend credit to a borrower without getting better information on the prospects for being repaid. Without such information, borrowers with worthwhile projects would get passed over. Depository institutions address these situations by incurring the costs of getting more information and forming judgments about whether to make loans to such borrowers and, if so, on what terms. The greater the extent of asymmetric information, the greater the cost to the lender. Depository lenders also must consider how the risks associated with one borrower relate to the risks of other borrowers and utilize managerial expertise in diversifying and managing loan portfolio risk.

Maturity Transformation

Borrowers from depository institutions typically want loans with longer durations (maturities) than the durations that depositors want for their deposits. Satisfying both sets of customers results in the duration of assets being longer than the duration of liabilities. In other words, these institutions engage in maturity transformation, which leaves them exposed to interest rate risk.

We can next see how these functions are at work in practice by examining the balance sheets of commercial banks, savings institutions, and credit unions, respectively.

THE BALANCE SHEET OF THE COMMERCIAL BANKING SYSTEM

Table 17.1 displays categories of assets and liabilities for all commercial banks operating in the United States—U.S. chartered and U.S. offices of foreign banks—as of end June 2013. On the asset side, the cash and liquid securities category is held by banks largely to provide liquidity to their customers.[4] These balances enable customers to meet unexpected needs for liquidity—either by drawing down transaction deposit balances or drawing on loan relationships, including lines of credit.

The next category of assets—GSE and agency securities—is holdings of securities that could be sold to meet liquidity needs, but possibly at a loss, and provide a flow of interest earnings to the banks. Many of these securities are based on mortgages, both residential and commercial. Because the duration of these assets exceeds that of deposits, they expose their bank holders to interest rate risk (and also to liquidity risk).[5] Commercial banks also hold relatively small amounts of tax-exempt securities—munis, on the next line—often issued by governments within the bank's primary market area.

The next three asset categories are the major types of loans that are made by commercial banks—business, consumer, and real estate (mortgage) loans. As noted, business loans have been the traditional form of bank lending. Today, a large share of these loans—roughly three-fourths—is made under loan commitments. Loan commitments expose the bank to uncertainty about when the borrower may choose to draw on its line of credit, but they also provide the bank with fee income based on the size of the line. Also, a large fraction of business loans are priced off a reference interest rate—the bank's prime rate or another, such as the London Interbank Offered Rate (LIBOR)—and this reference rate changes with

TABLE 17.1 Commercial Banking System Balance Sheet (as of end June 2013)

Assets	$ Billions	Liabilities and Net Worth	$ Billions
Cash and liquid securities	2,033	Transaction deposits	1,412
GSE and agency securities	1,506	Other retail deposits	6,279
Munis	262	Wholesale time deposits	628
Other securities	738	Other managed liabilities	1,141
Business loans	1,505	Other liabilities and net worth	3,890
Consumer loans	1,217		
Mortgages	3,575		
Other assets	2,514		
Total assets	13,350	**Total liabilities and net worth**	13,350

Source: Federal Deposit Insurance Corporation.

market conditions. More than two-fifths of business loans made by commercial banks are backed by collateral. The riskier the loan, the more likely it is to be collateralized.

Consumer loans include credit card balances (also drawn under credit lines), motor vehicle loans, and personal loans. They have varying maturities. Some are collateralized (motor vehicle loans), and some have interest rates that adjust to changes in a market-related reference rate. Mortgages take the form of both residential and commercial mortgages. All are collateralized and tend to have longer durations. Commercial banks tend to hold more of their ARM originations in their portfolio—including commercial mortgages—thereby mitigating interest rate risk. A portion of mortgage assets takes the form of home equity loans; many of these are drawn under home equity lines of credit and contribute to management uncertainty about the timing of customer liquidity demands.

On the liabilities side of the balance sheet, the bulk of bank funding is done through core deposits—transaction and other retail deposits. As noted in Chapter 3, the duration of these deposits is difficult to ascertain. Checkable deposit balances can be drawn down or added to at any time, as can savings deposits. Other core deposits—retail time deposits—have specific maturities that facilitate duration management. Wholesale deposits and other managed liabilities are used by banks largely to address mismatches between core deposit inflows and loan demands—related to the liquidity provision function of commercial banks.[6]

THE BALANCE SHEET OF SAVINGS INSTITUTIONS

The balance sheet of savings institutions, shown in Table 17.2, illustrates some notable differences from commercial banks. These institutions have about half of their assets concentrated in mortgages—heavily residential. They also have a larger share of assets in GSE and agency securities and in consumer loans than commercial banks.

TABLE 17.2 Savings Institution Balance Sheet (as of end June 2013)

Assets	$ Billions	Liabilities and Net Worth	$ Billions
Cash and liquid securities	95	Transaction deposits	91
GSE and agency securities	201	Other retail deposits	613
Munis	12	Wholesale time deposits	103
Other securities	59	Other managed liabilities	26
Business and other loans	58	Other liabilities and net worth	227
Consumer loans	93		
Mortgages	472		
Other assets	70		
Total assets	1,060	**Total liabilities and net worth**	1,060

Source: Federal Deposit Insurance Corporation.

On the liability side of their balance sheet, savings institutions rely more on core deposits and somewhat less on managed liabilities (combined with liquid assets). Their lesser need for managed liabilities reflects their smaller role as liquidity providers than commercial banks. The heavier concentration on mortgage and GSE assets (mostly mortgage related), with longer durations, exposes them to interest rate risk. This high degree of maturity transformation has been an endemic problem of the industry over its history—and, as noted earlier, nearly wiped them out in the 1980s—but has been tempered somewhat by holdings of ARMs.

THE BALANCE SHEET OF CREDIT UNIONS

The balance sheet of credit unions is shown in Table 17.3. On the asset side, mortgages and GSE and agency securities (mostly mortgage related) account for more than half of credit union assets—exposing the industry to some interest rate risk. However, a good share of mortgage assets takes the form of loans under home equity lines, having interest rates that adjust with market rates, and many of their regular home mortgages are ARMs.

On the liability side, credit unions rely more on retail savings and time deposits (shares) than savings institutions or commercial banks. They tend to address mismatches between core deposit inflows and new loans more by using cash and liquid assets on the asset side than do commercial banks and even savings institutions.

DEPOSIT INSURANCE

Federal deposit insurance has come to play an important role in the depository system today. It was introduced in the 1930s as a way to cut down on bank runs that had disrupted the United States over much of its history. It was thought that if depositors had the assurance that their deposits were protected by a federal government guarantee, they would be less inclined to pull out their funds if they became worried

TABLE 17.3 Credit Union Balance Sheet (as of end June 2013)

Assets	$ Billions	Liabilities and Net Worth	$ Billions
Cash and liquid securities	165	Transaction deposits	119
GSE and agency securities	174	Other retail deposits	787
Corporate and foreign bonds	4	Wholesale time deposits	3
Other loans	34	Other liabilities and net worth	147
Consumer loans	223		
Mortgages	325		
Other assets	26		
Total assets	**1,056**	**Total liabilities and net worth**	**1,056**

Source: National Credit Union Administration.

about the condition of their bank. Federal insurance has since been extended to all depository institutions—savings institutions and credit unions, as well as commercial banks. The amount of coverage is the same for all depository institutions—currently, $250,000 per account. Commercial banks and savings banks are covered by the Federal Deposit Insurance Corporation (FDIC), and credit unions by the National Credit Union Share Insurance Fund (NCUSIF).

The insurance funds collect premiums from the depository institutions that they insure. These premiums are assessed on the amount of the institution's deposits and are risk based. That is, they vary with the risk profile of the institution—being higher for those deemed to be more risky. The premiums are used to add to the insurance fund's reserves. The insurance fund then draws on those reserves when it needs to step in to resolve an institution that is on the brink of failure or that has failed (become insolvent). Typically, it will need to pay another depository institution from the insurance fund to take on the failed institution's deposits before it has been able to sell the failed institution's assets.[7]

Through deposit insurance, federal regulation of depository institutions has become highly standardized. Even for state-chartered institutions, federal regulators establish common minimum standards of regulation through the deposit insurance agencies.

REGULATION AND SUPERVISION OF DEPOSITORY INSTITUTIONS

Because of their special role in the economy, commercial banking organizations—and other depository institutions—have become heavily regulated and supervised. Banks and other depository institutions form the heart of the payment system and hold a large share of the public's financial assets (especially of households with limited means). Moreover, disturbances in this sector can reverberate to the rest of the financial system and to the macroeconomy. As a consequence, a safety net has been established for these institutions that has provided certain protections to them and their customers, intended to limit adverse consequences for their customers, the financial system, and the economy of any difficulties that they may experience. The safety net has taken the form of deposit insurance, access to the Fed's discount window, and access to the national payment system. In so doing, a moral hazard situation has been created that can result in excess risk taking. Regulation and supervision are intended to compensate for these distortions.

The terms *regulation* and *supervision* are sometimes used interchangeably, but they refer to distinct functions. Regulation refers to a set of rules and guidelines that all institutions in that category must comply with. Supervision refers to examining and monitoring individual institutions to ensure that they comply with laws and regulations and that they are not taking on too much risk.

The Regulators

In the United States, supervision and regulation of depository institutions is the responsibility of various public authorities. State-chartered commercial banks, savings institutions, and credit unions are regulated (and supervised) by both the state granting their charter and their federal deposit insurer—the FDIC or NCUSIF. The exception is state-chartered commercial banks that can elect to be members of the Federal Reserve System. Those that choose membership are regulated by the Fed. Federally chartered commercial banks and savings institutions are regulated by the OCC, which has separate departments for commercial banks and for savings institutions.[8] Federally chartered credit unions are regulated by the NCUA. These separate federal regulatory agencies are supposed to coordinate their regulatory and supervisory policies to ensure comparable standards and a level playing field for all depository institutions.[9]

In addition, bank holding companies are subject to umbrella (consolidated) supervision by the Federal Reserve Board. The law limits the activities of entities within a holding company to banking and activities closely related to banking. The latter includes securities underwriting, dealing, brokering, and various types of insurance. The Board has responsibility for ensuring compliance of financial holding companies with the law.

Furthermore, foreign banks operating in the United States are subject to the *national treatment* principle, under which they are granted the same powers as U.S.-chartered commercial banks and are subject to the same regulatory treatment. The Fed plays the major role in regulating these institutions, although the OCC and FDIC also have responsibilities.

The financial crisis brought to a head concerns about the *systemic risk* that can be posed by certain large financial institutions. As noted in Chapter 15, systemic risk refers to situations in which the difficulties of one financial institution spill over to others—because of the numerous interconnections among them—and disrupt the workings of the financial system and the economy. In response, the Dodd-Frank Act of 2010 established a federal Financial Stability Oversight Council (FSOC) made up of the various depository institution regulators, the Treasury Department, and some other financial system regulatory authorities, such as the SEC. It has responsibility for identifying conditions that could be contributing to a systemic crisis and for addressing them in a coordinated manner. It also can determine whether other financial institutions not subject to depository institution regulation might pose systemic risks, and, if so, are to be placed under Fed supervision. These institutions have come to be known as systemically important financial institutions (SIFIs).

The Focus of Regulation and Supervision

Regulation (and supervision) has been focused on the safety and soundness of individual institutions—and only recently to the systemic risk they pose to the financial system. In the course of supervision, a composite score is assigned to each supervised institution—the *CAMELS rating*—which is intended to capture the extent to which the institution poses safety and soundness concerns. The CAMELS rating consists of ratings assigned each of the following dimensions of the institution: capital adequacy (C), asset quality (A), management (M), earnings (E), liquidity (L), and sensitivity to market risk (S). The score can range from one (the best) to five (the worst). Institutions scoring poorly are subject to remedial measures by the supervisor.

Capital Standards

Of these six dimensions, depository capital has gotten considerable emphasis in recent decades. The reasoning is that capital acts as a buffer between the losses that are incurred on the loans and other assets of an institution and its insured deposit liabilities. Should the risky assets of the institution result in sizable losses, higher capital positions provide more scope for those losses to be absorbed by the institution's owners before they affect others. Indeed, the authorities have developed risk-based capital standards, under which the more risky the assets, the higher the required capital against it. Capital standards and other aspects of supervision and regulation have become more stringent for SIFIs on grounds that problems that they encounter will be more likely to spill over to other institutions and to the economy. In other words, they impose costs on others that are not internalized in the cost structure of the institution and thus not fully reflected in management decisions regarding risk. Supervisory capital standards are intended to compensate for this distortion.

Capital standards have become internationally coordinated over this period. This reflects the recognition that banking has become globalized and that banks chartered and supervised in one country can, if they get into difficulties, transmit those difficulties to banks in other banking markets. It also recognizes that regulation of financial institutions affects their ability to compete in their home and foreign markets, and there is a desire to level the playing field across borders through harmonized regulation. Bank supervisors from around the globe have been convening at the headquarters of the Bank for International Settlements (BIS) in Basel, Switzerland, to work on coordinated standards for bank supervision and regulation. The common capital standards have come to be known as Basel I (the initial agreement) and Basel II (its successor). Basel I assigned different levels of capital requirements on assets based on where they fell in a few broad categories, such as business loans, mortgages, and sovereign debt. Basel II made more distinctions in the degree of riskiness of assets within these categories.

A third stage, Basel III, has been adopted and is being phased in. It imposes a capital surcharge—a so-called conservation buffer—on SIFIs that is intended to reflect the extent to which they pose risks to other institutions. This is augmented by a countercyclical buffer that is to be built up in good times and can be drawn down in bad times. Basel III standards will be applied more than in the past to off-balance-sheet exposures that pose risks to the bank. In defining what can be included in measures of capital that can be used to satisfy capital requirements, regulators have included certain forms of subordinated debt issued by the bank. Such debt, by having a low claim on the earnings and assets of the bank, is risky to the investor, like common stock. It is thought that the willingness of investors to hold such debt will depend on the risk profile of the bank. By affecting the cost of such debt, these investors, it is thought, will apply market discipline on the managers of the bank to carefully manage risk.

Increasingly, these capital standards are being supplemented by stress tests overseen by banking regulators, noted in Chapter 15. Under stress tests, each systemically important financial institution is required to simulate the impact of various specified shocks, mostly associated with a serious downturn in the macroeconomy, on its balance sheet to determine if it might need even more capital than suggested by Basel-type standards.

Liquidity Standards

In addition, regulators have agreed to establish common standards for ensuring that institutions have adequate levels of liquidity. Maturity mismatches at major financial institutions placed serious strains on these institutions and on the financial system during the financial crisis as these institutions were losing their regular sources of funding. As noted in Chapter 15, these institutions had raised funds at shorter maturities than the assets that they financed. During the crisis, the institutions were faced with the prospect of having to sell those assets at fire sale prices or to get replacement funding from the discount window of the central bank—which turned out to be the primary way that they were able to avoid even greater losses. This situation was largely repeated in parts of the euro area once the subsequent sovereign debt crisis unfolded in that part of the world.

Beyond these, Basel III seeks to increase disclosure and transparency on the part of SIFIs. The reasoning for this has to do with the role of transparency in enhancing market discipline. The more information available to market participants, the more they will be able to assess the risk profile of these institutions and apply discipline on the management of those institutions that are pursuing excessively risky strategies, in part by raising the cost of risky strategies through insisting on more compensation for such risk. The market response to such information might also induce managers to boost capital.

DEPOSITORY INSTITUTIONS AND MONETARY POLICY

Depository institutions are at the heart of the transmission of monetary policy to the economy. Fed policy decisions are made regarding the setting of the federal funds rate—the policy interest rate in the United States—and this is the interbank rate. As noted earlier, commercial banks and other depository institutions face the federal funds market and the federal funds rate on a daily basis as they adjust to imbalances on their balance sheets between core deposit inflows and loan demand. As a consequence, monetary policy is transmitted promptly to the entire depository institutions sector. This will quickly affect decisions by commercial banks on the terms that they offer on loans—including the thresholds for which customers will get credit, the amounts that they can borrow, and the interest spreads on loans. It will also affect their decisions regarding bidding for liquid assets and foreign exchange, helping to transmit the policy more broadly throughout financial markets.

SUMMARY

1. Commercial banks continue to be the dominant financial institution in the United States, as they are elsewhere in the world. Savings institutions and credit unions have come to resemble commercial banks in many ways, but they are much smaller and still more focused on the household sector.
2. The United States has a very large number of separately chartered commercial banks, though the number has been declining. The vast majority of banks are owned by a (multibank) holding company. Increasingly, banking has come to be dominated by branch banks, as state and federal restrictions on branching have been lifted.
3. With so many separate banks, the interbank market plays an important role in distributing funds from banking offices where they are collected to where they

are most highly valued, and provides a vehicle for individual banks to deal with shocks. It also better ensures that monetary policy is having a uniform effect on credit pricing around the banking system.
4. Banking developments have been influenced heavily by economies of scale and scope. Economies of scale tend to encourage larger-scale banking organizations, which can be achieved most effectively through networks of branches or less through commonly owned separately chartered banks. Economies of scope are achieved by combining various related financial services under one roof. This can be seen in relationship banking, which reduces the effects of asymmetric information. Smaller banks tend to have certain advantages in getting useful information about payment prospects of customers in their market area.
5. In some other parts of the world, economies of scale and scope are achieved through universal banks, which combine branching and a variety of banking and other financial services within a single bank. This raises questions about whether financial activities outside of traditional banking pose undue risks on the bank when they are all housed in the same organization.
6. Savings institutions and credit unions were developed to provide basic deposit and credit services to households without access to such services. They have expanded the types of services that they offer, and now more closely resemble commercial banks than in the past. However, they still cater primarily to households.
7. Smaller commercial banks and savings institutions that focus on providing services to households and small businesses in their local markets are called community banks.
8. The primary functions provided by commercial banks (and other depository institutions) are payment services, provision of liquidity, provision of credit in situations characterized by asymmetric information, and maturity transformation.
9. The balance sheets of each of these types of institutions reflect their respective roles in serving these functions.
10. Federal deposit insurance has been a means by which retail deposits across institutions have been protected. It also has been a means of standardizing basic levels of federal regulation among the various types of depository institutions.
11. Commercial banks and other depository institutions have become highly regulated and supervised. This owes importantly to their prominent role in the payment system and as holders of the public's assets. Increasingly, it has also reflected the systemic risk that they pose to the financial system more broadly and to the economy.
12. Depository institutions are covered by a safety net that results in moral hazard. The purpose of supervision is to counter the moral hazard–related incentives to take on excessive risk.
13. Supervisors in the United States utilize a CAMELS system to rate individual depository institutions on their safety and soundness. A considerable amount of attention has been given to ensuring that institutions have adequate levels of capital commensurate with their risk profile. Systemically important financial institutions (SIFIs) have become subjected to more stringent regulatory standards to account for the greater risk that they pose to other institutions and thereby the financial system and the economy.

14. Increasingly, capital standards are being coordinated internationally. Most recently, banking supervisors have agreed to Basel III standards that are intended to harmonize treatment across borders. These capital standards are being supplemented by common liquidity standards and enhanced transparency.

QUESTIONS

1. Why are commercial banks deemed to be special? Why are they subject to more regulation and supervision than most other industries? Do the same arguments apply to savings institutions and credit unions?
2. Explain why the United States has so many more commercial banks than other countries?
3. How does a universal bank common in some other parts of the world compare with a commercial bank in the United States? How does the U.S. holding company structure compare with a universal bank?
4. What is meant by economies of scale? Economies of scope? How have they influenced banking developments in the United States?
5. Why have smaller commercial banks been able to survive alongside larger banks?
6. What role is played by the interbank system? Is the interbank system more important in the United States than in places dominated by large branch banks or universal banks?
7. What role do commercial banks play in the payment system? Other depository institutions?
8. What is meant by the liquidity provision function?
9. How do depository institutions address asymmetric information?
10. What is meant by maturity transformation? How is this related to interest rate risk? How can depository institutions reduce interest rate risk? How does maturity transformation lead to vulnerability to a financial crisis?
11. What is meant by systemic risk? How is this related to economic externalities? How is systemic risk being addressed by the regulatory authorities?
12. How is the CAMELS system used by regulatory authorities to assess a depository institution's safety and soundness? What does CAMELS stand for?
13. Why have bank supervisors from around the globe agreed to adopt common regulatory and supervisory standards? What is meant by Basel I, II, and III? What are some of the key features of Basel III?

NOTES

1. This prohibition also applied to dealer activities (making markets) in securities other than those of the federal and state and local governments.
2. During the 1960s and 1970s, the competitive position of thrift institutions was enhanced in the retail deposit market by interest rate ceilings that applied to thrifts and to commercial banks. These ceilings—sometimes called Regulation Q ceilings—were intended to hold down interest costs at depository institutions at a time when market interest rates were rising with rising inflation. The bottom

line of thrifts was most vulnerable to the general rise in interest rates because they were stuck with huge amounts of low-yielding long-term mortgages. To give these institutions a competitive edge in the retail deposit market, regulators allowed them to offer a slightly higher interest rate on deposits than commercial banks. However, the general level of these regulatory ceilings did not keep up with the rise in market interest rates, which encouraged households to seek returns that were more in line with the market—notably those offered by money market and bond mutual funds. In response to the disintermediation from thrifts and commercial banks that developed, Congress passed major banking legislation in 1980 that called for the phased removal of ceilings.

3. Credit unions are regarded for tax purposes as nonprofit organizations and are thus exempt from income taxes. Other depository institutions have complained loudly about this favorable tax treatment.
4. Included in cash and liquid securities are required reserves and excess reserves held at the Fed. The latter component has been very large owing to the Fed's aggressive measures that have expanded its balance sheet in the wake of the financial crisis. Also included in this category are holdings of Treasury securities—bills and coupons.
5. Banks in other parts of the world, notably Europe, tend to hold larger portions of their portfolios in bonds, especially government (sovereign) bonds. As acute fiscal stress has been faced by several of the sovereign issuers of these bonds, many European banks have taken substantial losses on their sovereign debt holdings.
6. Wholesale deposits for all the depository institutions include all time deposits in denominations that exceed $100,000. This is a rather low threshold for the designation of wholesale deposits and is something of an anachronism. Today, many retail depositors have time deposits with balances in excess of this amount, and they are insured up to $250,000.
7. The insurance agencies can also arrange for another depository institution to acquire the failed institution—a so-called purchase and assumption by another depository institution. In such a case, the agency must tap reserves to cover the negative net worth hole to make the deal worthwhile for the other depository institution.
8. Prior to 2011, a large segment of nationally chartered savings institutions was regulated by a separate federal regulator—the Office of Thrift Supervision (OTS). The Dodd-Frank bill moved the OTS to the OCC. This was based on what was thought to be overly lax regulation (and supervision) by OTS that led to large losses at institutions subject to OTS regulation, which, in turn, became losses to the FDIC.
9. To that end, Congress created the Federal Financial Examination Council (FFIEC), which coordinates and standardizes practices among federal regulators.

CHAPTER 18

Mutual Funds

WHAT YOU WILL LEARN IN THIS CHAPTER

- How mutual funds have become second in size only to commercial banks.
- The difference between open-end, closed-end, and exchange-traded funds.
- How the industry is regulated.
- Why open-end funds are dominated by large mutual fund complexes offering a variety of different investment products.
- Why large-cap equity funds have become a popular product of both open-end and exchange-traded funds (ETFs).
- How open-end fund shares are priced and traded.
- What is meant by money market mutual funds "breaking the buck" and why the pricing of money market mutual funds has prompted financial stability concerns.
- Why ETFs have been growing faster than other funds in recent years.
- What is the specialized role of closed-end funds.
- How mutual funds are involved in the transmission of monetary policy.

BACKGROUND

In just a couple of decades, the mutual fund sector transformed from being a small, backwater financial industry to becoming a big gorilla in financial markets. During the 1970s, assets of mutual funds were below $100 billion and there were fewer than 10 million shareholder accounts. A decade later, industry assets had soared to $1 trillion and the number of accounts exceeded 60 million. As we entered the new millennium, mutual fund assets had jumped to $7 trillion and the number of accounts reached nearly 250 million. The odds are decent that you currently are an investor in mutual funds. Indeed, you may own shares in more than one fund. Moreover, you may have retirement funds managed by a mutual fund and may not be aware of this. If you are a mutual fund investor, what prompted you to make that choice?

Aside from commercial banks, mutual funds are the largest institutional managers of assets in the United States. This variety of collective investment scheme offers participations or shares in pools of assets instead of deposits. The types of pools vary considerably from those holding money market assets, to those holding corporate, government or other bonds, to those holding domestic or foreign equities, and even some holding commodities. In addition, there are hybrids containing some or all of the others. The participations are called shares. As a shareholder, the investor is entitled to a proportionate share of all the cash flows and assets in the fund after expenses have been paid to the fund's managers. The investor's return depends on the performance of the assets in the pool. The risk of a fund varies considerably, depending on the underlying assets in the pool. Unlike retail deposits, the shares in mutual funds are not protected by federal insurance.

Today, more than 4 in 10 households in the United States own shares in at least one mutual fund and mutual fund shares account for nearly a fourth of all financial assets owned by households.[1] Fund shares are held in a variety of forms, including retirement accounts; indeed, close to a third of all defined contribution (DC) and individual retirement accounts (IRAs) are invested with mutual funds. In addition, a number of businesses and nonprofit organizations have opened mutual fund accounts for managing their cash, largely with money market mutual funds.

The United States has led the development of the global mutual fund industry. Today, mutual funds are available to investors on all continents. Notable among large centers of mutual fund activity are Luxembourg, France, Ireland, Australia, and Brazil. Nonetheless, the mutual fund industry in the United States accounts for roughly half of mutual fund assets globally.

In their role in U.S. securities markets, mutual funds have become a major player. They hold a fourth of all U.S. equity, a third of all municipal securities, and nearly half of all commercial paper outstanding. They are also involved in the monetary policy transmission process.

HISTORY

Mutual funds began in the United States in the early part of the twentieth century and focused primarily on offering investments in diversified equity portfolios to households. They originally appealed to investors with limited financial resources who would otherwise have been unable to assemble a diversified portfolio of assets. Participation in a pool allowed them to get a slice of a large, diversified portfolio with the limited funds that they had available.

This sector languished during the Depression of the 1930s and its aftermath. Devastation throughout the financial sector had left retail-type investors seeking the safety of federally insured deposits at commercial banks and other depositories. A step in the direction of building public confidence in mutual funds was the passage of the Investment Company Act of 1940, which established the regulatory framework for the industry and the Securities and Exchange Commission (SEC) as the primary regulator of investment companies (mutual funds).

Until the mid-1970s, this sector focused on equity funds, although it also offered investors shares in portfolios of bonds—mostly corporate bonds. However, mutual funds made only slow inroads with retail investors as memories of the debacle of the 1930s continued to lean them toward the protection of federally insured deposits.

Things started to change in the mid-1970s as market interest rates rose sharply with inflation and pushed well above the capped interest rates that depository institutions could pay on retail deposits.[2] In response, the mutual fund concept was extended to money market instruments and marketed to retail customers seeking better returns on their short-term funds. To enhance the appeal of these money market mutual funds, they provided very easy withdrawals—including by check. Thus, these high-yielding money market mutual funds became something of a hybrid savings and transaction account. Money market funds became popular almost overnight and many of the existing mutual fund organizations introduced money funds to complement and attract investors to their other offerings.

As the public became more familiar and comfortable with mutual funds, these organizations introduced a growing variety of funds. These included different types of equity investments—broad market and index-based funds, as well as narrower sector-based funds. They also added a variety of fixed-income (bond) funds—federal government based, government-sponsored enterprise (GSE) based, muni based, and corporate based. In addition to new funds focusing on domestic assets, the mutual fund complexes extended these concepts to foreign assets.

As previously noted, mutual fund growth picked up steam in the 1980s and exploded in the 1990s. Mutual fund complexes became a popular alternative to conventional deposits, especially to the growing portion of retail investors who had not experienced the trauma of investment losses during the Depression. Moreover, mutual fund complexes were introducing more investments with appeal to smaller and medium-sized businesses seeking the benefits of diversified pools. Adding to the attraction of mutual fund complexes was the capability of investors to transfer assets from one of the funds in the complex to another.

SEC REGULATION

The mutual fund industry is subject to the regulatory oversight of the Securities and Exchange Commission (SEC), as previously noted. The rationale for such regulation has been to protect investors. The focus of this regulation has been to ensure that investors have adequate information about the fund that they are considering, that the information is accurate, and that the fund complies with applicable laws and regulations, as well as to its stated objectives. Before the fund can offer an investment product to investors, it must register with the SEC. It must also furnish interested investors with a prospectus specifying the objectives of the fund, its governance, and the historical record of investor returns (after it has begun operations). Funds must be audited by approved outside auditors, and they are subject to SEC inspections to ensure compliance with laws, regulations, and the fund's prospectus.

More recently, concerns have been raised about whether the size of firms in the industry and their linkage with other major financial institutions may be posing risks to the broader financial system and to the economy—systemic risk. This attention has been directed primarily to the money market mutual fund component, which has been faced with bouts of panic that have spilled over to other parts of the financial system. This vulnerability has been caused by the unique way in which money funds are priced, to be discussed below. In light of this, a controversy has emerged over whether mutual funds—especially money market mutual funds—should be deemed to be systemically important financial institutions (SIFIs) and come under the more stringent Fed regulation applied to SIFIs.

ROLE OF MUTUAL FUND COMPLEXES

Today, most mutual funds are part of a large mutual fund complex that offers a wide variety of investment opportunities in different types of funds. By dealing with a fund that is part of a complex, the investor can easily shift investment assets from one type of fund to another, and this enhances other synergies that derive from dealing with different parts of the same organization. In other words, the mutual fund business can be characterized by having economies of scope that foster networks of different funds under the same umbrella organization. In addition to economies of scope, individual mutual funds evidently face economies of scale, resulting in declines in per unit costs as size increases. This favors large-scale funds, as larger funds will be able to pass on their lower per-unit costs to their customers in the form of lower fees.

In other words, economies of scale favor large-sized mutual funds, while economies of scope favor collections of different types of funds under a single roof. Economies of scale and scope explain why the share of assets managed by the five largest mutual fund complexes has risen over the past couple of decades, to around 40 percent.

Money market funds are a very distinctive type of mutual fund. They not only differentiate themselves from others by holding only short-term assets, as noted, they price investor shares differently than the others. As a consequence, they have faced a somewhat different set of challenges, as we will see shortly.

In practice, the provision of mutual fund products involves several separate functions, some performed outside the mutual fund complex. This is illustrated in the diagram in Figure 18.1.

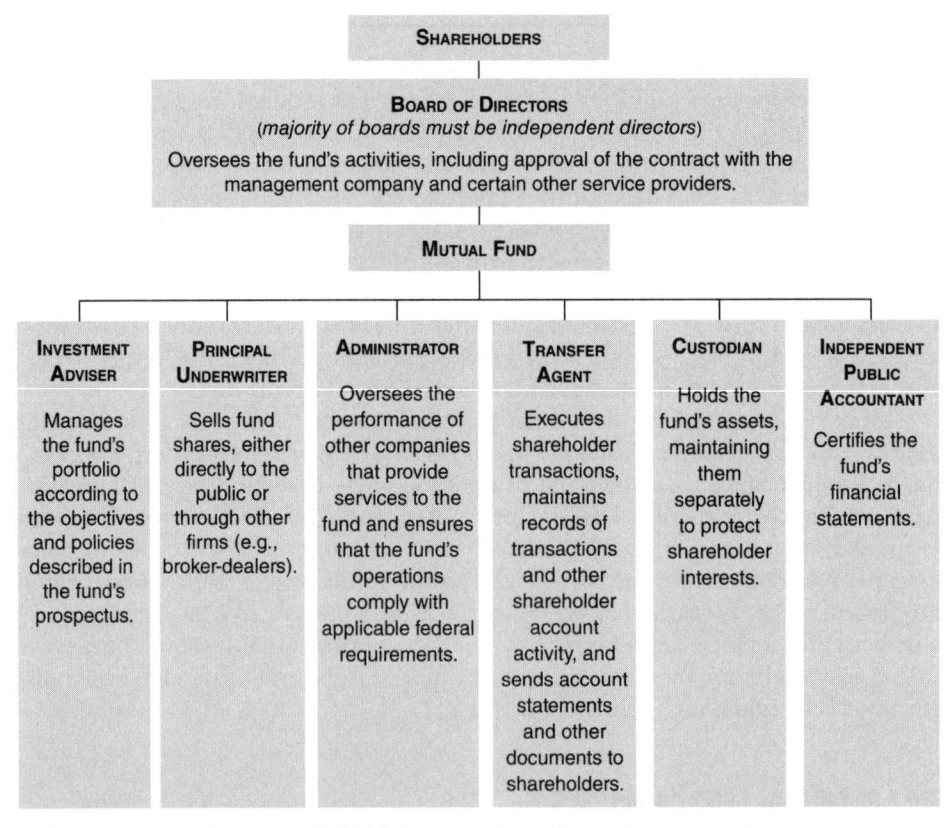

```
                    SHAREHOLDERS
                         |
                  BOARD OF DIRECTORS
        (majority of boards must be independent directors)
    Oversees the fund's activities, including approval of the contract with the
           management company and certain other service providers.
                         |
                    MUTUAL FUND
```

INVESTMENT ADVISER	PRINCIPAL UNDERWRITER	ADMINISTRATOR	TRANSFER AGENT	CUSTODIAN	INDEPENDENT PUBLIC ACCOUNTANT
Manages the fund's portfolio according to the objectives and policies described in the fund's prospectus.	Sells fund shares, either directly to the public or through other firms (e.g., broker-dealers).	Oversees the performance of other companies that provide services to the fund and ensures that the fund's operations comply with applicable federal requirements.	Executes shareholder transactions, maintains records of transactions and other shareholder account activity, and sends account statements and other documents to shareholders.	Holds the fund's assets, maintaining them separately to protect shareholder interests.	Certifies the fund's financial statements.

FIGURE 18.1 The Provision of Mutual Fund Products
Source: Investment Company Institute, *A Guide to Understanding Mutual Funds.*

The investors in a fund, shareholders, select a board to represent their interests in much the same way that shareholders who own stocks select a board in a regular corporation. The board contracts with the fund's investment adviser, who manages the portfolio in accord with the objectives of the fund as specified in the prospectus. In practice, the mutual fund complex provides the investment adviser. The mutual fund complex also typically provides the administrator function and the transfer function. The former involves ensuring that other fund vendors are discharging their duties and that the fund is complying with laws and regulations. The transfer agent function executes shareholder orders to buy and sell shares and it maintains records and provides statements to shareholders. The principal underwriter function involves distributing shares to investors, technically acquiring shares from the fund and selling them to the public.

The underwriter must be an SEC-registered broker-dealer, and this function typically is performed by a component of the mutual fund complex. The custodian is a separate financial institution that holds the fund's assets in safekeeping. As with other public firms, external public accounting firms audit mutual funds, a legal requirement.

TYPES OF FUNDS

In practice, there are three principal categories of institutions that fall under the mutual fund label. They are: open-end funds, the primary type; closed-end funds; and exchange-traded funds, the newest and most rapidly growing sector. There are also unit investment trusts—which fall in the mutual fund category—but they are small players.

The size of each type of fund is shown here (as of end December 2012).

Type of Investment Company	Assets, $ Billion
Open-end	13,045
Exchange-traded funds	1,337
Closed-end	265

Source: Investment Company Institute, *2013 Investment Company Fact Book.*

Open-end funds are clearly the largest category, with assets that exceed three-fourths of GDP. Exchange-traded funds (ETFs) are still much smaller than open-end funds, despite their rapid growth. Closed-end funds are a distant third.

Open-End Funds

Open-end funds are what are commonly thought of as mutual funds. As their name suggests, open-end funds can expand or contract with investor demand. Each separate fund has an objective, which dictates the types of assets that it holds. This results in a certain mix of assets in the fund. As investors demand more shares in the fund, the managers use the incoming cash to buy more assets, in rough proportion to the target composition. And as investor demand wanes, the managers liquidate assets in the portfolio to meet shareholder requests, again in rough proportion to the target mix. To be able to honor shifting investor demands for fund shares, especially withdrawals, mutual funds hold some of the fund's assets in very liquid form.

The distribution of assets among general categories of open-fund funds is shown here (as of end December 2012).

Type of Fund	Assets, $ Billion
Equity	5,934
Hybrid	991
Bond	3,426
Money market	2,694

Source: Investment Company Institute, *2013 Investment Company Fact Book.*

The largest category of mutual funds is equity funds, the traditional product of the industry. These days, fund complexes offer equity funds that track broad stock price indexes—so-called index funds—as well as funds that focus on specific sectors. The most popular of the stock index funds are those that attempt to mimic the Standard & Poor's (S&P) 500, although there are others that attempt to track the performance of mid-range firms (mid-cap indexes) and smaller firms (small-cap indexes). As we noted in Chapter 6, investors seeking to achieve a diversified portfolio of equities would want a portfolio that approximates the market, and the S&P 500 comes close to representing the market. Also, index funds of this sort have lower expenses because they follow a straightforward algorithm and do not require the costs of high-priced stock pickers and the associated transactions costs of churning the portfolio.

Sector funds include the tech and health sectors. As globalization has proceeded and investors have sought to avail themselves of the benefits of global diversification, the importance of global equity funds has grown and now such funds account for more than a fourth of all equity assets in open-end funds. Also in the equity fund category are actively managed funds that seek to improve investor returns by picking winners and losers. The theory and evidence regarding efficient markets suggests that these funds can do no better over time than those attempting to replicate the market.

Of the long-term mutual funds, bond funds are the next largest category. They, too, offer a considerable variety of investment opportunities to investors. The most popular are those holding portfolios of corporate bonds. Of these, the ones holding investment-grade corporate bonds are the largest. In the government category, those holding munis are largest. Some of these hold only munis of governmental units within a particular state, enabling household investors to take advantage of state tax exemptions of the interest on such bonds as well as the federal tax exemption. In addition, globalization has led to more demand for funds holding bonds issued outside the United States—both corporate and government (sovereign). Funds holding federal-level government bonds have fallen as a share of the total, but remain large in size.

Hybrid funds combine both stocks and bonds. These take the form of "fund of funds" in which the hybrid fund builds a more diversified portfolio by acquiring shares in other mutual funds, both bond and stock funds.

Increasingly, mutual fund complexes have offered so-called target funds, directed to persons preparing for retirement. These funds are offered with different target dates that correspond to the investor's expected date of retirement. Principles of finance suggest that the mix of assets in one's retirement portfolio should change over time, being heavily weighted toward equities—having high, but volatile returns—in the early years. However, the equity share should be decreasing and the fixed-income share, especially short-term assets, should be increasing as retirement draws near. This strategy involves accumulating assets with high, but volatile, returns during the early and middle working years, and then involves moving toward locking in accumulated asset values, at the expense of return, as the worker moves toward retirement. In other words, target funds are designed to adjust the mix of assets to move along the risk-return frontier by reducing risk and sacrificing expected return as the fund moves toward the target date.

The final category shown is money market mutual funds. These funds are restricted by regulation to hold only money market instruments (which can include longer-term coupon securities that are within a year of maturity) in their portfolios. The bulk of these funds hold taxable money market instruments, although some specialize in tax-exempt securities for investors in high marginal tax brackets for whom the exemption from taxation is worth more.

Money market mutual funds take the form of retail and institutional funds. Retail money funds cater primarily to individuals. Institutional money funds are the largest of the two and cater to businesses—primarily smaller and mid-sized—and to nonprofit organizations. For them, money market mutual fund accounts provide convenience for managing the organization's cash. Flows into and out of institutional money funds tend to be more volatile than those into and out of other (retail-type) money market mutual funds, in part because of the way they are priced (discussed in the next section). Pricing practices often lead to sizable divergences between the yield available on the money fund and the yield on market instruments—either above or below—providing an incentive to shift between money funds and the market.

Included in all of the above categories of open-end mutual funds are retirement balances. These take the form tax-favored IRA and DC assets. Some of these retirement accounts are offered directly to individuals and others are offered indirectly to individuals through their employers. Retirement funds are discussed in more detail in Chapter 20.

Pricing of Open-End Shares The price that investors pay for mutual fund shares (other than money fund shares) is determined by *net asset value* (*NAV*) per share. The net asset value is determined each day by valuing each component asset of the portfolio at its closing price and dividing the resulting total value of the portfolio by the number of shares outstanding in the mutual fund. This procedure for valuing the portfolio is referred to as "marking the portfolio to market." Investors must pay the NAV for the shares that they buy and they get the NAV for the shares that they sell. Each fund sets a cutoff time within the day for submitting buy or sell instructions to have the order executed that day at the NAV.

Some assets in the portfolio do not trade each day and this poses a problem for pricing. In these instances, funds tend to rely on pricing services that use algorithms for estimating the prices of such assets. Open-end funds do not hold large amounts of such inactively traded assets because of the difficulties of pricing them, not to mention difficulties in buying or selling them as customer demands for these funds expand or contract. Inactively traded assets are better candidates for closed-end funds, discussed in the final section of this chapter.

Pricing of Money Market Mutual Funds As noted, shares in money market mutual funds are priced differently from those in other open-end funds. Money funds are allowed to use a so-called amortized cost basis for pricing their shares. So long as the funds hold money market assets having solid credit quality, a high degree of liquidity, and relatively short maturities, they are permitted by the SEC to use this method instead of marking the assets to market each day. In essence, when the money fund acquires a money market asset—which, in accord with market practices, is purchased at a discount in relation to its face value and does not pay explicit interest—the fund can value that asset each day at that purchase price plus accrued appreciation. The accrued appreciation is read off a straight line between the purchase price and the value at maturity (its face value). In other words, the valuation of the money market asset increases each day by the total appreciation between the purchase date and the maturity date divided by the maturity measured in number of days. Following this method for all assets in the portfolio allows the money fund to price each share at $1, so that investors can count on receiving $1 for each share that they redeem. Meanwhile, the number of shares that the investor holds with the fund will grow by the accumulated dividends (interest) earned on the amount invested—that is, earnings are translated into new shares. Because investors have revealed a very strong preference for stability of the value of their short-term assets (NAV staying at $1), nearly all money market mutual funds use this pricing method.

A problem can occur when the underlying market value of the assets in the pool falls appreciably, causing the mark-to-market value (so-called shadow value) of a share to fall below $1. This can happen if the issuer of a money market security held by the fund defaults or if market interest rates rise quickly. In the latter case, some investors will want to redeem their shares at $1 to take advantage of more attractive yields on assets available in the market (the yield earned by staying in the fund will be determined by the amortized appreciation on the now lower-yielding assets in the fund's portfolio).[3] As this occurs in volume, the managers of the fund will need to begin selling money market instruments at a loss (because of the higher interest rates). Such a drop in asset value caused by a rise in interest rates has the same effect on the market value of the portfolio as a default. In these circumstances, the fund may need to redeem shares at less than $1—known as "breaking the buck." On the few occasions that this has happened at a money fund, it has led to investor concerns about the stability of share value at other money market funds and has sparked redemptions from those funds—which presses these funds to dump assets on weakened markets and pushes them closer to breaking the buck. In other words, there have been systemic spillovers to other funds.

During the worst of the financial crisis in 2008, a worrisome run on money market mutual funds developed (see Chapter 15). This was caused by a prominent fund—Prime Reserve—that experienced large losses on commercial paper issued by a major investment bank, Lehman Brothers, after it filed for bankruptcy. As the money fund wrote down its losses on Lehman paper, the value of its shares dropped below $1 (to $0.97). This prompted shareholders in other money funds to fear that they, too, might suffer losses, and they rushed to withdraw funds while they could at $1 per share. Those funds, in turn, faced the need to sell large numbers of assets—including commercial paper—at a time when the commercial paper market was seizing up because investors were reluctant to buy anything perceived to have risk. To avoid an impending large-scale run on money funds and full shutdown of the commercial paper market, the Fed, in a high-profile manner, stepped in to provide indirect access to its discount window to money funds facing large outflows.[4] This action helped to calm investor fears and stemmed outflows from the industry, keeping many other money funds from breaking the buck.

Holders of institutional money market funds tend to be more sharp-penciled than retail investors and are more responsive to fluctuations in interest rates that affect the market value of the fund's portfolio. That is, they respond more vigorously to differences between yields on money market funds and those prevailing in the market on money market instruments. As a consequence, flows out of and into institutional money funds display larger swings.

In view of the systemic disruptions that can be caused by money market mutual funds, they have attracted a lot of attention in the public policy arena in recent years. The SEC, which regulates money funds, has been considering alternatives to amortized cost pricing to reduce the scope for runs that can occur when investors fear that their money fund might be on the verge of breaking the buck. In addition, the Financial Services Oversight Council has been considering whether money funds should be designated systemically important financial institutions (essentially, shadow banks) and thereby come under Fed systemic risk regulation (see Chapter 15).

Open-End Fees Open-end funds earn fees from investors in two different forms. First, some charge *loads*. That is, they charge a fee to the investor either when the investor buys shares in the fund (a front load), sells shares (a back load), or at both ends. These are assessed on the value of the shares bought or sold. The more common of these is front-load fees, which can be as high as 5 percent on equity funds and 4 percent on bond funds. Loads are more prevalent among funds that are offered through brokers and other vendors that provide investment advice. A growing portion of mutual fund investments has been placed with funds that do not charge loads—so-called no-load funds. No-load funds typically deal directly with the investor and do not offer much personalized investment advice or counseling. Customers wanting investment advice gravitate toward funds with loads while those not needing such assistance gravitate toward no-load funds. The size of assets in no-load open-end funds has grown in relation to those of load funds and has come to exceed assets in load funds.

Second, funds charge ongoing fees to cover operating expenses. These fees cover the fund's expenses for managing the portfolio, back-office administration, and sales and marketing. They tend to vary with the type of fund. For equity funds, they average around 1 percent per year. Fees are higher for more actively managed funds and specialized funds—having high operating costs—than they are for funds that mimic stock price indexes, such as S&P 500 index funds. For bond funds, fees are lower, around 60 basis points.

Fees are even lower for money market mutual funds, averaging roughly 25 basis points. With these lower fees, money market mutual funds have faced difficulties in periods of very low interest rates on money market instruments. At these times, money market yields have been barely high enough to cover fees. If the fees assessed by the fund exceed interest earnings per share, then the difference needs to be made up by dipping into fund asset values and possibly breaking the buck. To avoid this, funds have frequently waived some of the fees and have gotten infusions from the mutual fund complex.

Both forms of fees—loads and operating expense fees—have been dropping over time, reflecting both economies of scale as the industry and competition among funds grows.

Exchange-Traded Funds

ETFs are the fastest-growing segment of the mutual fund industry. ETFs are traded on organized exchanges and can be purchased or sold throughout the business day at prices that vary with market forces, using the services of a broker. In this respect, they are something of a cross between an open-end fund and a regular stock in a publicly traded company. Most ETFs are fashioned to mimic an index, such as the S&P 500. However, some are actively managed and do not confine themselves to any standardized portfolio composition.

Basically, an ETF is a basket of securities—a so-called creation basket—that is assembled by a large institutional participant, commonly a specialist or market maker in other securities. Once created, the basket is then placed with a fund sponsor. From there, participations in the basket are offered for trading on an exchange just like any ordinary security. These creation baskets can be expanded or contracted with investor demand, as is the case with open-end funds.[5]

The largest category of ETFs is large-cap equity funds, which includes those structured to mimic the S&P 500 index. Next in size are bond funds, followed by emerging market equity funds. The rest are scattered among a variety of funds, including smaller-cap index funds and commodity funds.

Thus, ETFs have a number of similarities with open-end funds. The key difference is that the investor in ETFs can buy or sell within the day at the prevailing market price at the time of the order and they are traded in standardized lots. Shares in open-end funds, in contrast, can also be bought or sold within the day, but at a price determined by the market close, and the size of the transaction is customized to the investor's demand.

Closed-End Funds

Closed-end funds are only a fifth the size of ETFs, although they have been around for much longer. These funds, like ETFs, have shares that can be traded during the day on exchanges (or over the counter) at prices that vary with market conditions at the time of the trade. However, the number of shares does not expand or contract with investor demand, as with an ETF or open-end fund. The number of shares is fixed at the time the fund is launched. After the launch, investors can only acquire shares in the secondary market from another investor.

Closed-end funds have specific investment objectives and can be managed actively. They acquire a portfolio of assets that conforms to those stated objectives. Because the number of shares held by investors does not change after the launch, closed-end funds do not need to hold much in the form of liquid assets to meet investor withdrawals, as do open-end funds. Because returns on illiquid assets tend to be higher than those on liquid assets, concentrating on less liquid assets serves to boost gross returns for investors. Indeed, the structure of closed-end funds enables them to specialize in holding illiquid assets that may be hard to sell on short notice, as they do not confront investor withdrawals. More than half of all closed-end assets are held in bond funds—munis, domestic taxable, and foreign. Among closed-end equity funds, more than half of assets are held in domestic equities, but foreign equities are also a significant portion of equities in closed-end portfolios.

MUTUAL FUNDS AND MONETARY POLICY

Mutual funds, like other major financial institutions, are involved in the transmission of monetary policy. This is especially true of money market funds. An easing of monetary policy will lower money market yields, and, given the amortized-cost pricing of money market shares, will result in money fund shares having yields on new investments that initially drop by less than market yields. This will lead to stronger inflows to money funds—especially institution-only funds—and more buying of money market assets by these funds. In addition, the increase in the price of coupon securities and equities tends to draw more balances into these funds and results in more purchases of capital market assets by mutual funds.[6]

SUMMARY

1. Mutual funds have come to be a very large component of financial markets. They offer the public a large array of investment choices involving shares in portfolios of equities, bonds, money market instruments, and even commodities. Moreover, some funds are hybrids containing all of the above.
2. Mutual funds were originally developed as a way to provide the benefits of portfolio diversification to investors of limited means who were unable to assemble such portfolios on their own. Equity funds were the primary offerings of the industry, although shares in bond portfolios were also offered. The Depression of the 1930s dealt a major setback to the evolution of this industry.
3. As memories of the Depression faded and inflation soared in the 1970s, money market mutual funds were introduced, attracting substantial amounts from depository institutions. Growing familiarity with money funds led to greater retail investor interest and confidence in other funds, helping to propel growth in the industry.
4. The Investment Company Act of 1940 established the SEC as the primary regulator of mutual funds, primarily to protect the interests of retail investors. This largely involves minimum standards for information disclosure—through prospectuses and other communications—and verification of the accuracy of financial statements issued by the funds.

5. More recently, some have argued that mutual funds, especially money funds, pose systemic risk and should be designated as systemically important financial institutions and placed under Fed systemic risk regulation.
6. A large share of industry assets is held by a relatively small number of fund complexes, each offering investors a wide variety of investment choices. The industry can be characterized by having both economies of scale and scope.
7. The largest of the funds are open-end funds, accounting for nearly 90 percent of the industry's assets. Roughly half of open-end fund assets are held in equity funds, with the other half evenly split between bond and money market funds. Among equity funds, those that seek to track stock price indexes—such as the S&P 500—have become very popular, consistent with diversification principles and efficient market principles.
8. The industry also holds substantial amounts of retirement funds—both in the form of IRAs and DC accounts. Target date funds, which seek high returns in the early years and stability of principal in the later years, have become popular in recent years and also meet retirement objectives.
9. Open-end funds expand or contract with investor demand. Shares are bought and redeemed at each day's net asset value, calculated by pricing the portfolio at the closing price for each asset in the portfolio. The exceptions are money market mutual funds that value shares based on an amortized cost, which results in each share in the fund having a price of $1. That method of pricing, though, is vulnerable to breaking the buck in the event of a large drop in the value of underlying assets in the pool owing either to a default on pool assets or a big increase in interest rates. The risk posed by such pricing has led to calls for the SEC to require alternative methods of pricing and to Fed systemic risk regulation, noted above.
10. Investors in open-end funds are assessed fees to cover standard operating costs. In addition, a portion of the industry imposes loads—fees at the time of purchase or sale. Load funds appeal more to investors seeking investment guidance and have been losing some ground to no-load funds.
11. The fastest growing segment of the mutual fund industry is ETFs. Like open-end funds, ETFs can expand or contract with investor demand. However, they can be traded throughout the day, and at a price that reflects prevailing market conditions at the time of the trade.
12. Closed-end funds issue a fixed number of shares. After they have been issued, these shares trade in the secondary market in much the same way as ETFs or common stock. Closed-end funds tend to specialize in holding illiquid assets—having higher returns that compensate for less liquidity—more than open-end funds and ETFs.

QUESTIONS

1. Contrast the features of a mutual fund investment with those of retail deposits at commercial banks or other depository institutions. In particular, what are their differences in risk and return? Why do you think that the Great Depression led the retail public to favor deposits and shun mutual fund investments, with this aversion to mutual funds continuing for a very long time afterward?

2. Why do mutual funds generally appeal more to retail investors than large investors?
3. Why do money market mutual funds appeal to institutional investors more than other funds? Do you think that institutional funds appeal more to larger or smaller businesses?
4. How have economies of scale affected concentration of large mutual fund complexes in the mutual fund industry? How have economies of scope affected the configuration of products offered by funds in the industry?
5. Describe the various functions performed by a mutual fund. Which of these functions are performed by the complex itself, and which are outsourced to other institutions? Why this separation?
6. Why do you think that large-cap index funds have become a dominant product of the mutual fund industry? That is, which principles of economics and finance explain this phenomenon?
7. What is your outlook for mutual funds offering investments in foreign stocks in relation to those offering only domestic stocks? What about funds offering broad portfolios of domestic and foreign stocks? Explain.
8. What is the purpose for SEC regulation of mutual funds? Why might some observers believe that mutual funds are SIFIs and should be regulated as such?
9. How does the pricing of money market mutual funds differ from that of other (longer-term) funds? How does a loss resulting from default on a significant asset in a money fund's portfolio or a large increase in interest rates affect such pricing of money funds? What causes a money fund to break the buck?
10. Why do you suppose the money market mutual fund industry is dominated by funds that use amortized cost pricing of their shares (over those that mark their portfolios to market)? Why are amortized cost funds more vulnerable to swings in investor demand?
11. What has been happening to fees on open-end funds? Why?
12. Go to the Fidelity Fund website (www.fidelity.com). Name three index mutual funds that they offer; three muni bond funds; and three international equity funds. Can you identify a fund of funds?
13. Explain the objective of target-date mutual funds. What are they designed to accomplish? How do they achieve this?
14. How do shares in ETFs differ from those in open-end funds?
15. Visit the Bloomberg public website. What is the current price of an SPDR S&P 500 ETF? How has it changed? What about the S&P INDU SELECT?
16. Contrast a closed-end fund with an open-end fund. How would you expect their asset composition to differ? How can you, as an investor, be able to buy shares in an open-end fund? A closed-end fund?

NOTES

1. See Investment Company Institute, *2013 Investment Company Fact Book* (Washington, D.C.: Investment Company Institute, 2013).
2. Depository institutions faced ceilings on retail savings and time deposits—so-called Regulation Q ceiling, named after the Federal Reserve Board's regulation of that name. These ceilings were slow to be adjusted upward as market interest rates

rose, in part because depository regulators were concerned about the impact of higher rates on retail deposit interest costs and the earnings and stability of these institutions. Larger deposits—in excess of $100,000—were exempted from these ceilings to give depository institutions scope to bid for wholesale funds to replace outflows from retail accounts.

3. This works in the reverse direction, too. When market interest rates decline and the market value of money market assets increases, investors can sell their holdings of money market assets at a gain and use the proceeds to acquire money fund shares at $1 per share, below their market value. Looked at differently, these investors can move into money funds and thereby share in the higher yields on the fund's assets with the existing investors.

4. The Fed introduced some other temporary programs intended to relieve pressures on money funds and the commercial paper market.

5. When the price of the ETF basket exceeds the price of the underlying shares, it becomes worthwhile for the creator of the basket to form new baskets, profiting from the price difference. Conversely, when the value of the ETF basket drops below the value of the underlying assets, there is an arbitrage opportunity to buy the ETF basket in the market and sell the component assets.

6. While mutual funds are affected by monetary policy, they tend to passively respond to customer inflows and are not inclined to aggressively take positions based on actual or expected monetary policy actions. This contrasts with hedge funds, discussed in the next chapter.

CHAPTER 19

Hedge, Venture Capital, and Private Equity Funds

WHAT YOU WILL LEARN IN THIS CHAPTER

- What is meant by hedge funds, venture capital funds, and private equity funds.
- Why these are deemed to be alternative and risky investments.
- Why these funds are typically organized as limited partnerships.
- How hedge funds go about trying to achieve extraordinary returns on marketable instruments.
- How venture capital funds assist new and promising businesses, especially in the tech sector.
- How private equity funds seek to profit from restructuring underperforming established businesses
- How these funds seek greater returns through borrowed funds and leverage.
- How each of these funds creates economic value and enhances overall economic performance.
- How these funds are involved in the monetary policy process.

BACKGROUND

Ever wonder if highly successful firms, such as Apple, benefited from financing and other assistance as they were getting their start? Or what happens to established firms that took the wrong business path and fell into a ditch? Or what fosters nearly instantaneous adjustments to stock and other financial asset prices on the release of news? In such cases, an alternative investment fund likely was involved—a venture capital, private equity, or hedge fund.

No doubt you run across the terms *hedge funds, private equity funds,* and *venture capital funds* all the time. These funds are among the most mysterious and controversial financial institutions around the globe. Hedge funds and private equity funds, in particular, draw visceral reactions from a wide range of critics. They have been alleged to cause extreme market volatility as well as to plunder established firms, destroying good jobs in the process. In their current form, they are all relatively new intermediaries, although one could trace organizations performing their respective roles back to earlier times. Hedge, venture capital, and private equity funds in the United States have been on the cutting edge of major change in various sectors of the economy.

Each of these funds has been battered by external and internal forces, but has survived and evolved. This indicates that they have been creating economic value, though in different ways. All three have similar organizational structures and common investor bases, and engage in activities involving substantial amounts of risk. But they have distinctly different strategies. *Hedge funds* take positions in market instruments ahead of expected movements in the prices of those instruments—be they up or down. *Venture capital* funds try to identify promising start-up and early-stage firms—importantly in the information technology and biotechnology sectors—and provide financing and managerial assistance to them. *Private equity funds*, sometimes known as *buyout funds*, look for underperforming established firms—many seriously ailing—and attempt to turn them around to reach their potential. Each takes the form of investment pools in which investors acquire participations in a portfolio of assets, in much the same way as mutual fund investors. They all fall under the heading of collective investment schemes, as do mutual funds, discussed in the previous chapter.

The primary investors in these funds are pension funds (discussed in the next chapter), large private endowments (including major universities), and high-net-worth individuals. Each type of investor allocates a portion of its investment portfolio to such alternative investments to boost overall portfolio returns, but limits that portion to contain portfolio risk. They also scrutinize fund managers carefully because individual funds have very different performance records in delivering returns to their investors. These kinds of investment funds typically require that investors commit to the investment in the fund for longer periods than many alternative investments, and thus are less liquid than such alternative investments. They are called alternative investments because they get involved in activities that are unusually risky—well beyond the regular business model of standard financial intermediaries, such as commercial banks—and are not for the faint of heart.

Information on the size and composition of the portfolios of hedge, private equity, and venture capital funds tends to be sketchier than for the other intermediaries that we have discussed. This owes importantly to the tendency for these funds to sell shares to investors as private placements, as discussed below. Indeed, they follow strategies that they do not want to reveal to rivals and choose to go the private placement route to avoid disclosing information that could be of strategic value to their competitors. Nonetheless, estimates for the global assets under management of hedge funds exceed $2.5 trillion, with the bulk managed outside of the United States. For private equity funds, the amount under management is estimated to be on the order of $1 trillion, mostly held in the United States. The venture capital industry is a good bit smaller—roughly $200 billion—for reasons noted later in this chapter.

COMMONALITIES IN STRUCTURE

Hedge, venture, and private equity funds are investment pools that typically are organized as limited partnerships, and the shares that they offer investors, as noted, take the form of private placements. As private placements, they must limit the number of investors to 100 and demonstrate that each investor has sufficient financial capacity to withstand a large loss from this investment. By taking the form of private placements, they are able to avoid Securities and Exchange Commission (SEC) registration and disclosure requirements. In most cases, these funds—as noted—follow strategies that they wish to keep closely held to prevent rivals from copying their moves and sharing in the gains.

The limited partnership arrangement consists of a general partner and a number of limited partners. The general partner forms the fund, sets its general goals and strategies, raises cash from investors, and acts as the manager of the fund. Also, the general partner assumes liability for the debts of the partnership. The limited partners are the regular shareholders in the fund and do not assume responsibility for the fund's obligations; that is, their exposure is limited to the amount of the investment they place with the fund. In contrast to the general partner, the limited partners are passive investors.

The general partner assembles a staff to manage the fund's assets. To ensure that the general partner's interests are aligned with those of the other partners, the bylaws of the fund usually specify that the general manager must acquire a material ownership in the fund—has "skin the game." In addition, the compensation system for the general manager is designed to encourage the general manager to aggressively pursue higher returns for the fund. The fees received by the general manager usually have a *management fee* that is assessed as a percentage of the assets in the fund—commonly 2 percent. The management fee is intended to cover the expenses of the general partner and staff of the fund. In addition, they have a *performance fee* that is based on the fund's returns. Often, this performance fee is assessed on the fund's annual returns in excess of a benchmark or "hurdle" rate, such as the London Interbank Offered Rate (LIBOR). This is sometimes referred to as *carry*. The general partner normally receives 20 percent of carry when carry is positive—when the fund is generating profits. To discourage losses and earnings volatility, the base for the performance fee will usually contain "loss carry-forwards." That is, previous losses will be netted against current-year gains before the general manager earns a performance fee for the current period. Thus, the compensation arrangements for managers of these funds are set to encourage managers to diligently improve returns on the fund's assets, but without risking big losses or generating excess volatility of returns.[1]

HEDGE FUNDS

As previously noted, hedge funds take positions in financial instruments—securities or derivatives—that are traded in organized markets.[2] In this regard, they resemble mutual funds. However, hedge funds are focused on earning above-market returns by identifying situations of asset mispricing or situations in which market fundamentals will be leading to broader movements in asset prices—either up or down. This would seem to be hard to accomplish in a world characterized by efficient markets, as discussed in Chapter 6.

Hedge funds attempt to do so in various ways. In all cases, they depend on cutting-edge information and order execution systems that enable them to get news quickly and to act on that news before others. This includes scanning a vast array of real-time market prices using algorithms that help to identify mispricing. In other cases, the fund's management may form a view that the market price of a currency, a certain asset, or a certain class of assets is about to move, providing an opportunity to take a position ahead of this move and earn a good return. Hedge funds do not confine their activities to financial instruments, but many take positions in commodities as well. Being able to identify profit opportunities requires very good analysts who can—more often than not—use the information available to come up with a better assessment of value than that captured by prevailing market prices. Beyond this, occasionally some hedge fund managers attempt to get ahead of the market by coaxing information out of insiders before it is disclosed publicly. This has resulted in certain high-profile prosecutions for violations of securities laws, and the jails are filling with those convicted.

Role of the Prime Broker

Key to hedge fund operations is the *prime broker*. The prime broker executes trades for the fund, clears trades, lends securities for short sales,[3] provides credit, and often serves as the custodian of the fund's securities. Large commercial and investment banks perform this role. The riskiness of the hedge fund business has raised concerns about the risk exposure that prime broker banks absorb in their dealings with hedge funds.

Leverage

Hedge funds attempt to magnify returns by utilizing leverage, typically by borrowing funds from the prime broker. This, of course, adds to the fund's risk and to the risk exposure of the lender. In these circumstances, good risk management systems are needed on the part of both the fund and the lender to avoid disastrous outcomes.

Entry and Redemption

Unlike mutual fund investors who can enter or exit the fund daily, qualified hedge fund investors are permitted to enter or exit less frequently. Withdrawals typically are permitted after a so-called lockup period, a minimum initial investment interval after the fund starts its operations. Beyond the lockup period, the investor in most cases must submit notice of a request to withdraw, usually 30 to 60 days in advance. The reason for the lockup and notice of withdrawal is that many funds hold assets that are not very liquid and it takes time for them to sell those assets for cash to meet the withdrawal. The entry and exit price is the portfolio's net asset value as of the date of redemption, much like for open-end mutual funds.

Types of Hedge Funds

Hedge funds follow a variety of strategies. Some seek to make returns from positioning in front of macroeconomic developments that will be affecting currency values and bond and stock prices. These are referred to as *global macro funds*. Their analysts, for example, may be forecasting that the British economy will be facing more inflationary pressures than is suggested by interest rates in Britain and the prevailing exchange value of the pound. As their outlook unfolds, they envision that the Bank of England will be raising its policy rate sooner and by more than built into prevailing market prices. If correct, they will be able to get attractive returns by selling their current holdings of British securities or shorting them, before they drop in value. They will also want to take a long position in pounds, before the expected higher policy rate leads to an appreciation.

Other hedge funds seek attractive returns by discovering mispricing of individual securities. For example, a three-year once off-the-run Treasury note may have a current price that is abnormally low in relation to the current price of an on-the-run note; shorting the on-the-run note and going long in the off-the-run note will enable a return to be made if prices converge to a more normal relationship between these two securities. Alternatively, their algorithms may discover a price-earnings ratio for one firm in an industry that is anomalous in relation to other firms in the industry—say, it is exceptionally low—and there does not appear to be a good reason for this disparity. The fund may decide to take a long position in the shares of this firm and short its rivals. Still another situation involves the debt of distressed firms, often in the wake of a default. The fund may judge that investors have overreacted to the default and the price has fallen below the likely recovery value. In this case, the hedge fund would take a long position in the debt of this firm. Funds in this overall category fall under the names of *arbitrage, relative value, event-driven,* and *distressed debt funds.*

In addition, there are hedge *funds of funds* that acquire shares in several of the above types of hedge funds. In many respects, these resemble fund-of-fund mutual funds by achieving a greater degree of portfolio diversification.

To be able to offer existing investors above-market returns, managers will, at times, close off their funds to additional investments. If they do not see good profit opportunities for new investments, managers would dilute the returns of existing investors if they were to allow new investments in the fund. That is, if the marginal return on new fund investments falls short of the average return on existing investments, new investments will lower the returns to current investors.[4]

Economic Value and Hedge Fund Risk

An axiom of economics is that the acid test of whether an economic unit is creating value or not is whether it makes a profit or not. If it sells at a higher price than it buys, allowing for the costs involved, then it is regarded as having created economic value. If not, it is destroying economic value. Thus, if hedge funds are able to consistently beat market returns, they are adding economic value.

How have they done this? Usually, if they make a gain on a transaction—say, they shorted an overvalued security—they have taken an action that brings the asset's value into alignment with its fundamental value sooner. This will help to better guide resources to their more effective uses, as we discussed in the first chapter. Also, hedge funds take on risk, often acquiring it from investors who are less willing and less capable of managing the risk. Further, hedge funds are said to add liquidity to markets when they perceive that the price of an asset (or class of assets) has gone above or below its fundamental value and they take action to profit from this situation. For example, if the price of a particular bond has dropped below its perceived fundamental value, the hedge fund would buy this bond. Any further sales would be met by hedge fund purchases, limiting further declines in price. Sellers of the bond would find that there is a willing buyer at a better price than would be the case if the hedge fund did not act.

However, many observers are concerned that hedge funds pose serious systemic risks. They point to the exposure that prime broker banks have to hedge funds and the systemic impact of large losses at a hedge fund being pushed onto its prime broker. Others have expressed concern that hedge funds often display a herd instinct and take similar positions, resulting in a stampede effect on the prices of securities and derivatives—moving them sharply up or down. When they decide to sell, in addition to exacerbating price movements, they put a lot of strain on markets and on systemically important institutions exposed to those markets. In recognition of their potential threat to financial stability, the Dodd-Frank Act of 2010 requires all hedge funds with assets in excess of $150 million to register with the SEC and subjects smaller ones to more state regulation. At issue under the Dodd-Frank Act is whether the Financial Stability Oversight Council should designate the industry, or a portion of the industry, to be systemically important financial institutions (SIFIs) and come under Fed regulation and supervision (see Chapter 15).

From the perspective of monetary policy and the goal of financial stabilization, hedge funds, when they guess correctly on forthcoming monetary actions, serve to enhance the effectiveness of those actions by moving the corresponding asset price changes forward in time and thereby initiating the desired spending decisions by businesses and households sooner. Also, when they otherwise guess correctly on asset price movements, they tend to attenuate price volatility and reduce potentially destabilizing losses to important financial institutions. However, they have the opposite effect when they guess wrong.

VENTURE CAPITAL FUNDS

Venture capital (VC) funds apply the limited partnership model discussed above to newly formed and highly innovative firms, mostly in the information technology (IT) and biotechnology sectors of the economy. In particular, VC funds look for promising opportunities in IT hardware and software, medical devices, other areas of health and life sciences, and, more recently, clean technology. They also look for firms that have attractive new models of marketing and selling products. Many VC funds and the firms that they finance are located in the Silicon Valley area of California.

Types of Firms Selected for Financing

The businesses considered by VC funds for investment are built around promising but very risky concepts. They look for innovative products and marketing ideas. As noted, the venture capital industry is a good bit smaller than the hedge fund sector. This owes largely to the fledgling nature of the firms seeking financing through venture capital funds and the limited capacity of VC fund managerial teams to handle many such early-stage firms. The firms that venture capital funds seek to assist typically are start-up firms or those in the earlier stages of development. Thus, owing to their embryonic stage of development, they are much smaller than they will become at maturity when they will have publicly traded securities that might be objects of investments by hedge funds—or be targets of private equity firms. Nonetheless, VC funds finance a large number of firms.

Risks Involved

Because the preponderance of start-ups fail, the general partner of the hedge fund must carefully screen potential investments to weed out those least likely to survive and identify the most promising. In practice, they tend to weed out about 90 percent of the firms seeking venture capital. To do this well, the general partner hires a staff of specialists that may include engineers, medical doctors, and scientists, along with business specialists. VC funds tend to build expertise in certain sectors of business—for example, medical devices—and specialize in those areas. The general partner, on behalf of the VC fund, acquires an equity position in the new firm and usually also serves on the firm's board of directors. Often, the new company's founder has a very promising idea for a product that could be successful in the marketplace, but lacks the managerial and back office skills to translate this idea into a viable product. Moreover, the experts on the general partner's staff often can help with fine-tuning the entrepreneur's ideas and transforming them into products that are more usable and valued in the marketplace. The VC general partner's staff provides these complementary skills and seeks to actively nurture the firm to profitability, while advancing funds for expansion.

Even after new firms begin operations, around a third of VC-financed firms fail—well below the fraction of other new firms that fail. This implies that the survivors must provide substantial returns to the fund to make up for those losses and to provide the fund's investors with a satisfactory return. Related to VC funds are so-called angel investors, which also provide financing for start-ups and early-stage firms. However, angel investors tend to be more passive investors and do not take such a hands-on role in assisting the firm.

The VC manager strings a number of these new firm investments together and thereby achieves diversification benefits for the VC fund's overall portfolio. Because it takes considerable time to translate a promising idea into an established profit maker, VC funds are commonly set up for a lengthy period—10 years or more. That is, it usually requires a considerable amount of time to bring the new firm to the point where the venture capital firm can exit from its investment and the fund can get something close to an optimal return from that investment. Thus, investors in the fund make a long-term investment commitment. VC fund partners make an investment commitment at the time the fund is launched, but not all the committed balances are advanced at that time. This is because the general partner wants to have sufficient resources to be able to pursue promising investments, but must be careful to avoid rushing to undertake more marginal investments that will dilute the overall returns on the fund. Accordingly, the general partner draws on the remainder of the commitment as opportunities develop.

Size and Stages of Financing

Because businesses getting VC funds and assistance require a considerable amount of ongoing attention, this limits the overall size of the VC fund and the number of firms that one VC fund can manage at any one time. Indeed, the most common size of a VC fund is around $100 million, although some have more than $1 billion under management. Getting too large poses the danger that the general partner will not be able to adequately manage all the investments at the cost of the returns provided to investors. In other words, beyond that point, the VC fund faces diseconomies of scale.

VC funds will provide financing at the time the new firm starts up—seed capital—and at various points along the way. This follow-on financing is referred to as early stage, expansion, and later stage, with the bulk taking the form of early stage and expansion financing. Initial financing tends to average around $4 million and follow-on financing rounds usually are larger, on the order of $10 million.

Exit

To realize gains from these investments, the VC fund must look for the best way to exit the investment, either all at once or in stages. Exit can take the form of initial public offerings of shares (IPOs) or an acquisition by a more established firm. Indeed, many VC-funded firms have as a goal to be acquired by an industry leader, such as Cisco. Moreover, many established firms seek to improve or expand product lines and stay on the cutting edge of their industry by acquiring younger, innovative firms with promising new products. Often, the acquiring firm itself had been nurtured by a VC fund. In exiting, the VC fund can choose to liquidate its entire holding in that firm or retain some ownership. Of the two forms of exit, acquisitions account for the larger share.

A large number of start-up companies that were financed with venture capital have become household names and have made it into the S&P 500. These include Amazon, Amgen, Apple, Google, Intel, Jet Blue, Microsoft, Starbucks, and Whole Foods.

Economic Value Provided by VC Funds

The VC fund industry, over time, has provided attractive returns to its investors, and, from this, one can conclude that it adds value. This value is created by skillful screening of firms and selecting those with the most promising ideas. This is related to a considerable degree to the asymmetric information surrounding these start-up and early-stage firms. It requires not only probing for more information, but the use of sound, professional judgment in evaluating that information. Furthermore, VC funds provide critical financing for expansion of these firms, and also provide value in the form of managerial and technical expertise that often is the difference between life and death for the new firm. Finally, the VC fund bears much of the risk associated with the development of the firm before it has established a solid track record and becomes of interest to other investors. VC funds are structured to be able to absorb and manage the substantial risk associated with start-up and early-stage businesses. This is in contrast to commercial banks and other lenders that generally do not have the capital positions or the internal reward systems to be able to handle this type of risky financing without threatening the soundness of the institution.[5]

From the perspective of overall economic performance, hedge funds are thought to have been important facilitators of technical change in the United States. This, in turn, improves growth in productivity and growth of potential output. The United States has been the leader in this form of risk capital and a major beneficiary of its results.

PRIVATE EQUITY FUNDS

Private equity funds apply the limited partnership model to the acquisition of established firms that are underperforming and must be turned around—often through wholesale restructuring—to achieve their potential. In other words, these target firms have a current market value that is well below what its value would be if transformed to achieve its potential. Such funds also are called *buyout funds*. In many cases, the target firm is on the brink of failure.

Underperformance may be due to an outdated vision or business plan, diffusion of business activities beyond the firm's core line of business, bloated payrolls, or ineffective management. In some cases, the firm acquired had been a large conglomerate organization that had taken on many disparate and unrelated lines of business and was diverting management attention away from its core functions. Whatever benefits could be derived from diversification among many unrelated business activities were being more than offset by inefficiencies from diluting the ability of management to focus adequately on each component—effectively, a form of diseconomies of scale.

The private equity function of turning around underachieving businesses is not something new to the United States. It can be traced back to poorly run railroads in the nineteenth century and transformation of the U.S. steel industry in the early twentieth century, both of which required massive amounts of financial resources that were provided by major investment and commercial banks.

The modern-day private equity fund was begun in the late 1970s and gathered steam in the 1980s. It has since gone through very distinct ebbs and flows.

The private equity fund typically buys underperforming or struggling companies, retires their publicly traded shares, and takes them private. Once private, the managers of the fund are able to exert full control over the business and make all the necessary changes, without having to get the accession of other shareholders, as would be the case if it were still a public firm with shares in the hands of other investors. The transformation may involve the drafting of a new business plan, selling peripheral parts, reducing payrolls, updating product lines, and replacing management. Like VC funds, private equity funds usually take on a number of target companies at a time.

Investors in private equity funds must make a fairly long-term commitment, usually 10 years or longer at the time the fund is formed—possibly with extensions beyond that time. As with hedge and VC funds, not all of the limited partners' commitment is advanced at the time the fund begins operations. Instead, the general partner can call the remaining balance as needed. Often, the general partner will start another private equity fund a few years later that will acquire other firms in need of being turned around—resulting in a rolling set of new and departing private equity funds. In these ways, private equity funds also resemble VC funds.

Leverage

To magnify the fund's returns, private equity funds frequently take on leverage through loans from commercial banks, hedge funds, or by issuing bonds (ordinarily below-investment grade). Buyouts financed partly by debt are commonly called *leveraged buyouts*. Indeed, about 60 percent of private equity assets under management are financed with debt, and that portion varies with swings in the willingness of lenders and other creditors to provide financing. In other words, access to debt financing tends to vary with credit conditions more broadly. During the financial crisis, debt financing dried up and private equity acquisitions all but came to a halt.[6] Some observers have argued that leverage better ensures that discipline is being applied on the managers of the private equity fund. That is, with leverage, creditors, in addition to the limited partners, will carefully scrutinize the management of the private equity fund to ensure that it is staying on the right path.

Exit

As with venture capital funds, private equity funds seek to exit from their investments once the firms that they have acquired have been rehabilitated and have established good, well-documented performance. They do so through IPO stock offerings or by sale to another firm. In the latter case, the buying firm sees the turned-around firm to be an attractive strategic addition to its business profile. However, not all firms acquired by private equity firms survive, highlighting that private equity investment involves risk.

Economic Value Provided by Private Equity Firms

As with hedge funds and venture capital funds, private equity or buyout funds have provided their investors with attractive returns, indicating that they have been creating economic value. This has taken the form of identifying established firms that are underperforming, in some cases on the verge of collapsing. The private equity fund then takes full control of the target firm and begins to transform it by restructuring and redirecting the firm. At the same time, the buyout fund absorbs risk and manages this risk. The rehabilitation process frequently involves discharging redundant employees and trimming excessive labor and other costs.[7] In many cases, it also involves replacing and strengthening the management of the firm. When the general partner is able to sell the firm later at a higher price than its purchase price—especially after taking account of the opportunity cost of the funds that were tied up in the acquired firm while it was owned—investors, including the general partner, will have experienced a gain, and value has been created. In contrast, when the acquired firm is sold at a loss, value has been destroyed.

From a macroeconomic perspective, private equity firms, through improvements in managerial efficiency and productivity, have tended to increase potential output.

Private equity firms have also been controversial, as have hedge funds. This probably has to do with the major—often radical—changes they make to the businesses they acquire. These include employee layoffs and compensation reductions that are part of making the firms that they acquire leaner and more efficient. These are disruptive and painful for those affected. Moreover, not all the firms that they acquire survive, and their closure and liquidation invite charges that the target firms have been plundered.

ALTERNATIVE INVESTMENT FUNDS AND MONETARY POLICY

As noted, hedge funds play an important role in the transmission of monetary policy, especially so-called macro funds. Hedge funds are continually trying to determine the direction of monetary policy, and take positions when they deem that market prices do not reflect anticipated policy actions. In this way, they can transmit expected policy to asset prices, even before the central bank acts. When they guess correctly, they lead to policy having its intended impact on the economy and inflation sooner. Of course, when they guess incorrectly, they interfere with policy goals. Private equity funds are influenced by monetary policy as policy affects access to and the price of credit. A tighter monetary policy will promptly lead to a higher cost of debt and perhaps tighter restrictions on the amount that can be borrowed. This will tend to reduce the aggressiveness of private equity funds in the bidding for shares in target firms, and will tend to reduce the market value of equity and private spending. Beyond this, successful private equity and venture capital funds tend to foster a higher level of output and faster growth in output and thereby affect monetary policy decisions as they relate to the level and growth of potential output.

SUMMARY

1. Hedge funds, venture capital funds, and private equity funds are investment pools offered mostly to pension funds, large endowments, and high-net-worth individuals. They seek to provide these investors with above-market returns, but they are more risky and less liquid than other investor pools. These alternative investments perform very different kinds of economic functions.
2. Compared to other large financial institutions, these funds are relatively new on the scene and have gone through some tumultuous times. However, the underlying business concepts have survived, suggesting that they are performing a role that creates economic value.
3. These funds have many commonalities in their structure. They are organized as limited partnerships that avoid the kind of regulation that other large financial institutions face, and they have tight compensation systems for fund managers that align incentives for the manager with fund performance. The limited partnership form of organization involves a general partner, who manages the fund, and a number of limited partners, who provide the bulk of the funds for investment. The resources provided by partners often are augmented by borrowings that create leverage and add to risk.
4. Hedge funds have some resemblance to mutual funds. However, they attempt to provide better returns by following a variety of strategies, typically also involving market-traded financial instruments. Some try to profit from pricing anomalies, while others try to position ahead of more general asset price—macro—movements, be they up or down. They rely on cutting-edge information and trading systems to be able to get the jump on other investors when profit opportunities develop.
5. Hedge funds often seek to magnify returns to investors by utilizing leverage. They can borrow from their prime broker, which also provides various other key services.
6. Like other alternative investments, hedge funds create value when they make profits—above-market returns for their investors. This value takes the form of moving prices of financial assets closer to their fundamental values and absorbing and managing risk.
7. Venture capital (VC) funds specialize in providing financing and management expertise for innovative start-up and early-stage businesses—largely in the information and biotechnology sectors of the economy. They carefully screen potential businesses seeking assistance, provide critical financing, and also provide important managerial and specialized professional expertise.
8. Because this is a fairly long process, investors in VC funds make lengthy commitments, on the order of 10 years or more. Exit is provided through IPOs or

acquisitions by established firms looking to gain from the innovative products of the VC-assisted firm. VC funds create value by doing a good job of picking winners, providing essential financing for development of promising products, nurturing them to maturity, and absorbing and managing risk. Many major American businesses today have gotten assistance from VC funds. VCs have contributed to faster technical change in the United States and more rapid growth in potential output.
9. Private equity (sometimes called buyout) funds look for underperforming established firms and seek to turn them around. Like hedge funds, they often attempt to magnify returns to investors through leverage. Like VC funds, investors in private equity funds make long-term investment commitments to the fund, owing to the length of time it takes to successfully restructure target businesses and demonstrate sustained good performance. Also like VC exits, private equity exits take the form of IPOs or acquisitions by other firms.
10. Private equity firms create economic value by improving the performance of existing firms through restructuring them and increasing their efficiency. They get rid of extraneous parts, downsize bloated payrolls, upgrade product lines, and remove ineffective management. They also absorb and manage risk. However, the process of restructuring them tends to be disruptive to many and has created a considerable amount of controversy.
11. Hedge funds, VC funds, and private equity funds can enhance the effectiveness of monetary policy and overall macroeconomic performance. They do this when they are profitable.

QUESTIONS

1. Are successful hedge funds and efficient financial markets compatible? Explain why or why not.
2. How do hedge funds differ from open-end mutual funds? How are they similar?
3. Describe the organizational structure of hedge funds, VC funds, and private equity funds. How are the incentives of managers of these funds aligned with the goals of the (other) investors?
4. Describe the different types of hedge funds and how they are able to earn attractive returns. Why do you suppose that state-of-the-art information and order execution systems are vital to the success of hedge funds? What kinds of analysts do you think contribute to the success or failure of a hedge fund?
5. Describe how hedge funds create economic value. Does this help or hinder the goals of monetary policy? How could they cause financial instability?
6. Do hedge funds increase or reduce asset price volatility? How can you tell?
7. Why do VC funds require longer-term commitments from investors? Private equity firms?
8. What sectors of the economy do VC funds focus on? Why might VC funds be better suited than commercial banks for financing the types of firms that they focus on? At what point might these firms become better suited for financing from commercial banks?
9. How do VC funds provide attractive returns to their investors when roughly a third of the companies that they select for financing and other assistance fail?

10. How do VC funds create economic value? How do they affect macroeconomic performance?
11. How do private equity funds differ from VC funds?
12. Why is exit for VC and private equity funds regarded to be important? How is exit achieved for investors in each?
13. How do private equity firms create economic value? Affect macroeconomic performance?
14. How do hedge, VC, and private equity funds absorb and manage risk? How does the use of debt by hedge and private equity funds affect risk? How might leverage enhance monitoring of fund managers?
15. Why are private equity funds very controversial? Hedge funds?

NOTES

1. The management fee assessed on the amount of assets under management also serves as an incentive for general partners to provide attractive returns, because high returns will induce more investors to acquire shares in the fund and will expand the amount of assets under management.
2. Derivatives can take the form of futures, swaps, options, and credit default swaps (CDSs).
3. A short sale will be worthwhile when the price of an asset is expected to drop, after which the short seller can buy the security back at a lower price and return it to the lender. Profit comes from the difference between the sale and purchase price.
4. To the extent that there is only a limited amount of asset mispricing and other potential gains that can be exploited by hedge funds, the size of the hedge fund industry will be limited. In other words, hedge funds cannot be expected to have unlimited expansion in relation to the economy or the rest of the financial system. However, some analysts have seen no limit to the expansion of the hedge fund industry.
5. Some large banking organizations have a venture capital arm, but this is done through a separately capitalized subsidiary of the holding company and not put on the balance sheet of the commercial bank.
6. Access to leveraged financing of buyouts has been a fairly good barometer of the availability of credit from banks and other lenders.
7. The effect on employment will depend on the extent to which improvements to worker productivity are larger or smaller than the expansion in output coming from greater competitiveness. If the increase in output exceeds the increase in productivity (both expressed in percent terms), then employment will increase. Employment, however, will decrease if the expansion in output falls short of the increase in productivity.

CHAPTER 20

Large Institutional Investors

WHAT YOU WILL LEARN IN THIS CHAPTER

- The difference between defined benefit (DB) and defined contribution (DC) pension plans.
- Which party—employer or employee—bears investment risk in each type of plan.
- Why increasing employment mobility by workers and risk avoidance by employers has been leading to a shift from DB to DC plans.
- How Social Security is structured and the nature of pension plans offered to state and local government employees.
- Why life insurance companies (LICOs) and pension funds are major institutional investors.
- How actuarial expertise plays a major role in the pricing of life insurance and annuities by LICOs.
- What constitutes the difference between term and permanent policies offered by LICOs.
- How the savings component of permanent policies and the payment for annuities gives rise to substantial amounts of funds to be invested by LICOs.
- How permanent life insurance policies and annuities complement each other from the perspective of LICOs.
- How pension plans and LICOs play a role in the transmission of monetary policy.

BACKGROUND

Whether you realize it or not, pension funds will play a big part in your future, affecting the standard of living you will have at retirement, and, perhaps, even when you decide to retire. Moreover, LICOs, through their annuity products, will provide you with an opportunity to convert the assets that you have accumulated during your working years into a steady stream of income over your retirement years. In addition, of course, LICOs will provide your heirs with financial resources in the event of an untimely death, especially if that happens during your peak earning years, and they will provide you with a means of saving for your future.

As large institutional investors, pension funds and insurance companies play a key role in the financial system, although they have given some ground to mutual funds over recent decades. The products of pension funds and LICOs—sometimes referred to as contractual savings institutions—are geared primarily to individuals, either directly or indirectly. Also prominent are property and casualty (P&C) insurance companies that provide insurance to a wider variety of customers—individuals for home and motor vehicle insurance, and businesses for insurance on business real estate and equipment. Each of these institutions holds massive amounts of financial assets, and—given their longer-term nature—most of these are capital market instruments. Pension funds, and to a lesser extent LICOs, hold the public's retirement assets, which have grown in importance with the aging of the population.

The assets of these respective institutions are as follows as of end June 2013:

Institution	Assets $ Billions
Private pension funds	7,567
State and local pension funds	4,752
Federal government retirement fund	3,436
Life insurance companies	5,746
Property and casualty insurance companies	1,469

Source: Board of Governors of the Federal Reserve System, *Financial Accounts of the United States*, September 2013.

Pension and retirement funds—private, state and local, and federal—are the largest, amounting to more than $15 trillion in 2013. LICOs managed a little more than a third of this amount, and P&C companies managed a good bit less. We will discuss pension and retirement funds next, to be followed by life and P&C insurance companies.

PENSION FUNDS

We noted in Chapter 2 that there are two basic types of pension funds—defined benefit and defined contribution. While both are common, they differ importantly with regard to the party bearing investment risk—the employer or employee. They also differ with regard to the way in which pension benefits are paid out.

With a *defined benefit* (DB) plan, the employee makes a regular contribution to the plan out of earnings while in the workforce and the sponsor of the plan—the employer—is responsible for making regular monthly pension payments during retirement for the remainder of the employee's life (and perhaps the employee's surviving spouse). With a *defined contribution* (DC) plan, the employee also makes regular contributions out of earnings, but designates where they are to be invested.[1] At retirement, the employee can draw on the balances in the account for retirement or use the funds that were built up to buy an annuity that will make regular payments (like a DB plan) for the remainder of the employee's life. With a DB plan, the sponsor bears the investment risk. In contrast, with a DC plan, the employee bears the investment risk and may end up retiring with less (or more) than was counted on during his or her working years. In both types of plans, deductions from earnings for a qualified pension program avoid income taxation at the time the contribution is made, but the pension payments at retirement are subject to taxation. This is advantageous to the employee for two reasons: tax liabilities are deferred (lowering their present value) and earnings at retirement are usually a good bit lower and thus, under graduated tax rates, tax payments are lower.

The government sets standards for both employment-based DB and DC plans under the Employee Retirement Income Security Act (ERISA) of 1974, administered by the Department of Labor. ERISA establishes basic requirements for these pension plans.

DB plans long dominated private pension plans, but over the past few decades, DC plans have become much more popular. We will examine each of these private pension plans next.

Defined Benefit (DB) Plans

As noted, under a DB plan, the employee makes regular contributions out of earnings to the plan, and, in return, the sponsor (employer) commits to regular monthly benefits during the employee's retirement (and often partial benefits for a surviving spouse).[2] The benefits are based on an algorithm primarily involving the worker's tenure with the firm and the worker's earnings, with earnings in the latter years of employment commonly used. This algorithm results in retirement benefits being back-loaded. That is, the latter years of employment, when earnings are usually highest, get disproportionate weight in retirement benefits.[3] As a consequence, employees covered by DB plans have an incentive to stay with the employer until retirement. In essence, they are penalized—incurring a so-called accrual loss—for moving to another employer before retirement, as they receive a disproportionately lower retirement benefit. Moreover, the employee's position in the plan cannot be transferred to another employer—it is not portable. These features have acted to discourage employee mobility.

The employer (sponsor) of the fund is responsible for investing employee contributions in a way that will provide sufficient resources to be able to cover pension payments as workers retire. In other words, the employer is subject to so-called investment risk—the returns on investments must be large enough to build assets to the point that they will cover pension outlays. If not, the difference must be made up out of the company's profits.

In these circumstances, the sponsor faces a risk-return trade-off. If the employer concentrates on investments with higher returns and accompanying higher risk, there is a greater danger that asset prices will be depressed once the sponsor needs to sell them to meet pension payments. Conversely, if the sponsor wants to pursue a safer route and acquire assets that are less risky, there will be a danger that insufficient amounts of assets will be accumulated because of the accompanying lower investment returns. The sponsor also faces so-called longevity risk. If employees live longer than contemplated by the structure of the fund, the employer will have insufficient assets in the plan and will need to cough up more out of profits to cover the larger cash outlays.

Because of concerns that DB plans may not be adequately funded and there may not be adequate resources in the fund to provide promised benefits to employees, rules have been established for minimum funding levels of pension plans.[4] Determining whether a pension plan is adequately funded is not a simple task. Basically, the sponsor must compare the amount of the plan's liabilities—the present value of future benefits expected to be paid to employees—with the current level of assets. This requires making an assumption about the time profile of pension outlays, which, in practice, is highly uncertain. It entails making assumptions about when current employees will retire, their wage or salary at retirement, and their life expectancy after retirement. It also requires the selection of a discount rate for calculating the present value of projected pension outlays. Selecting one that is too high will cause the present value of pension fund liabilities to be too low, and selecting one that is too low will cause those liabilities to be too high. Sponsors may be tempted to choose a discount rate that is too high, which regulatory authorities seek to curb.

If the value of pension fund assets falls significantly below the amount of assets, the sponsor is required to make up some of the shortfall each year over several years. As we will see, pension DB plans hold a lot of equity, which, given the volatility of share prices, causes the funding status to swing widely over time. During the sharp run-up in stock prices in the late 1990s, private DB plans were, in the aggregate, overfunded. However, this situation changed dramatically after stock prices collapsed in the early 2000s. On balance over time, private DC plans, as a whole, have tended to be underfunded, which has been an ongoing policy concern.

DB plans hold about two-thirds of their assets in equity, a small portion of which takes the form of investments in private equity funds. Some also is held indirectly through investments in equity mutual funds. The heavy concentration in equity, as noted, adds to the volatility of their funding positions, but tends to improve asset returns over time—either enabling retirees to have larger benefits or employers to have larger profits (after pension contributions). About a fifth of DB assets are held in longer-term fixed-income assets—Treasury coupons, corporate bonds, and government-sponsored enterprise (GSE)-backed securities.

Defined Contribution (DC) Plans

DC plans have come to be the dominant form of private pension funds. Under a DC plan, the employer, as in a DB plan, withholds a portion of the employee's regular earnings—in many cases adding a matching contribution—and places it in a qualified investment vehicle. The investment choices include shares in the employer's own company stock, other domestic and international equities, fixed-income securities (corporate and government, domestic and international), money market instruments, or some combination of all of these.

Very commonly, the employer will offer DC investments through an open-end mutual fund. Mutual funds have exploited economies of scale associated with the detailed record keeping required of individual retirement funds, especially the aspects relating to the complicated tax dimension. They can offer such investments at a lower cost to the employer than the employer would incur by doing this itself.

Balances in the DC plan become the property of the employee, in contrast to those in DB plans under which the sponsor owns the fund's assets and the employee acquires a claim on the sponsor for retirement benefits. Balances in DC plans also are portable—after a specified vesting period—and remain with the employee after leaving the employer. At the same time, investment risk is absorbed by the employee—not the employer. If investment returns prove to be disappointing in relation to expectations, the employee's retirement benefits will suffer, while the employer's bottom line will be stronger.

Tax provisions for qualified DC plans play an important role in the design of DC plans. The plans often are called 401(k) plans, referring to the section of the tax code that governs the tax treatment of employee contributions and withdrawals.[5] When certain conditions are satisfied, the portion of the employee's income taking the form of the contribution to the DC plan can be excluded from current taxation. However, withdrawals from the plan are not permitted until the person approaches retirement age, except under penalty. Like DB plans, withdrawals from DC plans are subject to federal taxation at the time of the distribution, which usually lowers the present value of the individual's tax liability.

As noted, DC funds have long surpassed DB funds in size and coverage. These days, more than 60 percent of private pension fund assets and more than two-thirds of employees covered by a private pension plan are in DC funds.[6] This contrasts with only around 30 percent of assets in DB plans and one-third of private pension plan participants in the early 1980s. The change owes to greater job mobility by workers combined with the back-loaded nature of DB plans that favors long-tenured workers. The greater turnover in the labor market reflects less commitment to long-term employment relationships on the part of both employees and employers. In these circumstances, employees tend to get better returns on DC plans, because they are not inclined to stay with a single employer long enough to enjoy the better returns on a DB plan that come with job tenure. Also, many employers have sought to avoid the pension plan investment risk that accompanies DB funds. Moreover, a change in the composition of the U.S. industrial sector away from industries that had traditionally provided DB plans has accounted for some of the trend away from DB plans and toward DC plans.

The asset composition of DC plans has some notable differences with DB plans. While about the same 60 percent of assets are in equities, a larger portion of such shares is held as employer stock.[7] Also, DC plans utilize open-end mutual funds for DC investments more than DB plans. Adding to the appeal of open-end funds have been so-called target-date funds, discussed in Chapter 18. Target-date funds alter the mix of assets over time in keeping with the target date the employee expects to retire. They usually hold higher return and higher risk equity early in the period but move toward fixed income and shorter maturity fixed-income assets as the target date approaches. This limits the risk that the market value of pension assets will drop sharply just before retirement. Because the overall composition of assets in DB and DC plans have not differed much, the shift from DB to DC has not had much of an effect on relative asset prices.

As noted, DC plans do not provide a flow of monthly income for life at retirement, as do DB plans. Instead, the retiree owns the assets accumulated by the plan. These can be drawn down at the discretion of the employee during retirement, or the employee can use them to purchase an annuity from another institution with some or all of the proceeds—in both cases after paying taxes. LICOs, in particular, are major sellers of annuities, which we will discuss more fully later in this chapter.

In practice, the portion of retirees buying annuity plans is fairly low. In part, this reflects the pricing of annuities, which analysts have estimated to be high in relation to the present value of projected benefits. Some have argued that this unattractive pricing may reflect inadequate competition in this market. Others have argued that vendors of annuities are faced with an adverse selection problem: Retirees who are healthiest and expect to live the longest are the most likely to opt for annuities, resulting in higher costs to the annuity seller than if annuity buyers were more fully representative of their cohorts. When the sellers of annuities set prices that reflect adverse selection, they encourage more retirees to manage retirement assets by themselves or with the assistance of a financial adviser.

In any event, DC plans, as a group, place more responsibility on the shoulders of employees than DB plans. They must decide on the initial allocation of their DC contributions, whether to change the mix as they draw closer to retirement, and how to use those assets in their retirement years. Mistakes at any of these stages can be very costly in terms of the employee's standard of living during retirement. As a consequence, many observers have advocated placing more priority on improving the financial literacy of the American public.

A special type of tax-favored retirement plan is the *individual retirement account* (*IRA*). IRAs were authorized in the 1970s for persons who are self-employed or not covered by an employer's retirement plan. They are also intended for persons who have accumulated tax-advantaged retirement assets and are transferring employers, therefore needing another tax-advantaged type of retirement account. The latter are referred to as rollovers. Since the 1970s, special types of IRAs have been authorized for employees of small businesses, who typically had not been offered a retirement plan. IRAs have become very large, in excess of a quarter of all retirement assets. Like other DC programs, the employee directs the investment in an IRA.[8] The employee can choose among the various depository, life insurance, mutual fund, and brokerage institutions offering such accounts. In practice, the allocation of assets in IRAs is similar to other retirement plans.[9]

Social Security

DB and DC pension funds are not to be confused with the national retirement system—Social Security. In principle, Social Security resembles a DB pension plan in that the employee makes regular contributions to the system (the employer withholds a portion of the employee's regular pay and, after matching it, passes it along to the government) and, at retirement, the employee is entitled to a schedule of monthly benefits for life. Social Security was originally intended to be a self-sustaining pension plan for covered workers. Contributions in excess of retirement benefits have been invested by a trust fund in special-issue Treasury securities. However, benefits grew more generously than contributions. As a consequence, the buildup of assets has been insufficient to fund liabilities. In other words, it has evolved into an intergenerational transfer—so-called pay-as-you-go—program. In effect, current workers make regular payments to the system, which are then used to pay current retirees.

State and Local Government Pension Funds

State and local governments offer their employees DB pension plans. Usually, the employee makes a contribution out of regular earnings, as with other plans. The governmental unit—state or local—provides a guarantee of benefits at retirement, based on tenure and earnings. In comparison with private DB plans, these plans tend to provide more generous benefits (relative to the employee's contribution).

Standards for funding of these plans are less stringent than for private DB plans and they have, overall, been less adequately funded. Like private pension funds, state and local funds hold about 60 percent of their assets in equities, about a sixth of which take the form of investments in private equity funds. Much of the remainder is split between corporate bonds and GSE securities. As with private DB plans, swings in the stock market have a substantial effect on the extent to which state and local pension liabilities are funded.

Federal Government Retirement Funds

Employees of the federal government are provided a DC plan to supplement their regular federal pension, sometimes called the "thrift plan." Like many other DC plans, the employee designates a portion of earnings to be placed in the plan and the agency employer matches that contribution. Participants have designated that a large share of their DC contributions be allocated to accounts holding Treasury securities, and thus the composition of federal employee retirement funds differs markedly from other plans.[10]

LIFE INSURANCE COMPANIES

LICOs manage assets that are nearly as large in size as those of private pension funds. LICOs have been around longer than all other financial institutions apart from commercial banks. The first companies began operations in the United States in the second half of the eighteenth century and developed into prominence in the nineteenth century. These days, they have nearly $20 trillion of life insurance coverage in force.[11]

While the primary business of LICOs is insuring people's lives, they also engage in certain complementary activities—namely, providing annuities and health insurance. They rely on mortality statistics and actuarial expertise for structuring and pricing both their life insurance and annuity business lines and health statistics for their health insurances lines.

Life Insurance

The traditional line of business of these companies has, of course, been life insurance. There are two basic types of life insurance products that they offer: term and permanent (whole life) policies. Term policies insure a person for a specified length of time and then expire. They must be renewed to continue coverage, much like a car insurance policy. Permanent policies provide ongoing coverage for the remainder of the insured person's life.

By their design, permanent policies have a saving component. Premiums on the policy are level, although the actuarial cost of the underlying life insurance increases with age. That is, the likelihood of death and the need to pay death benefits to the policy's beneficiaries—the expected payout—increases with age. With term policies, this increasing expected cost is addressed through premiums that rise with age. Under permanent policies, the level premium exceeds the underlying cost of life insurance in the early years and the difference is applied toward a saving component called cash value. The cash value builds up owing to both the accumulation of premiums in excess of insurance costs and to investment returns on previous savings. At some point, the insurance cost will rise to match the premium and the cash value will then increase by the returns on the amount of cash value accumulated. Beyond this point, the increase in insurance cost may result in the cash value stabilizing or actually declining.

Insurance companies of all sorts must price their policies in such a way that the premiums they collect each year are sufficient to cover the expected claims during that year. This requires getting the most out of the information available on mortality rates. Because there will be errors in these estimates of claims, and claims during some years will exceed premiums, insurance companies must also have sufficient cash assets to tap when there is a premium shortfall. Beyond the need for these asset cushions, the cash value feature of permanent life policies boosts the amount of funds that LICOs have to invest in financial markets and the role they play in those markets.

Annuities

Complementing the writing of life insurance policies is the business of selling annuities—committing to pay a steady stream of income for the remaining life of the annuitant (or for some fixed period). Annuities are purchased by individuals themselves and by some employers with DB pension plans that outsource this task to LICOs. By outsourcing DB plans to LICOs, the employer may be able to lower plan administration costs and offload investment and longevity risk to the LICO. The same mortality tables that LICOs rely on for pricing life insurance policies can be used for pricing annuities. Moreover, one line of business can serve as a hedge to the other. For example, an increase in life expectancy will push off life insurance claims to the future, which is beneficial to the company's bottom line. But it also extends the period for which annuity payments must be made, which hurts the bottom line.

Annuities can be purchased as a lump sum all at one time—say, at retirement with funds from a DC pension plan. Alternatively, they can be purchased as a deferred annuity under which payments are made over a period of time before the annuity becomes effective. In either case, the LICO gets a substantial payment from the annuitant up front and, in return, commits to make payments over an extended period of time. This gives LICOs a lot of funds to invest, and they seek to invest them in a manner that will enable them to honor their annuity commitments without needing to dip into the companies' capital, which enlarges the role of LICOs in capital markets.

LICO Assets

The largest category of LICO assets is corporate bonds, accounting for one-third of the total. The bulk of these are publicly traded bonds with investment-grade ratings. Nevertheless, also important are privately placed bonds, discussed in Chapter 8. As noted in that chapter, borrowers in the private bond market can be characterized as being not well known—they reflect a high degree of asymmetric information. This provides a profit opportunity for those lenders with the ability to drill down for the information needed and to use that information for making a sound credit judgment—whether to buy the bonds of an issuer and, if so, on what terms. The importance of LICOs as providers of business financing is indicated by this industry being the largest creditor to businesses in both the public and private bond markets.

In addition to corporate bonds, LICOs have very large holdings of common stocks and also hold various types of mortgage-backed securities (MBSs). Further, they have significant holdings of regular mortgages—whole loans. These are predominantly for commercial properties. Indeed, LICOs are a primary source of credit for financing income-earning properties, along with commercial banks.

In their financial reports, LICOs often divide their balance sheet between so-called general accounts and separate accounts. General accounts contain what can be thought of as the traditional business of LICOs, regular life insurance and annuities. These products contain specific contractual amounts of payouts, which expose the insurance company to the risk that the assumptions underlying the pricing of these products may prove to be wrong. That is, the returns that they get on the invested funds may turn out to be lower—or higher—than projected, requiring that they dip into capital (net worth) to make good on their commitments. Depending on the underlying risks of their position, such losses could absorb large amounts of capital and even push the company into insolvency.

Separate accounts have developed for certain products that provide benefits to customers based on the returns on the assets that are held to finance those benefits. This effectively eliminates investment risk on that product for the company and lowers the amount of prudential capital that it needs to hold against to provide this product. These are sometimes referred to as pass-through arrangements because variations in returns on assets are passed through to the customer, on both separate account life insurance or annuity customer. Over recent decades, LICOs have offered variable life policies and variable annuities under separate accounts for which customer benefits vary with the returns on the assets held for these products. A much larger portion of the assets held in separate accounts is invested in equities. As a result, this has led to a growing share of equities on the combined balance sheet of LICOs as their separate account business has grown.

Reinsurance

LICOs, in their normal course of business, may find themselves with a larger-than-desired concentration of risk in certain areas. For example, a company may find that it has a disproportionate share of its life insurance policies issued to elderly males, and may be concerned that an adverse change in mortality for that group could cause major losses for the firm. An active market for *reinsurance* enables this company to transfer some of this risk to another company. This permits companies to lower their overall risk profiles through diversification, based on the diversification principles that we developed in Chapter 6.

PROPERTY AND CASUALTY INSURANCE COMPANIES

P&C companies have a massive amount of insurance in force, but do not hold nearly the volume of assets as life insurers because of the nature of the products that they offer. The insurance policies that they write have a fixed term and no investment component like those of permanent life policies. In this regard, they are similar to term life insurance policies. Also, P&C companies are not involved in the annuity business.[12]

As with term life policies, P&C companies must rely on actuarial statistics for pricing residential and commercial property insurance and motor vehicle insurance, their principal lines. Those statistics tend to be more reliable in predicting the amount of claims that will be experienced over a period of several years than for any single year by itself. That is, actual claims over several years will tend to match the actuarial amount, but not so much for any particular year. In any particular year, claims may exceed or fall short of the actuarial amount—which determines premiums. For example, natural disasters—such as tornadoes and hurricanes—are not uniform in numbers and severity from one year to the next. Moreover, the amount of property loss from any such event will depend on where it occurs, in a major population center or in a desolate place. To be prepared for those years in which claims will exceed premiums, P&C companies must, for business purposes, hold financial assets that can be liquidated easily to make up the difference.

A market for reinsurance is available for diversifying this risk. This often involves transferring risk to a foreign insurer that is primarily exposed to disasters in other parts of the world—enabling geographic diversification. Playing a prominent role in the global P&C reinsurance market is Lloyd's of London.

P&C companies hold assets to cover shortfalls of premiums from claims in various forms. Roughly half of their assets are held as corporate and muni bonds. The latter, which are tax-exempt, comprise a larger share of assets than is the case for other major financial institutions owing to the high tax rate on P&C interest earnings. Beyond these assets, P&C companies hold GSE securities and corporate equities, as well as shorter-term and more liquid assets. The latter provide the first layer of cushion for covering a shortfall arising from a spike in claims.

LARGE INSTITUTIONAL INVESTORS AND MONETARY POLICY

Large institutional investors play an important role in the transmission of monetary policy, largely in their capacity as professional asset managers. As professional managers, they make decisions based on an informed assessment of the value of different categories of assets that are candidates for their portfolios. Thus, when the outlook for monetary policy has changed—be it the result of an actual or prospective change in the policy interest rate or statements by the Fed that bear on the future path of the policy rate—large institutional portfolio managers will take actions that influence asset prices. For example, if the Fed chair made a statement signaling that the Fed soon would be raising the policy interest rate to reduce the risk of inflationary pressure building in the economy, asset managers of large institutions would bid less aggressively for bonds and stocks, if such an outlook had not already been built into market prices. In so doing, they would be transmitting this information into lower bond and stock prices—and higher asset returns—which would begin to affect spending decisions by businesses and households and take the edge off inflation.

SUMMARY

1. Pension funds (and insurance companies) offer various types of retirement plans to individuals—mostly through employers—and insurance companies provide various types of insurance on individuals' lives and a wide range of property. In the course of offering these products, they hold vast amounts of financial assets and play a key role in financial markets.
2. Pension plans can be DB plans or DC plans. DC plans have been displacing DB plans. Both involve regular contributions from the employee's earnings, and, with DC plans, often a matching contribution from the employer.
3. With a DB plan, the sponsor (employer) provides the employee with monthly retirement payments for life based on the employee's earnings (usually in the final years of employment) and tenure with the employer. Benefits schedules are back-loaded—providing disproportionally better benefits for those staying with the firm until retirement. This back-loading of benefits has tended to reduce job mobility, especially among those who have been with a single employer for a long period of time. DB plans have been offered more by established industrial firms and less by newer firms in the expanding sectors of the economy. The employer bears the investment risk in a DB fund.
4. With a DC plan, the employee owns the assets in the plan and the amount available at retirement will depend not only on contributions but also on investment returns. In other words, the employee bears the investment risk. Because of their portability and the absence of back-loading, DC plans have had more appeal among workers who view themselves to be mobile.
5. Both DB and DC funds hold around 60 percent of their assets in equity, including private equity funds. For DB funds, this results in large swings in funding positions, often causing the plans to be underfunded. Underfunding can lower the corporate sponsor's profits.
6. State and local employee retirement funds are DB plans, and these also hold a large share of their assets in equities. Because of their large concentrations of equities and the big swings in equity prices, the funding levels of state and local pension funds also have varied a great deal. Owing to state and local plans being more chronically underfunded, greater stress has been placed on such governments' budgets, as they must deal with more of their workforce retiring.
7. Looming much smaller are DC funds (thrift plans) for federal employees. In contrast to other pension plans, these plans hold large amounts of Treasury securities.
8. LICOs primarily provide life insurance policies and annuities to individuals, the pricing of both being based on actuarial expertise and mortality rates.
9. Life insurance policies take two basic forms: term and permanent (whole life). The former provides insurance for a specified term, with the premium rising with the age of the insured. Term policies provide coverage for life, typically at a level premium. The latter involves a saving component and results in LICOs' having more assets to manage.
10. LICOs offer annuities to individuals and to employers offering DB plans. These provide large sums to the LICOs at the time of purchase, and the assets acquired with these funds are managed to enable the company to honor its commitment to pay annuity benefits over time.

11. LICOs hold a large share of their assets in corporate bonds, both public and private. They also have large holdings in common stocks and MBS. The portion held as common stocks has grown with a shift of the product mix of LICOs toward those classified as special accounts—having pricing that is based on actual investment returns.
12. P&C companies insure a wide variety of properties owned by individuals and businesses. They resemble term life policies in the sense that they have fixed terms and are priced to ensure that premiums collected are in line with expected claims. However, to allow for those times when claims turn out to be exceptionally large, P&C companies hold financial assets that can be liquidated easily to meet the shortfall. Assets are held largely in munis, corporate bonds, and equities.
13. Both LICOs and P&C companies rely on the reinsurance market—offloading a portion of their risk concentrations to other insurers—to manage risk through diversification.
14. Large institutional investors play a significant role in the transmission of monetary policy. As professional asset managers, they take into account measures by the central bank—including the prospective path of the policy interest rate—when they bid for assets. This helps to ensure that such measures by the central bank are being reflected in asset prices and thereby spending decisions by businesses and households.

QUESTIONS

1. How do the products offered to individuals by pension funds and LICOs differ from those of mutual funds? What is the outlook for each of these institutions as a growing share of the U.S. workforce approaches retirement?
2. Why is it said that the benefits from DB plans are back-loaded? (Hint: Work through a numerical example in which the benefits formula is based on an algorithm involving the product of tenure with the employer and compensation, especially compensation in the years just before retirement.) How does expected labor force mobility affect worker preferences for DC plans versus DB plans?
3. Why is it said that investment risk is borne by the employer in a DB plan and a worker in a DC plan? Why might employers favor DC plans over DB plans? Which plan requires the greater level of financial understanding of the employee? Why?
4. How would very low interest rates affect the funding position of DB plans? Very high interest rates? Why does the very high concentration of DB plan assets in equities contribute to swings in the funding status of such plans?
5. Why would an individual favor accumulating assets in a DC plan rather than in a standard mutual fund? How are IRAs connected to DC funds?
6. Why do you think state and local government DB plans are generally less well funded than private DB plans?
7. For LICOs, how does the offering of annuities complement (involve economies of scope) the offering of life insurance? Does one line of activity act as a hedge for the other? If so, how?
8. Why does the pricing of permanent life insurance result in LICOs' having more funds to invest in securities? Apart from this consideration, why do LICOs need

financial assets to be able to provide their term and permanent policies (for these products to be sustainable over time)? P&C companies? What kinds of financial assets are needed for this purpose?
9. How might an individual combining a series of term insurance policies and a separate savings program be able to replicate the features of a permanent life insurance policy?
10. How would longer life expectancies affect the pricing of life insurance policies? Annuities?
11. What determines the pricing of P&C policies?
12. How does reinsurance affect the risk profiles of insurance companies—LICOs and P&C companies?
13. How do large institutional investors affect the transmission of monetary policy? How would they respond to information indicating that the central bank was about to pursue a more accommodative (easier) monetary policy?

NOTES

1. The deduction from employee paychecks for pension plans tends to be about 5 to 6 percent of gross earnings. At first, this may not seem sufficient to accumulate enough assets at retirement to provide for adequate benefits throughout the retirement years. As a general rule of thumb, however, a regular 6 percent contribution from gross earnings for 40 years will provide payments in retirement at three-fourths of gross preretirement earnings. The ratio of retirement to employment earnings is referred to as the replacement rate.
2. Not all DB plans are employer sponsored. Some are sponsored by trade unions, which assume responsibility for providing pension benefits for retired union members. Payroll deductions are transferred to the union, which in turn is responsible for running the plan and investing employee contributions.
3. Commonly, the algorithm uses the product of tenure and earnings for determining retirement benefits. In this case, that product gets progressively larger as years and earnings expand together.
4. ERISA also provided insurance for beneficiaries of DB plans—through the Pension Benefit Guaranty Corporation (PBGC)—in the event that the sponsor fails and the DB plan has inadequate assets to cover pension benefits. In these cases, minimum levels of benefits are paid by the PBGC. All employers offering DB plans are assessed a premium on their payrolls to cover the insurance. The premiums paid go to the PBGC and are used to build reserves to cover payments to employees of failed firms. Some firms with seriously underfunded DB plans have chosen to go into bankruptcy to offload their pension liabilities to the PBGC.
5. There are other provisions of the tax code that allow for similar-type plans for employees of state and local governments, such as 403(b). Nonetheless, these plans in popular vernacular also are commonly called 401(k)s.
6. See *Private Pension Plan Bulletin Historical Tables and Graphs,* U.S. Department of Labor, Benefits Security Administration, June 2013. The larger proportion of employees in DC plans than assets in such plans owes to the DC sector being newer and those covered by these plans having had less time to build up their pension assets.

7. These holdings are sometimes referred to as Employer Stock Option Plans (ESOPs). Often, the employer's matching contribution to the employee's DC plan takes the form of company stock with restrictions on subsequent sales. Employers have been criticized for trying to steer their employees to designate company stock for their DC plans. As a result, the portfolio composition in company stock is said to exceed that suggested by sound diversification principles. In the cases of the Enron failure in 2001 and the Lehman failure in 2008, employees held large portions of their DC assets in company stock and had much of their retirement assets wiped out by the failure of their employer.
8. In 1997, the Roth IRA was introduced as an alternative to the standard IRA described in this chapter. Under a Roth IRA, the employee's contribution is made with after-tax income, rather than before-tax income. However, withdrawals are tax free. This feature enables the returns on after-tax contributions to escape federal income taxes.
9. See Sarah Holden et al., "The Individual Retirement Account at Thirty: A Retrospective," Investment Company Institute, *Perspective* 11, no. 1 (February 2005).
10. Most of the Treasury securities held by these funds are nonmarketable and are customized by the Treasury to the requirements of the funds.
11. American Council of Life Insurers, *2013 Life Insurance Fact Book* (Washington, DC: American Council of Life Insurers.
12. Some insurance companies offer life and P&C insurance, but under separately chartered firms. That is, the holding company owns separate subsidiaries for each product line, but uses the same corporate name for all. Instead of taking the form of stock corporations, some these are mutual organizations, owned by their customers.

About the Author

Tom Simpson spent most of his career at the Board of Governors of the Federal Reserve System in Washington, DC. At the Board, he was a senior officer, with responsibilities in the area of monetary policy, economic forecasting, and financial markets, and served as an officer of the Federal Open Market Committee. In addition, he represented the Board in various outside organizations, including the Committee on Financial Markets of the Organization for Economic Cooperation and Development (OECD).

Dr. Simpson also has provided technical assistance to various central banks around the world, including the People's Bank of China and the Central Bank of Russia. Beginning in 2003, he played a key role in building a new monetary and financial system in Iraq and advised the Central Bank of Iraq on monetary policy. In recent years, he has also provided assistance to the central banks of Afghanistan, Angola, Honduras, Lesotho, Liberia, South Sudan, and Uganda.

In 2006, Dr. Simpson joined the faculty of the Department of Economics and Finance at the University of North Carolina–Wilmington (UNCW). At UNCW, he teaches upper-level and MBA courses on macroeconomics, financial markets and institutions, and monetary policy.

Dr. Simpson earned a BA from the University of Minnesota and a PhD in economics from the University of Chicago. He has published numerous professional articles on monetary and financial issues and a textbook on money and banking. He authors a quarterly newsletter on the U.S. economy (Economic Barometer, www.csb.uncw.edu/cbes/newsletter/index.htm), and makes frequent presentations on the economic outlook.

Index

ABCP. *See* Asset-backed commercial paper
ABSs. *See* Asset-backed securities
Accrual loss, 335
ACH. *See* Automated clearinghouse
Actual cash flows, from mortgages, 161, 162
Actual output, 221
Adjustable pegs, 280, 282
Adjustable-rate mortgages, 156, 157, 160, 164, 256, 291
Advances, Reserve Banks and, 206
Adverse feedback loop, 248, 250, 254, 258, 260
Adverse selection problem, 21–22
   annuities and, 338
   securitization and, 144–145
Age, earnings, and spending profile, 4–5
Aggregate consumption, 216
Aggregate demand, 2, 216–217, 221, 225, 240, 241
   categories of, 216–217
   inflation and, 219, 220, 221, 222
   interest rates and, 228
   monetary policy and, 212, 218–219
   mortgage market and transmission of monetary policy to, 164, 165
   shocks to, 232–233, 243
   shortfall in output and, 223
   wealth loss and downward shift in, 241–242
Aggregate P-E ratio, 175
Aggregate supply, 215–216, 221, 225
   inflation and, 219, 222
   shocks to, 233–234, 243
   shortfall in output and, 223
AIG, 140, 258
Alt-A mortgages, 148, 255
Alternative investments, 320, 328–329
Amazon, 326
Amgen, 326
Amortization:
   commercial mortgages, 163
   home mortgages, 156, 159–160, 164
Amortized cost basis for pricing money market mutual fund shares, 312
Amortized loans, 60
Anchor currency, 280
Angel investors, 325
"Animal spirits," 232
Annual percentage rate, 159
Annuities, 26, 333, 337, 340, 341, 343
Apple, 319, 326
Appreciation, of currency, 264

APR. *See* Annual percentage rate
Arbitrage, 267, 268, 323
ARMs. *See* Adjustable-rate mortgages
Asked price, 29, 32, 90
Asset-backed commercial paper, 116–117, 121, 256, 258
Asset-backed securities:
   auto lenders and, 148–149
   business credit and, 150–152
   common features of, 149
   credit cards and, 149
   financial crisis of 2008 and, 150
   structured securities and, 150, 151
Asset bubbles, 106–107, 109, 253
Asset prices, portfolio risk and, 104
Assets. *See also* Portfolio selection
   commercial bank balance sheet, 34, 35, 50
   current price of, 56
   providing uneven cash flows, calculating with financial calculator, 71–72
Asset values, financial crises and drop in, 253
Asymmetric information problem, 21, 22, 30, 86, 133, 135, 301
   bond market and, 129
   commercial banks and, 46, 50
   credit provision in presence of, 293
   letters of credit and, 119
   LICO assets and, 340–341
   monoline insurers and, 140
   private-label pools and, 148
   securitization and, 144, 145
   start-up firms and, 326
ATMs. *See* Automated teller machines
Auction rate securities, 140
Auctions, U.S. Treasury, 19, 90, 114, 121, 127
Auto ABSs, 148–149, 153
Automated clearinghouse, 40
Automated teller machines, 33, 194, 197, 263
Automobile loans, monthly payments, 61

Back-loaded retirement benefits schedules, 335, 337, 343
Bagehot, Walter, 205
Balance sheets:
   of commercial banks, 34–36, 294–295, 301
   of credit unions, 296
   of savings institutions, 295–296
   U.S. banking system, 34
Balance sheet shocks, 45
Balloon payments, mortgages, 159, 163

349

INDEX

Bank for International Settlements, 299
Bank holiday, 251, 252
Banking commissions, 195
Bank notes, 39
Bank of England, 184, 185, 186, 191, 193, 278
Bank of Japan, 184, 191, 194
Bank of the United States, 185, 186
Bank panics, 186, 188, 189, 248–250
Bank regulators, diversification and, 103
Bank reserves, money stock and, 43–44
Bank runs, 251–252, 296
Banks and banking, 1. *See also* Central banks; Commercial banks; Depository institutions; Federal Reserve System; Investment banks
   community, 292
   consolidation in, 290
   economies of scale in, 288, 301
   electronic delivery systems, 287
   emergence of, 39
   Internet, 37, 50, 194, 287
   shadow banking system, 49, 53, 257–258, 260
   too big to fail, 48
   universal, 290–291, 301
Banque de France, 184
Basel I, 299
Basel II, 49, 299
Basel III, 259, 299, 300, 302
Base period value, 179, 182
Basis points, 90
Bear Stearns, financial crisis of 2008 and, 257
Below-investment grade bonds, 130, 132, 137
Below-investment grade instruments, 87, 93
Benchmark interest rates:
   financial crisis of 2008 and, 255
   as real interest rate, 182
Benchmark yields, cyclical behavior related to, 88, 89
Best-efforts basis, 31, 140
Beta (β), asset risk and, 104, 108
Biddle, Nicholas, 186
Bid prices, 29, 32, 90
BIS. *See* Bank for International Settlements
Black market in foreign exchange, exchange controls and, 279
Bloomberg news service website, 12
Board of directors, 20
Board of Governors of the Federal Reserve System, 189, 190, 196, 203
Boeing, 178
Boesky, Ivan, 105
Bogey, 66
Bond duration, 64
Bond funds, 310, 314
Bondholders, tension between shareholders and, 130–131, 137
Bond indenture, covenants in, 131–132
Bond market, 3, 125–141
   background on, 125–126
   corporate bonds, 129–133
   government-sponsored enterprises, 135–136
   monetary policy and impact on, 136–137, 138
   munis, 133–135
   Treasury notes and bonds, 126–129
   underperformance problem and, 178
Bond ratings, 87
Bonds, 19, 20, 21, 24. *See also* Treasury notes and bonds
   call provisions and, 92
   convertible, 131–132
   corporate, 129–133, 340–341, 344
   coupon rate, 58
   maturities, 32
   par value of, 126
   portfolio selection and, 103
   serial, 135, 159
Bond trustees, 126
Borrowed reserves, 196, 197, 204
Borrowing costs, differences in, 75
Bovespa (Brazil), 178
Branching, removal of restrictions on, 290
Branch system, commercial banks, 288
Break-even rate, 67
"Breaking the buck," 312, 313, 314
British Bankers' Association, 123
British consols, 61, 62, 73
British pound, 264, 265
Brokers, 29–30
Businesses, financial system and, 5–6
Business plans, 20
Buyout funds, 320, 326, 328, 330

CAC (France), 178
Callability:
   bond indentures and, 132, 137
   of GSE bonds, 136
   muni yields and, 135, 138
Call option, 266
Call protection, 92, 132, 137
Call provision, 92
Calls, 266
CAMELS rating, 298, 301
Canadian dollars, 265, 266
Capital, commercial banks and, 11–12, 36
Capital gains, 181
Capitalization-weighted index, 178, 179, 180
Capital market instruments, 21, 30
Capital standards, 298–299, 302
Caps, on ARMs, 157
Captives, 24
Carry, 321
Cash management bills, auctioning of, 122
Cash value, 340
Caterpillar, 178
Cause (legal term), meaning of, 206
CBOs. *See* Collateralized bond obligations
CD. *See* Certificate of deposit
CDOs. *See* Collateralized debt obligations
CDSs. *See* Credit default swaps
Cell phones, mobile banking and, 37

Index

Central banks, 1, 3, 48, 250
  accountability and transparency and, 191–192, 206
  century and a quarter without, 185–186
  constitutional foundations of, in U.S., 184–185, 203
  expectations and credibility of, 239–240
  floating exchange rate regime and, 273
  forward guidance and, 85, 236, 243
  inflation expectations and, 221–223
  inflation targeting and, 240–241
  instrument independence and, 191
  investment expectations and credibility of, 239–240, 244
  investment spending decisions and, 6
  lags and, 234
  as lender of last resort, 184, 205
  modern, responsibilities of, 193–196, 203
  need for forward looking, 234
  net worth and independence of, 192–193
  origins of, 184
  policy interest rate and, 120, 121, 136, 138, 196, 274
  policy rules and guidance for, 237–239
  price stability and, 212
  roles and responsibilities of, 183–184
Certificate of deposit, 18, 35, 118, 121
Check clearing, 290
Check-imaging systems, 52
Checking accounts, commercial banks, 35
Cisco, 178, 326
Civil War (U.S.), 186
Clearinghouses, 40
CLO. *See* Collateralized loan obligation
Closed-end funds, 32, 314–315, 316
Closed-loop cards, 41, 52
CMBSs. *See* Commercial mortgage-backed securities
CMOs. *See* Collateralized mortgage obligations
Coinage, history behind, 38–39
Collateralization, bond indentures and, 132, 137
Collateralized bond obligations, 150, 153
Collateralized debt obligations, 150, 153
Collateralized loan obligations, 150, 153
Collateralized mortgage obligations, 151
Collective investment schemes, 26, 320
Commercial bank balance sheet, 34–36
  assets, 35
  liabilities, 35–36
  net worth, 36
  U.S. banking system, 34
Commercial banks, 3, 22, 33–53, 184, 195
  asymmetric information and, 46, 50
  background on, 33–34
  balance sheet for system of, 294–295, 301
  banking panics and, 248–249
  branch system and, 288
  capital and, 11–12
  diversification and, 103
  economic role of, 34, 50
  economies of scale and, 288, 301
  economies of scope and, 289, 301
  everyday transactions handled by, 33
  federal charters for, 186
  federal insurance for, 297
  financial crises and, 247, 248
  foreign exchange and, 265–266
  interbank market and, 287
  liquidity provision and, 44–46, 50
  maturity transformation and, 46–47, 50
  money market and role of, 117–119, 121
  organization of, 286–290
  payment services and, 293
  payment system and, 36–37, 40–42, 44, 50
  removal of restrictions on branching and, 290
  safety net, regulatory policy, and, 47, 51
  securitization and, 145
  separately chartered, in United States, 287, 300
  services provided by, 285, 301
  size of, measured by assets, 286
  universal banks and, 290–291
Commercial loans, 35
Commercial mortgage-backed securities, 150, 153, 163, 164
Commercial mortgages, 156, 163, 164
Commercial paper, 19, 20, 21, 24, 32, 46, 87, 115–117, 256
  asset-backed, 116, 121
  credit quality, 115
  maturities, 116
  placement, 117
  retreat of ABCP market, 116–117
Commercial paper market, financial crisis of 2008 and, 313
Commercial real estate bubble (1980s), 252
Commodity funds, 314
Common equity, 32
Common stock, 168, 180
Community banks, 292, 301
Compensation, 162, 164, 166
Competitive bids, Treasury auctions and, 114, 127
Comptroller of the Currency, 195
Conforming (or conventional) mortgages:
  maximum size of, 147, 154
  qualifying for, 157–158, 164
Conservation buffer, on SIFIs, 299
Conservatorship, Fannie Mae and Freddie Mac placed under, 136, 141, 147
Consignment agreement, 31
Consols. *See* British consols
Constitution. *See* U.S. Constitution
Consumer Finance Protection Bureau, 196
Consumer loans, 35
Consumer Price Index, 67, 127
Consumer price indexes, basis of, 215
Consumer protection, central bank responsibilities and, 194, 195–196, 203
Consumption, aggregate, 216
Contractual savings institutions, 24–26, 30, 334
Convertibility, bond indentures and, 131–132, 137

Convertible bonds, 131–132
Convertible preferred stock, 169
Cooperative movement, credit unions and, 292
Core banking software, 288
Core deposits, 35
Core inflation, 215
Core loans, 35
Corporate bonds, 19, 129–133, 310
   below-investment-grade market, 132–133
   credit default swaps, 132
   cyclical behavior related to, 88
   embedded options and, 92
   indentures and role of convenants, 131–132
   LICOs and, 340–341, 344
   placements, 130
   preferred shares and, 168
   private placements, 133, 137
   rating, 130
   secondary-market trading, 133
   tension between bond and shareholders, 130–131, 137
Corporate governance, 20
Corporate stocks, 19
Corporations:
   bond market as major financing source for, 126, 137
   corporate governance and, 20
Correspondent bank, 40
Correspondent relationships, 291
Countercyclical buffer, 299
Coupon rate, 58
Coupon securities, 126
   calculating current price of, with financial calculator, 71
   purposes for issuing, 129
Covenants, 126, 131–132
Covered interest arbitrage, 267
CP. *See* Commercial paper
CPI. *See* Consumer Price Index
Creation baskets, ETFs and, 314, 318
Credit:
   finance companies and, 24
   revolving lines of, 45, 117
Credit card ABSs, 149, 153
Credit cards, 40–41, 45, 50
Credit crunches, 218, 228, 254, 260
   financial crises and, 241, 250, 258
   Great Depression and, 251
Credit default swaps, 89, 93, 132, 256, 331
Credit enhancements, asset-backed securities, 149, 153
Credit markets, securities and integration of, 152
Credit rating agencies, 86–87, 93
   asset-backed securities and, 149
   commercial paper ratings and, 115
   complex financial products and, 256
   preferred shares rated by, 168
   private-label pools and, 148
   ratings scale for, 86
   securitized assets and, 145

Credit ratings:
   commercial paper, 115
   insured bonds, 135
   state and local government securities, 135
Credit risk, 3, 85–90, 93
   cyclical behavior of spreads and, 88–89
   munis *versus* Treasuries, 134
Credit score, conforming mortgage status and, 157
Credit unions, 23, 286, 292, 301, 303
   balance sheets of, 296
   federal insurance for, 297
   regulation of, 298
   separately chartered, in United States, 292
Cross-border financial transactions, 263, 264
Crossing these orders, 29
Cumulative preferred shares, 181
Currencies, 39
   anchor, 280
   appreciation of, 264
   conversions of, 263
   day-to-day fluctuations in, 197
   depreciation of, 264
   Fed, central banks and, 194
   floating exchange rate regime and, 273–275
   foreign exchange transactions and, 265
   Law of One Price and, 267
   overvalued, 278–279, 281
   relation between spot and forward exchange rates and, 266–267
   risk exposures and, 266
   undervalued, 275–276, 281
Currencies in foreign exchange market:
   demand schedule, 270–271
   equilibrium, 272–273
   supply schedule, 271–272
Currency boards, 280, 282
Currency swaps, 265, 281
Cutoff rate, 114

DAX (Germany), 178
Dealers, 29
Death benefits, 333
Debit cards, 37
Debt:
   capital standards and, 299
   equity *versus*, 20
   GSE, 136
   investment-grade *versus* below-investment grade, 87
Deep markets, 122
Default risk, variation among issuers, 85
Deficit units, 4, 5, 13
   complications in direction of funds from surplus to, 28
   depository institutions and, 23
   financial instruments and, 9
   indirect finance and, 22
   transfer of resources from surplus to, 4–8, 18

Defined benefit (DB) pension plans, 24–25, 334, 335–336, 343, 345
Defined contribution (DC) pension plans, 24, 25, 306, 334, 336–338, 343, 345
Deflation, 220
Demand for money, 43
Demand for reserves, 196, 197, 202–203, 207
Deposit insurance, 36, 47–48, 248, 252, 296–297
Depository institutions, 22–24, 30, 285–303
 background on, 285–286
 balance sheet of commercial banking system, 294–295
 balance sheet of credit unions, 296
 balance sheet of savings institutions, 295–296
 commercial banks, 22, 286–291
 credit unions, 23, 292
 economic functions of, 293–294
 federal insurance for, 296–297
 monetary policy and, 300
 organization of, 286–292
 regulation and supervision of, 297–300, 301
 savings institutions, 23, 291–292
Deposits, 32, 35, 39
Depreciation, of currency, 264
Depreciation allowances, 6
Derivatives, forms of, 331
Deutsche mark, 278
Direct finance, 18–22, 23, 30
 adverse selection, 21–22
 asymmetric information, 21
 debt *versus* equity, 20
 investment banks, 19
 money *versus* capital markets, 21
 moral hazard, 22
 Treasury auctions, 114
"Dirty float," 273
Discipline, financial system and, 11
Discipline on corporate management:
 equity market and, 176–177
 financial markets and, 176
Disclosure, SIFIs and, 300
Discount-basis yield, calculation of, 113
Discount rates, 56, 180
 pension plans and, 336
 setting, 206, 208
 share prices and, 170, 180
Discounts, Reserve Banks and, 205–206
Discount window, 48, 188, 189–190, 197, 204, 208, 250
Disinflation, 211, 220
Distressed debt funds, 323
Diversification:
 reinsurance and, 341
 risk reduction and, 100, 102
 securitization and, 143
Dividend payout ratio, 172, 182
Dividends, 5, 6, 32, 170
 earnings and, 171–172
 growth in, 170–171, 180

indentures, role of convenants, and, 131
 preferred shares and, 168, 181
DJIA. *See* Dow Jones Industrial Average
DM. *See* Deutsche mark
Dodd-Frank Act. *See* Wall Street Reform and Consumer Protection (Dodd-Frank) Act of 2010
Dollarization, 280, 282
Dollars, Canadian, 265, 266
Dollars (U.S.), 263, 265
 international financial system and, 194
 sale of yuan for, 275
Dollar-yen exchange rate, 264
Domestic assets, 102, 103
Dow Jones index, introduction of, 182
Dow Jones Industrial Average, 178, 179, 181
Duration:
 maturity and, 64–66, 68
 modified, 73

Early stage financing, venture capital funds and, 325
Earnings, life-cycle pattern of, 4–5
ECNs. *See* Electronic communications networks
Economic value:
 financial system and, 4
 hedge fund risk and, 323–324
 of private equity firms, 328
 venture capital funds and, 326
Economic well-being, financial system and, 4
Economies of scale, 288, 301, 308, 336
Economies of scope, 289, 301, 308
Efficient markets hypothesis, 104–108
 asset bubbles and, 106–107
 evidence, 107–108
 other implications of, 106
 random walk and, 106
Efficient portfolios, risk-return trade-offs and, 103–104, 108
Electronic communications networks, 29, 30, 169, 180
Electronic payments, 293
Embedded options, 91–92, 93
Emerging market equity funds, 314
Employee Retirement Income Security Act, 335, 345
Employee Stock Option Plans, 346
Employment, 212
 Federal Reserve System and, 212–213
 full, restoring, 224
 maximum, 213–214, 222, 224, 237, 241
 monetary policy and, 212
 policy response to shortfall in, 223
 private equity firms and, 328, 331
Enron, 346
Equilibrium, fixed exchange rate regimes, 277
Equilibrium exchange rate, 273, 281
Equity funds, 310, 313
Equity(ies):
 debt *versus*, 20
 kinds of, 32
 as source of corporate finance, 168

Equity market, 167–182
Equity premiums, 170, 173, 174–175, 180, 182
Equity (stock) market, 3
Equity tranches, 151, 152
ERISA. *See* Employee Retirement Income Security Act
Escrow account, home mortgages, 160, 164
ESOPs. *See* Employee Stock Option Plans
ETFs. *See* Exchange-traded funds
European Central Bank, 191, 193–194
European sovereign debt crisis (2010), 175
Euros/eurodollars, 118, 119, 121, 264, 265
Event-driven funds, 323
ex ante real rate of interest, 67, 68
Excess reserves, 196, 203, 204, 209, 303
Exchange controls, 279
Exchange rate regimes:
   fixed exchange rate regime, 267–268, 275–280, 281
   floating exchange rate regime, 267, 268, 273–275, 281
Exchange rate relationships, long-run, 267–269
Exchange rate risk, 103
Exchange rates, 3, 280
   demand schedule, 270–271
   determination of, in the shorter run, 269–273
   equilibrium, 272–273, 281
   floating, 273–275, 281
   foreign, 263–264
   globalization and, 263, 280
   interest rates and, 217
   measuring, 264
   nominal, 269, 280, 281
   real, 269, 281
   reporting, common ways for, 264
   spot and forward exchange relationship, 266–267, 281
   supply schedule, 271–272
   undervalued, 275, 281
Exchange-traded funds, 26, 179, 314, 316
Expansion financing, venture capital funds and, 325
Expectations hypothesis, 77–80, 92
Expected inflation component, TIPS and, 127
Expected path of short-term rates, importance of, 235–236
Expected return:
   calculating, 98
   portfolio selection and, 99
ex post real rate of interest, 66, 68
ExxonMobil, 179

Fallen angel, 87
Fannie Mae, 135, 136, 138, 147, 148, 153, 154, 157, 208, 291
Farm Credit Banks, 140
Farmer Mac, 140
Farm sector GSEs, 140
FDIC. *See* Federal Deposit Insurance Corporation

Federal Agricultural Mortgage Corporation. *See* Farmer Mac
Federal deposit insurance, 296–297, 301
Federal Deposit Insurance Corporation, 12, 36, 47, 169, 195, 252, 259, 297
Federal Financial Examination Council, 303
Federal funds, 118, 121, 122
Federal funds broker, 118
Federal funds rate, 85, 196, 203, 204, 209, 300
   setting through open market operations, 198, 199, 200
   target, two versions of Taylor rule prescriptions, 238–239
   zero-bound constraint on, 242, 244
Federal government, as chronic deficit unit, 6
Federal government retirement funds, 338, 343
Federal Home Loan Banks, 135, 136, 138
Federal Home Loan Mortgage Corporation. *See* Freddie Mac
Federal Housing Administration, 146, 158
Federal National Mortgage Association. *See* Fannie Mae
Federal Open Market Committee, 85, 189, 191, 198, 199, 203, 242
Federal Reserve Act, 187–188, 212
Federal Reserve Bank of New York, 12, 189, 194, 198, 200
Federal Reserve Banks, 188, 189, 190
Federal Reserve Board, 12, 187, 188, 298
Federal Reserve float, 208
Federal Reserve notes, 188
Federal Reserve System (the Fed), 42, 43, 44, 83, 85, 195, 259, 298
   Board of Governors of, 189, 196, 203
   creation of, 184, 186–188, 203, 250
   credit conditions and, 11
   discount window and, 188, 189–190, 197, 204, 208
   districts and reserve bank headquarters, 187
   dual mandate and, 212–213, 224, 241
   early years of, 188–189
   financial crisis of 2008 and policy responses of, 258
   GAO audits and, 191, 206
   independence of, 190–191, 203
   monetary policy and, 2
   net worth, 192, 193
   open market operations conducted by, 200, 204
   payment of interest on excess reserves, 201
   permanent *versus* temporary transactions and, 200
   primary dealer status and, 114
   reforms of the 1930s, 189–190, 203, 252
FFIEC. *See* Federal Financial Examination Council
FHA. *See* Federal Housing Administration
FHLBs. *See* Federal Home Loan Banks
Fibonacci series, 106
Fiduciary system, financial system as, 17
Field of membership, credit unions and, 292

Finance:
    direct methods of, 18–22, 30
    indirect methods of, 22–27, 30
Finance companies, 24, 30
Financial calculator, solutions calculated with, 70–72
Financial crises, 3, 48
    big drop in asset values and, 253
    broader, 252–254
    classic banking panics, 248–250
    common threads to, 259–260
    fire sales and, 253–254
    runs on suspected institutions and, 253
    in U.S. financial history, 247–248
Financial crisis of 2008, 252, 254. *See also* Great Recession
    asset-backed securities and, 150
    asset bubbles and, 107
    background factors related to, 255
    central banks, supervision of financial institutions, and, 195
    commercial real estate market and, 163
    Dodd-Frank and, 259
    growing exposures of key financial institutions and, 256–258
    home equity lines of credit and, 159
    housing bubble bursts and onset of, 107, 166, 248, 254, 260
    major credit crunch and, 258
    maturity mismatches and, 299–300
    monolone insurers and, 140
    nonstandard mortgages and, 255–256
    policy response to, 258
    reserves market and, 201–202, 204
    retreat of ABCP market and, 116
    run on money market mutual funds during, 313
    shadow banking stress and, 257–258
    structured product market and, 152
    subprime mortgages and, 148
    systemic risk and, 298
    unraveling of, 257
    zero-bound constraint and, 241–243
Financial institutions. *See also* Banks and banking; Depository institutions
    central banks and supervision of, 195
    financial crises and central role of, 248
    sound, 18
    systemic risk and, 256
Financial instruments, 9–10, 30, 32
Financial literacy, 338
Financial markets, 1
    pension industry and, 25
    types of, 3
Financial Stability Oversight Council, 313
Financial stability, central bank responsibilities and, 194, 203, 206
Financial Stability Oversight Council, 259, 298, 324
Financial system:
    businesses and, 5–6
    contributions made by, 4–11
    defined, 1
    discipline and, 11
    effective, features of, 17–18
    foreign sector and, 6
    forward-looking nature of, 11, 13
    globalization of, 12, 13
    governments and, 6
    households and, 4–5
    reallocation of risk and, 10
    recurring themes related to, 11–12
    standards of living and, 2, 13
    transfers of resources from surplus to deficit units and, 4–8
    trust and, 17–18, 30
    uncertainty and risk disliked by, 11, 13
Financial Times website, 12
Fire sales, financial crises and, 253–254
First Bank of the United States, 185, 194
First (senior) mortgages, 156, 158, 164
Fiscal agency, central bank responsibilities and, 194, 203
Fitch, 86, 87, 115
Fixed exchange rate regimes, 267–268, 275–280, 281
    dynamics of undervalued currency, 276–278
    overvalued currency, 278–279
    self-equilibrating nature of, 277
    undervalued exchange rate, 275
    variations on, 280
Fixed exchange rates, 43, 188
Fixed-income (bond) funds, 307
Fixed-income instruments, embedded options and, 91–92
Fixed-maturity time deposits, 291
Fixed monthly payments on loans, determining, present value formula and, 69–70
Fixed-payment loans, monthly payments on, calculating, 61
Fixed-rate mortgages, 156, 157, 159–160, 164
Flight to safety, 92, 94
    Great Recession of 2008 and, 174, 219
    munis *versus* Treasuries and, 134
    TIPS and, 127
Floaters, 136
Floating exchange rate regime, 267, 268, 273–275, 281
Floors, on ARMs, 157
FOMC. *See* Federal Open Market Committee
Foreign assets, 102, 103
Foreign banks:
    national treatment principle and, 298
    as universal banks, 290
Foreign-chartered commercial banking organizations, 290
Foreign currencies, 32
Foreign exchange market, 3
    background on, 263–264
    demand for currency in, 270–271
    equilibrium in, 272–273
    features of, 264–266

Foreign exchange market (*continued*)
  supply of currency in, 271–272
  wholesale transactions in, 264, 281
Foreign exchange rates, economic decisions and role of, 263–264
Foreign exchange swaps, 265
Foreign exchange transactions, daily volume of, 264
Foreign sector, financial system and, 6
Forward exchange rates, spot transactions and, 266–267, 281
Forward guidance, 85, 136–137, 138, 236, 242, 243, 244
Forward-looking behavior, in stock prices, 174
Forward markets, 84
Forward prices, 84
Forward transactions, 265, 266, 281
401(k) plans, 337, 345
403(b) plans, 345
FRBNY. *See* Federal Reserve Bank of New York
FRED. *See* St. Louis Fed Database
Freddie Mac, 135, 136, 138, 147, 148, 153, 154, 157, 208, 291
Free-rider problem, 176
Frictional unemployment, 213, 214
FRMs. *See* Fixed-rate mortgages
Front-load fees, 313
FSOC. *See* Financial Stability Oversight Council
FTSE (United Kingdom), 178
Futures, 331
Futures contracts, 266
Futures markets, 84, 95
Future value, 56, 67
  financial calculator and calculation of, 70
  higher interest rate, calculating, 70

GAO. *See* General Accountability Office
GDP. *See* Gross domestic product
General Accountability Office, 191, 206
General accounts, LICOs, 341
General obligations, 134, 138
Ginnie Mae. *See* Government National Mortgage Association
Glass-Steagall Act of 1933, 289
Global equity funds, 310
Globalization:
  capital standards and, 299
  exchange rates and, 263, 280
  of financial system, 12, 13
  foreign-chartered commercial banking and, 290
  mutual funds and, 310
Global macro funds, 322
Global saving glut, 15
GNMA. *See* Government National Mortgage Association
Goal independence, 191
Gold, 39
Goldman Sachs, 179
Gold standard, 184, 188, 275
  Great Depression and restraints on, 250–251, 262
  money supply and, 43
Google, 326
Gordon growth model, 182
GOs. *See* General obligations
Governance, corporate, 20
Government National Mortgage Association, 141, 146, 153
Governments, financial system and, 6
Government spending, 217
Government-sponsored enterprises, 135–136, 138, 147, 156, 163, 166, 208, 209
Gramm-Leach-Bliley Act, 289
Great Depression (1930s), 2, 250–252
  bank runs during, 251–252
  Federal Reserve System reforms and, 189–190, 203
  gold standard restraints and, 250–251, 260
  massive damage related to, 252
  mutual funds sector during, 306, 315
  stock market crash and onset of, 251
Great Moderation, 223, 255
Great Recession, 2, 107, 175, 232, 247. *See also* Financial crisis of 2008
  aggregate demand during, 219
  flight to safety and, 174
  large output gap during, 223
  long-term unemployed workers and, 214
  lower labor force participation during, 227
  negative output gap and, 221
  systemic risk and, 47
  zero-bound constraint and slow recovery from, 241–243, 244
Gross domestic product, 44, 237
  aggregate demand and, 216
  aggregate supply and, 215
  change in inventories and, 228
  index for, 214
  magnitudes of M1 and M2 and, 41
  mortgage market and, 164
  velocities of M1 and M2 and, 42
GSE bonds, features of, 136
GSEs. *See* Government-sponsored enterprises
Guarantees, forms of, 46

Hamilton, Alexander, 129, 185
Head-and-shoulders pattern, 106
Hedge fund risk, economic value and, 323–324
Hedge funds, 3, 26, 30, 105, 319, 321–324, 329, 330
  entry and redemption and, 322
  leverage and, 322
  prime broker's role and, 322
  as private placements, 320–321
  strategies of, 320
  types of, 322–323
Hedge funds of funds, 323
HELOC. *See* Home equity line of credit
High-yield bonds, 88, 89, 130, 132

High-yield instruments, 87, 93
Holding companies:
    multibank, 288
    savings institutions and, 292
    supervision of, 298
Holding periods, maturities *versus*, 63
Home-country bias, 102
Home equity line of credit, 158–159, 166
Home equity loans, 149, 166
Home mortgages, 156–163
    actual cash flows from, 161
    amortization of, 156, 159–160, 164
    conforming or nonconforming, 157–158, 164
    embedded options and, 91–92
    escrow account, 160, 164
    first *versus* second mortgages, 158
    FRM or ARM, 157
    home equity lines, 158–159
    interest rate specification, 159
    maturity of loan, 156–157
    monthly payments, 157, 159, 164
    points, 158, 164
    prepayment option, 161, 164
    prepayment risk and compensation, 162–163, 164
Hostile takeover, 177
Households, financial markets and, 4–5
Housing, investment in, 217
Housing bubble:
    financial crisis of 2008 and bursting of, 15, 107, 166, 248, 254, 260
    shortfall in setting of federal funds rate and, 239
Housing sector, government-sponsored enterprises and, 135–136
Hybrid ARMs, 157
Hybrid funds, as "fund of funds," 310, 311

IBM Corporation, 24
IBM Global Financing, 24
Illiquid instruments, defined, 90
Implicit forward rates of interest, 84–85, 93, 95
Income:
    consumption proportional to, 216
    life-cycle pattern of, 4–5
Indentures, 126
    role of covenants and, 131–132
    for tax-exempt bonds, 135
Indexes of prices, 214–215
Indexes of stock prices, 178–179, 180
Index funds, 98, 310, 314
Indicators, targets *versus*, 245
Indirect finance, 22–27, 28, 30
    collective investment schemes, 26–27
    contractual savings institutions, 24–26
    depository institutions, 22–24
    finance companies, 24
Individual retirement accounts, 306, 338
Industrial loans, 35
Indy Mac, 257

Inflation, 211, 212, 213, 225
    addressing, 221–223
    adjustable pegs and, 280
    aggregate demand and supply and, 219–220
    core, 215
    NAIRU and rate of, 214
    shocks and, 232–234
    targeting, 240–241, 244
    time lags and, 234
    unwanted, 221
Inflation compensation, 67, 127
Inflation expectations, 243
    central bank credibility and, 239–240, 244
    important role of, 220, 225
Inflation-protected issues, 127
Inflation rate, computing, 227
Inflation risk component, TIPS and, 127
Information technology:
    economies of scale and, 288
    unbundling, pooling of loans, and, 144, 153
Initial public offerings, 27, 133, 169, 178, 180, 326, 328, 329
Inside lag, 245
Insider trading, 105
Institutional money funds, 311, 313
Instrument independence, 191
Insurance, muni yields and, 135, 138
Insurance companies, private placements and, 133. *See also* Life insurance companies
Intel, 178, 326
Interbank market, role of, 287, 300–301
Interbank rate, 300
Interest rates, 3, 32. *See also* Term structure of interest rates
    aggregate consumption and, 216
    aggregate demand and, 216–217, 218–219, 228
    businesses and, 6
    commercial mortgages and, 163
    credit risk and, 85, 92
    cyclical behavior of credit risk and, 88–89
    demand for currencies and, 270–271
    demand for money and, 43
    depository institutions and, 23
    duration and, 65–66
    embedded options and, 91–92
    fixed-rate *versus* adjustable-rate mortgages and, 157
    floating exchange rate regime and, 273, 274
    future value and, 56
    global saving glut and, 15
    home mortgages and, 159, 160, 166
    households and, 5
    liquidity and, 90, 92
    maturity, price sensitivity, and, 61–62, 92
    money market mutual funds and, 312
    payment of, on excess reserves, 201, 204
    premium of forward over spot and, 267
    prepayments on mortgages and, 162
    securitization, credit markets, and, 152
    taxation differences and, 91, 92

Interest rates (*continued*)
  term structure of, 76–85
  thrift institution model and, 291
  TIPS and, 127
  transfer of funds from surplus to deficit units and, 7–8
  variation in, 75
International trade, letters of credit and, 119–120, 121
Internet banking, 37, 50, 194, 287
Inventories:
  change in, 228
  investment in, 217
Investment banks, 19, 145
Investment Company Act of 1940, 306, 315
Investment-grade bonds, 130, 132
Investment-grade instruments, 87, 93
Investment risk:
  annuities and, 340
  defined benefit (DB) plans and, 335
  defined contribution (DC) plans and, 336
Investments:
  aggregate demand and, 217
  alternative, 320
  expected return on, 98
  meanings of references to, in text, 3–4
Investment spending decisions, central banks and, 6
Investment yield basis, 113
Investors:
  changing tolerance for risk and, 90
  investment banks and, 19
  uncertainty faced by, 98
IPOs. *See* Initial public offerings
IRAs. *See* Individual retirement accounts

Jackson, Andrew, 186
January effect, 106
Japan, 227
Japanese yen, 264, 265
Jet Blue, 326
Job mobility:
  DB plans and reduction in, 335, 343
  DC plans and, 337
Jumbos/jumbo mortgages, 148, 255
Junior (second) mortgages, 156, 158, 164
Junior status, bond indentures and, 132, 137
Junk bonds, 130, 132, 133, 150
Junk (speculative-grade instruments), 87, 93

Keynes, John Maynard, 232

Labor force participation rate, 227
Labor market, turnover in, 213
Lags:
  central banks and, 234
  inside and outside, 245
Large-cap equity funds, 314
Large institutional investors:
  background on, 333–334
  life insurance companies, 339–341, 343–344
  monetary policy and, 342
  pension funds, 334–339, 343
  property and casualty insurance companies, 341–342, 344
Large-scale asset purchase programs, 242, 244
Large-Scale Asset Purchases, 84
Later stage financing, venture capital funds and, 325
Law of One Price, 267, 281
LBOs. *See* Leveraged buyouts
L/C. *See* Letters of credit
Leases, loans *versus*, 24
Legal infrastructure, strong, financial system and, 18, 30
Legal tender, 38
Lehman Brothers, 257, 313, 346
"Lemons problem," 144
Lender of last resort function, central bank as, 184, 205
Letters of credit, 46, 119–120, 121
Leveraged buyouts, 177, 327
Leverage restrictions, corporate bond market and, 131
Liabilities, commercial bank balance sheet, 35–36, 50
LIBOR, 95, 119, 123, 126, 136, 156, 157, 166, 294, 321
LICOs. *See* Life insurance companies
Life-cycle pattern, households and, 4
Life expectancy, annuity pricing and, 26
Life insurance companies, 3, 25–26, 30, 144, 333, 334, 337, 338–341, 343, 344
  annuities purchased through, 340, 343
  assets of, 340–341, 344
  commercial real estate market and, 163
  reinsurance and, 341, 344
Life insurance products, types of, 339
Limited liability company, 163
Limited partnership arrangement, hedge, venture, and private equity funds and, 320–321, 324, 326, 329
Line for banks, commercial banks and, 118
Line of credit, 45
Liquid instruments, defined, 90
Liquidity, 3, 53, 90, 93
  commercial banks and, 44–46, 117
  defined, 44–45
  money market and, 112
  munis *versus* Treasuries, 134
Liquidity premium hypothesis, 81
Liquidity provision, 44–46, 50, 293, 301
Liquidity standards, 299–300
LLC. *See* Limited liability company
Lloyd's of London, 342
Load funds, 313, 316
Loans, 32
  amortized, 60
  commercial banks and, 22, 35
  depository institutions and, 22, 23
  leases *versus*, 24
  personal, 24
  whole, 146

Index

Loan servicing, securitization and, 143–144
Loan-to-value:
   commercial mortgages and, 163, 164
   conforming mortgage status and, 157, 164
Local government pension funds, 338–339, 343
Local governments, 6
   bond market as major financing source for, 126
   serial bonds and, 135
London Interbank Offered Rate. *See* LIBOR
Longevity risk:
   annuities and, 340
   defined benefit pension plans and, 335
Long-term interest rates, 85
   under expectations hypothesis, 78
   under term premium hypothesis, 81
Loss carry-forwards, 321
Lottery choice, calculating with financial calculator, 71
LSAPs. *See* Large-Scale Asset Purchases
LTV. *See* Loan-to-value

Macaulay duration, 73
Macro funds, 328
Macro-prudential supervision, 194
Managed float, 273
Management, equity market and disciplining of, 176–177
Management fee, 321, 331
Managers, tension between shareholders and, 176–177
Manufactured home loans, securitization of, 149
Market equilibrium for reserves, 198, 199
Market for corporate control, 178
Market portfolio, 102, 103
Market segmentation hypothesis, 83–84
MasterCard, 40
Matched sale-purchase agreements, 200, 204
Matched sale purchases, 128
Maturities:
   bond, 20, 32
   commercial mortgages, 163
   commercial paper, 116
   depository institutions and, 24
   differences in yields and, 76
   duration and, 64–66
   holding periods *versus*, 63
   in money market, 112, 120
   mortgages, 156–157
   price sensitivity and, 61–62
   serial bonds, 135
   Treasury notes, 122, 126
Maturity mismatches
   financial crisis of 2008 and, 299–300
   interest rate risk and, 47
Maturity transformation, 50, 249
   defined, 46–47
   depository institutions and, 293–294, 301
Maximum employment, 213–214, 222, 224, 237, 241
MBSs. *See* Mortgage-backed securities
McDonald's, 178

Mergers and acquisitions, 177, 290
Mezzanine tranches, 152
Microsoft, 326
Milken, Michael, 105
Mobile banking, 37, 50, 287
Modified duration, 73
Modigliani-Miller Theorem, 131
M1, 41, 50, 52
Monetary policy, 1, 3, 21, 75, 184, 188
   aggregate demand and, 216, 218–219
   alternative investment funds and, 328–329
   background on, 211–213
   bond market and impact of, 136–137, 138
   central bank net worth and independence and, 192–193
   central bank responsibilities and, 193, 194, 203
   depository institutions and, 300
   disruptive, 226
   dual mandate in United States and, 212–213
   Federal Reserve System and, 2
   floating exchange rate regime and, 274–275
   forward guidance and, 236
   inflation and, 221–223
   inflation expectations and effectiveness of, 239–240
   large institutional investors and, 342
   maximum employment and, 213–214
   money market and effects of, 120
   mortgage market and, 163–164, 165
   mutual funds and, 315, 318
   output and prices and, 212
   price stability and, 212, 214–215, 224
   securitization and, 152–153
   shocks and, 232–234
   shortfall in output and employment and, 223–224
   stock market and, 175, 178, 180
   term structure relationship and, 85, 93
Money:
   evolution of, 38–39
   time value of, 56
Money demand, money supply and, 43–44
Money market, 3, 111–123
   background and basic features of, 111–112
   commercial banks and role in, 117–119, 121
   commercial paper, 115–117
   letters of credit and bankers' acceptances, 119–120
   maturities in, 112, 120
   monetary policy effects on, 120
   pricing, 112–113
   Treasury bills, 114–115
   as a wholesale market, 112
Money market funds, 307, 308, 316
Money market instruments, 21, 30, 118–119
Money market mutual funds, 311
   low fees for, 314
   pricing of, 312–313
Money stock, payments media in, 41
Money stock rule, 237, 243
Money supply, money demand and, 43–44

Monoline insurers, 140
Monthly payments:
  on fixed-payment loans, calculating, 61
  on home mortgages, 159
Moody's, 86, 87, 115
Moral hazard situations, 12, 22, 30, 32
  commercial banks, safety net backstop, and, 48, 51
  government-sponsored agencies and, 136, 138
  supervision and, 207
  tension between bond and shareholders and, 130–131
Mortgage-backed securities, 146, 208
  Fannie Mae and Freddie Mac, 147–148, 153
  Ginnie Mae, 146, 153
  LICO assets and, 341
  secondary trading of, 148, 153
  structured securities and, 150, 151
Mortgage interest, deductibility of, for income tax purposes, 156, 166
Mortgage loans, savings institutions and, 291
Mortgage market, 3, 155–166
  background on, 155–156
  commercial mortgages, 163
  home mortgages, 156–163, 164
  as largest credit market in United States, 156
  monetary policy and, 163–164
Mortgages, 21, 35
  conforming (or conventional), 147, 154
  defined, 156, 164
  monthly payments, 61
Mortgage sector, government-sponsored enterprises and, 135–136
MSP agreements. See Matched sale-purchase agreements
MSPs. See Matched sale purchases
M2, 41, 50, 52
Multibank holding companies, 288, 300
Multiples, 171
Municipal bonds, 19
Munis, 91, 93, 133–135
  credit risk and liquidity differences between Treasuries and, 134
  general obligations *versus* revenue bonds, 134, 138
  indentures, 135
  placement, 135
  ratings, 135, 138
  tax considerations between Treasuries and, 134
Mutual fund complexes:
  role of, 307–309
  S&P 500 index and, 179, 181
Mutual fund industry, SEC and oversight of, 307
Mutual fund products, provision of, 308
Mutual funds, 3, 26, 30, 305–318
  closed-end funds, 309, 314–315, 316
  economies of scale and, 336
  exchange-traded funds, 309, 314, 316
  history behind, 306–307, 315
  as large component of financial markets, 305, 315
  monetary policy and, 315, 318
  open-end funds, 309–314, 316
  types of, 309
Mutual organizations, 291

NAIRU, 214, 219, 220, 221, 223, 224, 225, 226, 227, 228, 244
Nasdaq, 29, 169, 178, 179
National Banking Act of 1863, 186
National banks, chartering of, 186
National City Bank, 257
National Credit Union Administration, 292, 298
National Credit Union Share Insurance Fund, 297
National treatment principle, 298
NAV. See Net asset value
NCUA. See National Credit Union Administration
NCUSIF. See National Credit Union Share Insurance Fund
Negative aggregate supply shock, 233
Negative convexity, 162
Negative demand shocks, 233
Negative supply shocks, 234
Net asset value, per share, 311
Net eurodollar liabilities, 207
Net exports, 217
Net profits, 6
Net worth (capital), commercial bank balance sheet, 36, 50
New York Stock Exchange, 29, 133, 169
New York Times, 179
Nikkei (Japan), 178
No-load funds, 313
Nominal exchange rate, 269, 280, 281
Nominal interest rates, 66–67
Nominal issues, 126–127
Nonaccelerating inflation rate of unemployment. See NAIRU
Nonborrowed reserves, 196–197, 201–202, 204, 208
Noncompetitive bids, Treasury auctions and, 114, 127
Noncumulative shares, 181–182
Nonpersonal time deposits, 207
Nonstandard mortgages, financial crisis of 2008 and proliferation of, 255–256
NOW accounts, 52
NYSE. See New York Stock Exchange

OCC, 298
Office of the Comptroller of the Currency (OCC), 186, 259, 286, 298
Office of Thrift Supervision, 303
Off-the-run securities, 128, 137
Okun, Arthur, 224
Okun's Law, 224, 225
144(a) provision, 133
One-off shocks, 233
On-the-run issues, 128
On-the-run securities, 90
On-the-run spread, 90

Index

On-the-run Treasuries, 128, 137
On-the-run yields, 128
Open-end fees, 313–314
Open-end funds, 32, 309–314, 310, 314, 316
Open-end mutual funds, for DC *versus* DB plans, 337
Open-end shares, pricing of, 311–312
Open-loop cards, 41, 52
Open market "Desk," 198, 200
Open Market Investment Committee, 206
Open market operations, 198, 199, 200, 203, 208
Operating expense fees, 314
"Operation Twist," 243
Optimists, price movement, fundamentals, and, 107
Options, 331
OTC market, for corporate bonds, 133
OTS. *See* Office of Thrift Supervision
Output:
  actual and potential, in practice, 221
  employment level and, 214
  monetary policy and, 212
  Okun's Law and, 224, 225
  potential, 214
  shocks and, 232–234
  shortfall in, addressing, 223
  time lags and, 234
  underlying aggregate demand and supply schedules and, 228
Outright forward transactions, 265, 281
Outright (permanent) transactions, 200
Outside lag, 245
Overcollateralization, consumer ABSs and, 149, 153
Over-the-counter (OTC) system, 29, 30, 169, 180
Overvalued currencies, 278–279, 281

Paper instructions, 39
Par value, 58, 126
Pass-through arrangements, 341
Pass-throughs, MBS, 146, 147, 153
Payment instructions, forms of, 37
Payment services, depository institutions and, 293, 301
Payments system, 2
  central bank responsibilities and, 194, 203
  commercial banks and, 36–37, 40–42, 44, 50
  infrastructure, 40
  reliable and efficient, 10, 18, 30
PBGC. *See* Pension Benefit Guaranty Corporation
PBOC. *See* People's Bank of China
Pension Benefit Guaranty Corporation, 345
Pension funds, 3, 32, 144, 320, 333, 334–339, 343
  defined benefit (DB) plans, 334, 335–336, 343
  defined contribution (DC) plans, 334, 336–338, 343
  federal government, 339
  state and local government, 338–339, 343
  types of, 24–25, 30
  zero-coupon notes and, 58

Pension plans, minimum funding levels of, 335–336
People's Bank of China, 275, 276, 277
P-E ratio. *See* Price-to-earnings (P-E) ratio
Performance fee, 321
Permanent insurance, 25, 339, 343
Permanent transactions, 200, 204
Perpetual coupon, 61
Persisting shocks, 233
Personal loans, 24
Pessimists, price movement, fundamentals, and, 107
PMI. *See* Private mortgage insurance
Point-of-sale (POS) systems, 194
Point-of-sale (POS) terminals, 37, 50
Points, home mortgages and, 158, 164
Poison pills, 177
Policy interest rate, 235, 242, 300
  central banks and, 120, 121, 136, 138, 196, 274
  determining, 196, 203
  open market operations and, 198, 200
Policy rules, 237–239
  money stock rule, 237, 243
  Taylor rule, 237–238, 243
Political risks, 103
Pooling of loans, unbundling and, 144
Portfolio selection, 99–103, 108
  calculating expected return and risk of portfolio of two assets, 101–102
  expected return, 99
  interpreting expression for risk, 100–101
  principles in practice for, 102–103
  risk and, 99–100
Positive demand shocks, 232, 233
Positive supply shocks, 234
Potential output, 221
Potential real GDP (or potential output), 214
PPP. *See* Purchasing power parity
Preferred equity, 32, 180
Preferred habitat, 83
Preferred habitat hypothesis, 83
Preferred shares, 168, 181
Preferred stock, 169, 180
Prepayment option, home mortgages, 161, 164
Prepayment penalties, home *versus* commercial mortgages, 156
Prepayment risk, home mortgages, 162–163, 164
Present value, 56–61, 67
  formula for, 56–57, 67
  other valuation applications, 59
  of single cash flow, calculating with financial calculator, 71
  solving for fixed payments, 60–61
  solving for yield to maturity, 59–60
  special case of a consol, 61
  value of a coupon security, 58–59
  value of a single future payment, 57–58
Price appreciation, money market instruments and, 112–113

Price discovery, Treasury securities and, 11
Price-level target, 246
Price (or interest rate) risk, 63
Price rationing, 8
Price risk, term premium hypothesis and, 81
Prices, monetary policy and, 212
Price sensitivity, maturity and, 61–62
Price stability, 222, 240, 243
   Federal Reserve and, 2, 212–213
   goal of, 212
   inflation targeting and, 241
   monetary policy and, 212, 224
   operational measure of, 214–215
Price-to-earnings (P-E) ratio, 171–172, 180, 182
   aggregate, 175
   comparing for different firms, 173
   converting expression for, into share price valuation relationship, 172
Price-weighted indexes, 179, 181
Pricing of financial assets, 55–73
   duration, 64–66
   holding periods *versus* maturities, 63
   maturity and price sensitivity, 61–62
   nominal *versus* real yields, 66–67
   present value, 56–61
   return *versus* yield, 63–64
Primary dealers, 114, 128, 208
Primary market:
   new shares placed in, 169
   transactions, 27–28, 30
Prime broker, hedge fund operations and, 322
Prime Reserve fund, 313
Principal, home mortgages, 159, 160, 166
Prior preferred stock, 169
Private equity firms, 177, 328
Private equity funds, 26, 27, 30, 319, 326–328
   exit, 328, 330
   history behind, 327
   leverage, 327
   as private placements, 320–321
   strategies of, 320
Private-label pools, 148
Private mortgage insurance, 158
Private placements, bonds issued as, 133
Productivity growth, 227–228
Profits, 5
Property and casualty (P&C) insurance companies, 334, 341–342, 344
Property tax payments, escrowing, 160, 164
Purchase and assumption, by another depository institution, 303
Purchasing power parity, 268–269, 281
Put (or call), 266

Quantitative easing (QE), 84, 242

Rajaratnam, Raj, 105
Random walk, 106
Rational bubble, 107, 109, 262
"Reaching for the yield," 255

Real estate:
   commercial, 163, 165
   mortgages as loans secured by, 156
   residential, 156, 165
Real estate bubble, financial crisis of 2008 and bursting of, 15, 107, 166, 248, 260
Real estate loans, 35
Real exchange rate, 269, 281
Real income, aggregate consumption and, 216
Real interest rate, 66–67
Real-time gross settlement, 52
Refinancing, of home mortgages, 161, 164
Regulation:
   capital standards and, 299
   of commercial banks, 48–49
   of depository institutions, 297–300, 301
   focus of, 298
   of mutual fund industry, 307, 315–316
   supervision and, 207
Regulation Q ceilings, 302, 318
Regulatory arbitrage, 145
Regulatory compliance, commercial banking and, 288
Regulatory policy, safety net and, 47–49
Reinsurance:
   active market for, 341
   property and casualty (P&C) insurance companies and, 342, 344
Reinvestment risk, 63
Relationship banking, 46, 289
Relative value funds, 323
Reopened issues, 128–129
Replacement earnings, 213–214
Replacement rate, 345
Repurchase agreements, 36, 118–119, 121, 128, 200, 204
Required reserves, 196, 203, 303
Reserves:
   borrowed, 196, 197, 204
   demand for, 196, 197, 202–203, 207
   excess, 196, 201, 203, 209
   market equilibrium and, 198, 199
   nonborrowed, 196–197, 201–202, 204, 208
   required, 196, 203, 303
   supply of, 196–198
Reserves market:
   financial crisis of 2008 and, 201–202, 204
   interaction of policy instruments in, 202–203
Residential investment, 217
Residential mortgages, 35. *See also* Home mortgages
Restrictive covenants, 126, 137
Retail customers, 23
Retail money funds, 311
Retained earnings, 139, 168, 172, 180
Retirement:
   labor force participation and, 227
   pension funds and quality of, 333
   target funds and preparing for, 311

Retirement accounts, invested with mutual funds, 306
Retirement benefits, back-loading of, 335, 337, 343
Retirement funds, assets in, as of June 2013, 333, 334. *See also* Pension funds
Return, yield *versus*, 63–64, 68
Revenue bonds, 134, 138
Reverse repurchase agreements, 200, 204
Revolving lines of credit, 45, 117
Riegle-Neal Act, 290
Riksbank (Sweden), 184
Risk:
　changing investor tolerance for, 90
　financial markets and, 11
　financial system and reallocation of, 10
　investors and aversion to, 98, 103, 112
　measuring, 98–99
　portfolio and interpreting expression for, 100–101
　portfolio selection and, 99–100
　reduction through diversification, 100, 102
　reinvestment or rollover, 63
　systemic, 47
　uncertainty *versus*, 110
Risk-free yields, cyclical behavior related to, 88
Risk premiums, 170, 173, 174, 180, 182
Risk-return tradeoffs, efficient portfolios and, 103–104, 108
Rollover risk, 63
Rollovers, 338
Roosevelt, Franklin D., 251
Roth IRA, 346
RPs. *See* Repurchase agreements
RTGS. *See* Real-time gross settlement
Russell 2000 index, 178, 179

Safety net, commercial banks, regulatory policy, and, 47–49, 51
Saving, household patterns of, 4, 5
Savings and loans crisis, 23
Savings deposits, 291
Savings institutions, 23, 286, 291–292, 301
　balance sheets of, 295–296
　federal insurance for, 297
SBA. *See* Small Business Administration
Scheduled cash flows, from mortgages, 161
Seasoned issue, 27
Seasoned offerings, 169, 180
SEC. *See* Securities and Exchange Commission
Secondary market:
　corporate bonds traded in, 133, 138
　GSEs traded in, 136, 138
　mortgage-backed securities traded in, 148
　shares trading in, 169, 180
　transactions, 28
　Treasury coupon securities traded in, 128
Second Bank of the United States, 186, 194
Second (junior) mortgages, 156, 158, 164

Securities and Exchange Commission, 27, 49, 115, 259, 298, 306, 321
　hedge funds and, 324
　mutual funds and, 26, 313, 315
　private placements and, 133
　website, 12
Securitization, 3, 21, 143–154
　adverse selection and, 144–145, 153
　asymmetric information problem and, 144, 145, 153
　auto ABSs and, 148–149, 153
　collateralized debt obligations and, 150
　collateralized mortgage obligations and, 151
　corrective measures, 145
　credit card ABSs and, 149, 153
　defined, 143
　government-sponsored enterprises and, 147–148, 153
　of home and commercial mortgages, 156
　integration of credit markets and, 152, 153
　monetary policy and, 152–153
　of mortgage-backed securities, 146
　other consumer ABSs, 149, 153
　other mortgage pools, 148
　regulatory capital on ordinary loans, 145–146
　secondary-market trading and, 148
　of secondary mortgages, 159
　senior-subordinated securities and, 152
　structured securities and, 150–151
Securitized financial assets, 255
Seed capital, venture capital funds and, 325
Seigniorage, 38, 280
Semiannual cash flows, present value formula and calculating contribution from, 69–70, 73
Senior claim, 87
Senior (first) mortgages, 156, 158, 164
Seniority, of bond, 126
Senior status, bond indentures and, 132, 137
Senior-subordinated securities, 152
Senior tranches, 152
Separate accounts, LICOs, 341
Separate Trading of Registered Interest and Principal of Securities. *See* STRIPS
September 11, 2001 terrorist events, sharp reaction to, 252
Serial bonds, 135, 159
Serial offerings, muni yields and, 135, 138
Shadow banking system, 49, 53
　Dodd-Frank and, 259
　financial crisis of 2008 and, 257–258, 260
Shadow value, 312
Shareholders, 6, 20
　debt *versus* equity and, 20
　primary-market transactions and, 27–28
　tension between bondholders and, 130–131, 137
　tension between managers and, 176–177
Share prices, indexes of, 178–179, 180
Share retirements, new issuance of equities *versus*, 168, 179–180

Shares:
    credit unions, 292
    mutual funds, 305, 306
    valuation of, 170–171
Shocks, 239
    to aggregate demand, 232–233, 243
    to aggregate supply, 233–234, 243
Short-run Phillips curve, 228
Short sales, 29, 322, 331
Short-term interest rates, 85
    under expectations hypothesis, 78–80
    expected path of, importance of, 235–236
    futures markets and, 95
    under term premium hypothesis, 81–82
SIFIs. *See* Systemically important financial institutions
Sinking funds, 131, 135, 137, 140, 159
SIVs. *See* Structured investment vehicles
Small Business Administration, 141, 150
Small businesses, financing, 24
Smaller-cap index funds, 314
Social Security, 32, 338
Sole proprietorship, 20
Sovereign debt, 76, 95
Sovereign issuers of debt, credit quality and, 129
Sovereign markets, characteristics of, 129
Sovereign yields, 129
Specialist system, 29, 30, 180
Special-purpose vehicles, 116, 117, 121, 122, 145
Speculative-grade bonds, 130, 132
    cyclical behavior related to, 88, 89
    spread on, over Treasury benchmark note, 89
Speculative-grade instruments, 87, 93
Spending, life-cycle pattern of, 4–5
Spot transactions, 265, 281
    forward exchange rates and, 266–267, 281
Spreads:
    cyclical behavior of credit risk and, 88–89
    on-the-run, 90
SPVs. *See* Special-purpose vehicles
St. Louis Fed Database website, 12
Stability, monetary policy and, 212
Stable prices, 237
Standard and Poor (S&P):
    commercial paper rating assigned by, 115
    ratings scale for, 86, 87
Standard and Poor (S&P) 500 index, 26, 102, 174, 178, 179, 181, 310
Standard of living, financial system and, 2, 13
Standard statistical distributions, expected return on investments and, 98–99
Starbucks, 326
Start-up companies, venture capital financing of, 326
State governments, 6
    bond market as major financing source for, 126
    serial bonds and, 135
State pension funds, 338–339, 343
Sterilized intervention, undervalued currency and, 278, 281

Stewart, Martha, 105
Stock index funds, 310
Stock market, 3. *See also* Equity market
    monetary policy and, 175, 178, 180
    news about economy, monetary policy and effect on, 175, 180
    valuation of, 173
Stock market crash (1929):
    Great Depression precipitated by, 251
    open market purchases by Reserve Banks and, 189
Stock market crash (1987), 252
Stock of money, 43–44
Stock price bubble, financial crisis of 2008 and bursting of, 248
Stock prices:
    cyclical behavior of, 174
    indexes of, 178–179
Stocks, 19, 21
    preferred, types of, 169
    prospective price volatility of, 175, 176
Stored value cards, 41, 50, 194
Stress tests, 259, 299
Strike price, 266
STRIPS, 128, 137
Strong, Benjamin, 206
Structural unemployment, 213, 214, 226
Structured investment vehicles, 256, 258
Structured securities, 150–151, 153
Student loans, securitization of, 149, 153
Subordinated (junior) claim, 87
Subprime mortgages, 148, 254, 255
Super-optimists, price movement, fundamentals, and, 107
Super-senior tranches, 152
Supervision:
    capital standards and, 299
    central bank responsibilities and, 194, 195, 203
    of depository institutions, 297–300, 301
    focus of, 298
    regulation and, 207
Supply and demand, interest rates, equilibrating process, and, 7–8, 13
Supply of reserves, 196–198, 201
Surplus to deficit units, complications in direction of funds from, 28
Surplus units, 4, 13
    depository institutions and, 23
    financial instruments and, 9
    indirect finance and, 22
    transfer of resources from, to deficit units, 4–8, 18
Swaps, 331
Systemically important financial institutions, 195, 259, 298, 301, 324
    Basel III and, 300
    conservation buffer on, 299
    mutual funds and, 307
Systemic risk, 47, 260, 298
    Dodd-Frank and containment of, 259
    hedge funds and, 323–324

Index

key financial institutions and, 256
money market mutual funds and, 307, 316

TALF program. *See* Term Asset-Backed Loan Facility (TALF) program
Target funds, 311, 337
Targets, indicators *versus*, 245
TARP. *See* Troubled Asset Relief Program
Taxes and taxation, 3
  defined benefit (DB) plans and, 335
  defined contribution (DC) plans and, 335, 337
  IRAs and, 338
  munis *versus* Treasuries and, 134
  yields and, 91, 93
Taylor, John, 237, 239
Taylor Principle, 246
Taylor rule, 237–238, 243
"Teaser" initial interest rate, ARMs and, 157
Tech bubble (late 1990s), 175, 248, 260
Temporary transactions, 200, 204
Tennessee Valley Authority, 141
Tenure and earnings algorithm, 345
Term Asset-Backed Loan Facility (TALF) program, 150
Term insurance, 25, 339, 343
Term premium hypothesis, 81–82, 85, 93
Term structure of interest rates, 76–85, 92
  expectations hypothesis, 77–80, 92
  implicit forward rates, 84–85
  market segmentation hypothesis, 83–84
  role of, 85
  term premium hypothesis, 81–82, 93
Thrift institutions, 291, 302–303
Thrifty plans, for federal employees, 338
Time lags, 234, 245
Time preference (or impatience), 56
Time value of money, 56
TIPS, 67, 127, 137
Too big to fail large banks, 48
Total equity/total assets, 37
Trading platforms, types of, 29
Tranches:
  credit card ABSs and, 149
  senior-subordinated, 152
  structured securities and, 150, 151, 153
Transaction accounts, 33, 52
Transparency, SIFIs and, 300
Travelers, 179
Treasury benchmark interest rates:
  ARMs and, 160
  mortgage market and, 162, 164
Treasury benchmark note, spread on speculative-grade bonds over, 89
Treasury benchmark yields, cyclical behavior related to, 88
Treasury bills, 20, 21, 112, 113, 118, 121
  auction procedures and, 114
  primary dealers and, 114
  purpose for issuing bills, 115

Treasury Inflation Protected Securities. *See* TIPS
Treasury notes and bonds:
  credit quality, 129
  maturities of, 122, 126
  placement of, 127
  purposes of issuing coupon securities, 129
  reopening of issue, 128–129
  secondary-market trading, 128
  STRIPS, 128
  TIPS, 127
  when-issued trading, 127–128
Treasury securities. *See* U. S. Treasury securities
Treasury yield curve, 76
Tri-party RP market, 262
Troubled Asset Relief Program, 169, 258
Trust, financial system and, 17–18, 30
TVA. *See* Tennessee Valley Authority

Unbundling process, 144, 153
Uncertainty, 98, 107, 234, 235, 260
  aggregate demand and, 217
  financial markets and, 11
  risk *versus*, 110
Underachieving businesses, turning around, private equity function of, 326–327
Underperforming corporate performance, equity markets and, 177–178
Undervalued currency, 275–276
  dynamics of, 276–278, 281
  sterilized intervention and, 278, 281
Undervalued exchange rate, 275
Underwriters, 19
  "best efforts" basis for bonds and, 140
  of credit default swaps, 132
  GSE bonds and, 136, 138
  IPO pricing and, 169
  mutual fund complexes and, 309
  public offerings of corporate bonds and, 130, 138
  tax-exempt securities and, 135
Underwriting criteria, securitized assets and, 145
Unemployment, frictional and structural, 213, 214, 226
Unemployment rate:
  calculating, 227
  Okun's Law and, 224, 225
Uneven cash flows, price of asset providing, calculating with financial calculator, 71–72
Unions, DB plans sponsored by, 345
Unit banking states, 287
United States:
  advocates of inflation targeting in, 241, 244
  credit unions in, 292
  dual mandate in, 212–213, 224
  high home ownership rate in, reasons for, 155–156
  inflation in (1970s), 223
  mutual fund industry in, 306
  separately chartered commercial banks in, 287, 300

Universal banks, 290–291, 301
U.S. Congress, creation of central bank and, 185
U.S. Constitution, central bank rooted in, 184–185, 203
U.S. Department of Veterans Affairs, 146
U.S. Treasury, 85
   auctions, 19, 90, 114, 121, 127
   bond market as major financing source for, 126
   financial crisis of 2008 and policy responses of, 258
U.S. Treasury securities, 118, 303
   Chinese authorities and accumulation of, 275, 278
   conducting open market transactions in, 200
   credit risk and liquidity differences with munis *versus*, 134
   as default-free instruments, 103, 129
   flights to safety and, 92, 94
   on-the-run, 90
   outsized deficits, government debt servicing, and, 110, 129
   price discovery and, 11
   tax considerations for munis *versus*, 134

Valuation, of share of common stock, 170
Valuation process, 55–56
Valuation relationship, variations of, 69–70
Variable life policies, 341
Variance of portfolio's returns, formula for, 100
Velocity, of M1 and M2 money stock, 42
Velocity (turnover of money), 42, 44, 53
Venture capital (VC) funds, 26, 27, 30, 319, 324–326, 329, 330
   economic value provided by, 326
   exit, 326, 329–330
   as private placements, 320–321
   risks involved with, 324–325
   size and stages of financing, 325
   strategies of, 320
   types of firms selected for financing, 324
Visa, 40
VIX Index, 175
Volcker, Paul, 223

Wachovia Bank, 257
Wall Street Journal website, 12

Wall Street Reform and Consumer Protection (Dodd-Frank) Act of 2010, 49, 195, 259, 289, 298, 303, 324
Wal-Mart, 178
War of 1812, 186
Washington, George, 185
Washington Mutual Bank, 257
Wealth, aggregate consumption and, 216
When-issued securities, 127–128, 137
Whole Foods, 326
Whole loans, 146
Wholesale time deposits, 118, 303
Wilshire 5000, 178, 179
Wilson, Woodrow, 187
Women, labor force participation and, 227
World War I, 188

Yield curve:
   expectations hypothesis and, 79, 80
   implicit forward rates of interest and, 84–85
   market segmentation hypothesis and, 83
   path of expected short-term rates and, 235–236
   term premium hypothesis and, 81, 82
   Treasury, 76
Yields:
   auctions, on-the-run issue, and, 139–140
   credit (default) risk embedded in, patterns of, 88–89
   embedded options and, 92
   flights to safety and, 92
   liquidity and differences in, 90
   maturity and differences in, 76
   on money market instruments, 112–113
   nominal *versus* real, 66–67, 68
   on-the-run, 128
   return *versus*, 63–64, 68
   sovereign, 129
   taxation and, 91
Yield to maturity:
   computing with financial calculator, 72
   solving for, 59–60
Yuan, 263, 275, 276

Zero-bound constraint, slow recovery from Great Recession and, 241–243, 244
Zero-coupon securities, 57–58, 62, 65, 68, 72–73, 128, 137
Z tranche, 149, 151